ISSA

MW00846114

Digital Forensics, Investigation, and Response

FOURTH EDITION

Chuck Easttom

JONES & BARTLETT
LEARNING

World Headquarters
Jones & Bartlett Learning
25 Mall Road, 6th Floor
Burlington, MA 01803
978-443-5000
info@jblearning.com
www.jblearning.com

Jones & Bartlett Learning books and products are available through most bookstores and online booksellers. To contact
Jones & Bartlett Learning directly, call 800-832-0034, fax 978-443-8000, or visit our website, www.jblearning.com.

24449-6

Production Credits

VP, Product Management: Christine Emerton
Director of Product Management: Laura Pagluica
Product Manager: Ned Hinman
Tech Editor: Jeffrey Parker
Content Strategist: Melissa Duffy
Content Strategist: Paula Gregory
Project Manager: Kristen Rogers
Senior Project Specialist: Dan Stone
Digital Project Specialist: Rachel DiMaggio
Marketing Manager: Suzy Balk
Product Fulfillment Manager: Wendy Kilborn

Composition: Straive
Cover Design: Briana Yates
Text Design: Kristin E. Parker
Content Services Manager: Colleen Lamy
Media Development Editor: Faith Brosnan
Rights & Permissions Manager: John Rusk
Rights Specialist: Benjamin Roy
Cover Image (Title Page, Part Opener, Chapter Opener):
   © phyZick/Shutterstock
Printing and Binding: McNaughton & Gunn

Library of Congress Cataloging-in-Publication Data
Names: Easttom, Chuck, author.
Title: Digital forensics, investigation, and response / Chuck Easttom.
Other titles: System forensics, investigation, and response
Description: Fourth edition. | Burlington, Massachusetts : Jones & Bartlett
   Learning, [2022] | Includes index.
Identifiers: LCCN 2021003216 | ISBN 9781284226065 (paperback)
Subjects: LCSH: Computer crimes—Investigation—Textbooks.
Classification: LCC HV8079.C65 E37 2022 | DDC 363.25/968--dc23
LC record available at https://lccn.loc.gov/20210032166048

Printed in the United States of America
25 24 23 22 21   10 9 8 7 6 5 4 3 2 1

Contents

CHAPTER 6

Recovering Data   151

CHAPTER 7

Incident Response 173

Preface

Purpose of This Book

This book is part of the *Information Systems Security & Assurance Series* from Jones & Bartlett Learning (www.jblearning.com). Designed for courses and curriculums in IT Security, Cybersecurity, Information Assurance, and Information Systems Security, this series features a comprehensive, consistent treatment of the most current thinking and trends in this critical subject area. These titles deliver fundamental information security principles packed with real-world applications and examples. Authored by Certified Information Systems Security Professionals, they deliver comprehensive information on all aspects of information security. Reviewed word-for-word by leading technical experts in the field, these books are not just current, but forward-thinking—putting you in the position to solve the cybersecurity challenges not just of today, but of tomorrow as well.

Computer crimes call for forensics specialists—people who know how to find and follow the evidence. But even aside from criminal investigations, incident response requires forensic skills. This book begins by examining the fundamentals of system forensics: what forensics is, an overview of computer crime, the challenges of system forensics, and forensic methods and labs. The second part of this book addresses the tools, techniques, and methods used to perform computer forensics and investigation. These include collecting evidence, investigating information hiding, recovering data, and scrutinizing email. It also discusses how to perform forensics in the Windows, Linux, and Macintosh operating systems; on mobile devices; and on networks. Finally, the third part explores incident and intrusion response, emerging technologies and future directions of this field, and additional system forensics resources.

New to This Edition

All aspects of the book have been updated, to include recent changes in Windows, Macintosh, and mobile devices. For example, Chapter 8, "Windows Forensics" has been expanded to include SRUM, BAM, and DAM registry entries. The updates to all chapters include changes to the underlying technology, changes to the law, and newer case studies. There is now a separate chapter regarding memory forensics, Chapter 14. Chapter 15, "New Trends," introduces a general methodology of smart TV forensics.

Cloud Labs

This text is accompanied by Cybersecurity Cloud Labs. These hands-on virtual labs provide immersive mock IT infrastructures where students can learn and practice foundational cybersecurity skills as an extension of the lessons in this textbook. For more information or to purchase the labs, visit go.jblearning.com/forensics4e.

Learning Features

The writing style of this book is practical and conversational. Each chapter begins with a statement of learning objectives. Step-by-step examples of information security concepts and procedures are presented throughout the text. Illustrations are used both to clarify the material and to vary the presentation. The text is sprinkled with Notes, Tips, FYIs, Warnings, and sidebars to alert the reader to additional helpful information related to the subject under discussion. Chapter assessments appear at the end of each chapter, with solutions provided at the back of the book.

Chapter summaries are included in the text to provide a rapid review or preview of the material and to help students understand the relative importance of the concepts presented.

Audience

This material is suitable for undergraduate or graduate computer science majors or information science majors, students at a two-year technical college or community college who have a basic technical background, or readers who have a basic understanding of IT security and want to expand their knowledge.

Dedication

This book is dedicated to all the forensic analysts who work diligently to extract the evidence necessary to find the truth in criminal and civil cases.

About the Author

Dr. Chuck Easttom is the author of 32 books, including several on computer security, forensics, and cryptography. He has also authored scientific papers on digital forensics, cyber warfare, machine learning, cryptography, and applied mathematics. He is an inventor with 22 computer science patents. He holds a Doctor of Science (D.Sc.) in cyber security, a Ph.D. in nanotechnology, a Ph.D. in computer science, and three master's degrees (one in applied computer science, one in education, and one in systems engineering). He is a senior member of both the IEEE and the ACM. He is also a Distinguished Speaker of the ACM and a Distinguished Visitor of the IEEE.

He also holds 55 industry certifications, including many cyber security and digital forensics certifications. He has both academic hands-on forensics experience. He has served as an expert witness in U.S. court cases since 2004. He is currently an adjunct lecturer at Georgetown University, where he teaches cyber security, systems engineering and cryptography, and an adjunct professor at University of Dallas, where he teaches a graduate course in digital forensics.

PART I

Introduction to Forensics

Introduction to Forensics

THIS CHAPTER INTRODUCES YOU TO THE FIELD of computer forensics. It covers some legal issues, the basic concepts of the forensic process, and a review of the basic computer and networking knowledge you will need. This chapter forms the basis for the subsequent chapters. It is important to be comfortable with the material in this chapter before proceeding.

Chapter 1 Topics

This chapter covers the following topics and concepts:

- What is computer forensics?
- What do you need to know about the field of digital forensics?
- What do you need to know for computer forensic analysis?
- What is the Daubert standard?
- What are the relevant laws?
- What are the federal guidelines?

Chapter 1 Goals

When you complete this chapter, you will be able to:

- Understand the basic concepts of forensics
- Maintain the chain of custody
- Understand basic hardware and networking knowledge needed for forensics
- Know the basic laws related to computer forensics

What Is Computer Forensics?

Before you can answer the question, "What is computer forensics?", you should address the question, "What is forensics?" *The American Heritage Dictionary* defines *forensics* as "the use of science and technology to investigate and establish facts in criminal or civil courts of law."

Essentially, forensics is the use of science to process evidence so you can establish the facts of a case. The individual case being examined could be criminal or civil, but the process is the same. The evidence has to be examined and processed in a consistent, scientific manner. This is to ensure that the evidence is not accidentally altered and that appropriate conclusions are derived from that evidence.

You have probably seen some crime drama wherein forensic techniques were a part of the investigative process. In such dramas, a bullet is found and forensics is used to determine which gun fired the bullet. Or perhaps a drop of blood is found and forensics is used to match the DNA to a suspect. These are all valid aspects of forensics. However, our modern world is full of electronic devices with the capacity to store data. The extraction of that data in a consistent, scientific manner is the subject of **computer forensics**. In fact, with the proliferation of smartphones, smartwatches, and other devices, some now refer to this field as **digital forensics**, emphasizing the wide range of different devices that can be included.

The U.S. Computer Emergency Response Team (US-CERT) defines computer forensics in this manner:

> Forensics is the process of using scientific knowledge for collecting, analyzing, and presenting evidence to the courts.... Forensics deals primarily with the recovery and analysis of latent evidence. Latent evidence can take many forms, from finger-prints left on a window to DNA evidence recovered from bloodstains to the files on a hard drive.

According to the website Computer Forensics World:

> Generally, computer forensics is considered to be the use of analytical and investigative techniques to identify, collect, examine and preserve evidence/information which is magnetically stored or encoded.

The objective in computer forensics (or digital forensics, if you prefer) is to recover, analyze, and present computer-based material in such a way that it can be used as evidence in a court of law. In computer forensics, as in any other branch of forensic science, the emphasis must be on the integrity and security of evidence. A forensic specialist must adhere to stringent guidelines and avoid taking shortcuts.

Any device that can store data is potentially the subject of computer forensics. Obviously, that includes devices such as network servers, personal computers, and laptops. However, computer forensics also encompasses devices such as smartphones, routers, tablets, printers, and global positioning system (GPS) devices. Remember that *any* device that can store data is a potential subject of computer forensics.

Although the subject of computer forensics, as well as the tools and techniques used, is significantly different from traditional forensics—like DNA analysis and bullet examination—the goal is the same: to obtain evidence that can be used in some legal proceeding. Computer forensics applies to all the domains of a typical IT infrastructure, from the User Domain and Remote Access Domain to the Wide Area Network (WAN) Domain and Internet Domain (see **FIGURE 1-1**).

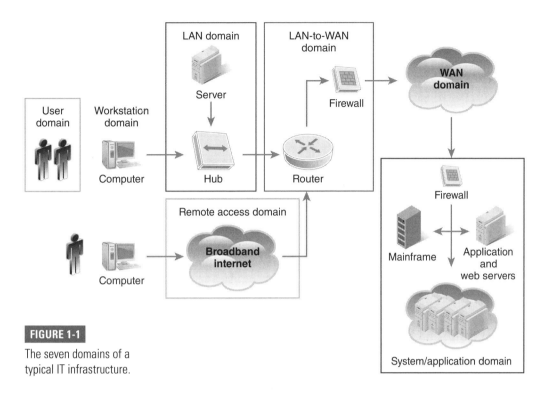

FIGURE 1-1

The seven domains of a
typical IT infrastructure.

Consider some elements of the preceding definitions. In particular, let's look at this sentence: "Forensics is the process of using scientific knowledge for collecting, analyzing, and presenting evidence to the courts." Each portion of this is critical, and the following sections of this chapter examine each one individually.

Using Scientific Knowledge

First and foremost, computer forensics is a science. This is not a process based on your "gut feelings" or personal whim. It is important to understand and apply scientific methods and processes. It is also important that you have knowledge of the relevant scientific disciplines. That also means you must have scientific knowledge of the field. Computer forensics begins with a thorough understanding of computer hardware. Then you need to understand the operating system running on that device; even smartphones and routers have operating systems. You must also understand at least the basics of computer networks. Indeed, one could argue that one issue with the current practice of forensics is that too many individuals want to enter the field without adequate computer backgrounds. Consider DNA forensics; you would not consider attempting such an endeavor if you did not have a solid working knowledge of biochemistry, genetics, and related subjects. The same is true with digital forensics. In this text, in addition to providing you with very specific forensic techniques and procedures, it will also be my goal to introduce you to enough working knowledge of computers for you to be effective as a forensic examiner.

If you attempt to master forensics without this basic knowledge, you are not likely to be successful. But if you find yourself starting in on a course and are not sure if you have the requisite knowledge, don't panic. First, you simply need a basic knowledge of computers and computer networks. If you have taken a couple of basic computer courses at a college or perhaps the CompTIA A+ certification, you have the baseline knowledge. Also, you will get a review of some basic concepts in this chapter. And, as previously stated, as we go through the book, you will be given technical details as needed. Material will be presented with the assumption that you have zero knowledge of computers. That is not likely to be true for all readers. If you already have substantial computer knowledge, then you can consider the technical material presented to be a review.

However, the more you know about computers and networks, the better you will be at computer forensics. There is no such thing as "knowing too much." Even though some technical details change quickly, such as the capacity and materials of hard disks, other details change very slowly, if at all, such as the various file systems, the role of volatile and non-volatile memory, and the fact that criminals take advantage of the advancements in computer and digital technology to improve their lives as much as the businessperson, student, or homeowner. A great deal of information is stored in computers. Keep learning what is there, where it is stored, and how that information may be used by computer user and computer criminal alike.

Collecting _Pg.18_

Before you can do any forensic analysis or examination, you have to collect the evidence. There are very specific procedures for properly collecting evidence. You will be introduced to some general guidelines later in this chapter. The important thing to realize for now is that how you collect the evidence determines if that evidence is admissible in a court.

3 Steps ⟶

Analyzing

Data analysis is one of the most time-consuming parts of a forensic investigation, and it can be the most challenging. Once you have collected the data, what does it mean? The real difference between a mediocre investigator and a star investigator is the analysis. The data is there, but do you know what it means? This is also related to your level of scientific knowledge. If you don't know enough, you may not see the significance of the data you have.

You also have to be able to solve puzzles. That is, in essence, what any forensic investigation is. It is solving a complex puzzle—putting together the data you have and finding out what sort of picture is revealed. You might try to approach a forensic investigation like Sherlock Holmes. Look at every detail. What does it mean? Before you jump to a conclusion, how much evidence do you have to support that conclusion? Are there alternative and, in fact, better explanations for the data? _Ensure evidence backs up conclusion. Consider possible alternative conclusions._

Presenting

Once you have finished your investigation, done your analysis, and obeyed all the rules and guidelines, you still have one more step. You will have to present that evidence in one form or another. The two most basic forms are the _expert report_ and _expert testimony_. In either case, it will be your job to interpret the arcane and seemingly impenetrable technical information using plain English that paints an accurate picture for the court. You must not use jargon and technobabble. Your clear use of language, and potentially graphics and demonstrations if needed, may be the difference between a big win and a lost case. So you should take a quick look at each of these.

The Expert Report

An **expert report** is a formal document that lists what tests you conducted, what you found, and your conclusions. It also includes your **curriculum vitae (CV)**, which is like a résumé, only much more thorough and specific to your work experience as a forensic investigator. Specific rules will vary from court to court, but as a general rule, if you don't put a specific subject in your report, you cannot testify about it at trial. So you need to make very certain that your report is thorough. Put in every single test you used, every single thing you found, and your conclusions. Expert reports tend to be rather long.

It is also important to back up your conclusions. As a general rule, it's good to have at least two to three references for every conclusion. In other words, in addition to your own opinion, you want to have a few reputable references that either agree with that conclusion or provide support for how you came to that conclusion. This way, your conclusion is not just based on your expert opinion, but also supported by other reputable sources. Make sure you use reputable sources. For example, US-CERT, the Federal Bureau of Investigation (FBI), the U.S. Secret Service, and the Cornell University Law School are all very reputable sources.

 WARNING

Court procedures vary from jurisdiction to jurisdiction, but in most cases, an expert cannot directly testify about anything not in his or her expert report. That is why it is critical to be thorough and to put into the report anything you feel might be pertinent to the case. In your work as an expert witness, you will often find additional items in an investigation—items that are peripheral to the main case. If you put those in your report, however, you will be able to testify about them at trial.

The reason for this is that in every legal case, there are two sides. The opposing side will have an attorney and perhaps its own expert. The opposing attorney will want to pick apart every opinion and conclusion you have. If there is an opposing expert, he or she will be looking for alternative interpretations of the data or flaws in your method. You have to make sure you have fully supported your conclusions.

It should be noted that the length and level of detail found in reports varies. In many cases, criminal courts won't require a formal expert report, but rather a statement from the attorney as to who you are and what topics you intend to testify about. You will need to produce a report of your forensic examination. In civil court, particularly in intellectual property cases, the expert report is far more lengthy and far more detailed. In my own experience, reports of 100, 200, or more pages are common. The largest I have seen yet was over 1500 pages long.

While not all cases will involve a full, detailed expert report, many will—particularly intellectual property cases. There are few legal guidelines on expert report writing, but a few issues have become clear in my experience. Let's cover what I have learned from years of working on court cases.

Expert reports generally start with the expert's qualifications. This should be a complete CV detailing education, work history, and publications. Particular attention should be paid to elements of the expert's history that are directly related to the case at hand. If the case involves Windows Server 2019, what is your experience and training related to that? If you use a particular forensics tool or technique, you should describe your experience and training that are related to that tool or technique. Then the report moves on to the actual topic at hand. An expert report is a very thorough document. It must first detail exactly what analysis was used: How did the expert conduct their examination and analysis? In the case of computer forensics, the expert report should detail what tools the expert used, what the results were, and the conditions of the tests conducted. You may wonder how much detail is required. The answer is simple: enough detail so that any competent forensics analyst could replicate your tests. Also, any claim an expert makes in a report should be supported by extrinsic reputable sources. This is sometimes overlooked by experts because they themselves are sources that are used, or because the claim being made seems obvious to them. For example, if an expert report needs to detail how domain name service (DNS) works to describe a DNS poisoning attack, then there should be references to recognized, authoritative works regarding the details of domain name service. The reason this matters is that at trial, a creative attorney can often extract nontraditional meanings from even commonly understood terms.

The next issue with an expert report is its completeness. The report must cover every item the expert wishes to opine on, and in detail. Nothing can be assumed. In some jurisdictions, if an item is not in the expert report, then the expert is not allowed to express an opinion about it during testimony. Whether that is the case in your jurisdiction or not, it is imperative that the expert report that is submitted must be very thorough and complete—and, of course, it must be error free. Even the smallest error can give opposing counsel an opportunity to impugn the accuracy of the entire report—as well as the expert's entire testimony. This is a document that should be carefully proofread by the expert and by the attorney retaining the expert.

Expert Testimony

As a forensic specialist, you will testify as an expert witness—that is, on the basis of scientific or technical knowledge you have that is relevant to a case, rather than on the basis of direct personal experience. Your testimony will be referred to as **expert testimony**, and there are two scenarios in which you give it. The first is a deposition, and the second is a trial. A *deposition*—testimony taken from a witness or party to a case before a trial—is less formal and is typically held in an attorney's office. The other side's lawyer gets to ask you questions. In fact, the lawyer can even ask some questions that would probably be disallowed by a trial judge. But do remember, this is still sworn testimony, and lying under oath is perjury, which is a felony.

Allow me to elaborate a bit on perjury. Telling an overt lie is not only a felony, but even if criminal charges are not brought, it will destroy your reputation. A forensics expert can survive a technical mistake or even being outright wrong. But your career cannot survive a lie. Some people try to shade the truth a bit—not overtly lying, but being evasive or trying to alter their answer to point in a particular direction. This is a significant mistake for a forensic analyst. First, you should remember that your goal is not to win or lose a case. Your goal is to present scientifically valid evidence in a manner that is acceptable to a court. If in your investigation you find evidence that would tend to undermine the case of whomever hired you, then your responsibility is to inform them of this as early as possible. It is not your responsibility to try and color your testimony in such a way as to obfuscate that evidence. Many people find testifying very stressful. I must confess that I, too, found it immensely stressful the first few times. However, I learned a secret that I will impart to you: If you do a really thorough and complete job, then all you have to do is to tell the truth. And that is not stressful at all.

U.S. Federal Rule 702 defines what an expert is and what expert testimony is:

"A witness who is qualified as an expert by knowledge, skill, experience, training, or education may testify in the form of an opinion or otherwise if:

a. the expert's scientific, technical, or other specialized knowledge will help the trier of fact to understand the evidence or to determine a fact in issue;

b. the testimony is based on sufficient facts or data;

c. the testimony is the product of reliable principles and methods; and

d. the expert has reliably applied the principles and methods to the facts of the case."[1]

This definition is very helpful. Yes, you do require training and experience in order to be an expert witness. However, regardless of your credentials, did you base your conclusions on sufficient facts and data? Did you apply reliable scientific principles and methods in forming your conclusions? These questions should guide your forensic work

During a deposition, the opposing counsel has a few goals. The first goal is to find out as much as possible about your position, methods, conclusions, and even your side's legal strategy. It is important to answer honestly but as briefly as possible. Don't volunteer information unasked. That simply allows the other side to be better prepared for trial. The second thing a lawyer is looking for during a deposition is to get you to commit to a position you may not be able to defend later. So follow a few rules:

- If you don't fully understand the question, say so. Ask for clarification before you answer. The opposing counsel will likely ask questions in such a way as to lead to a particular conclusion. Listen very carefully to the specific words he or she uses.
- If you really don't know, say so. Do not ever guess. Now, opposing counsel may try to make you feel awkward about not knowing something—try to badger you into giving some answer. But the fact is, no one knows everything. It is better to say you don't know than to take a guess.
- If you are not 100 percent certain of an answer, say so. Say, "to the best of my current recollection," or something to that effect.
- Whenever possible, review any document being referred to. Re-read your report and read any exhibit. If you have a document there, refer to it; do not testify from memory.

The other way you may testify is at trial. The first thing you absolutely must understand is that the first time you testify, you will be nervous. You'll begin to wonder if you are properly prepared. Are your conclusions correct? Did you miss anything? Don't worry; each time you do this, it gets easier. Next, remember that the opposing counsel, by definition, disagrees with you, and wants to trip you up. It might be helpful to remind yourself, "The opposing counsel's default position is that I am both incompetent and a liar." Now that is a bit harsh, and probably an overstatement. But if you start from that premise, you will be prepared for the opposing counsel's questions. Don't be too upset if he or she is trying to make you look bad. It's not personal.

The secret to deposition and trial testimony is simple: Be prepared. Not only should you make certain your forensic process is done correctly and well documented, including liberal use of charts, diagrams, and other graphics, but you should also prepare before you testify. Go over your report and your notes again. Often, your attorney will prep you, particularly if you have never testified before. Try to look objectively at your own report to see if there is anything the opposing counsel might use against you. Are there alternative ways to interpret the evidence? If so, why did you reject them?

The most important things on the stand are to keep calm and tell the truth. Obviously, any lie, even a very minor one that is not directly related to your investigation, would be devastating. But becoming agitated or angry on the stand can also undermine your credibility. When asked a question, answer it directly. Don't try to be evasive.

In addition to U.S. Federal Rule 702, there are several other U.S. Federal Rules related to expert witness testimony at trial. They are listed and very briefly described here.

- **Rule 703: Bases of an expert**[2]: An expert may base an opinion on facts or data that the expert has been made aware of or personally observed. If experts in the particular field would reasonably rely on those kinds of facts or data in forming an opinion on the subject, they need not be admissible for the opinion to be admitted. But if the facts or data would otherwise be inadmissible, the proponent of the opinion may disclose them to the jury only if their **probative value**—that is, the weight they carry in helping reach a valid judgment—in helping the jury evaluate the opinion substantially outweighs their prejudicial effect.
- **Rule 704: Opinion on ultimate issue**[3]: An opinion is not objectionable just because it embraces an ultimate issue. In other words an expert witness can, in many cases, offer an opinion as to the ultimate issue in a case.
- **Rule 705: Disclosing the facts or data underlying an expert**[4]: Unless the court orders otherwise, an expert may state an opinion—and give the reasons for it—without first testifying to the underlying facts or data. But the expert may be required to disclose those facts or data on cross-examination. Essentially, the expert can state his or her opinion without first giving the underlying facts, but he or she should expect to be questioned on those facts at some point.
- **Rule 706: Court-appointed expert witness**[5]: This rule covers the appointment of neutral experts used to advise the court. Such experts are working for neither the plaintiff nor the defendant; they work for the court.
- **Rule 401: Test for relevant evidence**[6]: Evidence is relevant if (a) it has any tendency to make a fact more or less probable than it would be without the evidence and (b) the fact is of consequence in determining the action.

Understanding the Field of Digital Forensics

The digital forensics field is changing very rapidly. First and foremost, standards are emerging. This means there are clearly defined ways of properly doing forensics. When computer forensics first began, most investigations were conducted according to the whims of the investigator rather than through a standardized methodology. But as the field has matured, it has also become standardized. Today, there are clear, codified methods for conducting a forensic examination.

Another change is in who is doing forensics. At one time, all forensics, including computer forensics, was the exclusive domain of law enforcement. That is no longer the case. Today, the following entities are also involved in and actively using computer forensics:

- **The military** uses digital forensics to gather intelligence information from computers captured during military actions.
- **Government agencies** use digital forensics to investigate crimes involving computers. These agencies include the Federal Bureau of Investigation (FBI), the U.S. Postal Inspection Service, the Federal Trade Commission (FTC), the U.S. Food and Drug Administration (FDA), and the U.S. Secret Service. They also include the U.S. Department of Justice's National Institute of Justice (NIJ), the National Institute of Standards and Technology (NIST) Office of Law Enforcement Standards (OLES), the Department of Homeland Security, and foreign government agencies, among others.
- **Law firms** need experienced system forensics professionals to conduct investigations and testify as expert witnesses. For example, civil cases can use records found on computer systems that bear on cases involving fraud, divorce, discrimination, and harassment.
- **Criminal prosecutors** use digital evidence when working with incriminating documents. They try to link these documents to crimes such as drug trafficking, embezzlement, financial fraud, homicide, and child pornography.
- **Academia** is involved with forensic research and education. For example, many universities offer degrees in digital forensics and online criminal justice.
- **Data recovery firms** use digital forensics techniques to recover data after hardware or software failures and when data has been lost.
- **Corporations** use digital forensics to assist in employee termination and prosecution. For example, corporations sometimes need to gather information concerning theft of intellectual property or trade secrets, fraud, embezzlement, sexual harassment, and network and computer intrusions. They also need to find evidence of unauthorized use of equipment, such as computers, fax machines, answering machines, and mobile phones.
- **Insurance companies** use digital evidence of possible fraud in accident, arson, and workers' compensation cases.
- **Individuals** sometimes hire forensic specialists in support of possible claims. These cases may include, for example, wrongful termination, sexual harassment, or age discrimination.

What Is Digital Evidence?

Information includes raw numbers, pictures, and a vast array of other data that may or may not have relevance to a particular event or incident under investigation. **Digital evidence** is information that has been processed and assembled so that it is relevant to an investigation and supports a specific finding or determination. Put another way, all the raw information is not, in and of itself, evidence. Data has to be first and foremost relevant to a case, in order to be evidence.

Investigators must carefully show an unbroken chain of custody to demonstrate that evidence has been protected from tampering. The **chain of custody** is the continuity of control of evidence that makes it possible to account for all that has happened to evidence between its original collection and its appearance in court, preferably unaltered. If forensic specialists can't demonstrate that they have maintained the chain of custody, then the court may consider all their conclusions invalid.

Courts deal with four types of evidence:

Quiz

- **Real** evidence is a physical object that someone can touch, hold, or directly observe. Examples of real evidence are a laptop with a suspect's fingerprints on the keyboard, a hard drive, a universal serial bus (USB) drive, and a handwritten note.
- **Documentary** evidence is data stored as written matter, on paper, or in electronic files. Documentary evidence includes memory-resident data and computer files. Examples are email messages, logs, databases, photographs, and telephone call-detail records. Investigators must **authenticate** documentary evidence—that is, demonstrate that it's genuine and was not created after the fact.
- **Testimonial** evidence is information that forensic specialists use to support or interpret real or documentary evidence. For example, they may employ testimonial evidence to demonstrate that the fingerprints found on a keyboard are those of a specific individual. Or system access controls might show that a particular user stored specific photographs on a desktop.
- **Demonstrative** evidence is information that helps explain other evidence—*any* other evidence. That could be testimonial evidence, documentary evidence, or real evidence. An example is a chart that explains a technical concept to the judge and jury. Forensic specialists must often provide testimony to support the conclusions of their analyses. For example, a member of an incident response team might be required to testify that he or she identified the computer program that deleted customer records at a specified date and time. In such a case, the testimony must show how the investigator reached his or her conclusion. The testimony must also show that the specialist protected against tampering with the information used in making the determination. That is, the testimony must show that the forensic investigator maintained the chain of custody. It must also show that the testifier based his or her conclusion on a reasonable, although not necessarily absolute, interpretation of the information. Further, the forensic specialist must present his or her testimony in a manner that avoids use of technical jargon and complex technical discussions and should use pictures, charts, and other graphics when helpful. Judges, juries, and lawyers aren't all technical experts. Therefore, a forensic specialist should translate technology into understandable descriptions. Pictures often communicate better than just numbers and words, so a forensic specialist may want to create charts and graphs.

Scope-Related Challenges to System Forensics

The scope of a forensic effort often presents not just an analytical challenge but a psychological challenge as well. Information systems collect and retain large volumes of data. They store this data in a dizzying array of applications, formats, and hardware components. In completing an analysis, forensic specialists face variations in the following:

- The volume of data to be analyzed
- The complexity of the computer system
- The size and character of the crime scene, which might involve a network that crosses U.S. and foreign jurisdictions
- The size of the caseload and resource limitations

Forensic specialists must be prepared to quickly complete an analysis regardless of these factors. The following sections discuss these factors in more detail.

Large Volumes of Data

Digital forensics is useful in identifying and documenting evidence. It is a disciplined approach that looks at the entire physical media, such as a hard disk drive, for all information representations. A system forensics specialist has access to all the information contained on a device—not just what the end user sees. A forensic analyst also examines *metadata*, which is data about information, such as disk partition structures and file tables. Metadata also includes file creation and modification times. Who authored a file and when it was revised or updated are also important pieces of metadata for a forensic analyst to document. An analyst also examines the often-critical unused areas of the media where information might be hidden. Examining all areas of potential data storage and examining all potential data representations generates extremely large volumes of information. A forensic specialist must analyze, store, and control all this information for the full duration of the investigation and analysis.

The total amount of information that is potentially relevant to a case offers a challenge to forensic analysts. Hard drives well in excess of 1 terabyte are quite common today. In fact, one can purchase a 4- or 5-terabyte drive for under $120 at any electronics store. While writing this chapter for the fourth edition of the book, I bought a 10-terabyte external drive for only $180. Sizes keep increasing and prices dropping. When working with such large volumes, a forensic specialist must do the following:

- Ensure that his or her equipment is capable of manipulating large volumes of information quickly.
- Provide for duplicate storage so that the original media and its resident information are preserved and protected against tampering and other corruption.
- Create backups early and often to avoid losing actual information and its associated metadata.
- Document everything that is done in an investigation and maintain the chain of custody.

In addition to all these tasks, a forensic specialist must work within the forensic budget. Manipulating and controlling large volumes of information is expensive. An investigator should show how budget cost items contribute to the analysis and to maintaining the chain of custody. Resource limitations increase the potential for analysis error and may compromise the analysis. For example, a forensic analyst may need to explain how the addition of data custodians or additional hard drives can multiply costs.

System Complexity

Modern computer systems can be extremely complex. This is not just a matter of the aforementioned size of storage, but rather the wide array of data and formats. Digital devices use multiple file formats, including Adobe Portable Document Format (PDF) files, Microsoft Word (DOC and DOCX) documents, Microsoft Excel spreadsheets (XLS), video files (MP4, AVI, MOV, etc.), and image files (JPEG, GIF, BMP, PNG, etc.), to name just a few. This does not even take into account formats of information "in motion" such as Voice over IP (VoIP), instant messaging protocols, or real-time video broadcast or two-way conferences. These systems connect to and share data with other systems that may be located anywhere in the world. In addition, the law may protect specific items and not others. No single forensic software application can deal with all the complexity.

Forensic specialists must use a set of software and hardware tools and supporting manual procedures. Further, a forensic specialist must build a case to support his or her interpretation of the "story" told by the information being analyzed. The specialist, there-fore, must have an understanding of all digital information and its associated technology. The specialist should also be able to show corroboration that meets the traditional legal evidence tests. Specific tests of legal evidence can vary from venue to venue and from juris-diction to jurisdiction—or both. There are a few basic tests that apply everywhere, but the chain of custody and the Daubert standard, both of which are discussed in this chapter, are nearly universal.

Individual pieces of information may have more than one possible interpretation. To reach a conclusion and turn raw information into supportable, actionable evidence, a foren-sic specialist must identify and analyze corroborating information. In other words, it is often the case that a single piece of information is not conclusive. It often takes the examination and correlation of multiple individual pieces of information to reach a conclusion. It is also a common practice for a forensic investigator to use more than one tool to conduct a test. For example, if you utilize one particular tool to recover deleted files, it can be a good idea to use yet another tool to conduct the same test. If two different tools yield the same result, this is compelling evidence that the information gathered is accurate and reliable. However, if the results differ, the forensic analyst has another situation to deal with.

Distributed Crime Scenes

Because networks are geographically dispersed, crime scenes may also be geographically dispersed. This creates practical as well as jurisdictional problems. Think about how difficult it is for a U.S. investigator to get evidence out of computers in China, for instance. Criminals take advantage of jurisdictional differences. A criminal may sell fake merchandise via the internet from a foreign country to Americans in several states. The criminal may then route his or her internet access, and the associated electronic payments, through several other countries before they reach their final destination.

Digital crime scenes can, and increasingly do, span the globe. Depending on the type of system connectivity and the controls in place, a forensic specialist may have to deal with information stored throughout the world and often in languages other than English. This could involve thousands of devices and network logs. Networks and centralized storage also present challenges because items of interest may not be stored on the target computer.

Gathering evidence from such a geographically far-flung digital crime scene requires the cooperation of local, state, and tribal governments, sometimes multiple national govern-ments, and international agencies in tracking down the criminals and bringing them to justice. If all the governments and agencies do not cooperate with one another, the investigation may fail.

Growing Caseload and Limited Resources

The number of forensic specialists today is too small to analyze every cybercrime. Regardless of the state of the economy, digital forensics specialists can be assured of two things: Their caseload will grow, and their resources will, relative to caseload, become more limited. It is a simple fact that anyone in law enforcement who works in digital crimes has a case backlog, and that backlog is increasing.

The digital forensics analysis workload is growing and will continue to grow as computers and related digital devices are used more and in different ways in the commission of crimes. Driving this growth is the increasing use of technology in all aspects of modern life, not just in support of business objectives. Criminals utilize technology not only to conduct crimes but also, in some cases, to hide the evidence. Forensic tools can also be used by criminals to eradicate evidence as easily as they can be used by investigators to locate, analyze, and catalog evidence.

Types of Digital System Forensics Analysis

Today, digital system forensics includes a number of specialties. The following are some examples:

- **Disk forensics** is the process of acquiring and analyzing information stored on physical storage media, such as computer hard drives, smartphones, GPS systems, and removable media. Disk forensics includes both the recovery of hidden and deleted information and the process of identifying who created a file or message.
- **Email forensics** is the study of the source and content of email as evidence. Email forensics includes the process of identifying the sender, recipient, date, time, and origination location of an email message. You can use email forensics to identify harassment, discrimination, or unauthorized activities. There is also a body of laws that deal with retention and storage of emails that are specific to certain fields, such as financial and medical.
- **Network forensics** is the process of examining network traffic, including transaction logs and real-time monitoring using sniffers and tracing.
- **Internet forensics** is the process of piecing together where and when a user has been on the internet. For example, you can use internet forensics to determine whether inappropriate internet content access and downloading were accidental.
- **Software forensics**, also known as *malware forensics*, is the process of examining malicious computer code.
- **Live system forensics** is the process of searching memory in real time, typically for working with compromised hosts or to identify system abuse. Each of these types of forensic analysis requires specialized skills and training.
- **Cell-phone forensics** is the process of searching the contents of cell phones. A few years ago, this was just not a big issue, but with the ubiquitous nature of cell phones today, cell-phone forensics is a very important topic. A cell phone can be a treasure trove of evidence. Modern cell phones are essentially computers with processors, memory, even hard drives

and operating systems, and they operate on networks. Phone forensics also includes VoIP and traditional phones and may overlap the Foreign Intelligence Surveillance Act of 1978 (FISA), the USA PATRIOT Act, and the Communications Assistance for Law Enforcement Act (CALEA) in the United States.

General Guidelines

Later in this chapter, you will read about specific federal guidelines, but you should keep a few general principles in mind when doing any forensic work, as discussed in the following sections.

Chain of Custody   *where it was, how it was stored, who had access to it*

This is the most important principle in any forensic effort, digital or nondigital. The chain of physical custody must be maintained. From the time the evidence is first seized by a law enforcement officer or civilian investigator until the moment it is shown in court, the whereabouts and custody of the evidence, and how it was handled and stored and by whom, must be able to be shown at all times. Failure to maintain the proper chain of custody can lead to evidence being excluded from trial.

Don't Touch the Suspect Drive

One very important principle is to touch the system as little as possible. It is possible to make changes to the system in the process of examining it, which is very undesirable. Obviously, you have to interact with the system to investigate it. The answer is to make a forensic copy and work with that copy. You can make a forensic copy with most major forensic tools such as AccessData's Forensic Toolkit, Guidance Software's EnCase, or PassMark's OSForensics. There are also open source software products that allow copying of original source information. To be specific, make a copy and analyze the copy.

There are times when you will need to interact directly with live evidence. For example, when a computer is first discovered, you will want to do an initial analysis to determine running processes and connections before you make an image. You may also need to perform live forensics in certain situations such as some cloud computing environments. We will discuss these as we encounter them in this book.

Document Trail

The next issue is documentation. The rule is that you document everything. Who was present when the device was seized? What was connected to the device or showing on the screen when you seized it? What specific tools and techniques did you use? Who had access to the evidence from the time of seizure until the time of trial? All of this must be documented. And when in doubt, err on the side of over-documentation. It really is not possible to document too much information about an investigation.

Secure the Evidence

It is absolutely critical to the integrity of your investigation as well as to maintaining the chain of custody that you secure the evidence. It is common to have the forensic lab be a locked room with access given only to those who must enter. Then, evidence is usually secured in a safe, with access given out only on a need-to-know basis. You have to take every reasonable precaution to ensure that no one can tamper with the evidence.

Knowledge Needed for Computer Forensics Analysis

To conduct computer forensics, a certain background body of knowledge is required, just as with traditional forensics. For example, you cannot examine DNA without some basic education in blood and genetics. This applies to computer forensics as well. You must have an understanding of the systems you are examining in order to successfully examine them.

This chapter assumes that you have a basic understanding of computer hardware, software, and operating systems. This section briefly discusses the highlights of these areas that you need to know, however. If you find you are lacking in one or more areas, you should take some time to brush up on these topics before continuing. For many readers, these items will be a review; for others, some information may be new. If this is new information for you, bear in mind that this is the absolute minimum of knowledge. The more you know about the underlying technology, the more effective you will be.

Hardware

In general, the good digital forensics examiners begin with a working knowledge of the hardware for the devices they want to examine. For PCs and laptops, this includes knowledge equivalent to the CompTIA A+ certification or a basic PC hardware course. If you are doing phone or router forensics, you need a similar level of knowledge of the hardware on those devices.

For PCs, this means a strong understanding of hard drives, memory, motherboards, and expansion cards. What exactly is a "strong understanding"? Think about random access memory (RAM). You are probably aware that RAM is **volatile memory** and it stores the programs and data you currently have open, but only for as long as the computer has power supplied to it. However, that level of knowledge is inadequate for forensics. A forensic examiner needs to go much deeper and understand the various types of RAM, how they work, the type of information that is contained in each, and how the computer uses them.

Random Access Memory

RAM can be examined in multiple ways. One way is to look at the method whereby information is written to and read from the RAM. These are presented in sequential order from older to newer technologies:

- **Extended data out dynamic random access memory (EDO DRAM)**—Single-cycle EDO has the ability to carry out a complete memory transaction in one clock cycle. Otherwise, each sequential RAM access within the same page takes two clock cycles instead of three, once the page has been selected.
- **Burst EDO (BEDO) DRAM**—An evolution of the EDO, burst EDO DRAM can process four memory addresses in one burst.

- **Asynchronous dynamic random access memory (ADRAM)**—ADRAM is not synchronized to the CPU clock.
- **Synchronous dynamic random access memory (SDRAM)**—SDRAM is a replacement for EDO.
- **Double data rate (DDR) SDRAM**—DDR SDRAM was a later development of SDRAM. DDR2, DDR3, and DDR4 are now available. DDR 5 is still under development at the time of this writing, but should be available soon, in fall of 2021.

SDRAM and, more specifically, DDR3 and DDR4, are the most common forms of RAM found in PCs and laptops.

Another way to look at RAM, and one that is particularly important from a forensic point of view, is to consider the volatility of the data stored. Volatility refers to how easily the data can be changed, either intentionally or unintentionally:

- **Random access memory (RAM)**—RAM is what most people think of when they say *memory*. It is easy to write to and read from. RAM is very volatile; as soon as power is discontinued, the data is gone.
- **Read-only memory (ROM)**—As the name suggests, ROM is not at all volatile; it cannot be changed. This is usually used for instructions embedded in chips and controls how the computer, option cards, peripherals, and other devices operate.
- **Programmable read-only memory (PROM)**—PROM can be programmed only once. Data is not lost when power is removed.
- **Erasable programmable read-only memory (EPROM)**—Data is not lost when power is removed. Again, EPROM is a technique for storing instructions on chips.
- **Electronically erasable programmable read-only memory (EEPROM)**—This form is how the instructions in your computer's basic input/output system (BIOS) are stored.

Hard Drives

A forensic specialist must also understand the following storage devices. The descriptions given here are for various types of connectors. The drives themselves are the same, but the method of attaching the drive, as well as the speed and efficiency of getting data to and from the drive, differ.

- **Small Computer System Interface (SCSI)**—SCSI has been around for many years, and it is particularly popular in high-end servers. This standard is actually fairly old, as it was established in 1986. SCSI devices must have a terminator at the end of the chain of devices to work and are limited to 16 chained devices.
- **Integrated Drive Electronics (IDE)**—IDE is an older standard, but it is one that was commonly used on PCs for many years. It is obvious you are dealing with an IDE or EIDE drive if you encounter a 40-pin connector on the drive.
- **Enhanced Integrated Drive Electronics (EIDE)**—This is an extension/enhancement of IDE.
- **Parallel Advanced Technology Attachment (PATA)**—PATA is an enhancement of IDE. It uses either a 40-pin (like IDE) or 80-pin connector.

- **Serial Advanced Technology Attachment (SATA)**—SATA is what you are most likely to find today. These devices are commonly found in workstations and many servers. The internals of the hard drive are very similar to IDE and EIDE, but the connectivity to the computer's motherboard is different. Also, unlike IDE or EIDE drives, this type of drive has no jumpers to set the drive.
- **Serial SCSI**—This is an enhancement of SCSI. It supports up to 65,537 devices and does not require termination.
- **Solid-state drives**—Solid-state drives (SSDs) are becoming more common, so it's worthwhile to discuss them in a bit more detail. Unlike the previously discussed drive types, these are not the same basic hard drive. These drives have an entirely different construction and method of storing data. SSDs use microchips that retain data in non-volatile memory chips and contain no moving parts. Since 2010, most SSDs have used NAND-based flash memory (NAND stands for "negated AND gate"), which retains memory even without power. Solid-state drives do not benefit from defragmentation. Any defragmentation process adds additional writes on the NAND flash, which already has a limited cycle life. High-performance flash-based SSDs generally require one-half to one-third the power of hard disk drives (HDDs); high-performance DRAM SSDs generally require as much power as HDDs and consume power when the rest of the system is shut down.

All of these, except for SSDs, refer to how the hard drive connects to the motherboard and transfers data, and do not define how information is stored on the disk. For all but SSDs, the following hard drive facts apply.

HDDs record data by magnetizing ferromagnetic material directionally to represent either a 0 or a 1 binary digit. The magnetic data is stored on platters; the platters are organized on a spindle with a read/write head reading and writing data to and from the platters. The data is organized as follows:

- A *sector* is the basic unit of data storage on a hard disk, which is usually 512 bytes. However, newer systems often use a 4096-byte sector size.
- A cluster is a logical grouping of sectors. Clusters can be 1 to 128 sectors in size. That means 512 bytes up to 64 kilobytes. The minimum size a file can use is one cluster. If the file is less than the size of a cluster, the remaining space is simply unused.
- Sectors are in turn organized by tracks.
- **Drive geometry** refers to the functional dimensions of a drive in terms of the number of heads, cylinders, and sectors per track.

That is a basic description of most hard drives (with the exception of solid-state drives). Forensic examiners should know the following terms, which are used with all hard drives, including solid-state drives (note these terms are the same, even though the structures of solid-state drives and traditional hard drives are different):

- **Slack space** is the space between the end of a file and the end of the cluster, assuming the file does not occupy the entire cluster. This is space that can be used to hide data. Discussing slack space brings us to an issue regarding SSDs. With SSDs, a technique called *wear leveling* is used to extend the life of the drive. The issue is that SSDs use flash memory (and related technology) with individual segments (as opposed to sectors). Each segment has a finite number of erase cycles before the segment is unreliable. Thus wear leveling spreads out the use of the SSD to avoid this problem. That means slack space is not particularly useful on SSDs.

- **Low-level format** creates a structure of sectors, tracks, and clusters.
- **High-level format** is the process of setting up an empty file system on the disk and installing a boot sector. This is sometimes referred to as a quick format.

It should be noted that SSDs have become the most common. At first, they were used largely for external drives and laptops. However, the use of that SSDs is continuing to grow. So you should expect to see these more often.

Software

Once you have a basic understanding of hardware, the next step is to learn about the software, and this begins with the operating system. It is imperative that you have a strong working knowledge of the operating system running on the device you want to examine.

Windows

There's a lot to know about Windows, but for now, here's a basic overview of how it works. The heart of Windows is the Windows Registry. The Windows Registry is essentially a repository of all settings, software, and parameters for Windows. If new software is installed, the Registry is updated to indicate the new software. If the background color of the desktop is changed, the Registry is updated to indicate the new color. From this Registry, you can get all kinds of information, including the password for wireless networks and the serial numbers for all USB devices that have been connected to that computer. This is really the most important part of Windows from both a technical support and a forensic point of view.

Windows also has other interesting places to look for forensic evidence. There are certain folders and files—the index.dat file, for instance—that are great places to find evidence. Even browser cookies and history can be useful. Given that Windows is such a common operating system, it is advisable to be very familiar with Windows.

Linux

Linux is particularly interesting from a forensic point of view. Even though it is not as widely used as Windows, it is a favorite in the security and forensics community. You will find that a lot of free forensic tools come with Linux. In fact, one specific Linux distribution called Kali Linux (formerly BackTrack in 2013) has an extensive collection of forensic, security, and hacking tools.

Linux is a UNIX clone, developed originally by Linus Torvalds. There are now well over 100 different distributions, or variations, of Linux. However, all have some commonalities. In the Linux world, work done from the command line, called the shell in Linux, is far more important than it is in Windows.

Mac OS

For many years, Apple Macintosh (currently branded as macOS) was a complete operating system. However, beginning with OS X, the Mac OS system has been based on FreeBSD, a

UNIX clone very similar to Linux. The graphical user interface is just that: an interface. The underlying operating system is a UNIX-like system.

This means that many forensic techniques you can use on Linux can also be used on Mac OS, from the shell prompt.

Files and File Systems

Computers store discrete sets of related information in files. Any document, spreadsheet, picture, video, or even program is a file. It is a very easy thing to change the extension of a file so that it looks like some other type of file. However, that will not change the file structure itself. There are tools that allow viewing of the actual file structure and the file header. This is very important from a forensic perspective. The file header gives you an accurate understanding of the file, regardless of whether the extension has been changed. A few basic facts about files are as follows:

- File headers start at the first byte of a file. This is particularly important when we look at file carving later in this book.
- In graphics file formats, the header might give information about an image's size, resolution, number of colors, and the like.
- The Executable and Linkable Format (ELF, formerly called Extensible Linking Format) is a common standard file format for executables, object code, and shared libraries for UNIX-based systems.
- Portable Executable (PE) is used in Windows for executables and dynamic-link libraries (DLLs). PE files are derived from the earlier Common Object File Format (COFF) found on VAX/VMS, a common operating system for mainframe computers.
- Area density is the data per area of disk.
- Windows Office files have a globally unique identifier (GUID) to identify them.

Files are organized on the computer based on the file system. There are many file systems, but they can be divided into two categories. Journaling is basically the process whereby the file system keeps a record of what file transactions take place so that in the event of a hard drive crash, the files can be recovered. Journaling file systems are fault tolerant because the file system logs all changes to files, directories, or file structures. The log in which changes are recorded is referred to as the file systems journal—thus the term *journaling* file systems.

There are actually two types of journaling: physical and logical. With physical journaling, the system logs a copy of every block that is about to be written to the storage device before it is written. The log also includes a checksum of those blocks, to make sure there is no error in writing the block. With logical journaling, only changes to file metadata are stored in the journal.

Here are some specific file systems:

- **File Allocation Table (FAT)** is an older system that was popular with Microsoft operating systems for many years. FAT was first implemented in Microsoft Standalone Disk BASIC. FAT stores file locations by sector in a file called the file allocation table. This table contains information about which clusters are being used by which particular files and which clusters are free to be used. The various extensions of FAT, such as FAT16 and FAT32, differ in the number of bits available for filenames.

- **New Technology File System (NTFS)** was introduced by Microsoft in 1993 as a new file system to replace FAT. This is the file system used by Windows NT 4, 2000, XP, Vista, 7, Server 2003, and Server 2008. One major improvement of NTFS over FAT was the increased volume sizes NTFS could support. The maximum NTFS volume size is $2^{64} - 1$ clusters. We will be discussing NTFS in more detail when we discuss Windows forensics later in this book.

- **ReFS or Resilient File System** is a new file system from Microsoft. It is available on Windows Server 2019, but not on Windows 10. As the name suggests, it is, in essence, a more resilient file system. This is accomplished with a variety of techniques, including checksums for both metadata and file data as well as proactive error correction. You can learn more at Microsoft's online documentation (https://docs.microsoft.com/en-us/windows-server/storage/refs/refs-overview).

- **Apple File System (APFS)** is the default file system for Apple computers using Mac OS 10.13. APFS supports encryption, snapshots, and other features. It is optimized for use with solid-state drives, but can also be used with traditional hard drives.

- **Extended file system** was the first file system created specifically for Linux. There have been many versions of EXT; the current version is 4. The EXT4 file system can support volumes with sizes up to 1 exabyte (10^{18} bytes, or 1 billion gigabytes) and files with sizes up to 16 terabytes. This is a huge file and volume size, and no current hard drives come even close to that volume size. For an administrator, one of the most exciting features of EXT4 is that it is backward compatible with EXT2 and EXT3, making it possible to mount drives that use those earlier versions of EXT.

- **ReiserFS** is a popular journaling file system, used primarily with Linux. ReiserFS was the first file system to be included with the standard Linux kernel, and first appeared in kernel version 2.4.1. Unlike some file systems, ReiserFS supported journaling from its inception, whereas EXT did not support journaling until version 3. ReiserFS is open source and was invented by Hans Reiser.

- The **Berkeley Fast File System** is also known as the UNIX file system. As its name suggests, it was developed at the University of California, Berkeley specifically for UNIX. Like many file systems, Berkeley uses a bitmap to track free clusters, indicating which clusters are available and which are not. Like EXT, Berkeley includes the FSCK utility. This is only one of many similarities between Berkeley and EXT. In fact, some sources consider EXT to just be a variant of the Berkeley Fast File System.

Networks

Digital forensics, like all branches of cybersecurity, breaks information into two types. There is information at rest and information in motion. Information at rest includes anything that is stored inside the computer, including in the file system or memory. Information in motion is information being transmitted between endpoints and includes the protocols and other information needed for transmission. The transmission of information across networks and the network components used make up a vast, quickly changing field. The modern forensic investigator, however, should be very familiar with the components and how they work, as well as the protocols and their operation, if information in motion is to be considered as a part of the investigator's skill set. The modern forensic analyst who will consider information in motion must also be very familiar with the concepts and operation of both the seven-layer Open Systems Interconnection (OSI) Reference Model and the five-layer Internet Engineering Task Force (IETF) model. If you lack this knowledge, you must acquire it before proceeding any further.

Addresses

The digital forensics analyst must be aware of the way that computer information is addressed and the proper vocabulary for discussing the different types of addresses and units of information transfer. It is also important for the digital forensics analyst to understand that not all addresses are a part of every communication. If they are present, the addresses are part of a hierarchy and are placed, one within the other, like envelopes.

Physical Ports

Physical ports are physical. You can touch them. Even a wireless physical port can be touched, although you must open the computer or other device to find the antenna first. The physical ports operate at OSI Layer 1, the Physical Layer. The units of information transfer are 1 and 0 bits grouped into fixed-length units called Layer 1 frames.

Media Access Control (MAC) Addresses

A MAC address is a 6-byte (or 48-bit) address used to identify a network interface card. The first three bytes identify the vendor, the second three identify the specific card. This can also be referred to as a computer's physical address.

A MAC address is supposed to be unique, is supposed to be tied to one—and only one—physical port, and is not supposed to be duplicated or reused for any reason. In practice, this is not always the case. Duplication of MAC addresses can occur due to bad quality control or can be done intentionally for a variety of malicious reasons. The keen forensic investigator will never be fooled by duplicate MAC addresses.

IP Addresses

IP addresses, sometimes called logical addresses, are assigned to a computer and can be easily changed. While IP version 6 has been available for quite some time, a majority of computers are still using IP version 4, which provides a 32-bit address. We will discuss IP version 4 and version 6 in more detail later in this book when we discuss network forensics.

Logical Port Numbers

Communication over a network depends on an IP address and a port number. You can think of the port as a channel. **TABLE 1-1** lists some common ports and their uses.

Uniform Resource Locators

As the internet grew and the number of servers and their IP addresses grew, the Domain Name System (DNS) was created to allow internet users to type a name instead of an IP address. This level of simplification is great, but it introduces a number of potential forensic issues. Issues range from changing the mapping of website name to IP address permanently or temporarily and many different forms of this that can be used to redirect browsers incorrectly and befuddle forensic efforts.

TABLE 1-1 Common ports and their uses.	
20, 21 – FTP (File Transfer Protocol)	Used for transferring files between computers. Port 20 is for data, and port 21 for control.
22 – SSH and secure FTP	Secure communications and file transfer
23 – Telnet	Used to remotely log onto a system. You can then use a command prompt or shell to execute commands on that system. Popular with network administrators.
25 – SMTP (Simple Mail Transfer Protocol)	Used for sending email
43 – WhoIS	A command that queries a target IP address for information
53 – DNS (Domain Name Service)	Translates URLs into web addresses
69 – TFTP	UDP-based file transfer
80 – HTTP (Hyper Text Transfer Protocol)	Displays web pages
88 – Kerberos Authentication	Authentication in environments using Kerberos authentication
109 – POP 2	Old email protocol
110 – POP3 (Post Office Protocol Version 3)	Used to retrieve email
137, 138, 139 – NetBIOS	Used in Windows networks
161 – SNMP (and 162)	Simple network management protocol
179 – BGP	Border gateway protocol. Used by gateway routers exchanging routing data.
194 – IRC (Internet Relay Chat)	Used in chat rooms
220 – IMAP	Email protocol
389 – LDAP	Lightweight directory access protocol
443 – HTTPS	Encrypted HTTP
445 – Active Directory, SMB	Used in Windows networks
464 – Kerberos	Used to change passwords
465 – SMTP over SSL	Encrypted email
636 – LDAPS (LDAP over SSL/TLS)	Encrypted LDAP

Addressing Review

In a complete, end-to-end internet communication, it is most common that user information, such as email text, would be formatted as specified by the email protocol. A URL would then be used to find the actual IP address of the recipient. The message would be formatted per the TCP protocol and sent with the proper TCP port number set to the IP addresses. The

IP packet containing all of this would be put into a special envelope built per the protocol rules of Ethernet, which would make its way onto the actual wire, or go across the wireless or optical connection, on its way through the cloud to its destination. At the destination, the process would be done in reverse and the email, or at least a part of it, would have gotten through to its destination.

Basic Network Utilities

You can execute some basic network utilities from a command prompt (Windows) or from a shell (UNIX/Linux). This text's discussion executes the commands and discusses them from the Windows command-prompt perspective; however, it must be stressed that these utilities are available in all operating systems. This section covers the `ipconfig`, `ping`, and `tracert` utilities.

Working with `ipconfig`

The first thing you need to do is to get information about your own system. To accomplish this fact-finding mission, you need to get to a command prompt. In Windows 10, you do this by going to the search box at the bottom left-hand side of the screen and typing `cmd`. For other versions of Windows, the process is identical, except the first option is called simply Programs rather than All Programs. Now you can type in `ipconfig`. You could input the same command in UNIX or Linux by typing in `ifconfig` from the shell. After typing in `ipconfig`—`ifconfig` in Linux—you should see something similar to what is shown in **FIGURE 1-2**.

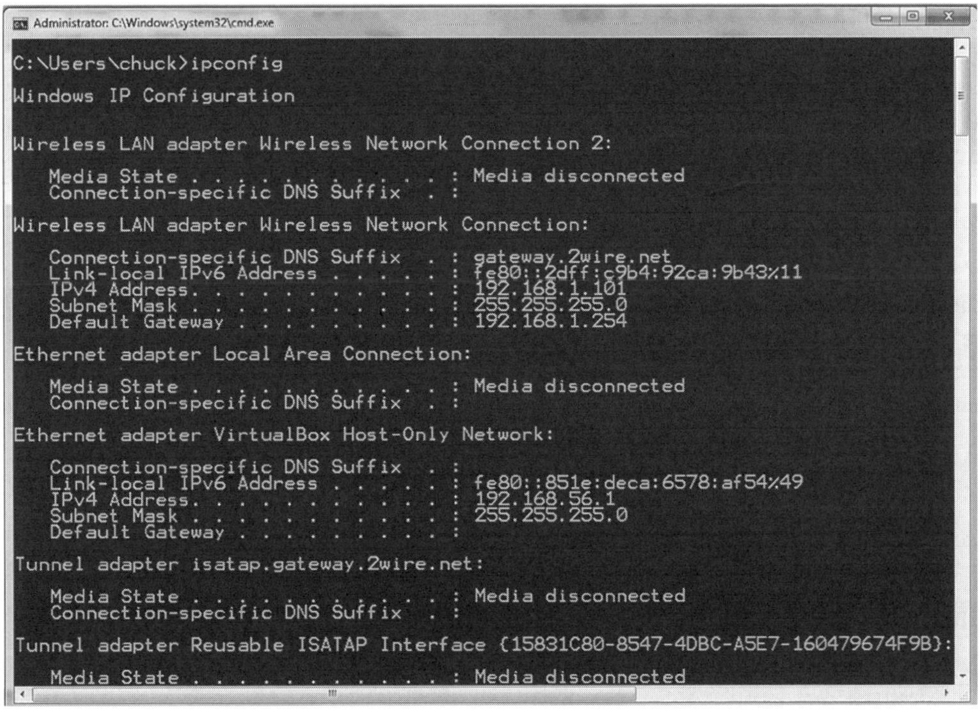

FIGURE 1-2
`ipconfig`.

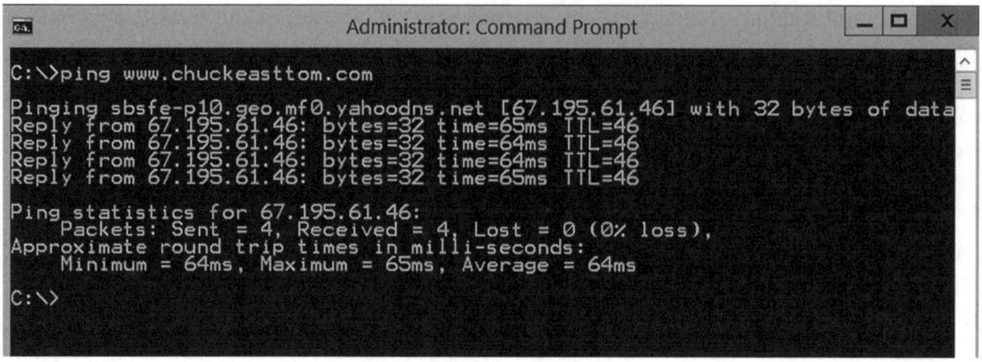

FIGURE 1-3

ping.

This command gives you some information about your connection to a network or to the internet. Most important, you find out your own IP address. The command also has the IP address for your default gateway, which is your connection to the outside world. Running the ipconfig command is a first step in determining your system's network configuration.

You can see that this option gives you much more information. For example, ipconfig/all gives the name of your computer, when your computer obtained its IP address, and more.

Using ping

Another commonly used command is ping, which is used to send a test packet, or echo packet, to a machine to find out if the machine is reachable and how long the packet takes to reach the machine. This useful diagnostic tool can be employed in elementary hacking techniques. The command is shown in **FIGURE 1-3**.

You can see in Figure 1-3 that a 32-byte echo packet was sent to the destination and returned. The TTL item means *time to live*. That time unit is how many intermediary steps, or hops, the packet should take to the destination before giving up. Remember that the internet is a vast conglomerate of interconnected networks. Your packet probably won't go straight to its destination. It will have to take several hops to get there. As with ipconfig, you can type in ping -? to find out various ways you can refine your ping.

Working with tracert

The final command this section examines is the tracert command. While tracert can be useful for some live network troubleshooting, the information reported by tracert is not useful or trustworthy for forensic examination. This same command can be executed in Linux or UNIX, but there it is called "traceroute" rather than "tracert." You can see this command in **FIGURE 1-4**.

This section is just a brief overview of the hardware, software, and networking knowledge you should have in order to study forensics. If you find you are lacking in one or more areas, do some review in those areas before you proceed.

Obscured Information and Anti-Forensics

Two more challenges in obtaining digital evidence are obscured information and anti-forensics.

```
Administrator: Command Prompt                          _  □  X

C:\>tracert www.chuckeasttom.com
Tracing route to sbsfe-p10.geo.mf0.yahoodns.net [67.195.61.46]
over a maximum of 30 hops:

  1    <1 ms    <1 ms    <1 ms  Tardis [192.168.1.1]
  2    <1 ms    <1 ms    <1 ms  192.168.0.1
  3     8 ms     8 ms     7 ms  142.254.141.53
  4    26 ms    20 ms    28 ms  tge0-0-4.plaotxso01h.texas.rr.com [24.28.90
  5    12 ms     9 ms    10 ms  agg21.plantxmp01r.texas.rr.com [24.175.49.2
  6    13 ms    13 ms    14 ms  agg27.crtntxjt01r.texas.rr.com [24.175.36.1
  7    46 ms    13 ms    13 ms  agg21.dllatxl301r.texas.rr.com [24.175.49.0
  8    11 ms    15 ms    14 ms  66.109.1.216
  9    10 ms     9 ms    10 ms  107.14.17.133
 10    10 ms    12 ms    11 ms  UNKNOWN-216-115-102-X.yahoo.com [216.115.10
 11    54 ms    64 ms    54 ms  ae-3.pat2.bfz.yahoo.com [216.115.97.209]
 12    64 ms    64 ms    64 ms  ae-6.pat2.gqb.yahoo.com [216.115.96.62]
 13    66 ms    64 ms    64 ms  et-18-1-0.msr2.gq1.yahoo.com [66.196.67.115
 14    64 ms    64 ms    65 ms  et-1-0-0.clr2-a-gdc.gq1.yahoo.com [67.195.3
 15    64 ms    64 ms    64 ms  te-8-1.bas2-1-flk.gq1.yahoo.com [67.195.1.1
 16    64 ms    65 ms    64 ms  p10pn-i.geo.vip.gq1.yahoo.com [67.195.61.46

Trace complete.

C:\>_
```

FIGURE 1-4

`tracert.`

Obscured Information

Information can be obscured in a number of ways. *Obscured information* may be scrambled by encryption, hidden using steganographic software, compressed, or in a proprietary format. Sometimes, cybercriminals obscure information to deter forensic examination. More often, companies use certain manipulation and storage techniques to protect business-sensitive information. Regardless of the reason for obscured data, collecting and analyzing it is difficult.

Data that has been obscured through encryption, steganography, compression, or proprietary formats can sometimes be converted with some serious detective work and the right tools. Forensic specialists often must do quite a bit of work to decrypt encrypted information. In many cases, the investigator cannot decrypt information unless the data owner provides the encryption key and algorithm. When digital evidence has been encrypted and is in use on a live system, an investigator might have to collect evidence through a live extraction process.

Anti-Forensics

Every investigation is unique. Investigations are not necessarily friendly activities. Forensic specialists may have to conduct the investigation with or without the cooperation of the information owner. And the information owner may or may not be the target of the investigation. Investigations are difficult with uncooperative information owners.

Attackers may use techniques to intentionally conceal their identities, locations, and behavior. For example, perpetrators may conceal their identities by using networked connections at a library, an internet café, or another public computer kiosk. Or they may use encryption or anonymous services to protect themselves. The actions that perpetrators take to conceal their locations, activities, or identities are generally termed **anti-forensics**.

Cybercriminals are becoming better at covering their tracks as their awareness of digital forensics capabilities increases. The following are examples of anti-forensics techniques:

- **Data destruction**—Methods for disposing of data vary. They can be as simple as wiping the memory buffers used by a program, or they can be as complex as repeatedly overwriting a cluster of data with patterns of 1s and 0s. Digital evidence can be destroyed easily. For example, starting a computer updates timestamps and modifies files. Attaching a hard disk or USB stick modifies file-system timestamps. Powering off a machine destroys volatile memory. Suspects may delete files and folders and defragment their hard drives in an attempt to overwrite evidence.
- **Data hiding**—Suspects often store data where an investigator is unlikely to find it. They may hide data, for example, in reserved disk sectors or as logical partitions within a defined, public partition. Or they may simply change filenames and extensions.
- **Data transformation**—Suspects may process information in a way that disguises its meaning. For example, they may use encryption to scramble a message based on an algorithm. Or they may use steganography to hide a message inside a larger message.
- **File system alteration**—Suspects often corrupt data structures and files that organize data, such as a Windows NT File System (NTFS) volume.

The Daubert Standard

One legal principle that is key to forensics and is all too often overlooked in forensics books is the Daubert standard. The Cornell University Law School defines the **Daubert standard** as follows:

[handwritten margin notes: 1. empirical testing 2. peer review 3. error rate and standard 4. generally accepted theory/technique]

> Standard used by a trial judge to make a preliminary assessment of whether an expert's scientific testimony is based on reasoning or methodology that is scientifically valid and can properly be applied to the facts at issue. Under this standard, the factors that may be considered in determining whether the methodology is valid are: (1) whether the theory or technique in question can be and has been tested; (2) whether it has been subjected to peer review and publication; (3) its known or potential error rate; (4) the existence and maintenance of standards controlling its operation; and (5) whether it has attracted widespread acceptance within a relevant scientific community.

What this means, in layman's terms, is that any scientific evidence presented in a trial has to have been reviewed and tested by the relevant scientific community. For a computer forensics investigator, that means that any tools, techniques, or processes you utilize in your investigation should be ones that are widely accepted in the computer forensics community. You cannot simply make up new tests or procedures.

This, naturally, brings up a question: How do new techniques become widely accepted? Let's suppose you have developed a new tool that extracts forensic information from the Windows Registry. A first step might be to provide a copy of that tool to a few professors of forensics, allowing them to experiment with it. You might also publish an article describing it. After it has been tested by the forensic community and articles about it have been read (and possibly rebutted), then your tool would be usable in real forensic investigations.

It is important to remember the Daubert standard because it will affect your forensic approach. It also reminds us of an even more basic concept: The evidence you collect is important only if it is admissible in court. So you have to pay attention to the techniques and tools you use and maintain the chain of custody.

If you fail to use widely accepted techniques, to fully document your methodology, and to use only those tools and techniques you are qualified to use, the opposing attorney might issue what is commonly called a "Daubert challenge." This is a motion to exclude all or part of your testimony due to it failing to meet the Daubert standard. Daubert challenges are quite common in civil cases, but are not common in criminal court. There has been a movement in the legal community in recent years to increase Daubert challenges in criminal court. The rationale behind this is that some people believe that "junk science" is making its way into criminal proceedings, and well-articulated Daubert challenges could reduce that.

U.S. Laws Affecting Digital Forensics

There are many laws that affect digital forensics investigation. For example, some jurisdictions have passed laws that require the investigator to be either a law enforcement officer or a licensed private investigator to extract the evidence. Of course, that does not prevent a forensic investigator from working with information someone else extracted or extracting evidence if the information owner gave his or her permission. It is important to be aware of the legal requirements in the jurisdiction in which you work.

The Federal Privacy Act of 1974

The Privacy Act of 1974 establishes a code of information-handling practices that governs the collection, maintenance, use, and dissemination of information about individuals that is maintained in systems of records by U.S. federal agencies. A system of records is a group of records under the control of an agency from which information is retrieved by the name of the individual or by some identifier assigned to the individual.

The Privacy Protection Act of 1980

The Privacy Protection Act (PPA) of 1980 protects journalists from being required to turn over to law enforcement any work product and documentary materials, including sources, before it is disseminated to the public. Journalists who most need the protection of the PPA are those who are working on stories that are highly controversial or that describe criminal acts, because the information gathered may also be useful to law enforcement.

The Communications Assistance to Law Enforcement Act of 1994

The Communications Assistance to Law Enforcement Act of 1994 is a federal wiretap law for traditional wired telephony. It was expanded in 2004 to include wireless, voice over packets, and other forms of electronic communications, including signaling traffic and metadata.

Unlawful Access to Stored Communications: 18 U.S.C. § 2701

This act covers access to a facility through which electronic communication is provided or exceeding the access that was authorized. It is broadly written to apply to a range of offenses. Punishment can be up to 5 years in prison and fines for the first offense.

The actual wording of the statute is as follows:

1. Offense. —Except as provided in subsection (c) of this section whoever—intentionally accesses without authorization a facility through which an electronic communication service is provided; or
2. intentionally exceeds an authorization to access that facility; and thereby obtains, alters, or prevents authorized access to a wire or electronic communication while it is in electronic storage in such system shall be punished as provided in subsection (b) of this section.

This law is used less frequently than the Computer Fraud and Abuse Act. However, it is written broadly enough to cover a number of acts. Primarily, the focus is on any facility, server, or device used to store electronic communications. It is sometimes the case that when employees leave a company, they seek to take information that they can use in competition with the company. This can include emails or other stored communications.

The Electronic Communications Privacy Act of 1986

The Electronic Communications Privacy Act of 1986 governs the privacy and disclosure, access, and interception of content and traffic data related to electronic communications.

The Computer Security Act of 1987

The Computer Security Act of 1987 was passed to improve the security and privacy of sensitive information in federal computer systems. The law requires the establishment of minimum acceptable security practices, creation of computer security plans, and training of system users or owners of facilities that house sensitive information.

The Foreign Intelligence Surveillance Act of 1978

The Foreign Intelligence Surveillance Act of 1978 (FISA) is a law that allows for collection of "foreign intelligence information" between foreign powers and agents of foreign powers using physical and electronic surveillance. A warrant is issued by the FISA court for actions under FISA.

The Child Protection and Sexual Predator Punishment Act of 1998

The Child Protection and Sexual Predator Punishment Act of 1998 requires service providers that become aware of the storage or transmission of child pornography to report it to law enforcement.

The Children's Online Privacy Protection Act of 1998

The Children's Online Privacy Protection Act of 1998 (COPPA) protects children 13 years of age and under from the collection and use of their personal information by websites. It is noteworthy that COPPA replaces the Child Online Protection Act of 1988 (COPA), which was determined to be unconstitutional.

The Communications Decency Act of 1996

The Communications Decency Act of 1996 was designed to protect persons 18 years of age and under from downloading or viewing material considered indecent. This act has been subject to court cases that subsequently changed some definitions and penalties.

The Telecommunications Act of 1996

The Telecommunications Act of 1996 includes many provisions relative to the privacy and disclosure of information in motion through and across telephony and computer networks.

The Wireless Communications and Public Safety Act of 1999

The Wireless Communications and Public Safety Act of 1999 allows for collection and use of "empty" communications, which means nonverbal and nontext communications, such as GPS information.

The USA PATRIOT Act

The USA PATRIOT Act is the primary law under which a wide variety of internet and communications information content and metadata is currently collected. Provisions exist within the PATRIOT Act to protect the identity and privacy of U.S. citizens.

The Sarbanes-Oxley Act of 2002

The Sarbanes-Oxley Act of 2002 contains many provisions about recordkeeping and destruction of electronic records relating to the management and operation of publicly held companies.

18 USC 1030 Fraud and Related Activity in Connection with Computers

This is one of the most widely used laws in hacking cases. It covers a wide range of crimes involving illicit access of any computer.

18 USC 1020 Fraud and Related Activity in Connection with Access Devices

This is closely related to 1030 but covers access devices (such as routers).

The Digital Millennium Copyright Act (DMCA)

This controversial law was enacted in 1998. It makes it a crime to publish methods or techniques to circumvent copyright protection. It is controversial because it has been used against legitimate researchers publishing research papers.

18 USC § 1028A Identity Theft and Aggravated Identity Theft

As the name suggests, this law targets any crime related to identity theft. It is often applied in stolen credit card cases.

18 USC § 2251 Sexual Exploitation of Children

This law covers a range of child exploitation crimes and is often seen in child pornography cases. Related to this rather broad law are several others, such as:

- 18 U.S.C. § 2260: Production of sexually explicit depictions of a minor for importation into the United States
- 18 U.S.C. § 2252: Certain activities relating to material involving the sexual exploitation of minors (possession, distribution, and receipt of child pornography)
- 18 U.S.C. § 2252A: Certain activities relating to material constituting or containing child pornography

Warrants

According to the Supreme Court, a "seizure of property occurs when there is some meaningful interference with an individual's possessory interests in that property" (*United States v. Jacobsen*, 466 U.S. 109, 113 [1984]). The Court also characterized the interception of intangible communications as a seizure, in the case of *Berger v. New York* (388 U.S. 41, 59–60 [1967]). That means that law enforcement need not take property in order for it to be considered seizure; merely interfering with an individual's access to his or her own property constitutes seizure. *Berger v. New York* extends that to communications. If law enforcement's conduct does not violate a person's "reasonable expectation of privacy," then formally it does not constitute a Fourth Amendment "search" and no warrant is required. There have been many cases where the issue of reasonable expectation of privacy has been argued. To use an example that is quite clear, if you save a message in an electronic diary, you clearly have a reasonable expectation of privacy; however, if you post such a message on a public bulletin board, you can have no expectation of privacy. In less clear cases, a general rule is that courts have held that law enforcement officers are prohibited from accessing and viewing information stored in a computer if it would be prohibited from opening a closed container and examining its contents in the same situation.

Warrants are not needed when evidence is in plain sight. For example, if a detective is talking to someone about a string of burglaries in the neighborhood and can clearly see child pornography on that person's computer screen, no warrant is needed. Another exception to the need for a warrant is consent. If someone who is authorized to provide consent (for example, the owner of a phone or computer) gives law enforcement that consent to a search, then no warrant is needed.

In computer crime cases, two consent issues arise particularly often. First, when does a search exceed the scope of consent? For example, when a person agrees to the search of a location, such as his or her apartment, does that consent authorize the retrieval of information stored in computers at the location? Second, who is the proper party to consent to a search? Can roommates, friends, and parents legally grant consent to a search of another person's computer files? These are all critical questions that must be considered when searching a computer. In general, courts have held that only the actual owner of a property can grant consent, or someone who has legal guardianship of the owner. For example, a parent of a minor child can grant consent to search the child's living quarters and computers. However, a roommate who shares rent can grant consent to search only shared living quarters and computers co-owned by both parties. A roommate cannot grant consent to search the private property of the other person.

There are other cases where investigators don't need a warrant. One such circumstance is border crossing. Anyone going through customs in any country may have their belongings searched. This can include a complete forensic examination of laptops, cell phones, and other devices. Another such instance where a warrant is not needed is if there is imminent danger that evidence will be destroyed. In the case of the *United States v. David*, the court held that "When destruction of evidence is imminent a warrantless seizure of that evidence is justified if there is probable cause to believe that the item seized constitutes evidence of criminal activity."

It is also important not to exceed the scope of a warrant. In *United States v. Schlingloff*, 2012 U.S. Dist. LEXIS 157272 (C.D. Ill. Oct. 24, 2012), Judge Shadid held that use of Forensic Toolkit's (FTK) Known File Filter (KFF) to alert on child pornography files was outside the scope of a warrant issued to look for evidence of identity theft. In this case, the owner of the device was suspected of identity theft, and a warrant was issued so that police could search for evidence of that crime. However, the investigator used the Known File Filter to search for child pornography, and indeed found illegal images on the computer in question.

Federal Guidelines

If you are setting up a forensic lab, or if you are new to forensics, a good place to start is the federal guidelines. Two agencies in particular—the FBI and the Secret Service—are particularly important.

The FBI

If an incident occurs, the FBI recommends that the first responder should preserve the state of the computer at the time of the incident by making a backup copy of any logs, any damaged or altered files, and any other files modified, viewed, or left by the intruder. This last part is critical. Hackers frequently use various tools and may leave traces of their presence. Furthermore, the FBI advises that if the incident is in progress, you should activate any auditing or recording software you might have available. Collect as much data about the incident as you can. In other words, this might be a case where you do not take the machine offline, but rather analyze the attack in progress.

The FBI computer forensics guidelines stress the importance of securing any evidence. They further stress that computer evidence can come in many forms. Here are a few common forms:

- Hard drives
- System logs

- Portable storage, such as USB drives and external drives
- Router logs
- Emails
- Chat room logs
- Cell phones
- SIM cards for cell phones
- Logs from security devices, such as firewalls and intrusion-detection systems
- Databases and database logs

What you secure will be dependent upon the nature of the cybercrime. For example, in the case of child predators, online stalkers, or online fraud, email may be very important, but router logs may be irrelevant. The FBI also stresses that you should work with a copy of the hard drive, not the original.

The FBI has a cybercrimes web page, which is a very useful resource for learning more about trends in cybercrime and in computer forensics.

The Secret Service

The U.S. Secret Service is the premier federal agency tasked with combating cybercrime. It has a website devoted to computer forensics that includes forensics courses. These courses are usually for law enforcement personnel.

FYI

Since 9/11, the U.S. Secret Service has been tasked with taking the lead in U.S. cybercrime efforts. There are electronic crime task force centers set up in several major cities, including Atlanta, Baltimore, Birmingham, Boston, Buffalo, Chicago, Dallas, Houston, and San Francisco. These electronic crime task force centers cooperate with other law enforcement agencies, including local police departments, in computer crime investigations.

The Secret Service also has released a guide for first responders to computer crime. The agency has listed its "golden rules" to begin the investigation. They are as follows:

- Officer safety: Secure the scene and make it safe.
- If you reasonably believe that the computer is involved in the crime you are investigating, take immediate steps to preserve the evidence.
- Determine whether you have a legal basis to seize the computer, such as plain view, search warrant, or consent.
- Do not access any computer files. If the computer is off, leave it off.
- If it is on, do not start searching through the computer. Instead, properly shut down the computer and prepare it for transport as evidence.
- If you reasonably believe that the computer is destroying evidence, immediately shut down the computer by pulling the power cord from the back of the computer.

- If a camera is available and the computer is on, take pictures of the computer screen. If the computer is off, take pictures of the computer, the location of the computer, and any electronic media attached.
- Determine whether special legal or privacy considerations apply, such as those for doctors, attorneys, clergy, psychiatrists, newspapers, or publishers.

These are all important first steps to both preserving the chain of custody and ensuring the integrity of the investigation from the very beginning.

The Regional Computer Forensics Laboratory Program

The Regional Computer Forensics Laboratory (RCFL) Program is a national network of forensic laboratories and training centers. The FBI provides startup and operational funding, training, staff, and equipment to the program. State, local, and other federal law enforcement agencies assign personnel to staff RCFL facilities.

Each of the 16 RCFLs examines digital evidence in support of criminal and national security investigations. The RCFL Program provides law enforcement at all levels with digital forensics expertise. It works with a wide variety of investigations, including terrorism, child pornography, fraud, and homicide.

The RCFL Program conducts digital forensics training. In 2008, for example, the program trained nearly 5000 law enforcement personnel in system forensics tools and techniques. For more information, see http://www.rcfl.gov.

CHAPTER SUMMARY

This chapter explored the basics of computer forensics. You have learned general principles, such as working only with a copy of the drive you're investigating and maintaining the chain of custody. The chapter also examined the types of digital forensics done as well as the laws regarding digital forensics. You should be familiar with the Daubert standard, warrants, federal forensic guidelines, and the general forensic procedure.

KEY CONCEPTS AND TERMS

Anti-forensics	Digital evidence	Live system forensics
Cell-phone forensics	Disk forensics	Network forensics
Chain of custody	Documentary evidence	Real evidence
Computer forensics	Email forensics	Software forensics
Curriculum vitae (CV)	Expert report	Testimonial evidence
Daubert standard	Expert testimony	Volatile memory
Demonstrative evidence	Internet forensics	

CHAPTER 1 ASSESSMENT

1. In a computer forensics investigation, this describes the route that evidence takes from the time you find it until the case is closed or goes to court.
   A. Rules of evidence
   B. Law of probability
   C. Chain of custody
   D. Policy of separation

2. If the computer is turned on when you arrive, what does the Secret Service recommend you do?
   A. Begin your investigation immediately.
   B. Shut the computer down according to the recommended Secret Service procedure.
   C. Transport the computer with power on.
   D. Unplug the machine immediately.

3. Why should you note all cable connections for a computer you want to seize as evidence?
   A. To know what outside connections existed
   B. In case other devices were connected
   C. To know what peripheral devices existed
   D. To know what hardware existed

4. What is the essence of the Daubert standard?
   A. That only experts can testify at trial
   B. That an expert must affirm that a tool or technique is valid
   C. That only tools or techniques that have been accepted by the scientific community are admissible at trial
   D. That the chain of custody must be preserved

5. When cataloging digital evidence, the primary goal is to do what?
   A. Make bitstream images of all hard drives.
   B. Preserve evidence integrity.
   C. Keep evidence from being removed from the scene.
   D. Keep the computer from being turned off.

6. Which of the following is important to the investigator regarding logging?
   A. The logging methods
   B. Log retention
   C. Location of stored logs
   D. All of the above

7. Your roommate can give consent to search your computer.
   A. True
   B. False

8. Evidence need not be locked if it is at a police station.
   A. True
   B. False

References

1. Cornell Law School Legal Information Institute. (n.d.) Rule 702. Testimony by Expert Witness. Retrieved from https://www.law.cornell.edu/rules/fre/rule_702 on January 27, 2021.

2. Cornell Law School Legal Information Institute. (n.d.) Rule 703. Bases of an Expert. Retrieved from https://www.law.cornell.edu/rules/fre/rule_703 on January 27, 2021.

3. Cornell Law School Legal Information Institute. (n.d.) Rule 704. Opinion on an Ultimate Issue. Retrieved from https://www.law.cornell.edu/rules/fre/rule_704 on January 27, 2021.

4. Cornell Law School Legal Information Institute. (n.d.) Rule 705. Disclosing the Facts or Data Underlying an Expert. Retrieved from https://www.law.cornell.edu/rules/fre/rule_705 on January 27, 2021.

5. Cornell Law School Legal Information Institute. (n.d.) Rule 705. Court-Appointed Expert Witness. Retrieved from https://www.law.cornell.edu/rules/fre/rule_706 on January 27, 2021.

6. Cornell Law School Legal Information Institute. (n.d.) Rule 401. Test for Relevant Evidence. Retrieved from https://www.law.cornell.edu/rules/fre/rule_401 on January 27, 2021.

Overview of Computer Crime

BEFORE DELVING INTO COMPUTER FORENSICS, it is important for you to understand the types of computer crimes that are likely to lead to forensic investigations. This chapter is not meant to be an exhaustive catalog of every computer crime that can be perpetrated, but rather a discussion of the most common computer crimes.

Chapter 2 Topics

This chapter covers the following topics and concepts:

- How computer crime affects forensics
- What the details of identity theft are
- Hacking
- Cyberstalking and harassment
- Fraud on the internet
- Non-access computer crimes
- Cyberterrorism: the new frontier

Chapter 2 Goals

When you complete this chapter, you will be able to:

- Describe common computer crimes
- Understand varying forensic approaches to different crimes
- Apply the appropriate forensic strategy based on the specific crime

How Computer Crime Affects Forensics

Many crimes today involve the use of computers and networks. A computer or another device can play one of three roles in a computer crime:

- It can be the target of the crime.
- It can be the instrument of the crime.
- It can be an evidence repository that stores valuable information about the crime.

In some cases, a computer can have multiple roles. It can be the instrument of a crime and also serve as a file cabinet that stores critical evidence. For example, an attacker may use a computer as a tool to break into another computer and steal files. The attacker may then store the stolen files on the computer used to perpetrate the theft. When investigating a case, it is important that the investigator know what roles a computer played in the crime and then tailor the investigative process to those roles.

Applying information about how a computer was used in a crime also helps when searching a system for evidence. If a computer was used to hack into a network password file, the investigator should look for password-cracking software and password files. If a computer was the target of a crime, such as an intrusion, the investigator should check audit logs and look for unfamiliar programs. Knowing how a computer was used in a crime helps narrow down the evidence collection process. Hard drives and other mass storage devices today are generally very large, reaching several terabytes. Therefore, checking and analyzing every piece of data a computer and associated media contain would take an impossibly long time if searched manually. Even when automated, more comprehensive searches can take a frustratingly long time. Often, law enforcement officials need information quickly. Having a general idea of what to look for on a suspect computer speeds the evidence collection process.

Computers can be involved in a variety of types of crimes, including white-collar crimes, violent crimes such as murder and terrorism, counterintelligence, economic espionage, counterfeiting, child pornography, and drug dealing, among others.

The internet has made targets much more accessible, and the risks involved for criminals are much lower than with traditional crimes. From the comfort of home or some other remote site, a cybercriminal can hack into a bank and transfer millions of dollars to a fictitious account. In essence, the criminal can rob the bank without the threat of being physically harmed while trying to escape.

Cybercrime can also involve modification of a traditional crime by using the internet in some way. It can be as simple as the illegal online sale of prescription drugs or as sophisticated as cyberstalking. Pedophiles use the internet to exchange child pornography and pose as children to lure victims into real-life kidnappings. Laws governing fraud apply with equal force, regardless of whether the activity is online or offline.

In the arena of computer forensics, the nature of the crime can have a significant effect on the forensic process. Certain crimes are more likely than others to yield certain types of forensic evidence. For example, identity theft is likely to leave email evidence via phishing emails, but hacking into a system and stealing data probably does not leave any email evidence. On the other hand, hacking into the system probably does leave evidence in the firewall and intrusion detection system logs, whereas phishing emails may not.

In order to select the appropriate forensic tests, the investigator must understand the types of computer crimes and how the crime affects the forensic process.

Most computer security books categorize computer attacks based on the nature of the attack. For example, such books look at denial-of-service attacks, malware, hacking into web pages, and so forth. However, for our purposes, this chapter categorizes computer attacks based on the type of crime being done, regardless of how it was performed. As you proceed through this chapter, you will see that this makes more sense for forensic examinations. This chapter examines the following categories:

- Identity theft
- Hacking systems for data
- Cyberstalking/harassment
- Internet fraud
- Non-access computer crimes
- Cyberterrorism

These are rather broad categories that encompass a great many activities. But the categories work well for investigating criminal behavior. It should also be noted that digital devices can be of interest in non-computer crimes. Certainly, examining drug traffickers' smartphones could yield information as to their colleagues, travel habits, and other information, even though the crime in question is not actually a computer crime.

Identity Theft

Identity theft is a growing problem. It is any use of another person's identity. Now that might seem like a pretty broad definition, but it is accurate. Most often, criminals commit identity theft in order to perpetrate some financial fraud. For example, a criminal might use the victim's information to obtain credit card information. If they use the card to make purchases, the victim is left with the bill.

The U.S. Department of Justice defines identity theft and identity fraud as:

> … terms used to refer to all types of crime in which someone wrongfully obtains and uses another person's personal data in some way that involves fraud or deception, typically for economic gain.

The simple act of wrongfully obtaining another person's personal data is the crime, with or without stealing any money. Notice that the Justice Department's definition states that it is *typically* for economic gain. However, a criminal might steal someone's identity for other reasons as well. Therefore, even non-financial identity theft is still a crime. For example, here is a real-world case. Some details have been changed to preserve confidentiality, but the essentials of the story are all true.

This crime occurred in a state that used Social Security numbers for driver's license numbers. No state does this anymore, for good reason. In this case, an individual worked at a local office of the Department of Motor Vehicles. When someone came in to renew a license, he or she surrendered the old license. The criminal in this case took some old licenses that he thought resembled him. He then put his picture on them and used one of them if he was pulled over for a traffic ticket. This caused the ticket to be issued to the individual who owned the license, along with a ticket for having an expired license. Eventually, however, an investigation tied the tickets to his car and license plate number.

This story illustrates one way in which criminals can accomplish identity theft—by getting official documents with someone else's information on them. It also shows an alternative reason for identity theft, one that does not involve bank accounts or credit. This is certainly not the most common example of identity theft, but it is one possible example. Criminals also use the following common methods to perpetrate identity theft:

- Phishing
- Spyware
- Discarded information

The following sections briefly examine each of these.

Phishing

Phishing is an attempt to trick a victim into giving up personal information. It is usually done by emailing the victim and claiming to be from some organization a victim would trust, such as his or her bank or credit card company. In one of its simplest forms, a perpetrator sends out an email to a large number of people. It claims to be from some bank—for the purposes of this example, consider a fictitious bank called Trustworthy Bank. The email claims that there is some issue with the recipient's account and states the recipient needs to click a link in the email to address the problem. However, the link actually takes the recipient to a fake website that simply looks like the real website. When the victim types in his or her username and password, this fake system displays some message like "login temporarily unavailable" or "error, please try later." What the perpetrator has done is tricked the victim into giving the criminal the victim's username and password for his or her bank account.

Clearly, in any mass email scenario, many recipients aren't customers of the financial institution being faked. And those recipients will likely just delete the email. Even many of those who are customers of the spoofed financial institution won't fall for the scam. They will delete the email, too. But, in this case, it is a numbers game for the criminal. If he or she sends out enough of these emails, it is certain that someone will fall for it. So the trick is to send out as many emails as possible, and know that only a small percentage will respond.

Phishing is generally a process of reaching out to as many people as possible, hoping enough people respond. In general, about as many people fall for scam emails as respond to other, legitimate, unsolicited bulk email, or spam. A good fictitious email gets a 1–3% response rate, according to the Federal Bureau of Investigation (FBI). An identity thief—if he or she uses the target organization's format, spells everything correctly, and uses logos and artwork that look legitimate—can count on a response of 10,000 to 30,000 clickthroughs per million emails sent.

Every year in the United States, shortly after federal taxes are due on April 15, tax-related fraud via phishing scams will begin. These phishing emails purport to be from the U.S. Internal Revenue Service (IRS), and they claim that there was an error with the person's online tax submission. The recipient is then directed to click on a link to fix the problem. What really occurs, if the victim clicks on the link, is that the perpetrator gets all their personal information, thus making identity theft quite easy.

Recent years have seen the growth of more targeted attacks. The first such targeted attack is called *spear phishing*. With spear phishing, the criminal targets a specific group. For example, the criminal may want to get information about the network of a specific bank, so he or she targets emails to the IT staff at that bank. The emails are a bit more specific, and thus more likely to look legitimate to the recipients.

Similar to spear phishing is *whaling*. This is phishing with a specific, high-value target in mind. For example, the attacker may target the CIO of a bank. First, the attacker performs a web search on that CIO and learns as much about him or her as possible. LinkedIn, Facebook, and other social media can be very helpful in this regard. Then, the attacker sends an email targeted to that specific individual. This makes it much more likely the email will appear legitimate and the victim will respond.

One scenario is to research the target, the CIO in this case, and find out his or her hobbies. For example, if the CIO is an avid fisherman, the attacker might send him or her an email offering a free subscription to a fishing magazine if he or she fills out a survey. The survey is generic, but requires the target to select a password. This is important because most people reuse passwords. Whatever password the CIO selects, it is likely he or she used that same password elsewhere as well. Even if it is not used as his or her network login password, it could be a password to a Hotmail, Gmail, LinkedIn, or Facebook account. This gives the attacker an inroad into that person's electronic life. From there, it is a matter of time before the attacker is able to secure the victim's network credentials. Information learned in phishing can also be used in social engineering or other highly targeted attacks such as advanced persistent threat attacks, which are ongoing attacks that make repeated and concerted attempts at phishing. It is usually for a specific, high-value target that several related phishing emails are sent.

Spyware

Spyware is any software that can monitor your activity on a computer. It may involve taking screenshots or perhaps logging keystrokes. It can even be as simple as a cookie—a tiny text file that simply records a few brief facts about your visit to a website. Normal web traffic is "stateless," meaning no information is passed from page to page without help. This is accomplished via cookies. For example, when you visit Amazon.com, the site remembers what you were last searching for. This is accomplished via cookies. Now, like most reputable sites, Amazon does not write your personal data to a cookie. Rather, there is an identifier that Amazon can utilize to match with your data it keeps on its back-end servers. Some people might object to website cookies being labeled as spyware, and it should be pointed out that cookies have many legitimate uses. However, it is up to whoever programmed the website to decide what information is stored in a website cookie and how it will be used. This means that, at least technically speaking, cookies could be considered spyware.

It has been claimed that 80% of all computers connected to the internet have spyware. Whether the number is really that high is hard to determine. However, it is a fact that spyware is quite prevalent. One reason (which may surprise you) is that such software itself is perfectly legal, if used correctly. There are two situations that allow a person to legally monitor another person's computer usage. The first is parents monitoring minor children. If a child is under the age of 18, it is perfectly legal for the parents to monitor their child's computer activity. In fact, some experts would go so far as to say it is neglectful *not* to monitor a young child on the internet. Another legal application of computer monitoring is in the workplace. Numerous court cases have upheld an employer's right to monitor computer and internet usage on company-owned equipment.

Because there are legal applications of "spying" on a person's computer usage, a number of spyware products are easily and cheaply available. Just a few are listed here:

- **Teen Safe**—This product can be found at *http://www.teensafe.net.*
- **Web Watcher**—This product can be found at *https://www.webwatcher.com.*
- **ICU**—This product can be found at *http://www.softpedia.com/get/Security /Security-Related/ICU-Child-Monitoring-Software.shtml.*
- **WorkTime**—This product can be found at *http://www.nestersoft.com/worktime /corporate/employee_monitoring.shtml.*

The only issue for a criminal who wants to misuse this software is how to get it onto the target system. In some cases, it is done via a Trojan horse. The victims are tricked into downloading the spyware onto their machines. In other cases, the spyware can be distributed like a virus, infecting various machines. It is also possible to manually put spyware on a machine. This is usually done when the spyware is being placed due to a warrant for a law enforcement agency to monitor a target system, or when a private citizen is legally placing spyware on a system.

Of course, spyware can also be placed on the target's machine by tricking the user into opening an attachment. You may get several emails every week that try to lure you into opening some attachment. These have either a virus, spyware, or Trojan horse. You can see one example of such an email in **FIGURE 2-1**.

The email entices the user into clicking on the attachment and downloading it. At that point, some sort of malware is installed on the user's machine. However, after the software is installed on the victim's computer, it then begins to gather information about that person's internet and computer activities. For criminals, the most interesting information is usually financial data, bank login passwords, and so forth.

Discarded Information

Another method that allows a hacker to gather information about a person's identity is discarded information. Any documents that are thrown out without first being shredded could potentially aid an identity thief. This usually doesn't leave much forensic evidence, but

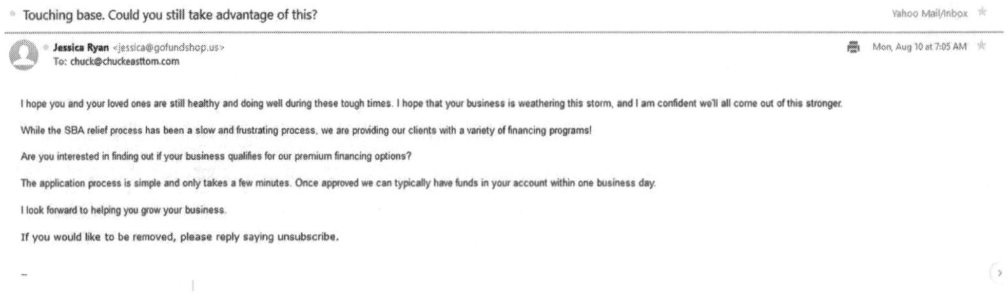

Touching base. Could you still take advantage of this?   Yahoo Mail/Inbox

Jessica Ryan <jessica@gofundshop.us>   Mon, Aug 10 at 7:05 AM
To: chuck@chuckeasttom.com

I hope you and your loved ones are still healthy and doing well during these tough times. I hope that your business is weathering this storm, and I am confident we'll come out of this stronger.

While the SBA relief process has been a slow and frustrating process, we are providing our clients with a variety of financing programs!

Are you interested in finding out if your business qualifies for our premium financing options?

The application process is simple and only takes a few minutes. Once approved we can typically have funds in your account within one business day.

I look forward to helping you grow your business.

If you would like to be removed, please reply saying unsubscribe.

FIGURE 2-1

Email attachment.

it does indicate that the perpetrator is local—they must be in order to access the victim's trash, a practice commonly known as dumpster diving.

How Does This Crime Affect Forensics?

If the crime being investigated is identity theft, then the first thing the investigator should be looking for is spyware on the victim's machine. While there are certainly other ways to get one's identity, this is an easy one to check. It is certainly possible that somewhere on the victim's machine is some type of spyware. If spyware exists, the investigator must start searching for where the spyware is sending its data. Yes, spyware collects data on the user's computer and internet activities, but ultimately that data must be communicated to the criminal. It could be something as simple as a periodic email with an attachment, or it could be a stream of packets to a server the criminal has access to. And since a firewall is more strict on blocking inbound communication rather than stopping outbound messages, sending data out to the criminal is easily done. Whatever the specific communication mechanism, there absolutely must be some way to get the information from the victim's computer to the attacker—and that will leave some forensic trace.

> **⚠ WARNING**
> It is important to remember the limits of monitoring employees and minor children. You can monitor employee activities, but only on company systems. Furthermore, the day a child turns 18, he or she is legally an adult and cannot be monitored. It is illegal for you to monitor other adults—even relatives living in your home.

> **▶ TIP**
> Dumpster diving is why paper must always be shredded or burned. A criminal could use any documents found in the trash to derive information that helps him or her perpetrate a crime, such as identity theft. Another issue the investigator should explore is that of phishing emails. It is important to check the email history for the victim's computer as well as the web history. If a phishing website was involved, it is important to gather information about that site.

Hacking

Hacking is a generic term that has different meanings to different people. In the hacking community, it means to experiment with a system, learning its rules or processes, in order to better understand the system or to fix the flaws. In most other contexts, it means circumventing a system's security. This section uses the latter definition. It is certainly possible to break into a system remotely. Attackers can use a number of techniques to do this. The following sections discuss a few of these techniques.

Structured Query Language Injection

Structured Query Language (SQL) injection may be the most common web application attack. It is based on inserting SQL commands into text boxes, such as the username and password text fields on the login screen. If the login fields expect only text and do not protect against SQL commands, the web attack is possible. According to the most recent Verizon Terremark Data Breach Investigations Report, SQL injection was once one of the most common types of web attack, but it has fallen off in recent years thanks to better website coding practices. Still, it is remarkable how many sites remain susceptible.

   To understand how SQL injection works, you have to first understand the basics of how data entry boxes should be guarding against unexpected text. A login screen requires the user to enter a username and password, and these then have to be validated. Most often, they are validated by checking a database that has a table of users to see if the password matches that user. All modern databases "speak" SQL, so if the programmer who created the login screen and validation process is not careful, the web page may be susceptible to SQL injection. Here is how that attack works. SQL looks a lot like English. For example, to check a username and password, you might want to query the database and see if there is any entry in the users table that matches the username and password that were entered. If there is, then you have a match. The SQL statements in the programming code for the website have to use quotation marks to separate the SQL code from the programming code. A typical SQL statement might look something like this:

```
SELECT * FROM tblUsers WHERE USERNAME = '" + txtUsername.Text
+' AND PASSWORD = '" + txtPassword.Text +"'.
```

If you enter username `'thisuser'` and the password `'letmein'`, this code produces the SQL command:

```
SELECT * FROM tblUsers WHERE USERNAME = 'thisuser' AND PASSWORD
= 'letmein'
```

This is fairly easy to understand even for nonprogrammers. Plus, it is effective. If there is a match in the database, that means the username and password match. If no records are returned from the database, that means there was no match, and this is not a valid login.

SQL injection is basically about subverting this process. The idea is to create a statement that will always be true and would cause the application to process a query. Before a true statement is considered, the entered text needs to "escape" the application reading it as text and instead process it as an instruction. For example, you enter in a single quote, such as `'`, then a statement that is always true, such as `1 = 1`, into the username and password boxes. This causes the program to execute whatever query that follows:

```
SELECT * FROM tblUsers WHERE USERNAME = '' or 1=1 AND PASSWORD =
'' or 1=1.
```

Here you are telling the database and application to return all records where the username and password are blank or if 1 = 1. The fact is that 1 always equals 1, so this works. Now if the programmer wrote the application properly—so that it does not allow any extra characters to escape out of being normal text—this does not work. But in all too many cases, it does work. And then the intruder has logged on to your web application and can do whatever any authorized user can do.

Technical TIP

SQL injection can be a lot more sophisticated than this section demonstrates. This chapter looks at the simplest implementation of SQL injection. Many other methods are available, including related attacks such as cross-site scripting, in which script—often JavaScript—is put into input boxes so it will be executed on the target website.

The example just described is the simplest version of SQL injection. There are more advanced SQL injection techniques. In fact, SQL injection is limited only by your own knowledge of SQL. Obviously, SQL injection attacks can be very sophisticated, involving a complex array of SQL statements, or they can be as simple as the example just discussed.

There are even tools that make the process of executing this attack—or testing your website to see if it is vulnerable to this attack—even easier. A few are listed here:

- Several tools at Database Security at *http://www.databasesecurity.com/sqlinjection-tools. htm*
- Sqlmap at *http://sqlmap.org/*
- SQL Ninja at *http://sqlninja.sourceforge.net/*

How Does This Crime Affect Forensics?

Regardless of the sophistication of the SQL injection attack, or the lack thereof, such attacks leave specific forensic evidence. The first place you should look is in the firewall logs. There should be some indication of where the connection came from. Second, search your database logs; some relational database engines log transactions, when they occurred, and what they were. This can be invaluable in your investigation.

Cross-Site Scripting

Cross-site scripting is another very common attack. In this attack, a legitimate website allows malicious script to act, and deliver content, as if it comes from the legitimate website. All that is needed for the perpetrator is to seek out some place on the target website that allows malicious script to wait for end users to fall victim from it. One example is to post text that other users will see. Product reviews are a great place for this. But instead of posting a review, or other text, the attacker will post JavaScript. If the website does not filter the user input before displaying it, then when other users navigate to this review, the website will instead execute that script. The attacker is only limited by his or her knowledge of JavaScript. One popular thing to do is to redirect the user to a phishing site. Phishing involves tricking an end user, generally by email, into giving up their account information. This practice of using technical means to redirect people to a very similar, but fake, phishing site is called *pharming*.

To better understand this attack, let us walk through a scenario. Before we do, I would point out to you that to the best of my knowledge, none of the major e-commerce or auction sites is vulnerable to this kind of attack. In this scenario, the attacker sets up a website that looks very much like the target site. He gives that site a name similar to the target site, off by only one letter. That makes it likely an end user will not notice the minor difference. Then the attacker infects the target site with cross-site scripting, a script that will redirect the user to the phishing site. Once at the phishing site, the malicious site simply displays a notice stating "your session has expired, please log in again." When the user logs in, the malicious site captures the login information, then sends the user back to the real site. Now the attacker has that user's login information. To the end user, it would appear as if they have always been on the same website.

How Does This Crime Affect Forensics?

Cross-site scripting can be a complex crime to investigate. The first item to look for is any scripts in the website. Certainly, websites have many scripts that are there intentionally for beneficial purposes, but this is the first place to search for any malicious scripts. In a large website, that search can be a very tedious task, and it is possible the attacker has removed the malicious script. A more efficient method is to search the web server's logs for any redirect messages (these are HTTP messages in the 300 range), then determine if any of these redirects cannot be accounted for via legitimate web coding.

Ophcrack ⎯ Live Cd to crack Sam database Passwords

Probably one of the most basic tools for physically accessing a Windows machine is Ophcrack. Ophcrack can be downloaded from http://ophcrack.sourceforge.net/. It is a tool to crack the local passwords on Windows systems. It is usually pretty effective. In fact, if an attacker can sit at a Windows machine on your network with an Ophcrack compact disc (CD) or USB flash drive for 10 minutes or less, chances are good that the attacker is going to get the local passwords. This is a significant problem on corporate networks that meet the following criteria:

- If physical security is lax, an outsider can get in the building, often by posing as a cleaning or maintenance person or a temporary employee.
- It is usually possible to find an unoccupied desk in the building.
- The network's focus is on domain accounts, not local accounts. There is a good chance that the local accounts for one Windows machine are the same throughout. The systems are usually just imaged from a base system.

It should be noted that Ophcrack is only one such tool. There are myriad similar tools available on the internet—some that work much better than Ophcrack.

How does Ophcrack work? First, let's discuss how Windows passwords work. When you choose your local Windows passwords, the password you choose is hashed and stored in the SAM file, which is found in the Windows\System32\ directory. The hash of the password is not the password itself, but is created from the password using a hashing algorithm that makes two identical hashes for different passwords very unlikely.

To make this work, all you have to do is put the Ophcrack CD into the system and reboot. During the boot-up process, press the key needed to enter the system's BIOS, often F2 or the DEL key, to change the boot order. Additionally, the F10 or F12 key might bring up a boot menu; then choose Boot from CD. Note that in **FIGURE 2-2**, the passwords that Ophcrack found are blocked out. There's a lot to know about hashes and cryptography, but for now, you just need to know that a hash is one-way; you don't "unhash" something. When you log on to Windows, the system hashes whatever you type in and compares it with whatever hash is in the SAM file. If there is an exact match, then you are given access.

The most basic way to extract passwords from hashes is a **rainbow table**, and that is what Ophcrack uses. To understand rainbow tables, consider a scenario where one wishes to extract Windows local passwords. Windows uses the NTLMv2 hashing algorithm to store passwords. Imagine you make a table of all common eight-character passwords in one column, and the NTLMv2 hash of them in the second column. Then you repeat this for all

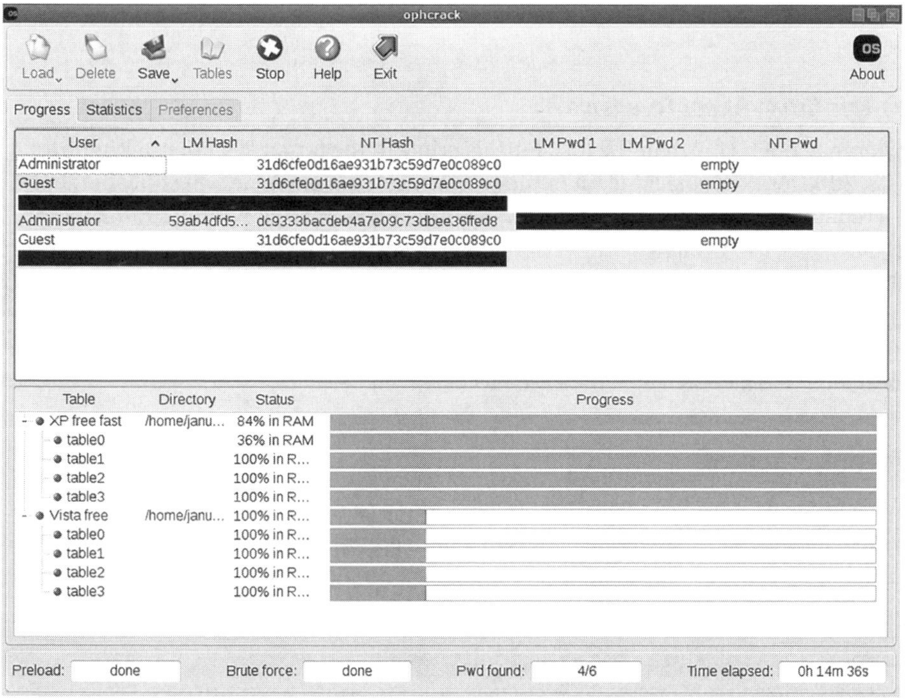

FIGURE 2-2

Ophcrack. Note: This screenshot was taken from a live machine, so all nonstandard user accounts and all passwords were redacted.

common nine-character passwords, then for all 10-character passwords. You can take this as far as you like, and as far as your computing resources will support. Then if you can extract a hash from the target machine, you search the tables for a match. If you find a match in the second column, whatever is in the first column must be that person's password. These tables get huge very fast, so most are no more than 8–10 characters in length, which works for most passwords. A sample of a rainbow table with both good and bad passwords is shown in **FIGURE 2-3**.

The problem is getting the SAM file to start with. When Windows boots up, long before you even get the login screen, the system locks the SAM file—preventing you from copying or editing it. Well, that is where Ophcrack comes in. It boots to a Linux Live CD and then scans its rainbow table searching for matches. It displays all the passwords it finds in an easy-to-use graphical user interface.

Once the attacker has a valid login account, particularly an administrator account, he or she can log on to that computer, even from a remote location. This doesn't let the attacker

Password	NTLM Hash
password	8846F7EAEE8FB117AD06BDD830B7586C
letmein	7156684CFA75A3D5678B3C144F64E14A
baspassword	24A4001F435CABC9914E34B8CAA9D01C
pa$$w0rd0!	03EDECCBCCA5A08A6581804ED776067D

FIGURE 2-3

Rainbow table.

join the domain, but he or she now has a foothold in your network. You can see this in Figure 2-2.

How Does This Crime Affect Forensics?

There may or may not be much in the logs for this crime. If the target system is a Windows Server 2003, 2008, or 2012 machine, then the rebooting of the machine will show in the log. If you see a reboot followed by a successful login with an account like Administrator, it is an indication that a tool like Ophcrack might have been used. Another issue to examine is physical security. If a physical intrusion is suspected, then traditional forensic methods, such as examining security cameras and even fingerprints, become important. Of course, having an account logged on at a time when the actual user who is assigned that account is not present is also a clear sign that a breach of some kind has occurred.

Tricking Tech Support

The following is a simple trick, and one that is a follow-up to using Ophcrack to break local accounts. After the attacker has gained access to a local account, he or she will really want to get domain admin privileges. The command net user can help do this. First, the attacker writes the following two-line script:

```
net user /domain /add localaccountname password
net group /domain "Domain Admins" /add localaccount
```

The attacker then saves that script in the All Users startup folder. The next step is to get a domain admin to log onto this machine. If that happens, the script runs—in the background and not visible—and your local account is now a domain admin. But how do you get a domain administrator to log on? Well, it just so happens that in many organizations, the tech support personnel are in the domain admin group. So the attacker merely needs to do something to render the machine not fully operational. When a tech support person logs on to fix that problem, the script is run.

How Does This Crime Affect Forensics?

Searching the system for any unrecognized scripts, particularly in any startup folders, is a good first step if you suspect a physical breach. Of course, the usage of the compromised account also yields clues. If the network admin account shows that it was used at a time when the network administrator was away, this suggests the account has been compromised. And, as with Ophcrack, physical security is an issue in this crime; therefore, investigating physical breaches of the premises is important.

Hacking in General

Entire books have been written on hacking techniques, and entire certification courses focus on such skills. The purpose here is to introduce you to some techniques that an attacker might use. To go into all the common hacking techniques attackers use is beyond the scope of this text. However, this section illustrates an important point: Computer crime investigators should have a strong working knowledge of hacking techniques. Your forensic investigations will be drastically improved if you have an understanding of the techniques that attackers use.

Cyberstalking and Harassment

Cyberstalking, cyberbullying, and online harassment are getting increasing attention in the media. As society becomes ever more wired, conduct online becomes more important. With many people using social media to interact with others, dating sites to find that special someone, and online discussion boards to talk, inappropriate behavior online becomes more noticeable. Some would say that bad behavior is becoming more common online. People feel more comfortable ranting at a faceless name on a screen than at a real person. But where does rudeness cross the line into stalking or harassment? Surely not every rude word on the internet constitutes a crime.

Cyberstalking or harassment is using electronic communications to harass or threaten another person. The U.S. Department of Justice puts it this way:

> Although there is no universally accepted definition of cyber stalking, the term is used in this report to refer to the use of the internet, e-mail, or other electronic communications devices to stalk another person. Stalking generally involves harassing or threatening behavior that an individual engages in repeatedly, such as following a person, appearing at a person's home or place of business, making harassing phone calls, leaving written messages or objects, or vandalizing a person's property. Most stalking laws require that the perpetrator make a credible threat of violence against the victim; others include threats against the victim's immediate family; and still others require only that the alleged stalker's course of conduct constitute an implied threat. While some conduct involving annoying or menacing behavior might fall short of illegal stalking, such behavior may be a prelude to stalking and violence and should be treated seriously.

Now, even after reading this description, you may still not know where the line between bad behavior and criminal behavior lies. Here are three criteria for law enforcement officers to bear in mind when considering cyberstalking and harassment cases. All three aren't necessarily essential to create a case of cyberstalking or harassment, but all three must be considered:

- **Is it possible?** If a person makes a threat, is that threat credible? To illustrate this question, consider two extremes. In the first scenario, you are playing a game online and another player, who lives in a different country, tells you he is so mad at you he is going to punch you in the nose. Given that you are probably not even using your real name, and this person is thousands of miles away, this is not a credible threat. At the other extreme, consider a scenario in which you receive an email threatening to kill you, but attached to the email is a recent photo of you leaving the front door of your home. That is clearly alarming and indicates the sender has the means and intent to commit harm.
- **How frequent?** Notice that the U.S. Department of Justice uses the term "repeatedly." People get angry and say things they later regret. Someone saying something rude and even violent, one time, is not necessarily stalking. Reasonable people calm down and

regret the harsh words they said, and then they don't repeat them. But repeated behavior is a pattern, not a mistake.

- **How serious?** Again, reasonable people can lose their temper and say things they don't mean. Many people have at some point uttered the words, "I could kill …"—but they don't act on them. Reasonable people do make vague statements in anger that they later regret and are embarrassed about. Specific and serious threats are more disconcerting. Someone saying, "I could just kill him," may be cause for concern, or may just be blowing off steam. Someone who makes such a statement and then goes on to detail just how he would go about killing the person, indicating that he has put thought into this, should be taken seriously as a threat.

Again, not all of these elements need to be present in order to constitute cyberstalking or harassment. However, all three need to be considered. Clearly, some people do make false reports to the police. Other people overreact to benign comments. On the other hand, cyberstalking can lead to real-world violent crimes.

Real Cyberstalking Cases

The following nine cases should give you a good overview of cyberstalking. Examining the facts in these cases might help you to get an idea of what legally constitutes cyberstalking. Some of these cases are quite recent. Others are older and are included because they were historically significant cases.

1. In 2019, North Carolina State Representative Cody Henson pled guilty to cyberstalking charges involving his ex-wife. The case involved threats to kill his ex-wife and her entire family. This case illustrates that cyberstalking can involve people from any segment of society.
2. In 2010, 70-year-old Joseph Medico met a 16-year-old girl at church. The girl was at the church volunteering, helping to prepare donations for homeless shelters. Mr. Medico followed the girl to her car and tried to talk her into going to dinner with him, and then back to his home. When she spurned his advances, he began calling and texting her several times a day. When she realized he was not going to stop, she called the police. Mr. Medico was arrested and charged with stalking. This case illustrates how easy it is for an unstable person to become obsessed with the victim. It also demonstrates the proper way to handle this sort of situation. This is definitely a case to report to the police. An adult who is making overtures like this to a minor is a matter of grave concern.
3. In the first successful prosecution under California's cyberstalking law, prosecutors in the Los Angeles District Attorney's Office prosecuted a 50-year-old former security guard who used the internet to solicit the rape of a woman who rejected his advances. The defendant terrorized his 28-year-old victim by impersonating her in various internet chat rooms and on online bulletin boards, where he posted, along with her telephone number and address, messages that she fantasized about being raped. On at least six occasions, sometimes in the middle of the night, men knocked on the woman's door saying they wanted to rape her. The former security guard pled guilty in April 1999 to one count of stalking and three counts of solicitation of sexual assault.
4. A local prosecutor's office in Massachusetts charged a man who, using anonymous remailers, allegedly engaged in a systematic pattern of harassment of a coworker, which

culminated in an attempt to extort sexual favors from the victim under threat of disclosing past sexual activities to the victim's new husband. (A remailer is an anonymous server that resends emails so they cannot be traced back to the original sender.)

5. In 2020, Samuel Trelawney Hughes was indicted by a federal grand jury on charges that he used cyberstalking to threaten to injure, rape, or kill at least 10 different people. He was also charged with seven counts of witness tampering. Hughes allegedly sent victims messages in which he expressed hope they would die or made specific threats to hurt them. In one example from October 2019, Hughes allegedly sent an email to a person who had reported prior threats, saying, "someone I can guarantee will come out and first bash you head in, rape you slash your throat and burn your car and house."

6. An honors graduate from the University of San Diego terrorized five female university students over the internet for more than a year. The victims received hundreds of violent and threatening emails, sometimes receiving four or five messages a day. The graduate student, who entered a guilty plea and faced up to six years in prison, told police he committed the crimes because he thought the women were laughing at him and causing others to ridicule him. In fact, the victims had never met him.

7. In England, Jason Smith continually harassed college student Alexandra Scarlett. He sent her as many as 30 messages a day threatening to slash her face, sexually assault her mother, or shoot her father. He was convicted and given a 12-month suspended sentence and a restraining order. However, within a week of this conviction, he used social networking sites to track down Ms. Scarlett and continue the campaign of harassment. Media in Britain have dubbed Mr. Smith "England's Most Obsessive Stalker." This case is also an example of stalking in response to unrequited romantic feelings. Mr. Smith had met Ms. Scarlett at a nightclub. She had given him her phone number. He then became convinced that they were in love and that they must be together. This led him to extreme jealousy, and eventually to the obsessive stalking.

8. Robert James Murphy was the first person charged under U.S. federal law for cyberstalking. He was accused of violating Title 47 of U.S. Code 223, which prohibits the use of telecommunications to annoy, abuse, threaten, or harass anyone. Murphy was accused of sending sexually explicit messages and photographs to his ex-girlfriend. This activity continued for a period of years. Mr. Murphy was charged and eventually pled guilty to two counts of cyberstalking.

9. In 2020, Kristian James O'Hara pled guilty to cyberstalking a woman he met while attending Fordham University. He is alleged to have initially started using the victim's phone number to have unsolicited late-night food orders delivered to her and make prank phone calls. He also left voicemails to the victim's family home in Delaware, in which he lied and accused her of giving him a sexually transmitted disease. The harassment escalated in both severity and frequency and lasted for 18 months. Mr. O'Hara has also admitting to cyberstalking at least eight other victims.

How Does This Crime Affect Forensics?

Cyberstalking and harassment is an interesting computer crime in that the computer is simply incidental. The intent of the crime is to target the human victim; the computer is just a vehicle. Fortunately, stalkers are often not the most technically savvy computer criminals. In stalking cases, you should begin with tracing emails and text messages. In many cases, they come directly from the perpetrator with little or no attempt to obfuscate their origin. Of course, if a suspect is arrested, any electronic devices in his or her possession should be examined for evidence. Stalking, by definition, indicates repeated, obsessive behavior. This means there is likely to be some evidence retained by the criminal.

Fraud

Fraud is a broad category of crime that can encompass many different activities. Essentially, any attempt to gain financial reward through deception is fraud. Two major subclasses of fraud are as follows:

- Investment offers
- Data piracy

The following sections briefly examine these classes of computer fraud.

Investment Offers

Investment offers are neither new nor necessarily illegal. In fact, cold-calling is a legitimate sales technique when selling stocks. However, the process can be used to artificially and fraudulently inflate the value of a target stock. The most common version of this is called the "pump and dump." In this scheme, the perpetrators buy significant amounts of stock in a company that is relatively cheap, often penny stocks. Then, they fuel false rumors that the company is on the verge of some large contract or other business deal that would increase its value significantly. This artificially drives up the price of the stock. Once the rumors have raised the stock as high as the criminals think it will go, they dump their stock at an inflated price, thus making substantial profits. Eventually, once it is clear the rumors were not true, the stock's value will drop again. The people who purchased the stock at an inflated price, but were not in on the scam and did not know to sell their stock before its value plummeted, lose significant amounts of money.

The growth of the internet did not create these scams—they existed long before the internet. But the widespread popularity and speed of the internet simply made scams easier to perpetrate. For example, with the pump and dump, the internet allows the perpetrator to create fake blogs, bulletin board postings, and emails, all claiming the target stock is likely to rise in value. The key to internet-based fraud of this kind is that, instead of cold-calling via the phone, the perpetrators send an enticing email to as many recipients as possible. Of course, they realize that most people will not respond to the email, but if the perpetrator sends out a million emails and even a tiny percentage of recipients respond, he or she can still pull in a significant amount of money.

One of the more common internet schemes involves sending out an email that suggests that you can make a large sum of money with a very minimal investment. It may be a processing fee you must submit in order to receive some lottery winnings, or perhaps legal fees in order to receive some inheritance. Perhaps the most famous of these schemes has been the "Nigerian prince" fraud. In this scenario, an email is sent to a large number of random email addresses. Each email contains a message purporting to be from a relative of some deceased Nigerian doctor or government official, always of significant social standing.

(It's more likely to convince victims that the arrangement is legitimate if it seems to involve people of good social standing.) The offer goes like this: A person has a sum of money he or she wants to transfer out of the country, and he or she cannot use normal channels. He or she wants to use your bank account to "park" the funds temporarily. If you allow the person access to your account, you will receive a hefty fee. If you do agree to this arrangement, you will receive, via normal mail, a variety of very official-looking documents—enough to convince most casual observers that the arrangement is legitimate. You will then be asked to advance some money to cover items such as taxes and wire fees. Should you actually send any money, however, you will lose it, and you will never hear from these individuals again. The FBI has issued a bulletin detailing this particular fraud scheme. Further FBI internet crime information is available at *https://www.fbi.gov/scams-and-safety /common-scams-and-crimes*.

How Does This Crime Affect Forensics?

The key in this sort of crime is to begin by tracing the communications. If it is a fake blog that is endorsing some investment, then someone had to register the domain for that blog. If there are emails involved, they had to come from somewhere. Of course, the more sophisticated the attacker, the less evidence there will be. Another way to seek evidence outside computer forensics is to follow the money. Someone is reaping financial rewards from the scheme.

Data Piracy

Intellectual property is a very real commodity. Large companies spend millions of dollars on filing patents and defending their patents and copyrights. The internet makes distribution of illegally copied materials, or data piracy, very easy. You are probably quite familiar with illegal music downloads; however, that is only one aspect of intellectual property theft.

Illegal copies of software can be found on the internet. There are websites that have such copies or the activation codes for software. These sites are colloquially referred to as warez (pronounced like wares) sites. As a consumer, the best advice to follow is, "If it seems too good to be true, it is probably not true." In other words, if a website boasts of a $400 software package for $89, it is probably illegally copied software.

How Does This Crime Affect Forensics?

The investigation of this sort of crime involves trying to trace the owners of the website that is distributing the intellectual property. This involves finding out who registered the domain and performing a WHOIS search on that domain. If the perpetrator is clever, he or she will hide behind several identities. However, the starting point is to track the website distributing the intellectual property.

 NOTE

Data piracy is frequently addressed via civil court rather than criminal. It is often a better option for the victim to sue the perpetrator rather than press criminal charges. This is one reason forensics is no longer just a law enforcement activity. There are myriad civilian reasons to utilize forensics.

Non-Access Computer Crimes

Non-access computer crimes are crimes that do not involve an attempt to actually access the target. For example, a virus or logic bomb does not require the attacker to attempt to hack into the target network. And denial-of-service attacks are designed to render the target unreachable by legitimate users, not to provide the attacker with access to the site.

Denial of Service

A **denial-of-service (DoS) attack** is an attempt to prevent legitimate users from being able to access a given computer resource. The most common target is a website. Although there are a number of methods for executing this type of attack, they all come down to the simple fact that every technology can handle only a finite load. If you overload the capacity of a given technology, it ceases to function properly. If you flood a website with fake connections, it becomes overloaded and unable to respond to legitimate connection attempts. This is a classic example of a DoS attack. Although these attacks may not directly compromise data or seek to steal personal information, they can certainly cause serious economic damages. Imagine the cost incurred if a DoS attack were to take eBay offline for a period of time!

Denial-of-service attacks are the cyber equivalent of vandalism. Rather than seek to break into the target system, the perpetrator simply wants to render the target system unusable. These attacks require minimal skill. For example, consider one of the most basic DoS attacks, called a SYN flood. This simple attack takes advantage of how connections to websites are established. So, first, let's take a look at how that works.

The client machine sends a Transmission Control Protocol (TCP) packet to the server with a synchronize flag turned on—it is a single bit that is turned to a 1. Because this is synchronizing, or starting the connection, it is called a SYN flag.

The server sets aside enough resources to handle the connection and sends back a TCP packet with two flags turned on: the acknowledgment flag (ACK) and the synchronize (SYN) flag. Essentially, this is acknowledging the request to synchronize. The client is supposed to respond with a single ACK flag to establish the connection and allow communications to begin. This is called the **three-way handshake**.

In the SYN flood attack, the attacker keeps sending SYN packets but never responds to the SYN/ACK packets it receives from the server. Eventually, the server has responded to millions of connection requests for a client that never fully connects. After several millions of connection requests in seconds, the server exhausts its resources and can no longer respond to legitimate users.

In addition to various DoS attack types, there are tools that can be used to create a DoS attack. One of the easiest to use is the Low Orbit Ion Cannon, shown in **FIGURE 2-4**. This tool is freely available on the internet and terribly easy to use. The prevalence of such easy-to-use tools is one reason why DoS attacks are so common.

The Tribal Flood Network (TFN) is probably the most widely used DoS tool. There is a newer version of it called TFN2K. The new version sends decoy information to make tracing more difficult. Both the original and the new version work by configuring the software to attack a particular target, and then getting the target on a specific machine. Usually, the attacker seeks to infect several machines with the TFN program in order to form a TFN. Instead of connection requests originating from one machine, the barrage is distributed across many. This attack variation is called a **distributed denial-of-service (DDoS) attack**.

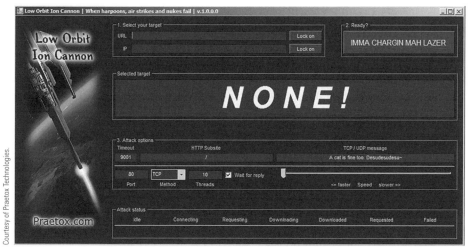

FIGURE 2-4

Low Orbit Ion Cannon.

You can get more details about TFN and TFN2K at these websites:

- Washington University at *http://staff.washington.edu/dittrich/misc/tfn.analysis.txt*
- Packetstorm Security at *http://packetstormsecurity.com/distributed / TFN2k_Analysis-1.3.txt*
- The Computer Emergency Response Team (CERT) at *http://www.cert.org/advisories /CA-1999-17.html*

Trin00 is another popular DoS tool. It was originally available only for UNIX but is now available for Windows as well. It is an alternative to TFN. One common technique attackers use is to send the Trin00 client to machines via a Trojan horse—a type of code that looks to the casual user like it is legitimate, but is really malware. Then, the infected machines can all be used to launch a coordinated attack on the target system.

A Smurf attack is a DoS attack that uses a combination of IP spoofing and ICMP to saturate a target network with traffic. Smurf consists of three elements: a source site, a bounce site, and a target site. The attacker (the source site) sends a modified ping to the broadcast address of a large network (the bounce site). The modified packet contains the source address of the target site—and everyone at the bounce site replies to the target site. A Fraggle attack is a variation of a Smurf attack where an attacker sends a large amount of UDP traffic to ports 7 (echo) and 19 (chargen) to a broadcast address, spoofing the intended victim's source IP address.

Dynamic Host Configuration Protocol (DHCP) starvation is another type of DoS attack. DHCP is used to dynamically assign network addresses to computers. This is widely used in most organizations. If enough requests flood onto the network, the attacker can completely exhaust the address space allocated by the DHCP servers for an indefinite period of time. There are tools such as Gobbler that will do this for the attacker.

An HTTP post DoS attack targets web servers. Such an attack sends a legitimate HTTP post message. Part of the post message is the `content-length`. This indicates the size of the message to follow. In this attack, the attacker then sends the actual message body at an extremely slow rate. The web server is then "hung" waiting for that message to complete.

For more robust servers, the attacker will need to use multiple HTTP post attacks simultaneously.

There are other DoS attacks targeting web servers and websites. The attacker could create a program that submits the registration forms repeatedly, adding a large number of spurious users to the application. The attacker may also choose to overload the login process by continually sending login requests that require the presentation tier to access the authentication mechanism, rendering it unavailable or unreasonably slow to respond.

A **permanent denial of service (PDoS)** is an attack that damages the system so badly that the victim machine needs an operating system reinstall or even new hardware. This is sometimes called *phlashing*. This will usually involve a DoS attack on the device's firmware.

Another type of DoS attack that has become more prevalent in recent years is the telephony denial of service (TDoS) attack. A TDoS attack is possible, and certainly has been documented, with traditional telephone systems by using an automatic dialer to tie up target phone lines. TDoS is flourishing, however, with the wide availability of Voice over Internet Protocol (VoIP) tools that make automated TDoS attacks against traditional and IP-based VoIP very easy to carry out. The way that a TDoS attack works is that a call center or business receives so many inbound calls that the equipment and staff are overwhelmed and unable to do business. A call to a supervisor or manager demands a certain amount of money be sent or a certain eradication service be purchased to stop the attacks.

How Does This Crime Affect Forensics?

When investigating DoS attacks launched from a single machine, the obvious task is to trace the packets coming from that machine. It is common for attackers to spoof some other IP address, but not as common for them to spoof a MAC address, which is related to the underlying hardware. If the attacker is not savvy enough to spoof the MAC address, then each packet contains evidence of the actual machine that it was launched from.

In DDoS attacks, the packets come from a multitude of machines. Usually, the owners of these machines are unaware that their machines are being used in this way. However, that does not mean the investigation is at a dead end. You can still trace back the packets and get a group of infected machines. You can then seek out commonalities on those machines. Did they all download the same free game from the internet or frequent the same website? Anything that all infected machines have in common is a candidate for where the machines got the software that launched the DDoS attack.

Viruses

Viruses are a major problem in modern computer systems. A **virus** is any software that self-replicates, like a human or animal virus. It is common for viruses to also wreak havoc on infected machines, but the self-replication is the defining characteristic of a virus. It should be noted that in modern times, most malware combines facets of different types of attacks (i.e., a virus and a Trojan horse). Some people now use the term *virus* to mean any malware. That is not technically accurate, but you should be prepared to see that in practice. Before discussing the forensics of viruses, it is a good idea to consider some recent viruses:

- **FakeAV.86**—This is a fake antivirus. It purports to be a free antivirus scanner, but is really itself a Trojan. This virus first appeared in July 2012. It affected Windows systems ranging from Windows 95 to Windows 7 and Windows Server 2003. This is not the only fake antivirus to have been found, but it is a widespread one.
- **Flame**—No modern discussion of viruses would be complete without a discussion of Flame, a virus that targeted Windows operating systems. The first item that makes this virus notable is that it was specifically designed for espionage. It was first discovered in May 2012 at several locations, including Iranian government sites. Flame is spyware that can monitor network traffic and take screenshots of the infected system. This malware stores data in a local database that is heavily encrypted. Flame is also able to change its behavior based on the specific antivirus software running on the target machine. This indicates that this malware is highly sophisticated. Also of note is that Flame is signed with a fraudulent Microsoft certificate. This means that Windows systems would trust the software.

These two pieces of malware give you some idea of the impact a virus can have on an organization's network. Viruses range from terribly annoying, like FakeAV, to sophisticated mechanisms for espionage, like Flame. A few other more recent viruses are discussed briefly here:

- **Gameover ZeuS** is a virus that creates a peer-to-peer botnet. This virus first began to spread in 2015. The virus creates encrypted communication between infected computers and the command and control computer, allowing the attacker to control the various infected computers.
- **Wannacry** hit the world in March 2017 with a storm of activity. However, this virus will be studied for many years to come. There are several reasons for this, but the main reason this virus is noteworthy is that there was a patch for the vulnerability it exploited, and that patch had been available for weeks. This illustrates why patch management is such an important part of cybersecurity.
- **Emotnet** came out in 2019; it was malware that pretended to be a scanned copy of Edward Snowden's memoir. Once the target clicks on the attachment, a Microsoft Word window opens with the message "Word hasn't been activated," prompting users to click on the "Enable Content" button. After the user clicks on the button, a PowerShell command is launched that attempts to download the botnet malware from one of the three URLs embedded in the application.
- **Ryuk** malware appeared throughout 2019 and affected millions of people all over the world. The ransomware targeted several state, local, and territorial government entities and demanded ransom in Bitcoin to decrypt files.
- The **Rombertik** virus began to be seen in 2015. This virus uses the browser to read user credentials to websites. It is most often sent as an attachment to an email. The virus can also either overwrite the master boot record on the hard drive, making the machine unbootable, or begin encrypting files in the user's home directory.
- The **Locky** virus began to show up in 2016. It is a ransomware virus that encrypts sensitive files on the victim computer and then demands ransom for the encryption key. Unlike previous ransomware viruses, this one can encrypt data on unmapped network shares.

Viruses can be divided into distinct categories. A list of major virus categories is provided here:

- **Macro**: Macro viruses infect the macros in office documents. Many office products, including Microsoft Office, allow users to write mini-programs called macros. These macros can also be written as a virus. This type of virus is very common due to the ease of writing such a virus.
- **Memory-resident**: A memory-resident virus installs itself and then remains in RAM from the time the computer is booted up to when it is shut down.
- **Multi-partite**: Multi-partite viruses attack the computer in multiple ways—for example, infecting the boot sector of the hard disk and one or more files.
- **Armored**: An armored virus uses techniques that make it hard to analyze. This is done by either compressing the code or encrypting it with a weak encryption method.
- **Sparse infector**: A sparse infector virus attempts to elude detection by performing its malicious activities only sporadically. With a sparse infector virus, the user will see symptoms for a short period, then no symptoms for a time. In some cases, the sparse infector targets a specific program but the virus only executes every 10th time or 20th time that target program runs.
- **Polymorphic**: A polymorphic virus literally changes its form from time to time to avoid detection by antivirus software. A more advanced form of this is called the Metamorphic virus; it can completely rewrite itself.

How Does This Crime Affect Forensics?

Viruses are remarkably easy to locate, but difficult to trace back to the creator. The first step is to document the particulars of the virus—for example, its behavior, the file characteristics, and so on. Then, you must see if there is some commonality among infected computers. For example, if all infected computers visited the same website, then it is likely that the website itself is infected. In addition, numerous sources of information about known viruses are available on the internet from software publishers and virus researchers, which is very useful in doing forensic research.

It is a slow and tedious process, but it is possible to track down the creator of a virus.

Logic Bombs

A **logic bomb** is malware that is designed to do harm to the system when some logical condition is reached. Often it is triggered based on a specific date and time. It is certainly possible to distribute a logic bomb via a Trojan horse, but this sort of attack is often perpetrated by employees. The following two cases illustrate this fact:

- In 2019, David Tinley, a contract programmer for Siemens, was charged with infecting his employer with a logic bomb. According to the U.S. Attorney's Office of the Western District of Pennsylvania's press release, Tinley pleaded guilty in federal court to a charge of intentional damage to a **protected computer**. He allegedly planted logic bombs in the spreadsheet. The logic bombs were timed to go off periodically, creating glitches that would require the company to call Tinley to fix the problem.

- Logic bombs are not new. In June 2006, Roger Duronio, a system administrator for the Swiss bank UBS, was charged with using a logic bomb to damage the company's computer network. His plan was to drive the company stock down due to damage from the logic bomb; thus, he was charged with securities fraud. Duronio was later convicted and sentenced to 8 years and 1 month in prison, as well as $3.1 million in restitution to UBS.

How Does This Crime Affect Forensics?

Logic bombs that are created by disgruntled employees are actually reasonably straightforward to investigate. First, the nature of the logic bomb gives some indication of the creator. It has to be someone with access to the system and with a programming background. Then, traditional issues such as motive are also helpful in investigating a logic bomb. If the logic bomb is distributed randomly via a Trojan horse, then investigating it follows the same parameters as investigating a virus.

Cyberterrorism

You cannot discuss cybercrime without having some discussion of cyberterrorism. Just a few years ago, the idea of cyberterrorism seemed completely hypothetical, perhaps even a bit sensationalist. Now, however, cyberterrorism is seen by many to surpass terrorism as a threat. There are definite reasons to take it seriously:

- In 2008 and 2009, there were several reports of attacks that were traced back to North Korea or China. Given that both nations are totalitarian regimes with very strict control on their populace, it is difficult to believe that the governments of those countries were not at least aware of those attacks.
- In December 2009, hackers broke into computer systems and stole secret defense plans of the United States and South Korea. The information stolen included a summary of plans for military operations by South Korean and U.S. troops in case of war with North Korea, though the attacks were traced back to a Chinese IP address.
- In December 2010, a group calling itself the Pakistan Cyber Army hacked the website of India's top investigating agency, the Central Bureau of Investigation (CBI).
- In March 2013, a cadre of the United States' top intelligence officials told Congress that cyberattacks led the numerous national security threats the United States faces. It is the first time since the September 11, 2001, terrorist attacks that anything other than an extremist physical threat has been the top concern in the Intelligence Community Worldwide Threat Assessment, which is presented annually to the Senate Select Committee on Intelligence. James Clapper, director of national intelligence at the time, told the panel that cyber and financial threats were being added "to the list of weapons being used against us." They help define a new "soft" kind of war.
- In 2015, 19-year-old hacker Ardit Ferizi was convicted of supplying the Islamic State insurgency (ISIS) with the data of 1300 use military personnel and government personnel so they could be targeted for attacks.

In 2020, many sources began expressing concern over cyberattacks on their nations' power grids. According to the North American Electric Reliability Corporation (NERC), another type of cyberattack on power grids involves exploiting vulnerabilities in firewall firmware. Such an attack happened in 2019 and caused communication outages between the control center and generation sites. These cases clearly illustrate that cyberterrorism and cyber-espionage are real threats that need to be examined and dealt with.

A critical topic in cyberterrorism is the subject of the China Eagle Union. This group consists of several thousand Chinese hackers whose stated goal is to infiltrate Western computer systems. There are a number of web resources regarding this group:

- *http://www.thedarkvisitor.com/2007/10/china-eagle-union/*
- *https://news.hitb.org/node/6164*
- *http://archives.cnn.com/2001/WORLD/asiapcf/east/04/27/china.hackers/index.html*

> **NOTE**
>
> Even at the time of this writing, the news was filled with more stories of the United States and China accusing each other of cyber-espionage and warfare. It is clear that there is now a significant cyber component to any international conflict. This makes computer security an issue of national security.

Members and leaders of the group insist that not only does the Chinese government have no involvement in their activities, but that they are breaking Chinese law and are in constant danger of arrest and imprisonment. However, most analysts believe this group is working with the full knowledge and support of the Chinese government. Throughout the first quarter of 2013, accusations of cyberattacks were leveled by both the U.S. and Chinese governments.

How Does This Crime Affect Forensics?

Because cyberterrorism and cyberespionage use the same techniques as any other cyber-crime, the actual technical portions of the investigation are the same. If it is a virus or DoS attack, you investigate it as you would any virus or DoS attack. However, the difference lies in the jurisdiction for the crime itself. Issues of cyberterrorism and cyberespionage are referred to the FBI.

CHAPTER SUMMARY

This chapter examined various ways in which the nature of a computer crime can affect the process of forensically investigating the crime. It is imperative that you be aware of the different crimes and how to investigate them. For example, seeking email evidence would be useful for investigating cyberstalking, but would not be useful for most DoS attacks. It is important that forensic investigators have a working knowledge of how these attacks are committed in order to properly investigate them.

KEY CONCEPTS AND TERMS

Cyberstalking

Denial-of-service (DoS) attack

Distributed denial-of-service (DDoS) attack

Fraud

Identity theft

Logic bomb

Rainbow table

Three-way handshake

Virus

CHAPTER 2 ASSESSMENT

1. When investigating a virus, what is the first step?

   A. Check firewall logs.
   B. Check IDS logs.
   C. Document the virus.
   D. Trace the origin of the virus.

2. Which of the following crimes is most likely to leave email evidence?

   A. Cyberstalking
   B. DoS
   C. Logic bomb
   D. Fraud

3. Where would you seek evidence that Ophcrack had been used on a Windows Server 2008 machine?

   A. In the logs of the server; look for the reboot of the system
   B. In the logs of the server; look for the loading of a CD
   C. In the firewall logs
   D. In the IDS logs

4. Logic bombs are often perpetrated by _____.

   A. identity thieves
   B. disgruntled employees
   C. terrorists
   D. hackers

5. Spyware is legal.

   A. True
   B. False

6. It is legal for employers to monitor work computers.

   A. True
   B. False

7. What is the primary reason to take cyberstalking seriously?

   A. It can damage your system.
   B. It can be annoying and distracting.
   C. It can be a prelude to real-world violence.
   D. It can be part of identity theft.

8. What is the starting point for investigating denial-of-service attacks?

   A. Firewall logs
   B. Email headers
   C. System logs
   D. Tracing the packets

Forensic Methods and Labs

I N THIS CHAPTER, YOU WILL LEARN SOME SPECIFIC APPROACHES to forensic investigation. These methodologies provide a framework for your investigations. You will also learn the requirements
for setting up a computer forensics lab. Finally, you will get a brief introduction to major
computer forensics software.

Chapter 3 Topics

This chapter covers the following topics and concepts:

- The methodologies used in forensic investigations
- Formal forensic approaches
- Proper documentation of methodologies and findings
- Evidence-handling tasks
- How to set up a forensics lab
- Common forensics software programs
- Common forensics certifications

Chapter 3 Goals

When you complete this chapter, you will be able to:

- Understand major forensic methodologies
- Set up a computer forensics lab
- Demonstrate an understanding of major forensics software

Forensic Methodologies

You will learn very specific techniques for computer forensics; however, it is important that you have a general framework for approaching forensics. This section examines general principles and specific methodologies you can apply to your own forensic investigations. First, here are some basic principles to consider.

Handle Original Data as Little as Possible

A forensics specialist should touch the original data as little as possible. Instead, information should be copied prior to examination. This means that the first step in any investigation is to make a copy of the suspected storage device. In the case of computer hard drives, you make a complete copy. That means a bit-level copy. Tools like EnCase, Forensic Toolkit, and OSForensics will do this for you; it is also possible to do this with basic Linux commands. In addition, it is a common practice to make two copies of the drive. This gives you one to work with and a backup in the event you need it.

The idea of handling original information as little as possible is a critical philosophy that should permeate your approach to forensics. But the real question is, why? Why is it so important that you not touch the actual original evidence any more than you have to? The first answer to that question is that each time you touch digital information, there is some chance of altering it. Even such a simple thing as changing the time/date stamp on a file is altering it. And if you alter the file, you cannot be certain that the evidence you find is valid.

Another reason is that there may be a need for another investigator to do his or her own examination. If you have worked with the original information, you may have altered it so that another person cannot now do a fresh analysis. There are many situations in which another examiner will need to review the original information. The most obvious situation is when the opposing counsel hires his or her own expert who wants to do his or her own examination.

This stems from a principle known in forensics as **Locard's principle of transference**. Edmond Locard was a pioneer in forensics. While he dealt with physical forensics (hair, blood, and so on) and lived long before the advent of the computer age, his concepts are still applicable. Essentially, he stated that you cannot interact in an environment without leaving some trace. This is true in computers. For example, the moment you log into a Windows system, you have changed a few Windows Registry keys, added to the log, and changed a few temp files.

There are times when live forensics may be needed. However, that is always a secondary choice. The preference is to work with an image of a drive, rather than the actual drive. If you must work with a live system, your report should explain why. One common place for live forensics is when you must extract evidence from cloud storage. It simply is not practical to image an entire cloud.

2 Comply with the Rules of Evidence

During an investigation, a forensics specialist should keep in mind the relevant rules of evidence. The chain of custody and the Daubert standard, for instance, are just two of these that you must follow.

Rules of evidence govern whether, when, how, and why proof of a legal case can be placed before a judge or jury. A forensics specialist should have a good understanding of the rules of evidence in the given type of court and jurisdiction.

As one example, the Federal Rules of Evidence (FRE) is a code of evidence law. The FRE governs the admission of facts by which parties in the U.S. federal court system may prove their cases. The FRE provides guidelines for the authentication and identification of evidence for admissibility under Rules 901 and 902. The following is an excerpt from Rule 901 of the FRE from Cornell University Law School (2011) with the portions relevant to computer forensics shown:

(a) **In General.** To satisfy the requirement of authenticating or identifying an item of evidence, the proponent must produce evidence sufficient to support a finding that the item is what the proponent claims it is....

(1) **Testimony of a Witness with Knowledge.** Testimony that an item is what it is claimed to be....

(3) **Comparison by an Expert Witness or the Trier of Fact.** A comparison with an authenticated specimen by an expert witness or the trier of fact....

(9) **Evidence About a Process or System.** Evidence describing a process or system and showing that it produces an accurate result.[1]

Item 1 refers to expert testimony. You as a forensic examiner may be called upon to authenticate evidence. Item 3 refers to a comparison between a given specimen and another item. This can be used to authenticate evidence. Item 9 is critical for computer forensics. Even if you use automated tools such as EnCase from Guidance Software or Forensic Toolkit from AccessData, you should understand how the tools work in detail so you can authenticate the process if necessary.

In Chapter 1, you were introduced to Federal Rule 702, which defines what constitutes an expert witness. There are other, related rules of which you should be aware.

Rule 703 discusses the bases of an expert opinion. Rule 703 states that an expert

may base an opinion on facts or data in the case that the expert has been made aware of or personally observed. If experts in the particular field would reasonably rely on those kinds of facts or data in forming an opinion on the subject, they need not be admissible for the opinion to be admitted. But if the facts or data would otherwise be inadmissible, the proponent of the opinion may disclose them to the jury only if their probative value in helping the jury evaluate the opinion substantially outweighs their prejudicial effect.[2]

Rule 705 states that, "unless the court orders otherwise, an expert may state an opinion—and give the reasons for it—without first testifying to the underlying facts or data. But the expert may be required to disclose those facts or data on cross-examination."[3] Now, this does not mean the expert does not have to have a reason for the opinion. In fact, you can rest assured that opposing counsel will probe this reasoning in some detail. The rule simply states you can give your opinion without *first* providing the reasons for it.

Individual jurisdictions may have some additional rules particular to that jurisdiction. It is critical that you be aware of the rules in your jurisdiction as well as general rules of evidence.

3 Avoid Exceeding Your Knowledge

A forensics specialist should not undertake an examination that is beyond his or her current level of knowledge and skill. This might seem obvious, but it is a problem that you can observe not just in forensics, but in the IT industry in general. Most other professions are more than happy to refer a client to a specialist. For example, if you see your family doctor and she discovers an anomaly regarding your heart, she will refer you to a cardiologist. Certainly she studied cardiology in medical school, but she will still send you to someone who specializes in cardiology. However, IT professionals all too often believe that if they have a little knowledge, that is enough to proceed.

> **FYI**
>
> In the field of forensics, your reputation is the most important thing you have. If you overextend beyond your actual skills, it is likely to come out at trial. The opposing side might have experts advising them—and when the other side's attorney cross-examines you, and your lack of knowledge becomes apparent, your reputation will be damaged. Consider adopting this standard: *Never testify or write an expert report unless you are very sure of your expertise in the relevant technologies and very comfortable with the conclusions you are presenting.* Even one occasion of being found to have been exaggerating, fabricating, or overextending yourself during testimony can ruin your reputation and your career.

This can be very problematic in forensics. Suppose you are a very skilled forensic examiner, and you have extensive experience with Microsoft Windows and Linux. But a computer is brought to you that runs Mac OS. Now, it is very likely that your skills would allow you to extract data. And it is true that Mac OS is based on a Linux-like system (FreeBSD). But is that enough? Very likely, it is not. It is also very likely that if you insist on doing the investigation yourself, you may miss key evidence—or at the very least, the opposition's attorney can claim in court that you have.

These basic principles should guide your forensic investigation. These are not specific procedures, but rather general philosophical approaches to investigation. It may seem that this point is being overstated, but there are numerous instances of expert witnesses going well beyond their actual skills. Here is one such story from the Expert Witness Institute:

> My worst experience with an expert witness concerned a misdiagnosis of precancerous cells in the uterus. All went well on direct examination. However, during cross-examination my expert had testified that one of the things he did to prepare for his testimony was to "google" the condition that was the subject of the entire lawsuit. Let's just say the defense attorney had a ball with him after that and my expert lost all credibility with the jury. That is one of the worst things an expert witness can say on the stand because the judge reminds the jurors not look up the medical conditions at issue in the case on Google or on the internet—one of the reasons being that there is a lot of wrong information on the web. I had prepared that expert witness for days leading up to the trial, but did not take it upon myself to advise him not to discuss "google" or the internet. Ever since that experience, I specifically advise my experts to never mention Google or the internet when discussing how the expert prepared for his or

her testimony. You would think this is obvious, but my experience proved otherwise. Experts, no matter how experienced, need to be properly prepared with respect to every single aspect of their testimony, even the most obvious aspects.[4]

If the witness had true expertise in this area, he would not have needed to "google" information on it. That is what a layperson does when curious about a topic.

Create an Analysis Plan

Before you begin any forensic examination, you should have an analysis plan. This plan is a guide for your work. How will you gather evidence? Are there concerns about evidence being changed or destroyed? What tools are most appropriate for this specific investigation? Is this a federal or state case? Will this affect admissibility rules? You should address all of these issues in your data analysis plan. It is advisable to have a standard data analysis plan that you simply customize for specific situations.

Creating an Order of Volatility

Much of the evidence on a system does not last very long. Some evidence resides in storage that requires a consistent power supply. *Volatility* refers to how easy it is for data to change. Registers are very volatile, whereas a CD-ROM is not. Other evidence might sit in media locations that are continuously changing. You must start with collecting the most volatile evidence and proceed to the least volatile. To determine what evidence to collect first, draw up an order of volatility—a list of evidence sources ordered by their relative volatility. The following is an example of an order of volatility:

1. Registers and cache
2. Routing tables
3. ARP cache
4. Process table
5. Kernel statistics and modules
6. Main memory
7. Temporary file systems
8. Secondary memory
9. Router configuration
10. Network topology

The standards document, RFC 3227, presents guidelines for evidence collection and archiving.[5] These are not regulatory requirements, but rather suggested guidelines. This exact order may not be applicable to every investigation.

- Volatile data
- File slack
- File system
- Registry
- Memory dumps
- System state backup
- Internet traces

3

Forensic Methods
and Labs

Technical Information Collection Considerations

System forensics specialists must keep in mind three main technical data collection considerations. These are understanding the life span of information, collecting information quickly, and collecting bit-level information.

Considering the Life Span of Information

In planning collection efforts, a forensics specialist must be aware that information has a life span. **Life span** refers to how long information is valid. The term is related to volatility. More volatile information tends to have a shorter life span. The nature of the information as well as organizational policies and practices determine the information's life span. For example, data regarding network traffic and the messages themselves may exist only for the time the transmission is passing through a router. This may be only milliseconds. Information stored in computer memory, such as the complete packet, may have a life span of 1 millisecond. Or, in the case of a cached IP address, the life span may last 20 minutes. In either case, memory is volatile because it lasts only for as long as the device is powered, so the forensics specialist must act accordingly.

As information life spans increase, the life span determinant is typically related to organizational practice. For example, an organization may establish an "email retention" policy that an email message may be stored within the email system for only 30 days. After 30 days, any message that is not moved to alternate storage is deleted. Log files may be retained for months or years, in accordance with an organization's audit policy. Finance and accounting information may have a multiple-year life span that corresponds with requirements established by state or federal governments.

In planning a collection effort, forensics specialists must be aware of the life span of the information with which they are working. They must use collection techniques appropriate to the information's life span.

Collecting Information Quickly

Once the collection effort is announced or in process, it is important to collect the evidence as quickly as possible. It is frequently not possible or practical to determine who made a change or when. In addition, the target of an investigation may try to conceal information, which further obscures changes. Networking systems also increase the potential for unauthorized changes. The person making a change on a network does not have to be local to the device on which the information is stored.

Collecting Bit-Level Information

To be useful, 1 and 0 bits must be converted through hardware and software into text, pictures, screen displays, videos, audio, or other usable formats. Investigators also look for whether unrelated bits were inserted, such as trade secrets buried within other files. Forensics specialists must therefore have tools that allow manipulation and evaluation of bit-level information. Use of bit-level tools also enables an investigator to reconstruct file fragments if files have been deleted or overwritten.

Basically, **bit-level information** is information at the level of actual 1s and 0s stored in memory or on the storage device, as opposed to going through the file system's interpretation. Whatever operating system is being used simply shows its representation of the data. Going to a bit-level view gives the most accurate view of how the information is actually stored on the hardware. If you use the file system to copy a suspect drive, you probably won't get slack space or hidden partitions. But you will get those items with a bit-level copy.

Formal Forensic Approaches

Several organizations have established formal guidelines for approaching a forensic investigation. You should become familiar with these guidelines. Depending on your work environment, you might implement one of these or use one of these as a base and adjust it to your own plan.

DoD Forensic Standards

The U.S. Department of Defense (DoD) coordinates and supervises agencies and functions of the government related to national security and the U.S. armed forces. The DoD uses system forensics to evaluate and examine data related to cyberattacks. The DoD estimates the potential impact of malicious activity. It also assesses the intent and identity of perpetrators. The DoD Cyber Crime Center (DC3) sets standards for digital evidence processing, analysis, and diagnostics. DC3 is involved with DoD investigations that require computer forensics support to detect, enhance, or recover digital media. DC3 is also involved in criminal law enforcement forensics and counterintelligence. It assists in criminal, counterintelligence, counterterrorism, and fraud investigations. In addition, it supports safety investigations, commander-directed inquiries, and inspector-general investigations.

DC3 provides computer investigation training. It trains forensics examiners, investigators, system administrators, and others. It also ensures that defense information systems are secure from unauthorized use, criminal and fraudulent activities, and foreign intelligence service exploitation. DC3 partners with government, academic, and private industry computer security officials. For more information on DC3, see *http://www.dc3.mil.*

The DFRWS Framework

The Digital Forensic Research Workshop (DFRWS) is a nonprofit volunteer organization. Its goal is to enhance the sharing of knowledge and ideas about digital forensics research. DFRWS sponsors annual conferences, technical working groups, and challenges to help drive the direction of research and development. In 2001, the DFRWS developed a framework for digital investigation that is still applicable and followed. The DFRWS framework is a matrix with six classes:

- Identification
- Preservation
- Collection
- Examination
- Analysis
- Presentation

The SWGDE Framework

The Scientific Working Group on Digital Evidence (SWGDE) promotes a framework process that includes four stages. The stages are:

- Collect
- Preserve
- Examine
- Transfer

That final step means any sort of transfer—even moving evidence from the lab to a court or returning evidence when no longer needed.

FYI

Although all forensic methodologies and texts recommend you make a copy of the suspect drive to work with, you may want to consider actually making two copies—each with a different imaging tool. Then, if time permits, use different tools on each copy. If both copies, made with different tools and examined with different tools, yield the same evidentiary results, that is a very powerful indication that the evidence is accurate. It would be exceedingly difficult for opposing counsel to find an issue with your examination.

An Event-Based Digital Forensics Investigation Framework

In 2004, Brian Carrier and Eugene Spafford, researchers at the Center for Education and Research in Information Assurance and Security (CERIAS) at Purdue University, proposed a model that is more intuitive and flexible than the DFRWS framework.

This model has five primary phases, each of which may contain additional subphases. The primary phases are the Readiness phase, the Deployment phase, the Physical Crime Scene Investigation phase, the Digital Crime Scene Investigation phase, and the Presentation phase. The Readiness phase contains the Operations Readiness subphase, which involves training people and testing investigation tools, and the Infrastructure Readiness subphase, which involves configuring the equipment. The Deployment phase includes the Detection and Notification subphase, in which someone detects an incident and alerts investigators, and the Confirmation and Authorization subphase, in which investigators receive authorization to conduct the investigation.

Documentation of Methodologies and Findings

Documentation of forensic processing methodologies and findings is critical. Without proper documentation, a forensics specialist has difficulty presenting findings. When security or audit findings become the object of a lawsuit or a criminal investigation, the legal system requires proper documentation. Without documentation, courts are unlikely to accept investigative results. Thus, a system forensics specialist must know the ins and outs

documentation

of computer evidence processing methodology. This methodology includes strong evidence-processing documentation and good chain-of-custody procedures.

Disk Structure

A system forensics specialist should have a good understanding of how computer hard disks, flash drives, and compact discs (CDs) are structured. A specialist should also know how to find data hidden in obscure places on CDs and hard disk drives. In fact, as technology progresses, it will be important for the digital forensics examiner to be familiar with any sort of media in common use. This is also an area wherein one might have to use multiple tools to get at the data.

File Slack Searching – *Autopsy*

A system forensics specialist should understand techniques and automated tools used to capture and evaluate file slack. A hard disk or CD is segmented into clusters of a particular size. Each cluster can hold only a single file or part of a single file. If you write a 1-kilobyte (KB) file to a disk that has a cluster size of 4 KB, the last 3 KB of the cluster are wasted. This unused space between the logical end of file and the physical end of file is known as **file slack** or **slack space**.

Most computer users have no idea that they're creating slack space as they use a computer. In addition, pieces of a file may remain even after you delete it. This residual information in file slack is not necessarily overwritten when you create a new file. File slack is therefore a source of potential security leaks involving passwords, network logins, email, database entries, images, and word processing documents. A forensics specialist should know how to search file slack, identify what information is or is not useful, and document any findings.

Evidence-Handling Tasks

A system forensics specialist has three basic tasks related to handling evidence:

- **Find evidence**—Gathering computer evidence goes beyond normal data recovery. Finding and isolating evidence to prove or disprove allegations can be difficult. Investigators may need to investigate thousands of active files and fragments of deleted files to find just one that makes a case. System forensics has therefore been described as looking for one needle in a mountain of needles. Examiners often work in secure laboratories where they check for viruses in suspect machines and isolate data to avoid contamination.
- **Preserve evidence**—Preserving computer evidence is important because data can be destroyed easily. The 1s and 0s that make up data can be hidden and vanish instantly with the push of a button. As a result, forensic examiners should assume that every computer has been rigged to destroy evidence. They must proceed with care in handling computers and storage media.
- **Prepare evidence**—Evidence must be able to withstand judicial scrutiny. Therefore, preparing evidence requires patience and thorough documentation. Failing to document

where evidence comes from and failing to ensure that it has not been changed can ruin a case. Judges have dismissed cases because of such failures.

Evidence-Gathering Measures

Here are principles to use when you gather evidence:

- **Avoid changing the evidence**—Photograph equipment in place as you find it before you remove it. Label wires and sockets so that you can put everything back as it was once you get computers and other equipment into your lab. Transport items carefully and avoid touching hard disks or CDs. Make exact, bit-by-bit copies and store them on a medium such as a write-once CD.
- **Determine when evidence was created**—You should create timelines of computer usage and file accesses. This can be difficult, because there are so many ways to falsify data. But timelines can make or break a case.
- **Trust only physical evidence**—The 1s and 0s of data are recorded at the physical level of magnetic materials. This is what counts in system forensics. Other items may be corrupt.
- **Search throughout a device**—You need to search at this level of 1s and 0s across a wide range of areas inside a computer.
- **Present the evidence well**—Forensic examiners must present computer evidence in a logical, compelling, and persuasive manner. A jury must be able to understand the evidence. In addition, the evidence should be solid enough that a defense counsel cannot rebut it.

Expert Reports

An expert report is a formal document that details the expert's findings. Often this document is filed in a case prior to trial. If there are depositions, then the expert report will probably be used as the basis for some of the questions you are asked during deposition. When writing an expert report, you should consider several issues. An expert report will always be needed in civil cases, but may or may not be required in criminal cases. When you do need to write an expert report, it is critical that you do so properly.

The first issue is the format of the report. You usually list all items, documents, and evidence you considered. You also detail tests you performed, analysis done, and your conclusion. You should list your entire curriculum vitae (CV)—an extensive document detailing your experience and qualifications for a position—in an appendix. Keep in mind that a CV is much more thorough than a résumé. You should list every publication, award, or credential you have earned. A CV should also include more detail on work history and educational history.

Another issue for your report is thoroughness. In most jurisdictions, if it is not in your report, you are not allowed to testify about it at trial. So be very thorough. Anything you leave out may become a problem at trial. It is critical that you be detailed in what you write and that you document all the analysis done. For example, if you performed three tests and all three support a specific conclusion, make sure you list all three tests. If you list just one, then that is the only test you can testify about at trial.

Finally, back up everything you say. Clearly, you are an expert in forensics or else you would not be asked to testify. But remember that there is an opposing counsel whose job it is to disagree with you. The opposing counsel may have his or her own expert who will testify to different conclusions. It's good to have well-respected references to support any important claims you make. This way, it is not just your opinion, but rather your opinion along with the support of multiple credible sources. I recommend your report be replete with citations from reputable sources—but ensure that you actually *read* those sources. The opposing counsel will. By citing them, you are making a statement that you agree with them, so be careful in selecting your sources.

How to Set Up a Forensics Lab

The detailed specifics of any given lab are based on the needs of the lab, the budget, and the types of cases that lab is likely to handle. A state law enforcement agency with a high volume of cases has different needs from a small forensics lab that deals only with civil matters. However, some general principles apply to all labs.

Equipment — minimum RAID 1 but recommend RAID 5

First and foremost, you must have adequate equipment for the job. Among other things, this means adequate storage for the data. Remember, you might analyze a system, but it could be months before the case goes to trial. A server with the most storage you can afford is in order. Also, that server must have redundancy. It should have a bare minimum of one redundant array of independent disks or RAID 1 (disk mirroring), but RAID 5 is recommended. And it should be backed up at least once per day. It is likely you will need multiple servers to accommodate your storage needs.

You also need a variety of computers capable of attaching various types of drives—for example, external universal serial bus (USB), internal Small Computer System Interface (SCSI), Enhanced Integrated Drive Electronics (EIDE), and Serial Advanced Technology Attachment (SATA) drives. The exact number depends on the workload expected for the lab. You should also have power connectors for all types of smartphones, laptops, routers, and other devices. Both legacy and state of the art equipment

Security

Security is paramount for forensics. Above all, the machines being examined should not be connected to the internet. You can have a lab network that is not attached to the internet and is separate from your working network where you check email and use the internet. It is also important to have the lab in a room that is shielded from any electromagnetic interference. This means that cellular and wireless signals cannot penetrate the room housing the lab.

After you have established network and electronic security, physical security is the next concern. It is imperative to limit access to the lab. Allow only people with a legitimate need to enter the lab. It is recommended that the lab entrance have some sort of electronic method of recording who enters and when they enter. Swipe-card access is ideal for this. Furthermore, the room itself should be difficult to forcibly access. That means the windows and doors are very secure and would be extremely difficult to force open.

The lab also requires the means to secure evidence when it is not being used. An evidence safe is the best way to do this. The safe should be highly fire resistant as well, so that in case of fire, the evidence is preserved.

In addition to the general guidelines already listed, you should consider various international standards that are published and updated by the International Organization for Standards (ISO). A few are briefly described here:

- ISO/IEC 27037:2012—Information technology—Security techniques—Guidelines for identification, collection, acquisition and preservation of digital evidence. This is one common standard for digital forensics. This standard regards forensic practices and processes, particularly for capturing forensic evidence.
- ISO/IEC 27041:2015—Information technology—Security techniques—Guidance on assuring suitability and adequacy of incident investigative method. This standard is about forensics methods and tools.
- ISO/IEC 27042:2015—Information technology—Security techniques—Guidelines for the analysis and interpretation of digital evidence. This standard provides guidance on processing and analyzing digital evidence.

The National Institute of Standards and Technology (NIST) has a Computer Forensics Tool Testing Program that is used to test forensic tools. It would be a very good idea to see if your favorite tool has been tested and found adequate.

American Society of Crime Laboratory Directors

The American Society of Crime Laboratory Directors (ASCLD) provides guidelines for managing a forensics lab. It also provides guidelines for acquiring crime lab and forensics lab certifications. The ASCLD offers voluntary accreditation to public and private crime laboratories in the United States and around the world. It certifies computer forensics labs that analyze digital evidence and other criminal evidence, such as fingerprints and DNA samples. The ASCLD/LAB certification regulates how to organize and manage crime labs. Achieving ASCLD accreditation is a rigorous process. A lab must meet about 400 criteria to achieve accreditation. Typically, an unaccredited lab needs two to three years to prepare for accreditation. It spends this time developing policies, procedures, document controls, analysis validations, and so on. Then, the lab needs another year to go through the process. The lab manager submits an application. The lead assessor and a team spend one to two months reviewing the application and the policies and procedures to make sure the lab is ready. The assessment takes about a week. The assessment team generates findings that require corrective action. The lab typically requires several months to make corrections to the satisfaction of the lead assessor. Once the facility has made all corrections, the lead assessor recommends the lab to the board of directors for accreditation. Finally, the ASCLD/LAB board of directors votes on whether to accredit the lab.

The ASCLD/LAB program includes audits to ensure that forensics specialists are performing lab procedures correctly and consistently for all casework. The society performs these audits in computer forensics labs to maintain quality and integrity. One recommendation for labs is to follow the DoD guidelines on electromagnetic radiation (EMR). The DoD shields computers to prevent would-be infiltrators from detecting them via their EMR emission under its TEMPEST program. You can find out more about TEMPEST at *http://www.gao.gov /products/NSIAD-86-132.* Shielding all computers would be impossible because of the high cost involved. To protect high-risk investigations, however, a lab might also consider implementing TEMPEST protection.

TEMPEST certifies equipment that is built with shielding that prevents EMR release. In some cases, TEMPEST can be applied to an entire lab. Shielding a lab is an extremely high-cost approach that includes the following measures:

* Lining the walls, ceiling, floor, and doors with specially grounded, conductive metal sheets
* Installing filters that prevent power cables from transmitting computer emanations
* Installing special baffles in heating and ventilation ducts to trap emanations
* Installing line filters on telephone lines
* Installing special features at entrances and exits that prevent the facility from being open to the outside at all times

Creating and maintaining a TEMPEST-certified lab is expensive. Such a lab must be inspected and tested regularly. Only large, regional computer forensics labs that demand absolute security from eavesdropping should consider complete TEMPEST protection. For smaller facilities, use of TEMPEST-certified equipment is often a more effective approach. You can find out more about TEMPEST at *http://www.gao.gov/products/NSIAD-86-132.*

Common Forensic Software Programs

After setting up the lab and the equipment, the next thing to address is the software. Several software tools are available that you might want to use in your forensics lab. This section takes a brief look at several commonly used tools. However, this section gives extra attention to Guidance Software's EnCase and AccessData's Forensic Toolkit because these two programs are very commonly used by law enforcement.

EnCase

EnCase from Guidance Software is a very widely used forensic toolkit. This tool allows the examiner to conncct an Ethernet cable or null modem cable to a suspect machine and to view the data on that machine. EnCase prevents the examiner from making any accidental changes to the suspect machine. This is important: Remember the basic principle of touching the suspect machine as little as possible. EnCase organizes information into "cases." This matches the way examiners normally examine computers. **FIGURE 3-1** shows a sample EnCase case file.

The EnCase concept is based on the evidence file. This file contains the header, the checksum, and the data blocks. The data blocks are the actual data copied from the suspect machine, and the checksum is done to ensure there is no error in the copying of that data and that the information is not subsequently modified. Any subsequent modification causes the new checksum to not match the original checksum. As soon as the evidence file is added to the case, EnCase begins to verify the integrity of the entire disk image. The evidence file is an exact copy of the hard drive. EnCase calculates an MD5 hash when the drive is acquired.

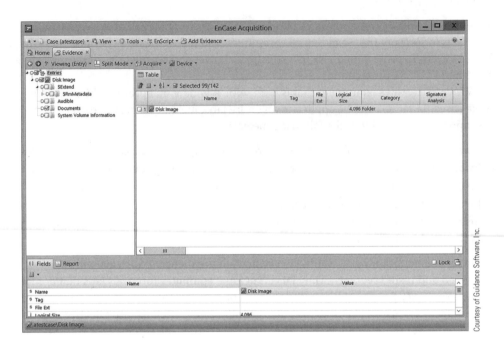

FIGURE 3-1

EnCase case file.

This hash is used to check for changes, alterations, or errors. When the investigator adds the evidence file to the case, it recalculates the hash; this shows that nothing has changed since the drive was acquired.

You can use multiple methods to acquire the data from the suspect computer:

- **EnCase boot disk** is a method that boots the system to EnCase using DOS mode rather than a GUI mode. You can then copy the suspect drive to a new drive to examine it.
- **EnCase network boot disk** is very similar to the EnCase boot disk, but it allows you to perform the process over a crossover cable between the investigator's computer and the computer being investigated.
- **LinEn boot disk** is specifically for acquiring the contents of a Linux machine. It operates much like the boot disk method, but it is for target machines that are running Linux.

After you have acquired a suspect drive, you can then examine it using EnCase.

The EnCase Tree pane is like Windows Explorer. It lists all the folders and can expand any particular element in the tree (folders or subfolders). The Table pane lists the subfolders and files contained within the folder that was selected in the Tree pane. When you select an item, it is displayed in the View pane, as shown in **FIGURE 3-2**.

EnCase allows you to filter what you view, narrowing your focus to specific items of interest. You can also search data using the EnCase Search feature, shown in **FIGURE 3-3**.

The Filter pane is a useful tool that can affect the data you view in the Table pane.

This is just a very brief introduction to EnCase. It is a very popular tool with law enforcement, and the vendor, Guidance Software, offers training for its product. You can visit the vendor website for more details at *http://www.guidancesoftware.com/*.

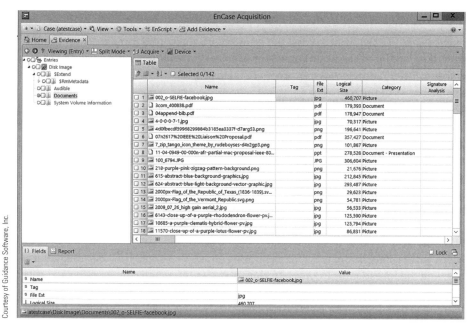

Courtesy of Guidance Software, Inc.

FIGURE 3-2

EnCase View pane.

3

Forensic Methods
and Labs

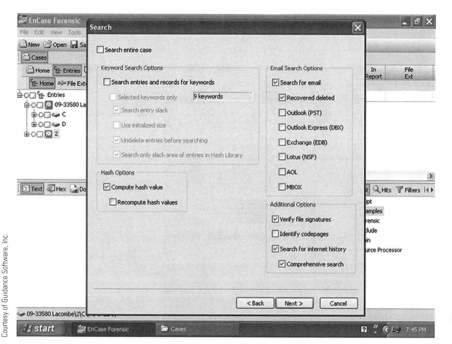

Courtesy of Guidance Software, Inc.

FIGURE 3-3

EnCase Search.

✻ Forensic Toolkit

The Forensic Toolkit (FTK) from AccessData is another widely used forensic analysis tool that is also very popular with law enforcement. You can get additional details at the company's website, *http://accessdata.com/product-download/digital-forensics*, but this section reviews some basics of the tool.

With FTK, you can select which hash to use to verify the drive when you copy it, which features you want to use on the suspect drive, and how to search, as shown in **FIGURE 3-4**.

Forensic Toolkit is particularly useful at cracking passwords. For example, password-protected Portable Document Format (PDF) files, Excel spreadsheets, and other documents often contain important information. FTK also provides tools to search and analyze the Windows Registry. The Windows Registry is where Windows stores all information regarding any programs installed. This includes viruses, worms, Trojan horses, rootkits, hidden programs, and spyware. The ability to effectively and efficiently scan the Registry for evidence is critical.

FTK gives you a robust set of tools for examining email. The email can be arranged in a timeline, giving the investigator a complete view of the entire email conversation and the ability to focus on any specific item of interest, as shown in **FIGURE 3-5**.

Another feature of this toolkit is its distributed processing. Scanning an entire hard drive, searching the Registry, and doing a complete forensic analysis of a computer can be a very time-intensive task. With AccessData's Forensic Toolkit, processing and analysis can be distributed across up to three computers. This lets all three computers perform the three parts of the analysis in parallel, thus significantly speeding up the forensic process. In addition, FTK has an Explicit Image Detection add-on that automatically detects pornographic images. This is very useful in cases involving allegations of pornography and is a particularly useful tool for law enforcement. FTK is available for Windows or Mac OS.

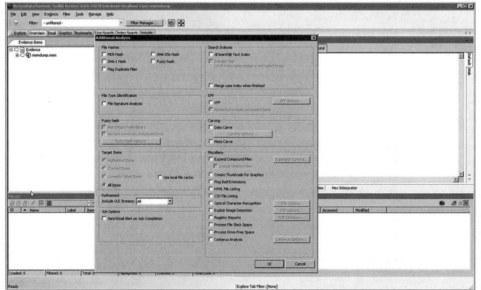

FIGURE 3-4

FTK features.

Courtesy of AccessData Group, Inc.

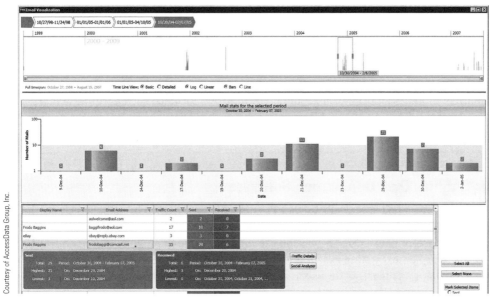

FIGURE 3-5

Email analysis.

OSForensics

The OSForensics tool from the company PassMark Software in Australia has been widely used since about 2010. One of the first attractive aspects of this tool is its cost. The full product is US$899, which is a fraction of the cost of many other tools. There is also a fully functional 30-day trial version. Furthermore, it is very easy to use. It will do most of what EnCase and FTK will do, but lacks a few of those products' specialized features. For example, OSForensics does not have a Known File Filter, as does FTK. You will see some labs using OSForenics in this book.

Helix

Helix is a customized Linux Live CD used for computer forensics. The suspect system is booted into Linux using the Helix CDs and then the tools provided with Helix are used to perform the analysis. This product is robust and full of features, but simply has not become as popular as AccessData's FTK and Guidance Software's EnCase. For more information, check out its website at *http://www.e-fense.com/products.php*.

Kali Linux

Kali Linux (formerly called BackTrack) is a Linux Live CD that you use to boot a system and then use the tools. Kali is a free Linux distribution, making it extremely attractive to schools teaching forensics or to laboratories on a strict budget. It is not used just for forensics, however, as it offers a wide range of general security and hacking tools. In fact, it is probably the most widely used collection of security tools available.

AnaDisk Disk Analysis Tool

AnaDisk from New Technologies Incorporated (NTI) turns a PC into a sophisticated disk analysis tool. The software was originally created to meet the needs of the U.S. Treasury Department in 1991. AnaDisk scans for anomalies that identify odd formats, extra tracks, and extra sectors. It can be used to uncover sophisticated data-hiding techniques.

AnaDisk supports all DOS formats and many non-DOS formats, such as Apple Mac OS and UNIX TAR. If a disk will fit in a PC CD drive, it is likely that AnaDisk can be used to analyze it. For information on AnaDisk, see *http://www.retrocomputing.org/cgi-bin/sitewise.pl?act=det &p=776&id=retroorg*.

CopyQM Plus Disk Duplication Software

CopyQM Plus from NTI essentially turns a PC into a disk duplicator. In a single pass, it formats, copies, and verifies a disk. This capability is useful for system forensics specialists who need to preconfigure CDs for specific uses and duplicate them. In addition, CopyQM Plus can create self-extracting executable programs that can be used to duplicate specific disks. CopyQM is an ideal tool for use in security reviews because once a CopyQM disk creation program has been created, anyone can use it to make preconfigured security risk-assessment disks. When the resulting program is run, the disk image of the original disk is restored on multiple disks automatically. The disk images can also be password-protected when they are converted to self-extracting programs. This is helpful when security is a concern, such as when disks are shared over the internet. CopyQM Plus is particularly helpful in creating computer incident response toolkit disks.

CopyQM Plus supports all DOS formats and many non-DOS formats, such as Apple Mac OS and UNIX TAR. It copies files, file slack, and unallocated storage space. However, it does not copy all areas of copy-protected disks—extra sectors added to one or more tracks on a CD. AnaDisk software should be used for this purpose. For information on CopyQM Plus, see *http://vetusware.com/download/CopyQM%203.24/?id=6457*.

✳The Sleuth Kit

The Sleuth Kit is a collection of command-line tools that are available as a free download. You can get them from this site: *http://www.sleuthkit.org/sleuthkit/*. This toolset is neither as rich nor as easy to use as EnCase, FTK, or OSForensics but can be a good option for a budget-conscious agency. The most obvious of the utilities included is ffind.exe.

There are options to search for a given file or to search for only deleted versions of a file. This particular utility is best used when you know the specific file you are searching for. It is not a good option for a general search. A number of utilities are available in Sleuth Kit; however, many people find using command-line utilities to be cumbersome. Fortunately, a graphical user interface (GUI) has been created for Sleuth Kit. That GUI is named Autopsy and is available at *http://www.sleuthkit.org/autopsy/download.php*. You can see Autopsy in **FIGURE 3-6**.

You will see Autopsy used frequently in this book. Since this tool is a free download, it is cost effective for the reader to use. It is also worthwhile to learn Autopsy even if you have a commercial forensics toolkit. Autopsy can be a second tool used to validate the results you derive from your primary tool.

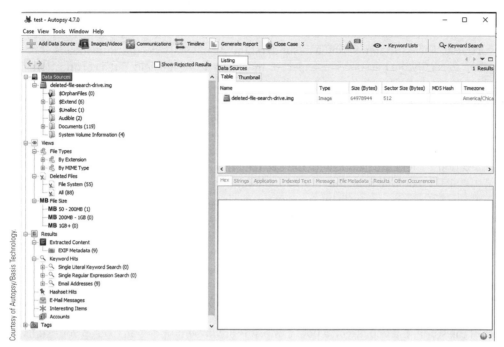

FIGURE 3-6

Autopsy.

⋇Disk Investigator

This is a free utility that comes as a GUI for use with Windows operating systems. You can download it from *http://www.theabsolute.net/sware/dskinv.html*. It is not a full-featured product like EnCase, but it is remarkably easy to use. When you first launch the utility, it presents you with a cluster-by-cluster view of your hard drive in hexadecimal form.

From the View menu, you can view directories or the root. The Tools menu allows you to search for a specific file or to recover deleted files.

Entire books could be written about the various forensic utilities available on the internet. It is a good idea for any investigator to spend some time searching the internet and experimenting with various utilities. Depending on your own skill set, technical background, and preferences, you might find one utility more suitable than another. It is also recommended that after you select a tool to use, you scan the internet for articles about that tool. Make certain that it has widespread acceptance and that there are no known issues with its use. It can also be useful to use more than one tool to search a hard drive. If multiple tools yield the same result, this can preempt any objections the opposing attorney or his or her expert may attempt to present at trial. And remember—as always—to document every single step of your investigation process.

Forensic Certifications

You have a lab, you have software, but what about personnel? When considering potential candidates, looking for candidates who have taken a forensics class is a very good first step, but you should also look for candidates who have earned industry certifications. Before looking at specific certifications, let's discuss computer certifications in general.

Certifications have always been a controversial topic. Some people swear by them and won't even interview a candidate who does not have a few. Other people are convinced they are worthless. The issue stems from a misunderstanding of what a certification means. It is not meant to certify the person as an expert or master in a specific field. But a certification would imply a person has a working knowledge comparable to that certification. It is meant to demonstrate a baseline of competence.

Think about a medical degree. Simply having an MD does not guarantee the person is a brilliant physician. It just shows that the person achieved a certain minimum skill level. There is certainly a wide variation in skills among physicians. The same thing occurs with IT certifications. There are people with the Certified Information Systems Security Professional (CISSP®) credential from the International Information Systems Security Certification Consortium (ISC)²® who are brilliant security professionals with a very deep understanding of security and a wide set of skills. There are others with that credential who are only moderately competent.

Another issue with certifications is the boot camp. These programs are usually four or five days of intense study where the materials needed to pass a certification test are crammed into the students. On the final day, when it is all still fresh in their minds, they take the relevant certification test. This does lead to many boot camp attendees forgetting everything a few months later; however, this can be seen not as a failure of the training, but rather of the student. If you attend a boot camp, it is incumbent upon you to keep your skills up after the training is over.

Regardless of your personal feelings on certifications, it is a fact that they can only help your résumé as a forensic analyst. That doesn't mean, however, that you should ever hire any IT professional based solely on certifications—they are but one part of the total résumé. A combination of the right certifications along with formal education and experience make an ideal candidate.

So what are the right certifications? Forensics is a very broad topic and requires analysts to have both a broad and deep knowledge. Some of this knowledge is obtained in a formal degree program, whereas some is obtained on the job. But anywhere you have a gap in your knowledge, or simply want to enhance your résumé, is a good place to add a certification. You need to know the following areas:

- **PC hardware**—This can be obtained in a basic hardware course at a college or via the CompTIA A+ certification.
- **Basic networking**—Most computer science–related degrees include a course in basic networking. This satisfies your needs as a forensics expert. However, you might consider the CompTIA Network+ or the Cisco Certified Network Associate certifications.
- **Security**—You must have a general knowledge of security. This can be best demonstrated with the (ISC)² CISSP certification or the CompTIA Security+ certification.
- **Hacking**—Yes, you do need to know what the hackers know. A few certifications for this area of study exist. One is Offensive Security's test. That test requires hands-on hacking. Additionally, there are the Certified Ethical Hacker from EC Council and the Global Information Assurance Certification (GIAC) Penetration Tester (GPEN) from SANS. There are also Offensive Security certifications that are all hands-on hacking tests.

   Now that you have learned about certifications in general, it's time to consider specific forensics certifications. The following sections examine two vendor certifications. Clearly, if your lab uses a specific tool, it is a good idea to have analysts who are certified in that tool. Subsequent sections explore a couple of general forensic certifications. These tests are about forensic methodologies rather than a specific tool.

EnCase Certified Examiner Certification

Guidance Software, the creator of EnCase, sponsors the EnCase Certified Examiner (EnCE) certification program. EnCE certification is open to the public and private sectors. This certification focuses on the use and mastery of system forensics analysis using EnCase. For more information on EnCE certification requirements, visit *http://www.guidancesoftware.com*.

AccessData Certified Examiner

AccessData is the creator of Forensic Toolkit (FTK). AccessData sponsors the AccessData Certified Examiner (ACE) certification program. ACE certification is open to the public and private sectors. This certification is specific to the use and mastery of FTK. Requirements for taking the ACE exam include completing the AccessData boot camp and Windows forensics courses. For more information on ACE certification, visit *http://www.accessdata.com/*.

OSForensics

OSForensics also has a certification test. This test covers a few basics of forensic methodology, but focuses on the use of the OSForensics tool. This certification does not have specific educational requirements. You can take an online course, self-study, or take an in-person course. For more information, visit *http://www.osforensics.com/*.

EC Council Certified Hacking Forensic Investigator

The EC Council Certified Hacking Forensic Investigator (CHFI) certification is a good general forensics certification. EC Council is more widely known for its Certified Ethical Hacker test, but its forensics test is a solid choice. It covers the general principles and techniques of forensics rather than specific tools like EnCase or FTK. This is a good starting point for learning forensics. You can learn more at its website at *http://www.eccouncil.org/Computer-Hacking-Forensic-Investigator/index.html*.

GIAC Certifications

The Global Information Assurance Certification (GIAC) certifications are well respected in the IT industry. They include security, hacking, and forensic certifications. GIAC provides several levels of certification, beginning with the GIAC Certified Forensic Analyst (GCFA) and culminating with the GIAC Certified Forensic Examiner (GCFE). You can learn more about its certifications at the GIAC website at *http://www.giac.org/certified-forensic-analyst-gcfa*.

CHAPTER SUMMARY

This chapter provided an overview of the forensic process. You examined general concepts as well as specific forensics frameworks. It is important that you fully understand these concepts before you move forward.

The chapter also looked at some widely used forensic tools. Even if you already have a tool that you prefer to use or that is mandated at your lab, it is worthwhile for you to at least have a basic familiarity with other forensic tools that are available. Kali Linux, in particular, is a tool you should become familiar with because it is free to use.

KEY CONCEPTS AND TERMS

Bit-level information
File slack

Life span
Locard's principle of transference

Rules of evidence
Slack space

CHAPTER 3 ASSESSMENT

1. To preserve digital evidence, an investigator should _____.

A. make two copies of each evidence item using a single imaging tool

B. make a single copy of each evidence item using an approved imaging tool

C. make two copies of each evidence item using different imaging tools

D. store only the original evidence item

2. Bob was asked to make a copy of all the evidence from the compromised system. Melanie did a DOS copy of all the files on the system. What would be the primary reason for you to recommend for or against using a disk-imaging tool?

A. A disk-imaging tool would check for internal self-checking and validation and have an MD5 checksum.

B. The evidence file format will contain case data entered by the examiner and encrypted at the beginning of the evidence file.

C. A simple DOS copy will not include deleted files, file slack, and other information.

D. There is no case for an imaging tool because it will use a closed, proprietary format that if compared with the original will not match up sector for sector.

3. It takes _____ occurrence(s) of overextending yourself during testimony to ruin your reputation.

A. only one (if it is a major case)

B. several

C. only one

D. at least two

4. The MD5 message-digest algorithm is used to _____.

A. wipe magnetic media before recycling it

B. make directories on an evidence disk

C. view graphics files on an evidence drive

D. hash a disk to verify that a disk is not altered when you examine it

5. You should make at least two bitstream copies of a suspect drive.

    A. True

    B. False

6. What is the purpose of hashing a copy of a suspect drive?

    A. To make it secure

    B. To remove viruses

    C. To check for changes

    D. To render it read-only

7. What is the most important reason that you not touch the actual original evidence any more than you have to?

    A. Each time you touch digital data, there is some chance of altering it.

    B. You might be accused of planting evidence.

    C. You might accidentally decrypt files.

    D. It can lead to data degradation.

References

1. Cornell Law School Legal Information Institute. (n.d.). Rule 901. Testimony by Expert Witness. Retrieved from https://www.law.cornell.edu/rules/fre/rule_901 on January 27, 2021.

2. Cornell Law School Legal Information Institute. (n.d.). Rule 703. Bases of an Expert. Retrieved from https://www.law.cornell.edu/rules/fre/rule_703 on January 27, 2021.

3. Cornell Law School Legal Information Institute. (n.d.). Rule 705. Disclosing the Facts or Data Underlying an Expert. Retrieved from https://www.law.cornell.edu/rules/fre/rule_705 on January 27, 2021.

4. Rahman, M. (2020). 15 attorneys share their expert witness horror stories. Expert Institute: Working with Experts [blog]. Retrieved from https://www.expertinstitute.com/resources/insights/15-attorneys-share-their-expert-witness-horror-stories/ on January 29, 2021.

5. Internet Society Network Working Group. (2002). Guidelines for evidence collection and archiving. Retrieved from https://tools.ietf.org/html/rfc3227 on January 29, 2021.

PART II

Forensics Tools, Techniques, and Methods

Collecting, Seizing, and Protecting Evidence

N THIS CHAPTER, YOU SEE SPECIFIC and practical steps that must be taken when seizing evidence, imaging drives, and preparing suspect drives for analysis. You are also introduced to some concepts such as forensic file formats.

Chapter 4 Topics

This chapter covers the following topics and concepts:

- Using proper forensic procedure
- Handling evidence appropriately
- Different storage formats
- The process of forensically imaging a drive
- Acquiring RAID

Chapter 4 Goals

When you complete this chapter, you will be able to:

- Properly seize a suspect computer
- Prepare that computer for forensic examination
- Understand the various storage formats
- Image a drive
- Acquire RAID drives

Proper Procedure

It is important to follow proper procedure when examining a suspect machine. This chapter covers specific details on the proper procedure to follow when collecting, seizing, and protecting evidence.

Shutting Down the Computer

At one time, it was recommended that the investigator shut down the computer as a first step. However, it soon became apparent that one could lose valuable evidence found in running processes or memory. It also may be the case that the computer is using hard drive encryption. If you simply shut the system down, you may not be able to get back into the system. Before you shut the system down, at a minimum, you need to see what is currently running on the computer. Remember, you want to touch it as little as possible, so it is important to be careful. But you do need to find out if someone is currently accessing the computer—or if there is malware running on the computer—before you shut it down. Although the specifics may vary depending on the installed operating system, this section focuses on Windows because it is the most common desktop operating system.

The first thing to do is to check for running processes. In Windows (all versions), you press the Ctrl+Alt+Delete keys simultaneously, then select Task Manager. The Task Manager window opens; select the Processes tab. The Windows 10 version of this is shown in **FIGURE 4-1**. You should note that this looks much the same in Windows Server.

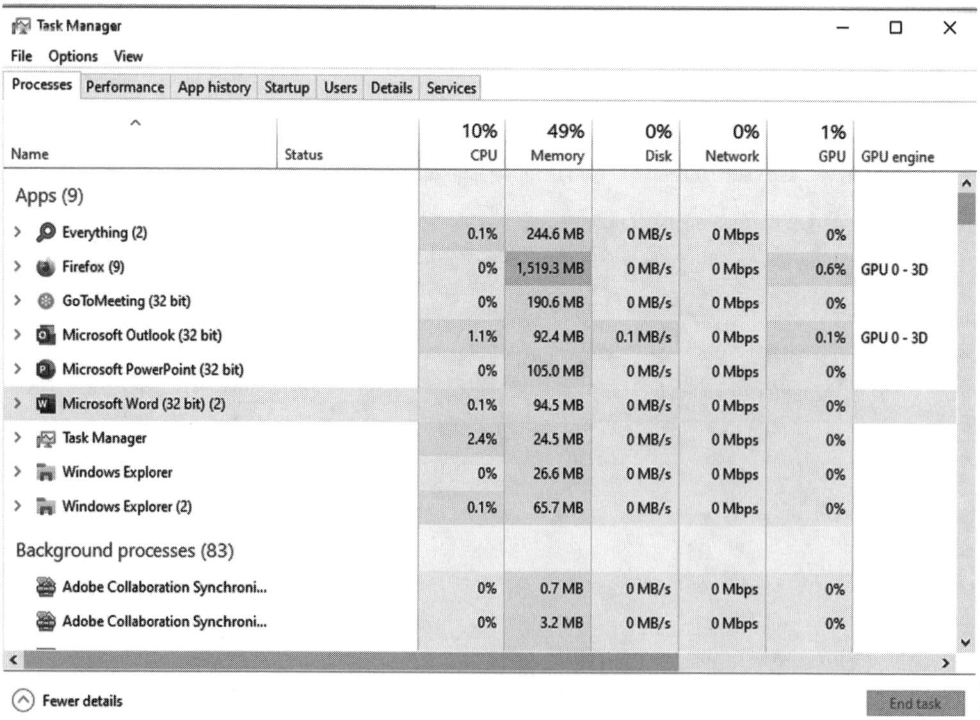

		10%	49%	0%	0%	1%	
Name	Status	CPU	Memory	Disk	Network	GPU	GPU engine
Apps (9)							
> Everything (2)		0.1%	244.6 MB	0 MB/s	0 Mbps	0%	
> Firefox (9)		0%	1,519.3 MB	0 MB/s	0 Mbps	0.6%	GPU 0 - 3D
> GoToMeeting (32 bit)		0%	190.6 MB	0 MB/s	0 Mbps	0%	
> Microsoft Outlook (32 bit)		1.1%	92.4 MB	0.1 MB/s	0 Mbps	0.1%	GPU 0 - 3D
> Microsoft PowerPoint (32 bit)		0%	105.0 MB	0 MB/s	0 Mbps	0%	
> Microsoft Word (32 bit) (2)		0.1%	94.5 MB	0 MB/s	0 Mbps	0%	
> Task Manager		2.4%	24.5 MB	0 MB/s	0 Mbps	0%	
> Windows Explorer		0%	26.6 MB	0 MB/s	0 Mbps	0%	
> Windows Explorer (2)		0.1%	65.7 MB	0 MB/s	0 Mbps	0%	
Background processes (83)							
Adobe Collaboration Synchroni...		0%	0.7 MB	0 MB/s	0 Mbps	0%	
Adobe Collaboration Synchroni...		0%	3.2 MB	0 MB/s	0 Mbps	0%	

FIGURE 4-1

Windows 10 running processes.

Now take a picture of the screen so you have a record of the running processes. In this case, "take a picture" means taking an actual photo with a camera, not taking a screenshot. In many cases, your photos are also subject to the rules of the chain of custody for evidence. You should assume that they are. Next, it is important to see if there are live connections to this system. Fortunately, there are built-in commands (most work in Linux as well as Windows) that will help you with that. The following sections cover a few of those commands.

Using `netstat`

The `netstat` command shows network statistics and any current connections. Normally, there are connections. For example, a Windows 7 computer that is part of a homegroup will have communications with other members of that group. What you are looking for are external connections, particularly ones from outside the local network. You can see an example of `netstat` in **FIGURE 4-2**.

Using `net sessions`

The `net sessions` command is actually more helpful than `netstat`. The `netstat` command shows even meaningless connections, such as your computer opening a web browser. But `net sessions` shows only established network communication sessions, such as someone logging on to that system. You can see an example of `net sessions` in **FIGURE 4-3**.

The `openfiles` Command

The `openfiles` command is very useful. It tells you if any shared files or folders are open and who has them open. Before shutting down the suspect machine, this is a critical command to run. You can see an example of `openfiles` in **FIGURE 4-4**.

You should run each of these commands and photograph the results before shutting down the machine. Also document that you ran them, the time you started them, and the

```
C:\Windows\system32\cmd.exe - netstat

Microsoft Windows [Version 6.2.9200]
(c) 2012 Microsoft Corporation. All rights reserved.

C:\Users\chuckeasttom>netstat

Active Connections

  Proto  Local Address          Foreign Address        State
  TCP    127.0.0.1:1030         ChucksLaptop:5354      ESTABLISHED
  TCP    127.0.0.1:1104         ChucksLaptop:27015     ESTABLISHED
  TCP    127.0.0.1:5354         ChucksLaptop:1030      ESTABLISHED
  TCP    127.0.0.1:27015        ChucksLaptop:1104      ESTABLISHED
  TCP    192.168.1.5:1539       server-54-240-170-126:http  CLOSE_WAIT
```

FIGURE 4-2

Using `netstat`.

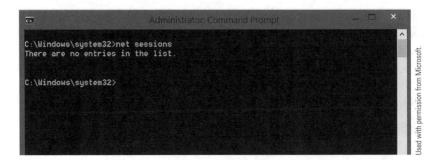

FIGURE 4-3

Using net sessions.

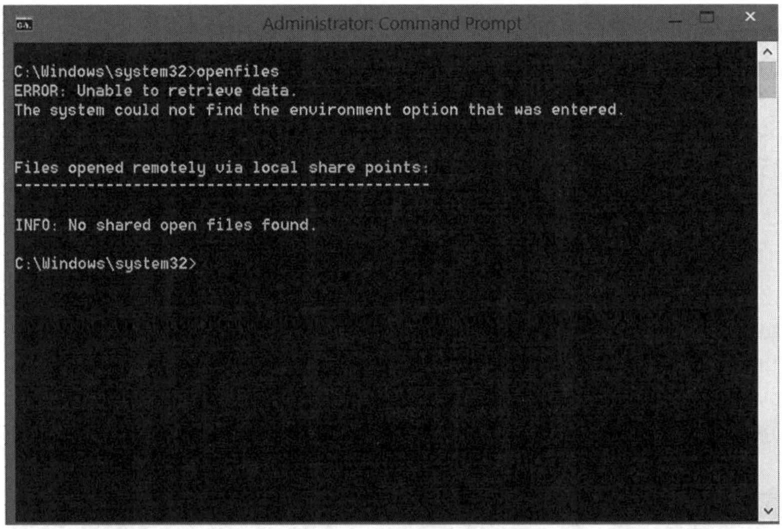

FIGURE 4-4

Using openfiles.

results. Then power down the machine. Most sources recommend you simply pull the plug. This may be contrary to how you usually power down a machine, but the idea is to interrupt normal operations. It is possible, though not likely, that there is some malware on the machine that would delete files, clear the swap, or otherwise destroy evidence during a normal power-down or the subsequent power-up of a machine.

Capturing Memory

If you believe that you may wish to analyze the system's memory at a later time, then it is imperative that you capture the memory now. Many tools exist that will capture memory. Remembering Locard's principle of transference—that interacting with an environment changes it—you will want to run these tools from a USB device, not actually on the suspect system. OSForensics can be installed to USB and can capture the system's memory. You can see this in **FIGURE 4-5**.

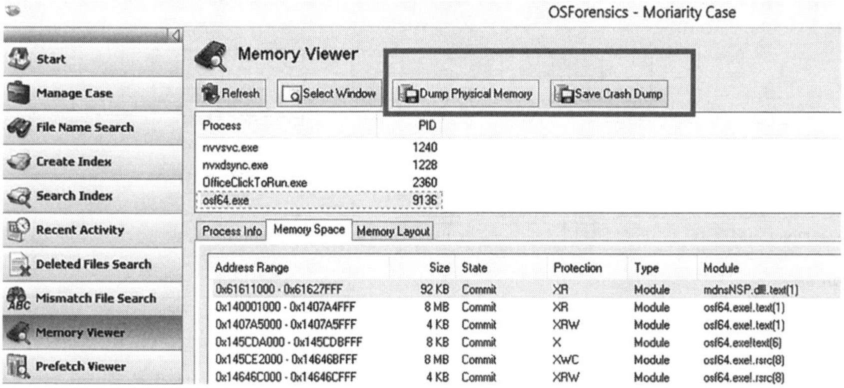

FIGURE 4-5

Capturing memory with OSForensics.

Magnet RAM Capture and DumpIt are two free tools that will capture memory. Both can be easily found on the internet using your favorite search engine. AccessData's FTK (which we will see later used to capture a drive image) can also be used to capture memory.

You will also want to document the surroundings of the device. Was there a printer attached, or any external device? Document any cables that are attached, as these may indicate there were external devices or drives were previously attached. Just remember that more information and detail are always better.

Transporting the Computer System to a Secure Location

Seized computers are often stored in less-than-secure locations. Both law enforcement agencies and corporations sometimes fail to transport and store suspect systems properly. It is imperative that you treat a subject computer as evidence and store it out of reach of curious computer users. Sometimes, individuals operate seized computers without knowing that they are destroying potential evidence and the chain of custody. A seized computer left unattended can easily be compromised. Someone could plant evidence or destroy crucial evidence. Lack of a proper chain of custody can make a savvy defense attorney's day. Without a proper chain of custody, you can't ensure that evidence was not planted on the computer after the seizure.

During the transport, you must be aware that this seized computer is evidence. It should be locked in a vehicle and the vehicle should be driven directly to the lab. This is not a time to stop for lunch! Any period of time in which you cannot account for the evidence is a break in the chain of custody. And it is certainly possible for someone to break into the vehicle while you are stopped at your favorite lunch spot.

Preparing the System — Photograph everything to ensure it hasn't been tampered with

If the device you have seized is a computer, you need to remove the drive(s) from the suspect machine even if the drive(s) is not currently attached to any cabling. Create a chain of custody form. You can see a sample evidence form in **FIGURE 4-6A**.

Some forensic examiners have a separate chain of custody form. **FIGURE 4-6B** shows one from an actual police department. Tools such as OSForensics include a chain of custody

Single Evidence Form

Case No.   Evidence No.

PLEASE COMPLETE FORM IN UPPERCASE

Section B: Evidence Collection

Date/Time Collected D D / M M / Y Y H H : M M   Collected by

Site Address

Section C: Evidence Details

Date/Time Stored D D / M M / Y Y H H : M M

Storage Location

Device Type	Capacity
Manufacturer	Model

Serial No.

MD5 Sum

SHA-1 Sum

Additional Information ...

Note any damage, marks and scratches | Digital Image Taken ☐ Yes ☐ No

Section D: Image Details

Date/Time Imaged D D / M M / Y Y H H : M M   Imaged by

Storage Location

Image Filename	Image Size	(inc. unit)

Additional Information ...

FIGURE 4-6A

Evidence form.

form, which is shown in **FIGURE 4-6C**. The chain of custody is integrated into the case file, making case management much easier.

Now, the specifics of your chain of custody form will vary depending on your jurisdiction and your organizational policies. You typically need to use a separate chain of custody form for each drive you have removed. Depending on your level of comfort in reliably describing and re-creating the technology present in the suspect system, you may want to take photographs of all of the drive connections, cable connections to the case, and general work area for future use. Photos are not required for admittance into court, but you should take

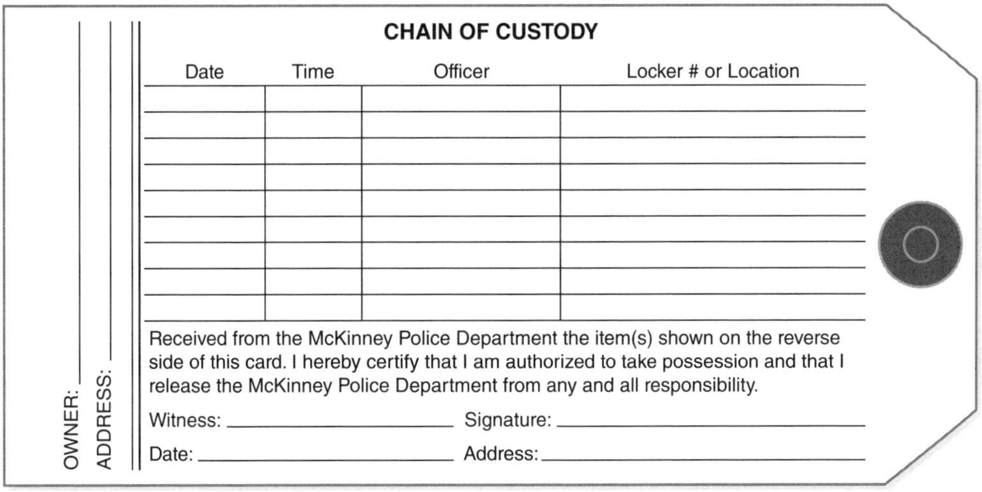

CHAIN OF CUSTODY

Date	Time	Officer	Locker # or Location

Received from the McKinney Police Department the item(s) shown on the reverse side of this card. I hereby certify that I am authorized to take possession and that I release the McKinney Police Department from any and all responsibility.

Witness: _____ Signature: _____

Date: _____ Address: _____

OWNER:
ADDRESS:

FIGURE 4-6B

Sample police department chain of custody form.

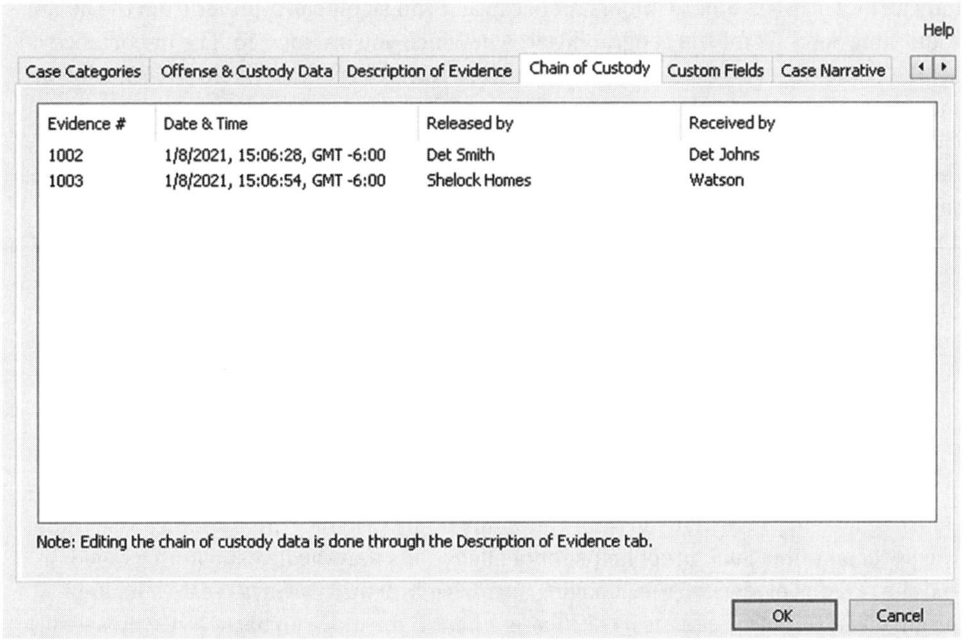

Case Categories	Offense & Custody Data	Description of Evidence	Chain of Custody	Custom Fields	Case Narrative

Help

Evidence #	Date & Time	Released by	Received by
1002	1/8/2021, 15:06:28, GMT -6:00	Det Smith	Det Johns
1003	1/8/2021, 15:06:54, GMT -6:00	Shelock Homes	Watson

Note: Editing the chain of custody data is done through the Description of Evidence tab.

OK   Cancel

FIGURE 4-6C

OSForensics chain of custody form.

4

Collecting, Seizing, and Protecting Evidence

photographs whenever possible. Any time you can use photographs to enhance your investigation or your reporting, you should do so. You can also leave the drives in the system and acquire their data with some forensically safe boot disks, CD-ROMs, or thumb drives.

In the case of phones, it is sometimes necessary to remove the SIM card (though this is not always required). It is certainly possible to examine a phone without removing the SIM card, and most modern phone forensic software allows you to simply dock the phone into the device.

Documenting the Hardware Configuration of the System

Before dismantling the computer, it is important to take pictures of the computer from all angles to document the system hardware components and how they are connected. Labeling each wire is also important, so that you can easily reconnect each one when the system configuration is restored to its original condition. You should also record basic input/output system (BIOS) information. Note that modern systems use Unified Extensible Firmware Interface (UEFI) rather than BIOS, but you can get the same information from UEFI that you would otherwise retrieve from BIOS.

time and date →

At this point, the drives are removed and you have identified and removed the media from the system. You can now safely boot up the system to check the BIOS information. In the chain of custody form, enter information about the BIOS of the system; you can typically access this information by pressing Esc, Delete, F2, F9, F10, or F11 during the initial boot screen (the specific key depends on the system, but F2 seems to be the most common). This varies depending on the system manufacturer, so always try to search the system manufacturer's website ahead of time to determine how to access this information. Once you've accessed the BIOS information, you need to record the system time and date in the chain of custody form. The BIOS time is important because it can significantly differ from the actual time and time zone set for the geographic area in which you are located. The importance of the BIOS time varies by the file system (the New Technology File System [NTFS] used in Windows stores Greenwich Mean Time, for example) and operating system, and some update the time using network time servers. If the BIOS time is different, you need to note this and then adjust the times of any files you recover from the image to determine the actual time and date they were created, accessed, or modified. After the power has been restored to the system, eject all media contained in drives that cannot be operated without power (such as some CD-ROMs and DVD-ROMs) and remove them. Then fill out a separate chain of custody form for each of the items removed. If you forget to eject the CD-ROM before powering it down, do not worry, because most CD-ROM drives can be opened by sticking the end of a paper clip in the tiny hole near the eject button.

Mathematically Authenticating Data on All Storage Devices

You must be able to prove that you didn't alter any of the evidence after taking possession of a suspect computer. Such proof helps rebut allegations that the investigator changed or altered the original evidence. After imaging any drive, you must always create a **hash** of the original and the copy (see the *FYI* "What is a hash?" for more on hashes). Compare the hashes. If they do not match exactly, then something was altered. You must also document what hashing algorithm you used (SHA1 is the most common, but SHA2 is being increasingly used) and what the results were. Linux has built-in tools for hashing, but many forensic tools such as EnCase and Forensic Toolkit (FTK) hash the suspect drive after it is imaged to check for copy errors. OSForensics will also create a hash of the suspect drive when imaging is complete.

In Linux, the following command hashes a partition:

```
md5sum /dev/hda1
```

FYI

What is a hash?

Although you might already have some knowledge of hashing algorithms, it is important to make certain you are completely clear on what a hash is. A hash is not encryption. There are three criteria for an algorithm to be considered a hash:

1. It must be nonreversible. Things are so scrambled they cannot be "unhashed." You don't "decrypt" or "dehash" a hash. You can compare it with another hash to see if it matches.

2. Variable-length input produces fixed-length output. No matter how much you put in, the hash is always the same size, and the size of the resulting hash value depends on the specific hashing algorithm.

3. There are few or no collisions. It should be extremely rare that you can put in two different values and get the same hash. Ideally, this should never occur.

MD5 has been a popular hash for many years. SHA1 and SHA2 are currently the most widely used hashing algorithms.

This assumes the partition is hda1. If your partition is different, then substitute your partition name. If you want to send that hash to a target machine (such as your forensic server), use this command:

```
md5sum /dev/hda1 | nc 192.168.0.2 8888 -w 3
```

This says to create the hash of the partition, then use netcat to send it to IP 192.168.0.2 port 8888. Obviously, your IP address and port could be different.

Handling Evidence

Once you have appropriately transported the device and prepared it for forensic examination, you have to handle the evidence. There are specific steps to use.

Preserving computer evidence requires planning and training in incident discovery procedures. The following sections describe tasks related to handling evidence and measures to take when gathering evidence. To review, a system forensics specialist has three basic tasks related to handling evidence:

- Find evidence
- Preserve evidence
- Prepare evidence

Collecting Data

There are three primary types of data that a forensic investigator must collect: volatile data, temporary data, and persistent data. As an investigator, you must attempt to avoid permanently losing data. Therefore, you must carefully secure the physical evidence first; then you can collect volatile and temporary data. Such data is lost whenever a system is used, so you should collect it first to minimize corruption or loss. The following are examples of volatile data:

- **Swap file**—The swap file is used to optimize the use of random access memory (RAM). Data is frequently found in the swap file. The details of how to extract data from the swap file vary depending on the installed operating system. While we still call this the swap file, in modern Windows systems it is actually pagefile.sys.
- **State of network connections**—This data is captured before the system is shut down.
- **State of running processes**—This data is captured before the system is shut down.

After collecting volatile data, you collect **temporary data**—data that an operating system creates and overwrites without the computer user taking a direct action to save this data. The likelihood of corrupting temporary data is less than that of volatile data. But temporary data is just that—temporary—and you must collect it before it is lost. Only after collecting volatile and temporary data should you begin to collect persistent data.

Documenting Filenames, Dates, and Times

From an evidence standpoint, filenames, creation dates, and last-modified dates and times can be relevant. Therefore, it is important to catalog all allocated and "erased" files. Sort the files based on the filename, file size, file content, creation date, and last-modified date and time. Such sorted information can provide a timeline of computer usage. The output should be in the form of a word processing–compatible file to help document computer evidence issues tied to specific files.

Identifying File, Program, and Storage Anomalies

Encrypted, compressed, and graphics files store data in binary format. As a result, text search programs can't identify text data stored in these file formats. These files require manual evaluation, which may involve a lot of work, especially with encrypted files. Depending on the type of file, view and evaluate the content as potential evidence. Reviewing the partitioning on seized hard disk drives is also important. Evaluate hidden partitions for evidence and document their existence. With Windows operating systems, you should also evaluate the files contained in the Recycle Bin. The Recycle Bin is the repository of files selected for deletion by the computer user. The fact that they have been selected for deletion may have some relevance from an evidentiary standpoint. If you find relevant files, thoroughly document the issues involved. Those issues can include the following:

- How did you find the files?
- What condition were they in (i.e., did you recover the entire file or just part of the file)?
- When was the file originally saved?

Remember that the more information you document about evidence, the better.

Evidence-Gathering Measures

Forensic specialists should take the following measures when gathering evidence:

- **Avoid changing the evidence**—Before removing any equipment, forensics specialists should photograph equipment in place and label wires and sockets so that computers and peripherals can be reassembled in a laboratory exactly as they were in the original location. When transporting computers, peripherals, and media, forensics specialists must be careful to avoid heat damage, jostling, or touching original computer hard disks and compact discs (CDs). Forensics specialists should also make exact bit-by-bit copies, storing the copies on an unalterable medium, such as a DVD-ROM.

- **Determine when evidence was created**—Timelines of computer usage and file accesses can be valuable sources of computer evidence. The times and dates when files were created, last accessed, or modified can make or break a case. However, forensics specialists should not trust a computer's internal clock or activity logs. It is possible that the internal clock is wrong, that a suspect tampered with logs, or that simply turning on the computer changes a log irrevocably. Before logs disappear, an investigator should capture the time a document was created, the last time it was opened, and the last time it was changed. The investigator can then calibrate or recalibrate evidence, based on a time standard, and work around log tampering.

- **Search throughout a device**—Forensic specialists must search at the bit level (the level of 1s and 0s) across a wide range of areas inside a computer. This includes email, temporary files, swap files, logical file structures, and slack and free space on the hard drive. They must also search software settings, script files, web browser data caches, bookmarks and history, and session logs. Forensic specialists can then correlate evidence to activities and sources. Don't be overly concerned about how difficult this process will be. Modern forensics tools will automate a great deal of the search process for you. You will see that first hand in Chapter 8.

- **Determine information about encrypted and steganized files**—Investigators should usually not attempt to decode encrypted files. Rather, investigators should look for evidence in a computer that tells them what is in the encrypted file. Frequently, this evidence has been erased, but unencrypted traces remain and can be used to make a case. For steganized information—that is, information concealed within other files or buried inside the 1s and 0s of a picture, for example—an investigator can tell that the data is there, even though it is inaccessible. The investigator can compare nearly identical files to identify minute differences. We will be exploring this in some detail in Chapter 5.

- **Present the evidence well**—Forensic examiners must present computer evidence in a logical, compelling, and persuasive manner. The jury must be able to understand the evidence, and the evidence must be solid enough that a defense counsel cannot rebut it. The forensic examiner must be able to create a step-by-step reconstruction of actions, with documented dates and times. In addition, the forensic examiner must prepare charts, graphs, and exhibits that explain what was done, describe how it was done, and withstand scrutiny. The forensic examiner's testimony must explain simply and clearly what a suspect did or did not do. The forensic examiner should remember that the jury and judge are rarely savvy computer technologists, and the ability of a forensic examiner to explain technical points clearly in plain English can make or break a case.

What to Examine

This chapter has so far discussed general preparations involved in the initial seizing, duplication, and finding of digital evidence. There's much more to learn, especially about examining data to find *incriminating evidence*—evidence that shows, or tends to show, a person's involvement in an act, or evidence that can establish guilt. One of the three techniques of forensic analysis is *live analysis*, which is the recording of any ongoing network processes. The remaining two techniques are **physical analysis** and **logical analysis**, which both deal with hard drive structures and file formats.

Physical imaging is making a physical copy of the disk. This is a bit-by-bit copy. Forensics tools will do this for you, and it is always the way to image a computer drive. In some cases, you cannot perform a physical imaging of phones. **Logical imaging** uses the target system's file system to copy data to an image for analysis. This can miss deleted files, files no longer in the file system but on the drive, and similar data.

Two of the easiest things to extract and analyze are a list of all website uniform resource locators (URLs) and a list of all email addresses on the computer. The user may have attempted to delete these, but you can reconstruct them from various places on the hard drive. Next, you should index the different kinds of file formats.

The file format you start with depends on the type of case. For example, you might want to start with graphics file formats or document formats in a pornography or forgery case. There are lots of other file formats: multimedia, archive, binary, database, font, game, and internet-related. Computers generally save things in file formats beyond the user's control. For example, all graphics files have header information. Collectors of pornography usually don't go to the trouble of removing this header information, so it's an easy matter of finding, for example, one graphics header at the beginning of a JPEG (Joint Photographic Experts Group) file and doing a string search for all other graphics of that type.

The following sections describe some of the places that an investigator must physically analyze.

> **NOTE**
>
> Of most interest forensically is the fact that swap files are not erased when the system shuts down. They work on a queue system. Data stays in the swap file and is not overwritten until that space is needed. That means it is possible to find data in the swap file that was live in memory and not stored on the suspect drive.

The Swap File

You read briefly about the swap file earlier in this chapter. A swap file is the most important type of ambient data. Windows uses a swap file on each system as a "scratch pad" to write data when additional RAM is needed. A swap file is a virtual memory extension of RAM. Most computer users are unaware of the existence of swap files. The size of these files is usually about 1.5 times the size of the physical RAM in the machine. Swap files contain remnants of word processing documents, emails, internet browsing activity, database entries, and almost any other work that has occurred during past Windows sessions. Swap files can be temporary or permanent, depending on the version of Windows installed and the settings selected by the computer user. Permanent swap files are of the greatest forensic value because they hold larger amounts of information for longer periods of time. However, temporary, or dynamic, swap files are more common. These files shrink and expand as necessary. When a dynamic swap file reduces its size close to zero, it sometimes releases the file's content to unallocated space, which you can also forensically examine. Modern Windows systems call this file pagefile.sys, but it has the same function.

Unallocated (Free) Space

Unallocated space, or free space, is the area of a hard drive that has not been allocated for file storage. It's the leftover area that the computer regards as unallocated after file deletion. When a file is deleted, only the header or reference point is deleted, while the file data remains. Space taken by that file data is now considered unallocated space, made available again for new data. If no data gets rewritten, then that space often contains fragments of the previously deleted files. The only way to clean unallocated space is with cleansing devices known as **sweepers** or **scrubbers**. While "scrubber" implies they clean, they are actually writing over the unallocated old fragments to remove that evidence. However, a few commercial products scrub free space to Department of Defense (DoD) standards. The fragments of old files in free space can be anywhere on the disk, even on a different partition, but they tend to fall next to partition headers, file allocation tables (FAT), and the last sectors of a cluster.

You may indeed find data in obvious places. There are cases where child pornography was found in the pictures folder of a Windows computer. However, you should not expect it to be that easy. Criminals do not wish to be caught, at least not usually. They use various tactics to hide what they've been doing. For example, perpetrators often use unusual file paths. In addition, many try to thwart investigators by using encryption to scramble information or steganography to hide information, or both together. Or they may use **metadata** to combine different file formats into one format. You can also expect to find lots of deleted, professionally scrubbed data.

FYI

What is metadata?

Metadata is essentially data about the data. In the case of files, it can include creation time/date, size, last modified date, and even file header information. This information can be as useful as the data itself.

A JPEG file might, for example, show evidence of a crime, but the date and time it was taken can be useful information as well. Image files, for example, have Exif data. Exif is shorthand for "exchangable image file format" and applies to a range of images. To illustrate, I begin with a picture of one of my dogs.

There is a great deal of Exif data one can gather from the image shown in **Figure 4-7A**. Information such as the device the picture was taken from, the date and time of the image, and even GPS latitude and longitude can be found in the Exif data **Figure 4-7B**.

FIGURE 4-7A

Exif sample
image.

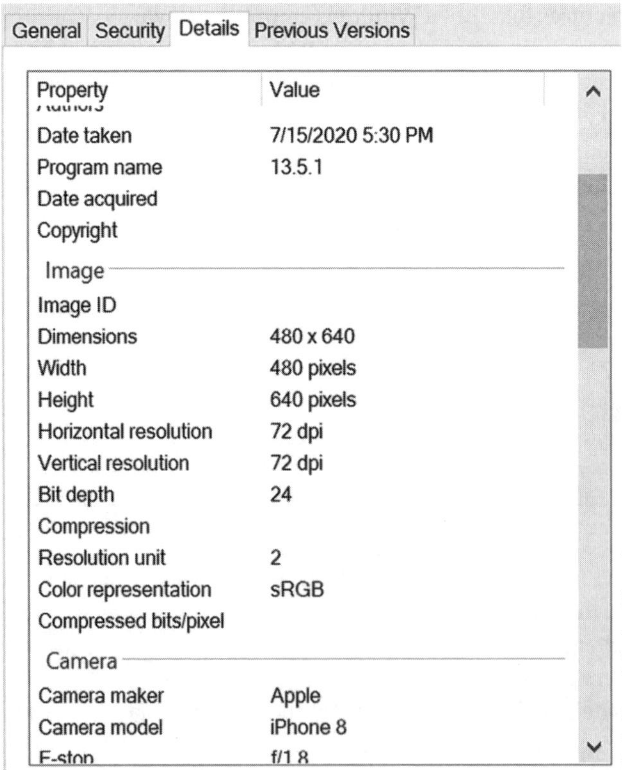

Property	Value
Authors	
Date taken	7/15/2020 5:30 PM
Program name	13.5.1
Date acquired	
Copyright	
Image	
Image ID	
Dimensions	480 x 640
Width	480 pixels
Height	640 pixels
Horizontal resolution	72 dpi
Vertical resolution	72 dpi
Bit depth	24
Compression	
Resolution unit	2
Color representation	sRGB
Compressed bits/pixel	
Camera	
Camera maker	Apple
Camera model	iPhone 8
F-stop	f/1.8

General   Security   Details   Previous Versions

FIGURE 4-7B

Exif data.

Creating a Timeline

To reconstruct the events that led to corruption of a system, create a timeline. This can be particularly difficult when it comes to computers. Clock drift, delayed reporting, and different time zones can create confusion. Never change the clock on a suspect system. Instead, record any clock drift and the time zone in use. It is also common to use the timeline format or TLN pipe-delimited format (a "pipe" is a vertical line character like this: |) with five values: Time | Source | System | User | Description. So the record might look something like this:

10-04-2020 | 15:45:23 | Chrome Browser | Windows 10 Computer | Jsmith | Visited a site that allows one to download source code for viruses.
10-6-2020 | 05:03:54 | FileZilla FTP Client | Windows 10 Computer | Jsmith | Uploads a virus to the server of the victim company.
10-7-2020 | 10:14:20 | Call App | Samsung S9 Phone | Jsmith | Calls victim company.

Now this is a very brief excerpt, but you can see that putting things in order gives one a very clear view of the activities and an understanding of the crime, even if evidence came from different devices. In this case, the perpetrator appears to have downloaded virus code, then two days later uploaded it to the target. Then he called the target the next day. That call is likely to have been made to look like a random sales call advertising PC repair services. This is actually a not uncommon scam: The perpetrator causes the problem that they then purport to repair.

Storage Formats

Working with forensics, you need to be familiar with a variety of storage formats. Specifically, you should be familiar with the various hard drive types, file systems, and journaling. This section reviews a variety of storage and file formats and explores additional issues with storage formats.

Magnetic Media

Although mobile devices like smartphones and tablets are a growing part of forensics work, computers are still the biggest target of forensic investigations. Most computers utilize magnetic media. Hard drives and floppy drives are types of magnetic media. Essentially, the data is organized by sectors and clusters, which are in turn organized in tracks around the platter. A typical sector is 512 bytes, although newer drives use 4096-byte sectors, and a cluster can be from 1 to 128 sectors.

Because the data is stored magnetically, the drives are susceptible to magnetic interference. This can include being demagnetized. If a drive has been demagnetized, there is no way to recover the data. You should transport drives in special transit bags that reduce electrostatic interference. This reduces the chance of inadvertent loss of data.

There are five types of drive connections, whether the drive is magnetic or solid state (which will be discussed a bit later in this chapter):

- Integrated Drive Electronics (IDE)
- Extended Integrated Drive Electronics (EIDE)

- Parallel Advanced Technology Attachment (PATA)
- Serial Advanced Technology Attachment (SATA)
- Serial SCSI

These drive types refer to the connection between the drive and the motherboard as well as the total capacity of the drive. SATA drives have become the norm, and what you will find most often. Serial SCSI can be found in some servers. However, IDE, EIDE, or PATA would only be found in very old systems.

It is important to remember that because magnetic drives have moving parts in them, they are also susceptible to physical damage. If you drop a drive, you may render the data inaccessible. This is one reason you must take care when handing magnetic drives.

Solid-State Drives

Solid-state drives (SSDs) use microchips, which retain data in non-volatile memory chips and contain no moving parts. Most SSDs use Negated AND (NAND) gate–based flash memory, which retains memory even without power. Because there are no moving parts, these drives are usually less susceptible to physical damage than magnetic drives are. They have become the standard for many internal drives and for all external drives.

One reason these drives are so popular is because they generally require one-half to one-third the power of hard disk drives. The startup time for SSDs is usually much faster than for magnetic storage drives. They are often used in tablets and in some laptops. This means that you are likely to encounter them at some point in your forensics career.

If these drives are internal, they can use the same interfaces magnetic drives use, including SCSI and SATA. However, if connected externally, it is most common for them to have a universal serial bus (USB) connection.

Both magnetic and solid-state drives include a few features that are important for forensics:

- **Host protected area (HPA)**—This was designed as an area where computer vendors could store data that is protected from user activities and operating system utilities, such as delete and format. To hide data in the HPA, a person would need to write a program to access the HPA and write the data.
- **Master boot record (MBR)**—This requires only a single sector, leaving 62 empty sectors of MBR space for hiding data.
- **Volume slack**—This is the space that remains on a hard drive if the partitions do not use all the available space. For example, suppose that two partitions are filled with data. When you delete one of them, its data is not actually deleted. Instead, it is hidden.
- **Unallocated space**—An operating system can't access any unallocated space in a partition. That space may contain hidden data.
- **Good blocks marked as bad**—Suppose that someone manipulates the file system metadata to mark unused blocks as bad. The operating system will no longer access these blocks. These blocks can then be used to hide data.
- **File slack**—File slack is the unused space that is created between the end of file and the end of the last data cluster assigned to a file.

Digital Audio Tape Drives

Although many organizations are moving from electronic backups to optical media or even direct network backups to an off-site location, digital audio tape (DAT) drives are still sometimes used. DAT drives are among the most common types of tape drives. DAT uses 4-mm magnetic tape enclosed in a protective plastic shell. Even though this looks very similar to audio tapes, the recording is digital rather than analog.

From a forensic point of view, it is important to remember that these tapes do wear out, just like audio tapes. If you are old enough to remember cassette or 8-track tapes, you'll recall that these tapes would, from time to time, become stretched and worn and no longer usable. The same thing happens with the DAT tapes. In fact, network administrators are admonished to replace them periodically.

When working with DAT drives, most likely they will contain archived/backup data that you need to analyze. Make certain you first forensically wipe the target drive so you can be sure that there is no residual data on that drive. You then need to restore it to the target hard drive (magnetic or solid state) in order to analyze it.

Digital Linear Tape and Super DLT

Digital Linear Tape (DLT) is another type of tape storage, more specifically a magnetic tape. The DLT technology relies on a linear recording method. The tape itself has either 128 or 208 total tracks. This technology was first invented by Digital Electronics Corporation (DEC). This tape, like DAT, is used primarily to store archived data. So, as with DAT, you need to make sure you have a forensically wiped hard drive to restore the data to and then restore the data to that hard drive in order to analyze it. These tapes have become relatively uncommon, but you may still find them.

Optical Media

Like hard disks, optical media such as CD-ROMs, DVD, and Blu-ray disks use high and low polarization to set the bits of data; however, CDs have reflective pits that represent the low bit. If the pit is nonexistent, the data is a 1; if the pit exists, it's a 0. The laser mechanism actually detects the distance the light beam has traveled in order to detect the presence or absence of a pit. This is why scratches can be problematic for optical media.

Since the advent of the original compact disc, there have been enhancements. These enhancements still utilize the same optical process, but have larger capacity. The DVD (or digital video disc) can hold 4.7 gigabytes (GB) for a one-sided DVD and 9.4 GB for a double-sided DVD. This technology uses a 650-nm wavelength laser diode light as opposed to 780 nm for CDs. The smaller wavelength allows DVDs to use smaller pits, thus increasing storage capacity.

Blu-ray discs are the successor to the DVD and store up to 25 GB per layer, with dual-layer discs storing up to 50 GB. There are also triple- and quadruple-layer discs such as the Blu-ray Disc XL that allow up to 150 GB of storage. Although Blu-ray discs are primarily associated with movies, you can certainly store data on them. And for smaller organizations, the Blu-ray disc can be an attractive backup medium.

Just like all other storage devices, a Blu-ray device should be forensically copied to a clean, forensically wiped drive for analysis. No matter what the medium, you never work with the original suspect storage if it is at all possible to avoid it.

Using USB Drives

USB, or universal serial bus, is actually a connectivity technology, not a storage technology. USB can be used to connect to external drives that can be either magnetic or solid state. Small USB flash drives, also known as thumb drives, are quite common. These drives can be easily erased or overwritten. It is important to copy the data from the USB drive to a target forensic drive for analysis. You must, of course, document the copying process and ensure nothing was missed or altered.

USB thumb drives have no moving parts. USB thumb drives or external drives utilize solid-state drive technology. Because there are no moving parts, these drives are resilient to shock damage (i.e., dropping them probably won't hurt them). From a forensics point of view, you should remember that many of these drives come with a small switch to put them in read-only mode. Use this whenever you are extracting data for investigation. If the drive is in read-only mode, it is unlikely you will accidentally alter the data.

The current most widely used USB standard is USB 3.2. However, you will still find a great many USB 2.0 devices. The USB 4.0 specification was released in August 2019. The differences in USB specifications primarily affect the speed of data transfer and will have little, if any, direct impact on your investigations.

File Formats

In addition to physical means of storing data, there are a variety of file formats for storing forensic data on a given storage device. It is important that you have a working knowledge of these formats for forensic analysis.

The Advanced Forensic Format

The advanced forensic file format (abbreviated AFF) was invented by Basis Technology. It is an open file standard with three variations: AFF, AFM, and AFD. The AFF variation stores all data and metadata in a single file. The AFM variation stores the data and the metadata in separate files, while the AFD variation stores the data and metadata in multiple small files. The AFF file format is part of the AFF Library and Toolkit, which is a set of open-source computer forensics programs. Sleuth Kit and Autopsy both support this file format.

EnCase

The EnCase format is a proprietary format that is defined by Guidance Software for use in its EnCase tool to store hard drive images and individual files. It includes a hash of the file to ensure nothing was changed when it was copied from the source.

The Generic Forensic Zip

Gfzip is another open-source file format used to store evidence from a forensic examination.

Forensic Imaging

Once you have acquired a physical storage medium of some type, you need to image the suspect data. You always work with an image whenever possible. Even if the medium is an optical storage device like a Blu-ray disc, you should make a forensic image of the drive and work with the image. It is possible to create a forensic image utilizing open-source tools, specifically Linux commands. This section explains all the details behind each step.

First, you must forensically wipe the target drive (which is the drive to which you will copy the suspect drive contents) to ensure there is no residual data left from a previous case. Forensically wiping is not simply deleting files; it involves actually overwriting *every single bit* with some pattern. That pattern can be random, or all zeros. I personally first format the drive, then perform a forensic wipe. Many forensic tools and software have the option to do a forensic wipe for you. You can also do this with the Linux dd command:

```
dd if=/dev/zero of=/dev/hdb1 bs=2048
```

This command is literally using /dev/zero as an input file and writing its contents out to the partition hdb1 as the output file. If you are not familiar with Linux, /dev/zero is a special file on UNIX-like systems that reads out as many nulls as are required. So this command is overwriting everything on the target drive with null values.

If your partition is different, you can use fdisk -l to list the partitions on your system.

The primary purpose of dd, a common UNIX program, is the low-level copying and conversion of raw data. Low-level copying means at the bit level. If you do your copy through the file system/operating system, then you can see only the data that the operating system sees. You won't get deleted files or slack space. That is why a basic file system copy is inadequate for forensic analysis. You must get a bit-level copy, and the dd utility is perfect for that. While most forensic tools will do imaging for you, this process can be done with a Linux live CD and the dd and netcat commands.

You also need to use netcat to set up the forensic server to listen, so you have a Linux live CD boot up the suspect drive to copy it to the forensic server. At this point, both the suspect drive and the target forensic server have been booted into Linux using any Linux live distribution.

The netcat command reads and writes bits over a network connection. The command to run on the forensic server is as follows:

```
# nc -l -p 8888 > evidence.dd
```

This sets up the listen process on the forensic server prior to sending the data from the subject's computer. The process listens (the -l flag) on port 8888 (the -p 8888 command) and takes all input and writes to a file called evidence.dd. You can always use another port or another filename if necessary. You must ensure the target drive is at least as big as the suspect drive.

> **NOTE**
>
> Many Linux distributions have dd and netcat, so you do not have to utilize Kali Linux. However, Kali Linux is designed for computer security. This Linux distribution has a host of security, hacking, and forensic tools on it. It is a very good idea to start getting comfortable with Kali Linux early in your forensic training.

On the suspect computer, use the dd command to read the first partition:

```
# dd if=/dev/hda1 | nc 192.168.0.2 8888 -w 3
```

You then pipe the output of the dd command to netcat, which sends the bits over the network to the specified network address and port on the listening forensic computer. The argument -w 3 indicates that netcat should wait 3 seconds before closing the connection upon finding no more data. This assumes that the suspect partition is hda1, but it might be a different partition.

This process can be accomplished with most major forensic tools, including EnCase from Guidance Software, OSForensics from PassMark Software, and Forensic Toolkit from AccessData.

Imaging with EnCase

EnCase is a forensic tool that is widely used by law enforcement. Once you have the suspect's hard drive disconnected from the suspect machine, you can connect that drive to the forensic computer. In some cases, you first connect to a device that prevents writing to the suspect device. FastBlock and Tableau are two such devices that are widely used in forensics.

At the top of the EnCase window, click New on the toolbar to start the new case you will be working. The Case Options dialog box opens, as shown in **FIGURE 4-8**.

This dialog box allows you to type in the case name and the examiner's name. Tracking evidence by case and examiner is one convenient feature of EnCase that helps make it popular with law enforcement agencies. The text boxes are filled in automatically, but you have to

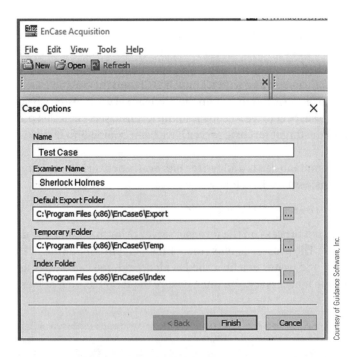

FIGURE 4-8

EnCase Case Options dialog box.

Courtesy of Guidance Software, Inc.

click on the button on the right side next to each of the lower text boxes to select the paths. After selecting the paths, click the Finish button.

Now that you have created the case, you need to save it by clicking the Save icon on the EnCase toolbar. Select a path for the save location when prompted. Now, you are ready to acquire evidence. On the EnCase toolbar, click the Add Device button. The Add Device window appears in EnCase, asking which device to add, as shown in **FIGURE 4-9**.

The left pane lists devices with subfolders, Local and Evidence Files. The right pane lists Local Drives, Palm Pilot, Parallel Port, and Network Crossover (note these options may differ on different systems). In this procedure, you check the Local Drives in the right pane. After EnCase reads the local drives, another window appears. Once you have added the device, it shows in the case, as shown in **FIGURE 4-10**.

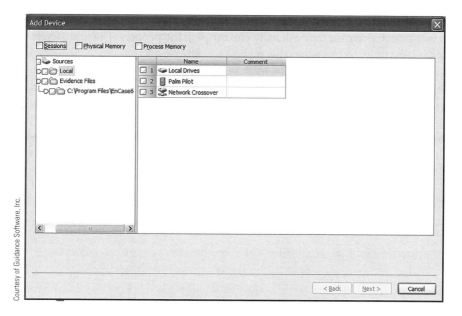

Courtesy of Guidance Software, Inc.

FIGURE 4-9

EnCase Add Device window.

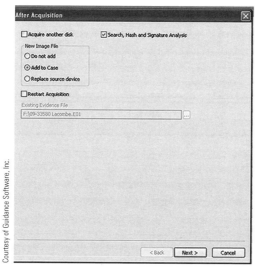

Courtesy of Guidance Software, Inc.

FIGURE 4-10

EnCase After Acquisition dialog box.

One of the first things you should note is that you can add multiple devices to a single case. This makes sense because many cases will have more than one seized device that requires examination.

Imaging with the Forensic Toolkit

The Forensic Toolkit (FTK) from AccessData is another popular forensic tool that is widely used by law enforcement. You can purchase FTK or you can request a free download of the FTK Imager from this website: *https://marketing.accessdata.com/imager4.3.1.1*. The current version of FTK Imager, as of February 2021, is 4.5. The main screen of FTK Imager is shown in **FIGURE 4-11**.

You now have to select specifically what you want to image. The first step is to select the create image option from the dropdown box (**FIGURE 4-12**).

This will launch a wizard that will walk you through the process. The first step is to select what it is you wish to image. This is shown in **FIGURE 4-13**.

The most common scenario is to select to image a physical drive. If you select that, the next step will be to select which physical drive. This is shown in **FIGURE 4-14**.

The next screen is quite important. Notice that the Verify Image option is checked by default. This will cause FTK Imager to create a cryptographic hash of the source drive and the image and compare them. This screen is also where you will select the drive destination, which is presumably another drive you have forensically wiped. This screen is shown in **FIGURE 4-15**.

After that, it is just a matter of waiting for the imaging process to complete. The larger the drive, the longer this process will take. It is often the case that it takes several hours to image an entire drive. That is true regardless of the specific imaging tool you use.

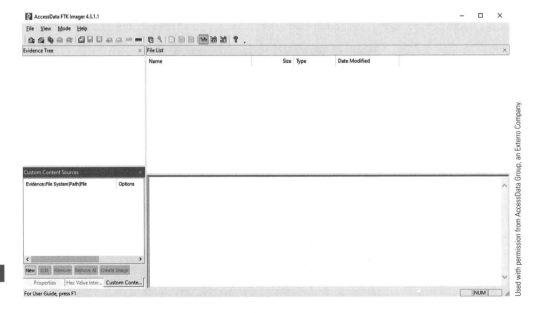

FIGURE 4-11

FTK Imager.

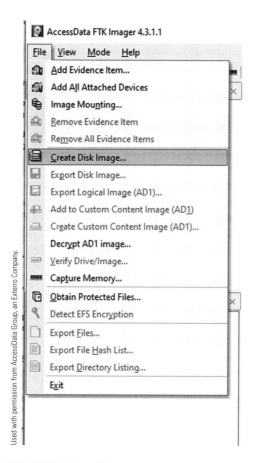

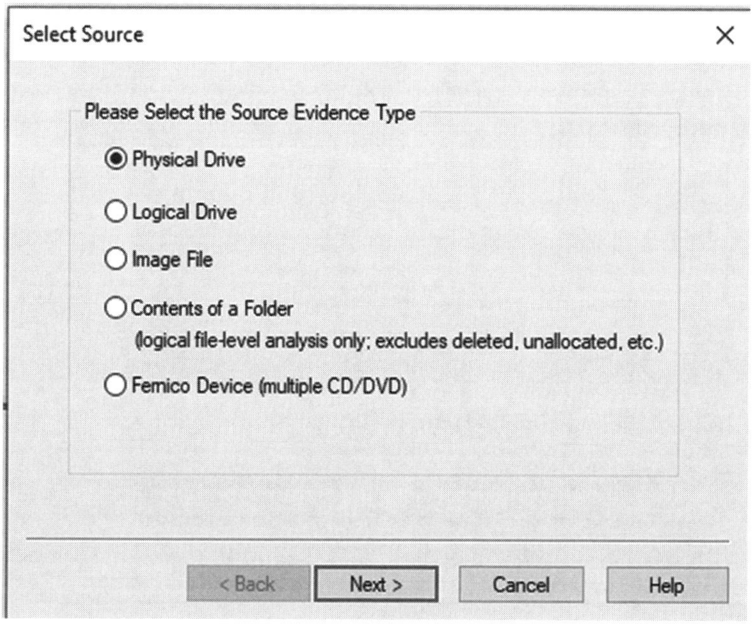

Used with permission from AccessData Group, an Exterro Company.

FIGURE 4-12

FTK Imager create image option.

FIGURE 4-13

FTK Imager selecting image source.

4

Collecting, Seizing, and Protecting Evidence

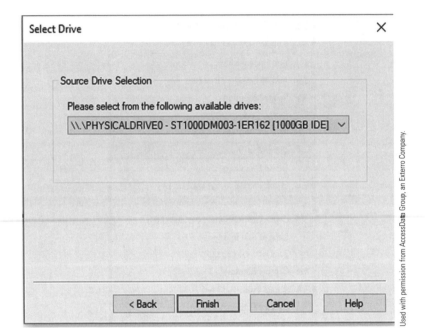

FIGURE 4-14

FTK Imager
selecting a drive.

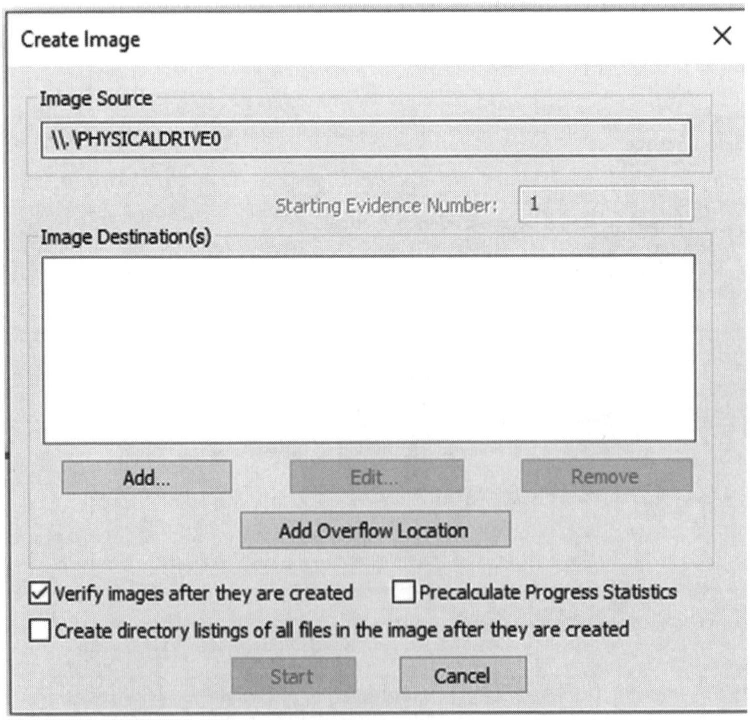

FIGURE 4-15

FTK Imager
Verify Image
option.

Imaging with OSForensics

OSForensics allows you to mount images created with other tools, but also allows you to create an image. The first step is to select Drive Imaging from the menu on the left, shown in **FIGURE 4-16**.

Then you will select the source drive you wish to image, and the target where the image will be put. Notice that "verify image" is checked by default (**FIGURE 4-17**). You should not uncheck this.

You now just start the process, and an image of the source drive will be created and verified for you.

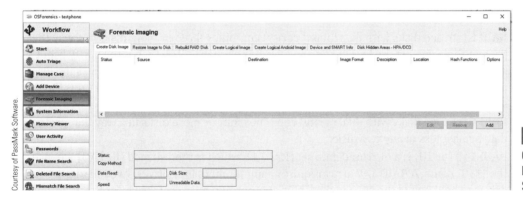

FIGURE 4-16

OSForensics Drive Imaging Step 1.

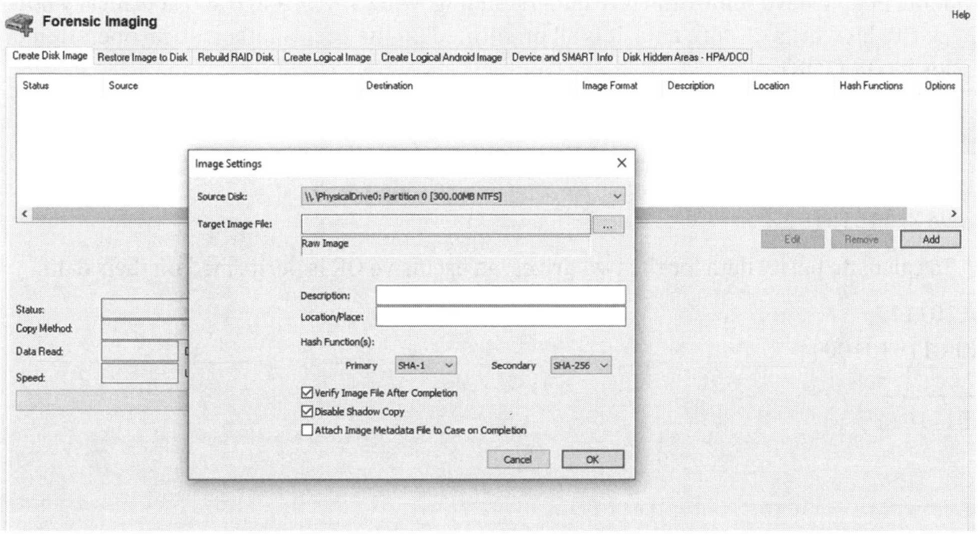

FIGURE 4-17

OSForensics Drive Imaging Step 2.

4

Collecting, Seizing, and Protecting Evidence

RAID Acquisitions

RAID stands for "redundant array of independent disks." You may already be comfortable with the concept of RAID; however, if you are not, this section provides a brief overview. The most common RAID levels are as follows:

- RAID 0 (**disk striping**) distributes data across multiple disks in a way that gives improved speed for data retrieval.
- RAID 1 mirrors the contents of the disks. The disk is completely mirrored so there is an identical copy of the drive running on the machine.
- RAID 3 or 4 (striped disks with dedicated parity) combines three or more disks in a way that protects data against loss of any one disk. Fault tolerance is achieved by adding an extra disk to the array and dedicating it to storing parity information. The storage capacity of the array is reduced by one disk.
- RAID 5 (striped disks with distributed parity) combines three or more disks in a way that protects data against the loss of any one disk. It is similar to RAID 3, but the parity is not stored on one dedicated drive; instead, parity information is interspersed across the drive array. The storage capacity of the array is a function of the number of drives minus the space needed to store parity.
- RAID 6 (striped disks with dual parity) combines four or more disks in a way that protects data against loss of any two disks.
- RAID 1+0 (or 10) is a mirrored data set (RAID 1), which is then striped (RAID 0)—hence the "1+0" name. A RAID 1+0 array requires a minimum of four drives: two mirrored drives to hold half of the striped data, plus another two mirrored drives for the other half of the data.

No matter what version of RAID you are using (except for RAID 1), what you have is an array of disks with data distributed across them. With RAID 1, the two disks are mirror copies of each other.

Some people have some difficulty understanding RAID 3, 4, 5, and 6 and specifically how the parity bit works to store data. It is all predicated on the basic mathematical operation of exclusive OR (XOR).

For example, suppose two drives in a three-drive RAID 5 array contained the following data:

Drive A: 01101111
Drive B: 11010100

To calculate parity data for the two drives, an exclusive OR is performed on their data:

01101111
XOR 11010100
─────────
10111011

The resulting parity data, 10111011, is then stored on Drive C.

Now if either Drive A or B fails, the data can be recreated. Let us assume that Drive B fails. We just exclusively OR the data stored on Drive C, with the data still on Drive A.

Drive A: 01101111

Drive c: 10111011

And you get back 11010100, which is the data originally on Drive B. This is how parity bits work in RAID.

Acquiring a RAID array has some challenges that are not encountered when acquiring a single drive. Some people recommend acquiring each disk separately. This is fine for RAID 1. Each disk is a separate entity. However with RAID 0, 3, 4, 5, and 6, there is data striping. The data is striped across multiple disks. In these situations, acquiring the disks separately is not recommended. Instead, make a forensic image of the entire RAID array—which requires you to copy it to a rather large target drive.

 NOTE

FTK, OSForensics, and EnCase provide built-in tools for acquiring RAID arrays.

CHAPTER SUMMARY

In this chapter, you were introduced to some very specific procedures. These procedures govern how you will seize evidence, transport it, and prepare it for analysis. When you perform forensic analysis on drives, you gather very specific information and/or evidence. However, if the procedures outlined in this chapter are not followed carefully, any evidence subsequently gathered may be suspect. Failure to properly seize, transport, and handle evidence may even render the evidence inadmissible in a court of law.

KEY CONCEPTS AND TERMS

Disk striping	Physical analysis	Temporary data
Hash	Scrubber	Unallocated space
Metadata	Swap file	Volatile data
Logical analysis	Sweeper	

4

Collecting, Seizing, and Protecting Evidence

CHAPTER 4 ASSESSMENT

1. What is the most commonly used hashing algorithm?

A. MD5

B. Whirlpool

C. SHA1

D. CRC

2. What Linux command can be used to create a hash?

A. SHA

B. MD5

C. MD5sum

D. Sha3sum

3. What Linux command can be used to wipe a target drive?

A. Del

B. Delete

C. nc

D. dd

4. RAID 4 should be acquired as individual disks.

A. True

B. False

5. Which of the following drives would be least susceptible to damage when dropped?

A. SCSI

B. SSD

C. IDE

D. SATA

6. It is acceptable, when you have evidence in a vehicle, to stop for a meal, if the vehicle is locked.

A. True

B. False

7. Which of the following might contain data that was live in memory and not stored on the hard drive?

A. Swap file

B. Registry Hive

C. Backup File

D. Log file

CHAPTER LAB

1. Download a trial version of OSForensics from www.OSForensics.com.

2. Make an image of a machine using the steps outlined in this chapter. Note: You will need someplace to copy the image to, such as an external portable drive.

Understanding Techniques for Hiding and Scrambling Information

TECHNICALLY SAVVY CRIMINALS will try to hide evidence on their computers. There are any number of techniques one can use to either hide or protect information. That way, even if the computer is seized and searched, investigators are less likely to find the evidence. This chapter introduces the two ways of hiding and scrambling information: steganography and cryptography. These techniques predate modern computers. In fact, they are so old that they can trace their origins to ancient Greece. Steganography comes from the Greek *steganos*, meaning covered or protected. Cryptography comes from the Greek *kryptos*, to hide. Encrypted information is clearly scrambled, and not hidden, per se.

Chapter 5 Topics

This chapter covers the following topics and concepts:

- Understanding the use and detection of steganography
- Encryption

Chapter 5 Goals

When you complete this chapter, you will be able to:

- Understand steganography
- Use steganography
- Detect steganography
- Understand basic cryptography
- Utilize basic cryptography
- Understand general cryptanalysis techniques

Steganography

Steganography is the art and science of writing hidden messages. The goal is to hide information so that even if it is intercepted, it is not clear that information is hidden there. The most common method today is to hide messages in pictures. One of the most common methods of performing this technique is the **least significant bit (LSB)** method (when the last bit or least significant bit is used to store data). To be clear, this is not the only technical method for performing steganography, just the most common. The LSB method depends on the fact that computers store things in bits and bytes. Now consider for a moment an 8-bit byte. For example, consider 11111111. If you convert this to a decimal number, it equals 255. Now if you change the first 1 to a 0, you get 01111111. This equals 127 in decimal numbers, which is a pretty major change.

However, what if—instead of changing the first 0—you change the last 0? That would give you 11111110, which is equal to 254 in decimal numbers. This is a trivial change. That is why this last bit is called the least significant bit. Changing the least significant bit from a 0 to a 1 or from a 1 to a 0 makes the smallest change in the original information. Also, consider that if the steganographic software overwrites the least significant bit with a 0 and it was already a 0, or overwrites the least significant bit with a 1 and it was already a 1, then there is no change to the original information.

Colored pixels in a computer are stored in bits. In Windows, for example, 24 bit is the normal color resolution. If you examine the Windows color palette, you'll find that you define a color by selecting three values between 0 and 255 in the Red, Green, and Blue text boxes shown in **FIGURE 5-1**.

Now consider what happens if you change just one bit. In **FIGURE 5-2**, you see a color that is defined by three numbers: 252, 101, and 100.

You can change the 101 by just one bit and make it 100, as you see in **FIGURE 5-3**.

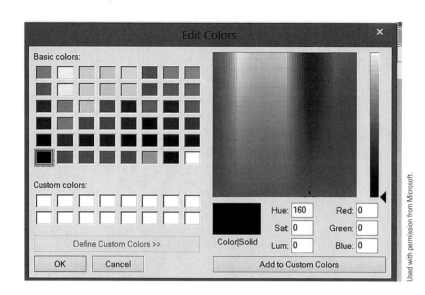

FIGURE 5-1

The Windows color palette in the Edit Colors dialog box.

Used with permission from Microsoft.

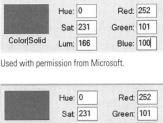

FIGURE 5-2

Windows color.

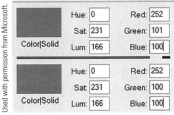

FIGURE 5-3

Windows color changed by one bit.

Your eye cannot really tell the difference; even if this book were in color, the difference would be impossible to detect. This is the basis for modern image steganography. If you change the least significant bit in a pixel, the image still looks the same. But a picture is made up of thousands—sometimes millions—of pixels. So by changing the least significant bit of many pixels, you can hide data in an image. If someone finds the image, even by using a tool such as Photoshop or GIMP (GNU Image Manipulation Program) to magnify the image, that person will not be able to see that data is hidden in it. Only by comparing the original image, bit by bit, to the steganized image can it be determined that information *may* be hidden within.

FYI

The following are some basic steganography terms you should know:

- **Payload** is the information to be covertly communicated. In other words, it is the message you want to hide.
- The **carrier** (or carrier file) is the signal, stream, or file in which the payload is hidden.
- The **channel** is the type of medium used. This may be a passive channel, such as photos, video, or sound files, or even an active channel, such as a Voice over IP (VoIP) voice call or streaming video connection.

It used to be the case that steganography required someone to be able to write specific computer program code to manipulate the bits in an image. This took training and skill; therefore, steganography was used only by computer professionals. However, a number of tools are now available on the web that will hide information within an image for you:

- **QuickStego** is very easy to use, but very limited.
- **Invisible Secrets** is much more robust, with both a free and a commercial version.
- **MP3Stego** hides a payload in MP3 files.
- **Stealth Files 4** works with sound files, video files, and image files.
- **StegVideo** hides data in a video sequence.
- **Deep Sound** hides data in sound files.

5

Understanding Techniques for Hiding and Scrambling Information

Historical Steganography

Obviously, using digital images and files to hide messages did not exist prior to the advent of modern computers. However, hiding messages is not new. It has been done since ancient times. The following methods were once used to hide messages:

- The ancient Chinese wrapped notes in wax and swallowed them for transport. This was a crude but effective method of hiding messages.
- In ancient Greece, a messenger's head might be shaved, a message written on his head, then his hair was allowed to grow back. Obviously, this method required some time to work effectively.
- The German scholar Johannes Trithemius (1462–1516) wrote a book on cryptography and described a technique where a message was hidden by having each letter taken as a word from a specific column.
- During World War II, the French Resistance sent messages written on the backs of couriers using invisible ink.

NOTE

It is a common practice for pornographers, cybercriminals, terrorists, and others to cache steganized files on the servers or file stores of unsuspecting third parties and to use such locations as "dead drops"—a place where the criminal can deliver the data to its intended recipient without actually physically meeting the recipient—without the knowledge of the third party.

Steganophony

Steganophony is a term for hiding messages in sound files. This can be done with the LSB method; however, another method that can be used for steganophony is the echo method. This method adds extra sound to an echo inside an audio file. It is that extra sound that contains information. Steganophony can be used with static files, such as MP3 files, but can also be used dynamically with VoIP and similar multimedia technologies, also utilizing the LSB method and imperceptibly changing the sound being transmitted.

Video Steganography

Information can also be hidden in video files, a practice called *video steganography*. There are various ways to do this, including the LSB method. Whatever method is used, it is important to realize that video files are obviously larger than other file types. This provides a great deal of opportunity for hiding information.

More Advanced Steganography

While simply using least significant bits, particularly with an image, is rather common and widely used steganography, it is not the only option. One other option is Bit-Plane Complexity Segmentation Steganography (BPCS).

Since the carrier is often an image that stores colors in 24 bits, this fact can be used to increase the storage area for payload. The complex areas on the bit planes are replaced with the payload. A bit plane of any discrete digital file is the set of bits that correspond to a given bit position. For example, in 24-bit files, there are 24 bit planes. This can be applied to signals as well as files.

Steganalysis

Steganalysis is the process of analyzing a file or files for hidden content. It is a difficult task. At best, it can show a likelihood that a given file has additional information hidden in it. A common method for detecting LSB steganography is to examine close-color pairs. Close-color pairs consist of two colors that have binary values that differ only in the LSB. If this is seen too frequently in a given file, it can indicate that steganographically hidden messages may be present.

Before we dive into technical methods for detecting steganography, there are some easy-to-use indicators of steganography that are important. The first is examining metadata about a given image or sound file. Two pieces of data are of greatest interest: the created date and the last-modified date. The created date is not when the file was originally created, but rather when it was created *on that device*. If you download an mp4 file, then the date/time you download it to your computer will be the created date. The last-modified date indicates when it was last changed. Most people do not modify music files; they usually just download music, perhaps from Google Play or Apple Music. Either the last-modified date and created date will be the same, or the last-modified date will be older. If the last-modified date is newer, this indicates the file has been modified since it was downloaded. If that person has music editing software and is known to mix music, then that explains the date discrepancy. However, if that is not the case, then steganography should be considered.

Many steganography tools don't do a really good job of steganography and actually bloat the target file's size. This means seeing a file with an incongruous size could indicate possible steganography. If a suspect has a collection of 100 vacation pictures, all of which are roughly 2 megabytes in size, but one is 4 megabytes in size, it may be worthwhile to analyze that image.

Aside from these indicators, there are several technical methods for analyzing an image to detect hidden messages. The raw quick pair method is one. It is based on statistics of the numbers of unique colors and close-color pairs in a 24-bit image. Basically, it performs a quick analysis to determine if there are more close-color pairs than would be expected.

Another option uses the chi-square method from statistics. Chi-square analysis calculates the average LSB and builds a table of frequencies and a second table with pairs of values. Then it performs a chi-square test on these two tables. Essentially, it measures the theoretical versus the calculated population difference. When analyzing audio files, you can use steganalysis, which involves examining noise distortion in the carrier file. Noise distortion could indicate the presence of a hidden signal.

Many modern forensic tools also check for the presence of steganographically hidden messages. Forensic Toolkit (FTK) and EnCase both check for steganography, and FTK has an entire image detection engine devoted to this task. Details about this feature of FTK can be found at *https://accessdata.com/blog/image-detection-or-image-recognition-quin-c-does-both*.

There are several free or inexpensive tools for detecting steganography:

- McAfee has an online steganography detection tool: *https://www.mcafee.com/enterprise/en-us/downloads/free-tools/steganography.html*
- Steg Secret is another tool: *http://stegsecret.sourceforge.net/*
- StegSpy has fewer limitations than StegDetect: *http://www.spy-hunter.com/stegspydown-load.htm*

Be aware that none of these methods is perfect. A great deal depends on the size of the payload compared with the size of the carrier file. This determines what percentage of the bits need to be changed. For example, if you have a 10-kilobyte text message in a 2-megabyte image file, it will be hard to detect. However, if you hide a 1-megabyte image in a 4-megabyte image, it will be easier to find.

It is also the case that the specific steganographic tool you use will determine how reliable steganalysis tests are. Some stego tools are more efficient than others. Depending upon how well information has been hidden, and if it is encrypted, it may be impossible to detect.

Invisible Secrets

A forensic examiner must be very familiar with steganography. This means you should be able to do steganography. Many tools are available on the web. In this section, you will learn about a tool called Invisible Secrets. This tool is very inexpensive and a free trial version is available. It is also easy to use.

You can download Invisible Secrets from *https://www.east-tec.com/invisiblesecrets /download/*. First, you must choose whether you want to hide a file or extract a hidden file. For this example, suppose you want to hide a file. You select your chosen option in the Invisible Secrets Select Action dialog box, shown in **FIGURE 5-4**, and then click the Next button.

Now select an image you want to use as the carrier file. You can see this in **FIGURE 5-5**. Select the file you want to hide. It can be a text file or another image file. You can also choose to encrypt as well as hide. This is shown in **FIGURE 5-6**.

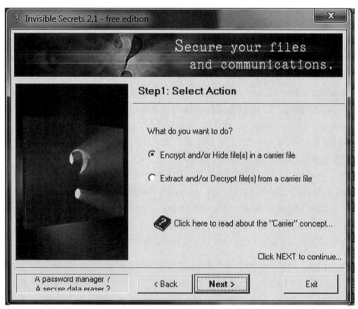

FIGURE 5-4

Choose to hide a file or extract a hidden file in the Invisible Secrets Select Action dialog box.

Courtesy of NeoByte Solutions.

FIGURE 5-5

Select an image to use as the carrier file in the Invisible Secrets Select Carrier File dialog box.

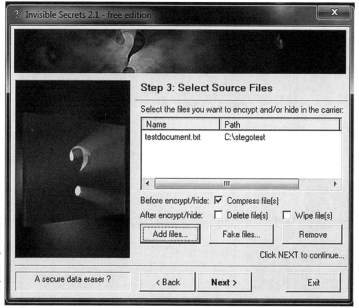

FIGURE 5-6

Select the file to hide in the Invisible Secrets Select Source Files dialog box.

Now, select a password for your hidden file, as shown in **FIGURE 5-7**.

Next, pick a name for the resulting file that contains your hidden file, as shown in **FIGURE 5-8**.

That's it. You have just done steganography. Now consider this for just a moment. If it is that easy and tools are available on the internet, then this is something many criminals

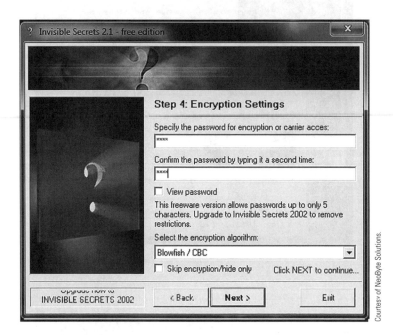

FIGURE 5-7

Select a password in the Invisible Secrets Encryption Settings dialog box.

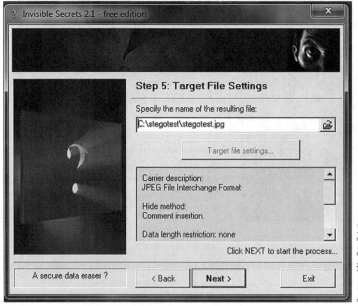

FIGURE 5-8

Name the new file in the Invisible Secrets Target File Settings dialog box.

probably use. Fortunately, not all criminals are tech savvy, so you will still find many computers with evidence that is not hidden with steganography. However, during your career as a forensic examiner, you will come across steganography from time to time, and more often in complex cases involving organized crime, spying, and terrorism.

FYI

During the raid on Osama Bin Laden's compound, which resulted in his death, a number of computer hard drives were found. On those hard drives, a number of pornographic videos were discovered. It was later determined, using computer forensics, that these videos contained steganographically hidden messages. It is clear that Bin Laden was communicating with terrorist cells via steganography.

MP3Stego

You can download the program MP3Stego from *http://www.petitcolas.net/steganography /mp3stego/*. This program is used to hide data in MP3 files. It takes the information (usually text) and combines it with a sound file to create a new sound file that contains the hidden information. The MP3Stego readme file provides these instructions:

- `encode -E data.txt -P pass sound.wav sound.mp3`—Compresses sound. wav and hides data.txt, using the password "pass." This produces the output called sound. mp3. The text in data.txt is encrypted using `pass`.
- `decode -X -P pass sound.mp3`—Uncompresses sound.mp3 into sound.mp3. pcm and attempts to extract hidden information. The `-P` flag denotes the following password "pass." The hidden message is decrypted, uncompressed, and saved into sound.mp3.

This is a very simple program to use and it is freely available on the internet.

Deep Sound

This tool is a free download from *http://jpinsoft.net/deepsound*. It allows one to hide files in mp3, wav, cda, and other file formats. It is very easy to use. A screenshot of the main screen of Deep Sound is shown in **FIGURE 5-9**.

Like many steganography tools, this one is very easy to use. It is self-explanatory. The ease of use, along with the product being free, makes finding steganographically hidden evidence more likely than it was in the past.

Additional Resources

The information provided here is enough steganography for you to work as a forensic examiner, but if you want to learn more, you might find the following resources of value (a full citation and URL for each reference can be found in the references list at the end of the chapter):

- The online publication *Towards Data Science* published an article on steganography with Python in May 2020.[1]
- InfoSec Institute published an article on steganography tools in July 2020.[2]

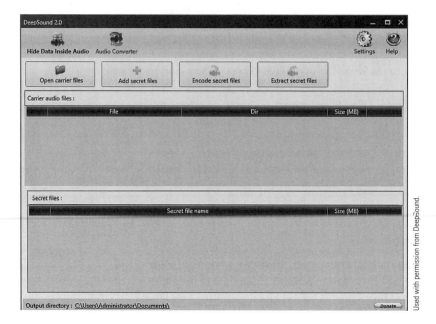

FIGURE 5-9

Deep Sound
main screen.

- A 2019 technical paper by two Egyptian researchers published in an open access forum describes a steganography technique.[3]
- An undated article from a digital security company describes detecting steganography in images.[4]

Encryption

Cryptography is not so much about hiding a message, as with steganography, but rather about obfuscating the message so that it cannot be read. In other words, with steganography, the examiner may not even be aware a message is present. With cryptography, it is obvious there is a message present, but the examiner cannot easily decipher the message. The word cryptography is derived from word *kryptós*, which means *hidden*, and the verb *gráfo*, which means *I write*. Therefore, cryptography is the study of writing secret messages.

● NOTE

Technically speaking, cryptography is the study of encryption and decryption methods; cryptanalysis is the study of breaking ciphers; and cryptology is the combination of cryptography and cryptanalysis. But, like many books, we will use cryptography and cryptology synonymously.

FYI

Cryptography is an area in which many security professionals, including forensic examiners, are weak. Even the major security certifications give only a cursory coverage of cryptography. It is particularly important for forensic examiners to be more knowledgeable about cryptography. This section provides a thorough introduction to the field.

The History of Encryption

Encrypting communications is almost as old as writing. Throughout history, people have wanted to keep their communications private. Although for much of human history this has been a requirement primarily for governments, militaries, and businesses, in modern times private individuals also have had a need for cryptography.

The concept of cryptography is actually pretty simple. Messages must be changed in such a way that they cannot be read easily by any party that intercepts them but can be decoded easily by the intended recipient. Modern methods usually depend on some combination of mathematics and information theory. First, it is a good idea to start by examining a few historical methods of encryption. Keep in mind that these historical methods are no longer considered secure. They can be cracked in seconds by modern computers. But they are very useful for the novice to begin learning the encryption process.

The Caesar Cipher

The **Caesar cipher** is purported to have been used by the ancient Roman Caesars, such as Julius Caesar—hence the name. This method is also referred to as a substitution cipher. Almost every introductory cryptography book in existence mentions the Caesar cipher. It is even mentioned in the course material for several prominent network security certifications. It is actually quite simple to do. You choose some number by which to shift each letter of a text and substitute the new alphabetic letter for the letter you are encrypting. For example, if the text is

A CAT

and you choose to shift by two letters, then *C* replaces *A*, *E* replaces *C*, *C* replaces *A*, and *V* replaces *T*. The encrypted message is

C ECV

Or, if you choose to shift by three letters, the encrypted message becomes

D FDW

You can choose to shift by any number of letters, either left or right. If you choose to shift 2 to the right, that would be a +2; if you choose to shift 4 to the left, that would be a −4. If you get to the end of the alphabet, just keep going back to the beginning. So if you are shifting to the right and need to go past Z, just start over at A. Julius Caesar was reputed to have used a shift of 3 to the right.

Because this is a very simple method to understand, it is a good place to start your study of encryption. It is, however, extremely easy to crack using the two major forms of attacking text for decryption. The first is a **brute-force attack**. If a Caesar cipher is suspected, modern computers can simply try all possible combinations and see if recognizable text emerges. Frankly, you could do this with pen and paper. With any cipher there is the concept of key space, which is the total number of possible keys. With a Caesar cipher applied to the English language, there are only 26 possible keys. You could easily try all of those in just a few minutes.

The second approach is based on the attacker's knowledge of the underlying language. The Caesar cipher is easy to crack using an academic approach because of letter and word frequency. Any language has a certain letter and word frequency, meaning that some letters or words are used more frequently than others. In the English language, the most common single-letter word is *a*. The most common three-letter word is *the*. Those two rules alone could help you decrypt a Caesar cipher. For example, if you saw a string of seemingly non-sense letters and noticed that a three-letter word was frequently repeated in the message, you might easily surmise that this word was *the* and the odds are highly in favor of this being correct. Furthermore, if you frequently noticed a single-letter word in the text, it is most likely the letter *a*. You now have found the substitution scheme for *a*, *t*, *h*, and *e*. You can now either translate all of those letters in the message and attempt to guess the rest, or simply analyze the substitute letters used for *a*, *t*, *h*, and *e* and derive the substitution cipher that was used for this message.

Decrypting a message of this type does not even require a computer. Someone with no background in cryptography could do it in less than 10 minutes using pen and paper. A popularized example is in the movie *A Christmas Story*, where schoolboy Ralphie decrypts the message "Be sure to drink your Ovaltine." There are other rules that help make cracking this code even easier. For example, in the English language, the two most common two-letter combinations are *ee* and *oo*. That gives you even more to work with.

The substitution scheme you choose (e.g., +2, +1) is referred to as a substitution alphabet (i.e., *b* substitutes for *a*, *u* substitutes for *t*, and so on). Thus, the Caesar cipher is also referred to as a monoalphabet or single-alphabet substitution method, meaning that it uses a single substitution for the encryption. That just means that all letters in the plaintext are shifted by the same number.

In any cryptographic algorithm, be it a simple one like the Caesar cipher or a more modern one, the number that is used by the algorithm to encrypt or decrypt a message is called the *key*, because it unlocks the scrambled information. In the case of the Caesar cipher, it is a single digit (like +2), and in the case of modern algorithms like Advanced Encryption Standard (AES), it is a 128-bit number. Even though the Caesar cipher may have a much simpler algorithm (shift the letters by whatever number and direction is in the key) and a smaller key (a single digit, or at most two digits, as in +12 or –11), it is still an example of the basic concepts you see in more sophisticated modern cryptographic algorithms.

The Caesar cipher also introduces two more basic concepts of cryptography. The text you want to encrypt is referred to as the *plaintext*. After it has been subjected to the algorithm and key, the resultant text is called the *ciphertext*. So, although simple, the Caesar cipher introduces cryptography algorithms, keys, plaintext, and ciphertext.

This example gives you a primitive introduction to cryptography and encryption. It must be stressed that the Caesar cipher is no longer a secure method of encrypting messages, but it is an interesting exercise to begin introducing the basic concepts of encryption.

The Atbash Cipher

Hebrew scribes copying the book of Jeremiah used the Atbash cipher. This cipher is very simple—just reverse the alphabet. This is also, by modern standards, a very primitive and easy-to-break cipher. But it will help you get a feel for how cryptography works.

The Atbash cipher is a Hebrew code that substitutes the first letter of the alphabet for the last letter and the second letter for the second-to-last letter, and so forth. It simply reverses the alphabet. This, like the Caesar cipher, is a single-alphabet substitution cipher. A becomes Z, B becomes Y, C becomes X, and so on.

The ROT13 Cipher

The ROT13 cipher is another single-alphabet substitution cipher. It is, in fact, the simplest of all of them. It is really just a permutation of the Caesar cipher. All characters are rotated 13 characters through the alphabet. The phrase

A CAT

becomes

N PNG

It is essentially the Caesar cipher, but always using a rotation or shift of 13 characters. This is very simple and not sophisticated enough for any real security. But, again, it can be done with pen and paper, or with a simple computer program.

The Scytale Cipher

The *scytale*, which rhymes with Italy, was a cylinder or baton used by the Greeks, and is often specifically attributed to the Spartans. This physical cylinder was used to encrypt messages. Turning the cylinder produced different ciphertexts. Although it is not clear exactly how old this cipher is, it was first mentioned in the 7th century BC by the Greek poet Archilochus. The recipient used a rod of the same diameter as the one used to create the message. He then wrapped the parchment to read the message. To encrypt, he simply wrote across a leather strip attached to a rod. To decrypt, the recipient would just wrap the leather strip around the rod and read across. This was a simple process; it just required both parties have the same size rod and the leather "key."

The Playfair Cipher

The Playfair cipher was invented in 1854 by Charles Wheatstone; however, it was popularized by Lord Playfair, so it bears his name. While it was first rejected by the British government as being too complex, it was actually used by the British military in World War I and to some extent in World War II. This cipher works by encrypting pairs of letters, also called digraphs, at a time.

The Playfair cipher uses a 5 × 5 table that contains a keyword or key phrase. To use the Playfair cipher, one need only memorize that keyword and four rules. First break the plaintext message into digraphs. Thus, "Attack at Dawn" becomes "At ta ck at da wn." If the final digraph is just a single letter, you can pad it with a letter z.

Any square of 5 × 5 letters can be used. You first fill in the keyword, then start, in order, adding in letters that did not appear in the keyword. I/J are combined. You can see this in the table on the next page. In this example the keyword is "falcon,"

F	A	L	C	O
N	B	D	E	G
H	I/J	K	M	P
Q	R	S	T	U
V	W	X	Y	Z

Since the 5 × 5 matrix is created by starting with a keyword, then filling in letters that did not appear in the keyword, the matrix will be different when different keywords are used. The next step is take the plaintext, in this case "attack at dawn," and divide it into digraphs. If there are any duplicate letters, replace the second letter with an X. For example, "dollar" would be "dolxar." Playfair does not account for numbers or punctuation marks, so you will need to remove any punctuation from the plaintext and spell out any numbers. Next, you take the plaintext—in our case

At ta ck at da wn

and find the pairs of letters in the table. Look to the rectangle formed by those letters. In our example, the first letters are AT, thus forming the rectangle shown below, with A in the upper left-hand corner and T in the lower right-hand corner.

A	L	C
B	D	E
I/J	K	M
R	S	T

Then you will take the opposite ends of the rectangle to create the ciphertext. A is in the upper left-hand corner, so you replace it with whatever appears in the upper right-hand corner, which in this case is the letter C. T is in the lower right-hand corner, so you replace it with whatever letter is in the lower left-hand corner, which in this case is the letter R. So AT gets enciphered as CR. Continuing on, the next pair of letters is TA and will form the same rectangle. However, since T is the first letter of the plaintext, R will be the first letter of the ciphertext, yielding RC. Next we have CK. Those letters form the rectangle shown here.

A	L	C
B	D	E
I/J	K	M

C becomes A, and K becomes M, so we have AM. If you continue this process through to the end of the plaintext, you will have "Attack at dawn" encrypted to yield

CRRCLMCRBLVB

If you really wish to learn the Playfair cipher you should work with this by hand, with pencil and paper. But you can check your work with online Playfair calculators:

https://planetcalc.com/7751/

https://www.geocachingtoolbox.com/index.php?lang=en&page=playfairCipher

Multialphabet Substitution

Eventually, a slight improvement on the Caesar cipher was developed, called multialphabet substitution. In this scheme, you select multiple numbers by which letters in the plaintext will be shifted; in other words, multiple substitution alphabets are created. For example, if you select three substitution alphabets (+2, −2, +3), then A CAT becomes C ADV. Notice that the fourth letter starts over with another +2, and you can see that the first *A* was transformed to *C* and the second *A* was transformed to *D*. This makes it more difficult to decipher the underlying text. Although this is harder to decrypt than a Caesar cipher, it is not overly difficult. It can be done with simple pen and paper and a bit of effort. It can be cracked very quickly by a computer. In fact, no one would use such a method today to send any truly secure message, because this type of encryption is considered very weak.

The Vigenère Cipher

One of the most widely known multialphabet ciphers was the **Vigenère cipher**. This cipher was invented in 1553 by Giovan Battista Bellaso. It is a method of encrypting alphabetic text

	A	B	C	D	E	F	G	H	I	J	K	L	M	N	O	P	Q	R	S	T	U	V	W	X	Y	Z
A	A	B	C	D	E	F	G	H	I	J	K	L	M	N	O	P	Q	R	S	T	U	V	W	X	Y	Z
B	B	C	D	E	F	G	H	I	J	K	L	M	N	O	P	Q	R	S	T	U	V	W	X	Y	Z	A
C	C	D	E	F	G	H	I	J	K	L	M	N	O	P	Q	R	S	T	U	V	W	X	Y	Z	A	B
D	D	E	F	G	H	I	J	K	L	M	N	O	P	Q	R	S	T	U	V	W	X	Y	Z	A	B	C
E	E	F	G	H	I	J	K	L	M	N	O	P	Q	R	S	T	U	V	W	X	Y	Z	A	B	C	D
F	F	G	H	I	J	K	L	M	N	O	P	Q	R	S	T	U	V	W	X	Y	Z	A	B	C	D	E
G	G	H	I	J	K	L	M	N	O	P	Q	R	S	T	U	V	W	X	Y	Z	A	B	C	D	E	F
H	H	I	J	K	L	M	N	O	P	Q	R	S	T	U	V	W	X	Y	Z	A	B	C	D	E	F	G
I	I	J	K	L	M	N	O	P	Q	R	S	T	U	V	W	X	Y	Z	A	B	C	D	E	F	G	H
J	J	K	L	M	N	O	P	Q	R	S	T	U	V	W	X	Y	Z	A	B	C	D	E	F	G	H	I
K	K	L	M	N	O	P	Q	R	S	T	U	V	W	X	Y	Z	A	B	C	D	E	F	G	H	I	J
L	L	M	N	O	P	Q	R	S	T	U	V	W	X	Y	Z	A	B	C	D	E	F	G	H	I	J	K
M	M	N	O	P	Q	R	S	T	U	V	W	X	Y	Z	A	B	C	D	E	F	G	H	I	J	K	L
N	N	O	P	Q	R	S	T	U	V	W	X	Y	Z	A	B	C	D	E	F	G	H	I	J	K	L	M
O	O	P	Q	R	S	T	U	V	W	X	Y	Z	A	B	C	D	E	F	G	H	I	J	K	L	M	N
P	P	Q	R	S	T	U	V	W	X	Y	Z	A	B	C	D	E	F	G	H	I	J	K	L	M	N	O
Q	Q	R	S	T	U	V	W	X	Y	Z	A	B	C	D	E	F	G	H	I	J	K	L	M	N	O	P
R	R	S	T	U	V	W	X	Y	Z	A	B	C	D	E	F	G	H	I	J	K	L	M	N	O	P	Q
S	S	T	U	V	W	X	Y	Z	A	B	C	D	E	F	G	H	I	J	K	L	M	N	O	P	Q	R
T	T	U	V	W	X	Y	Z	A	B	C	D	E	F	G	H	I	J	K	L	M	N	O	P	Q	R	S
U	U	V	W	X	Y	Z	A	B	C	D	E	F	G	H	I	J	K	L	M	N	O	P	Q	R	S	T
V	V	W	X	Y	Z	A	B	C	D	E	F	G	H	I	J	K	L	M	N	O	P	Q	R	S	T	U
W	W	X	Y	Z	A	B	C	D	E	F	G	H	I	J	K	L	M	N	O	P	Q	R	S	T	U	V
X	X	Y	Z	A	B	C	D	E	F	G	H	I	J	K	L	M	N	O	P	Q	R	S	T	U	V	W
Y	Y	Z	A	B	C	D	E	F	G	H	I	J	K	L	M	N	O	P	Q	R	S	T	U	V	W	X
Z	Z	A	B	C	D	E	F	G	H	I	J	K	L	M	N	O	P	Q	R	S	T	U	V	W	X	Y

FIGURE 5-10

Vigenère table.

by using a series of different monoalphabet ciphers selected based on the letters of a keyword. This algorithm was later misattributed to Blaise de Vigenère, and so it is now known as the Vigenère cipher, even though Vigenère did not really invent it.

You use the table (shown in **FIGURE 5-10**) along with a keyword you have selected. Match the letter of your keyword on the top with the letter of your plaintext on the left to find the ciphertext. Using the table shown in Figure 5-10, if you are encrypting the word *cat* and your keyword is *horse*, then the ciphertext is *jok*.

Multialphabet ciphers are more secure than single-alphabet substitution ciphers. However, they are still not acceptable for modern cryptographic usage. Computer-based cryptanalysis systems can crack historical cryptographic methods (both single-alphabet and multialphabet) very easily. This chapter presents the single-alphabet substitution and multialphabet substitution ciphers just to show you the history of cryptography and to help you get an understanding of how cryptography works.

The Enigma Machine

In World War II, the Germans made use of an electromechanical rotor-based cipher system known as the Enigma machine. The Enigma machine is pivotal in the history of cryptography. It is a multialphabet substitution cipher using machinery to accomplish the encryption. There are multiple variations on this machine.

The machine was designed so that when the operator pressed a key, the encrypted ciphertext for that plaintext was altered each time. So, if the operator pressed the *A* key, he or she might generate an *F* in the ciphertext, and the next time it might be a *D*. Essentially, this was a multialphabet cipher, consisting of 26 possible alphabets.

Allied cipher machines used in World War II included the British TypeX and the American SIGABA. Both of these were quite similar to the Enigma machine, but with improvements that made them more secure. The Enigma machine and its variations were essentially mechanical implementations of multialphabet substitution.

Modern Cryptography

The History of Encryption section was designed to give you a feel for cryptography. Some forms, like the Caesar cipher, can even be done with pen and paper. Modern cryptography methods, as well as computers, make decryption a rather advanced science. Therefore, encryption must be equally sophisticated to have a chance of success. It is also important to realize that cryptographic methods have evolved quite a bit since the days of these ancient ciphers.

Modern cryptography is separated into two distinct groups: symmetric cryptography and asymmetric cryptography. Symmetric cryptography uses the same key to encrypt and decrypt the plaintext, while asymmetric cryptography uses different keys to encrypt and decrypt the plaintext. In this section, you will learn about both methods.

FYI

Beware of Algorithms Too Good to Be True

As you are discovering in this chapter, the basic concepts of encryption are very simple. Anyone with even rudimentary programming skills can write a program that implements one of the simple encryption methods examined here. However, these methods are not secure and are only included to illustrate fundamental encryption concepts.

From time to time, someone new to encryption discovers these basic methods and, in their enthusiasm, attempts to create their own encryption method by making some minor modifications. Although this can be a very stimulating intellectual exercise, it is only that. Users without training in advanced math or cryptography are extremely unlikely to stumble across a new encryption method that is effective for secure communications.

Amateurs frequently post claims that they have discovered the latest, unbreakable encryption algorithm on the Usenet newsgroup sci.crypt (if you are not familiar with Usenet, those groups are now accessible via the Groups link on *http://www.google.com*). Their algorithms are usually quickly broken. Unfortunately, some people implement such methods into software products and market them as secure.

Some distributors of insecure encryption methods and software do so out of simple greed and are intentionally defrauding an unsuspecting public. Others do so out of simple ignorance, honestly believing that their method is superior. Methods for evaluating encryption claims are discussed later in this chapter.

Kerckhoffs' Principle

Kerckhoffs' principle states that the security of a cryptographic algorithm depends only on the secrecy of the key, not the algorithm itself. For practical purposes, this means that the details of a cryptographic algorithm can be made public. In fact, all the major algorithms discussed here are published. You can get all the details online or in books. This does not undermine the security of the algorithm. In fact, it enhances it. Publishing the algorithm allows cryptographic researchers to analyze the algorithm and to search for flaws in it.

> The opposite of Kerckhoffs' principle is an application of the principle of "security by obscurity" to the underlying cryptographic algorithm—that is, the algorithm is kept secret. Although this is a fairly common practice, it does not contribute to the secrecy of encrypted information—in fact, quite the opposite.

Symmetric Cryptography

Symmetric cryptography refers to those methods where the same key is used to encrypt and decrypt the plaintext. One step that has been used widely is to use two different encryption keys, one from sender to receiver and one from receiver to sender. This is still symmetric cryptography because the same key is used for encryption as is used for decryption—having different keys in both directions just provides additional security if the keys are learned or disclosed. This is historically the type of encryption that has been used exclusively until recently.

Substitution and Transposition.

Substitution is changing some part of the plaintext for some matching part of the ciphertext. The Caesar and Atbash ciphers are simple substitution ciphers. The Vigenère cipher is a bit more complex, but is still a substitution cipher. They are substitution ciphers because each single character of plaintext is converted into a single character of ciphertext.

Transposition is the swapping of blocks of ciphertext. For example, if you have the text "I like ice cream," you could transpose or swap every three-letter sequence (or block) with the next and get:

ikeI l creiceam

Of course, modern transposition is at the level of bits, or rather blocks, or contiguous groups, of bits. However, this illustrates the concept. All modern block-cipher algorithms use both substitution and transposition. The combination of substitution and transposition increases the security of the resultant ciphertext. Modern symmetric ciphers perform a complex series of substitutions and transpositions.

Block Ciphers and Stream Ciphers

There are two types of symmetric algorithms: block ciphers and stream ciphers. A **block cipher** literally encrypts the data in blocks; 64-bit blocks are quite common, although some algorithms (like AES) use larger blocks. For example, AES uses a 128-bit block. **Stream ciphers** encrypt the data as a stream, one bit at a time.

There are a few basic facts that are generally applicable to all block ciphers. Assuming the actual algorithm is mathematically sound, then the following is true:

- Larger block sizes increase security.
- Larger key sizes increase security against brute-force attack methods.
- If the round function is secure, then more rounds increase security to a point.

Now, the real caveat here is the "assuming the algorithm is mathematically sound" part. If the algorithm is mathematically sound, these facts hold true. If the algorithm is not sound, a larger block size or larger key size may have little impact on security. This takes us back to Kerckhoffs' principle, mentioned previously. It is important that any cryptographic algorithm be rigorously examined by mathematicians and cryptographers to ensure that it is sound.

The Feistel Function

This function is named after its inventor, the German-born physicist and cryptographer Horst Feistel. At the heart of many block ciphers is a **Feistel function**. So this makes it a good place to start your study of symmetric algorithms. This function forms the basis for many, if not most, block ciphers. This makes it one of the most influential developments in symmetric block ciphers. It is also known as a Feistel network or a Feistel cipher. Any block cipher that is based on Feistel will essentially work in the same manner; the differences will be found in what is done in the round function.

The Feistel function starts by splitting the block of plaintext data (often 64 bits) into two parts (traditionally termed L_0 and R_0). Usually the split is equal—both sides are the same size. However, there are variations where this is not the case.

The round function F is applied to one of the halves. The term *round function* simply means a function performed with each iteration, or round, of the Feistel cipher. The details of the round function F can vary with different implementations. Usually, these are relatively simple functions, to allow for increased speed of the algorithm.

The output of each round function F and the remaining half of the data are then run through the exclusive OR (XOR) function. This means, for example, that you take L_0, pass it through the round function F, then take the result and XOR it with R_0.

Then, the halves are transposed, or their positions switched. This means L_0 gets moved to the right and R_0 gets moved to the left. This process is repeated a given number of times. The main difference between different cryptographic algorithms that are Feistel ciphers is the exact nature of the round function F and the number of iterations. A simple diagram of this process is shown in **FIGURE 5-11**.

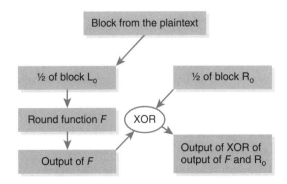

FIGURE 5-11

Feistel function.

A Brief Review of Binary Operations

When working with binary numbers, there are three logical operations not found in normal math: AND, OR, and XOR operations. Each is illustrated below.

AND

To perform the AND operation, you take two binary numbers and compare them one place at a time. If both numbers have a 1 in both places, then the resultant number is a 1. If not, then the resultant number is a 0, as you see here:

```
1 1 0 1
1 0 0 1
---------
1 0 0 1
```

OR

The OR operation checks to see whether there is a 1 in either or both numbers in a given place. If so, then the resultant number is 1. If not, the resultant number is 0, as you see here:

```
1 1 0 1
1 0 0 1
---------
1 1 0 1
```

XOR

The exclusive OR (XOR) operation affects your study of encryption the most. It checks to see whether there is a 1 in a number in a given place, but not in both numbers at that place. If it is in one number but not the other, then the resultant number is 1. If not, the resultant number is 0, as you see here:

```
1 1 0 1
1 0 0 1
---------
0 1 0 0
```

The XOR function has a very interesting property in that it is reversible. If you XOR the resultant number with the second number, you get back the first number. And if you XOR the resultant number with the first number, you get the second number.

```
0 1 0 0
1 0 0 1
---------
1 1 0 1
```

Data Encryption Standard

One of the oldest of the modern symmetric ciphers is the Data Encryption Standard (DES). DES was developed by IBM in the early 1970s. DES is a block cipher. It was a U.S. government standard until the 1990s. IBM had originally developed a cipher called

Lucifer, which was designed by Horst Feistel. When the U.S. government began seeking a standardized encryption algorithm, IBM worked with the National Security Agency (NSA) to alter Lucifer to fit the government's needs; thus DES was created. As you might guess, DES is a Feistel cipher.

The basic concept of DES is as follows:

1. Data is divided into 64-bit blocks.
2. That data is then manipulated by 16 separate steps of encryption involving substitutions, bit-shifting, and logical operations using a 56-bit key.
3. Data is then further scrambled using a swapping algorithm.
4. Data is finally transposed one last time.

Those four steps provide a simplified, high-level view of DES. As you can see, it works on splitting the block into two sections, as with all Feistel ciphers. The idea is to continually scramble the underlying message to make it appear as random as possible.

To generate the keys for each round, the 56-bit key is split into two 28-bit halves, and those halves are circularly shifted after each round by 1 or 2 bits. In other words, the halves are first subjected to a round function, then the keys are shifted by 1 to 2 bits each time so they can be used in the next round as a different key. Then 48 bits from those two halves are selected and permuted to form the round key. This means there is a different round key for each round—but it is related to the previous round key. In fact, it is derived from the previous round key.

DES uses eight S-boxes. The term *S-boxes* means substitution boxes. They are simply lookup tables. Each S-box basically has a table that determines, based on the bits passed into it, what to substitute for those bits. Each item passed into the box is substituted with the item that matches it in the lookup table. This is a very common tactic in symmetric key algorithms. Each one of the DES S-boxes takes in 6 bits and produces 4 bits. The middle 4 bits of the 6-bit input are used to look up the 4-bit replacement.

The round *F* function works as follows:

>
>
> **NOTE**
>
> **The Vulnerabilities of DES**
>
> DES is no longer considered secure because of its small key size. The algorithm is sound, but the key size is not. DES uses short keys compared with later algorithms and is therefore considered vulnerable to brute-force attacks. A brute-force attack is one in which the attacker tries to decrypt a message by simply applying every possible key in the key space.

1. Expand the 32-bit half that was input to 48 bits; this is done by replicating some bits.
2. XOR the resultant 48 bits with the 48-bit round key.
3. Split the result into eight 6-bit sections.
4. Pass each of these 6-bit portions through a different S-box. Each S-box produces a 4-bit output, giving a total of 32 output bits. Note in Step 1 the expansion of the 32 bits into 48; it's now taken back to just 32 bits, which demonstrates yet another way to scramble the resultant ciphertext.
5. Transpose the output bits.

This is done for each round of DES. DES has 16 rounds. So this is an effective way to scramble the plaintext.

The only reason DES is no longer considered secure is the short key. The 56-bit key is simply not long enough to prevent brute-force attacks. Brute force is trying every possible key.

DES has a total number of possible keys (also called a **key space**) of 2^{56}. A modern computer system can break this in a reasonable amount of time.

Triple DES

Eventually, it became obvious that DES would no longer be secure. The U.S. federal government began a contest seeking a replacement cryptography algorithm. However, in the meantime, Triple DES (3DES) was created as an interim solution. Essentially, it does DES three times, with three different keys. 3DES uses a "key bundle," which comprises three DES keys: K_1, K_2, and K_3. Each key is a standard 56-bit DES key. It then applies the following process:

DES encrypt with K_1, DES *decrypt* with K_2, then DES encrypt with K_3.

FYI

You might ask, "If DES was the first DES, and 3DES is currently popular, what happened to 2DES—and is there a 4DES?" Whereas 3DES basically does DES three times, there was an interim step, which was to do DES twice. This was called 2DES; however, it was not much more secure than DES and it took more time and computer resources to implement, so it was not widely used. On the other hand, 4DES was never implemented because early simulations indicated that 4DES was too scrambled—so scrambled, in fact, that blocks of the original plaintext appeared in the final ciphertext. This was one of the driving factors behind searching for a new algorithm not in the DES line.

There are three options for the keys. In the first option, all three keys are independent and different. In the second option, K_1 and K_3 are identical. In the third option, all three keys are the same, so you are literally applying the exact same DES algorithm three times, with the same key. Option 1 is the most secure, and Option 3 is the least secure.

Advanced Encryption Standard

The Advanced Encryption Standard (AES), also known as the Rijndael block cipher, was officially designated as a replacement for DES in 2001 after a five-year process involving 15 competing algorithms. AES is designated as Federal Information Processing Standard 197 (FIPS 197).

AES can have three different key sizes: 128, 192, or 256 bits. The three different implementations of AES are referred to as AES 128, AES 192, and AES 256. All three operate on a block size of 128 bits.

The AES algorithm was developed by two Belgian cryptographers, Joan Daemen and Vincent Rijmen. Unlike both DES and 3DES, AES is not based on a Feistel network. AES uses a substitution-permutation matrix instead. AES operates on a 4 × 4 column matrix of bytes, termed the *state* (versions of AES with a larger block size have additional columns in the state). The general steps of AES are as follows:

1. **Key expansion**—Round keys are derived from the cipher key using Rijndael's key schedule. The specifics of that key schedule are not important for this book, but essentially it generates a different key in each round, based on the original key. This is much like DES.

2. **Initial round**
   a. **AddRoundKey**—Each byte of the state is combined with the round key using bitwise XOR. In other words, the plaintext is arrayed bit by bit in a matrix that is XOR'd with the key.
3. **Rounds**
   a. **SubBytes**—A nonlinear substitution step where each byte is replaced with another according to a lookup table. Basically, each byte in the matrix is then fed into a substitution box. However, with AES, this box also transposes the bits as well as substituting them, so it is called a permutation box.
   b. **ShiftRows**—A transposition step where each row of the state is shifted cyclically a certain number of steps.
   c. **MixColumns**—A mixing operation that operates on the columns of the state, combining the 4 bytes in each column.
   d. **AddRoundKey**—A step where the key is XOR'd with the matrix again.
4. **Final round (no MixColumns)**
   a. **SubBytes**—Same as above
   b. **ShiftRows**—Same as above
   c. **AddRoundKey**—Same as above

Some details about these steps are as follows:

- In the SubBytes step, each byte in the matrix is substituted for another byte using an 8-bit substitution box, called the Rijndael S-box.
- The ShiftRows step works by shifting the bytes in each row by a certain amount. The first row is left unchanged. The second row is shifted one to the left, the third row is shifted by two, and so on.
- In the MixColumns step, the columns are mixed, similar to the shifting rows. However, rather than just shifting them, they are actually mixed together.
- In the AddRoundKey step, the subkey is XOR'd with the state. For each round, a subkey is derived from the main key using Rijndael's key schedule; each subkey is the same size as the state.

This algorithm is a bit more complex than DES or 3DES.

AES can use three different key sizes: a 128-bit, a 192-bit, or a 256-bit key. The longer the key, the more resistant the resultant ciphertext will be to brute-force attacks. The National Security Agency has approved 256-bit AES for use with Top Secret data; therefore, it is secure enough for commercial applications.

Other Symmetric Algorithms

There are many other symmetric algorithms. A few examples include the following:

- Blowfish
- Serpent
- Skipjack

However, AES is the most commonly used symmetric algorithm today, and DES is one of the most widely known and an excellent example of a Feistel cipher. If you study these two, you will be reasonably well informed on symmetric ciphers.

Cryptographic Hashes

Cryptographic hashes were discussed earlier in this book, but not in any detail. In this section, we will explore hashes in more detail. A *hash* is a type of cryptographic algorithm that has some specific characteristics. First and foremost, it is one-way, not reversible. That means you cannot "unhash" something. The second characteristic is that you get a fixed-length output no matter what input is given. The third is that the algorithm must be collision resistant. A *collision* occurs when two different inputs to the same hashing algorithm produce the same output (called a hash or digest). Now ideally, we would like to have no collisions. But the reality is that with a fixed-length output, a collision is possible. So the goal is to make it so unlikely as to be something we need not think about.

Cryptographic hashes are how many systems, including Microsoft Windows, store passwords. For example, if your password is "password", then Windows will first hash it, producing something like this:

0BD181063899C9239016320B50D3E896693A96DF

Windows will then store that hash in the SAM (Security Accounts Manager) file in the Windows System directory. When you log on, Windows cannot unhash your password. Instead, what Windows does is take whatever password you type in, hash it, and then compare the result with what is in the SAM file. If they match (exactly), then you can log in.

There are various hashing algorithms. The two most common are MD5 and SHA (the latter was SHA-1, but since then, later versions like SHA-256 have become more common.).

Asymmetric Cryptography

Asymmetric cryptography is cryptography wherein two keys are used: one to encrypt the message and another to decrypt it.

RSA

The RSA algorithm was publicly described in 1977 by Ron Rivest, Adi Shamir, and Leonard Adleman at MIT. The letters RSA are the initials of their surnames. RSA is perhaps the most widely used public key cryptography algorithm in existence today.

It is based on some interesting relationships of prime numbers. The security of RSA derives from the fact that it is difficult to factor a large integer composed of two or more large prime factors.

To create the key, two large random prime numbers, p and q, of approximately equal size are generated. Next, two numbers are chosen so that when multiplied together the product will be the desired size—for example, 1,024 bits, 2,048 bits, and so on.

Now p and q are multiplied to get n.

The next step is to multiply **Euler's Totient** for each of these primes. Euler's Totient is the total number of coprime numbers. Two numbers are considered coprime if they have no common factors. For example, if the original number is 7, then 5 and 7 would be coprime. It just so happens that for prime numbers, this is always the number minus 1. For example, 7 has six numbers that are coprime to it. Therefore,

$$m = (p - 1)(q - 1)$$

Now another number is selected. This number is called e and e is coprime to m.

At this point, the key is almost generated. Now a number d is calculated that when multiplied by e and modulo m would yield a 1.

Find d, such that $[d \times e]\mathrm{mod}(m) = 1$.

Now you have the public keys, e and n, and the private, or secret, keys, d and n. To encrypt, you simply take your message raised to the e power and modulo n.

$$= M^e \, \mathrm{mod}(n)$$

To decrypt, you take the ciphertext, raise it to the d power modulo n, or

$$P = C^d \, \mathrm{mod}(n)$$

> **NOTE**
>
> *Modulo* refers to dividing two numbers and returning the remainder. For example, 8 modulo 3 would be 8/3 with a remainder of 2. The modulo would, therefore, be 2. This is a rather simplified explanation of the modulus concept, but sufficient for the purposes of a forensic analyst understanding RSA.

You can get a better understanding of RSA by walking through the algorithm utilizing small integers. Normally, RSA would be done with very large integers.

RSA is based on large prime numbers. Now you might think, couldn't someone take the public key and use factoring to derive the private key? Hypothetically, yes. However, factoring really large numbers into their prime factors is difficult. There is no efficient algorithm for doing it. RSA can use 1,024-, 2,048-, 4,096-bit and larger keys. Those make for some huge numbers. Of course, should anyone ever invent an efficient algorithm that will factor a large number into its prime factors, RSA would be obsolete.

Diffie-Hellman

The Diffie-Hellman algorithm is a cryptographic protocol that allows two parties to establish a shared key over an insecure channel. In other words, Diffie-Hellman is often used to allow parties to exchange a symmetric key through some insecure medium, such as the internet. It was developed by Whitfield Diffie and Martin Hellman in 1976. An interesting twist is that the method had actually already been developed by Malcolm J. Williamson of the British Intelligence Service, but it was classified, and therefore could not be publicly disclosed at the time of its creation. Diffie-Hellman enabled all secure communications between parties that did not have a preestablished relationship, such as e-commerce, and facilitated communications even between parties with a preestablished relationship, such as e-banking.

Other Asymmetric Algorithms

RSA is the most widely used asymmetric algorithm, so it is the only one this chapter covers in detail. However, you can study other asymmetric algorithms if you desire:

- MQV
- Elliptic Curve
- DSA

Each of these is based on some aspect of number theory.

Breaking Encryption

Cryptanalysis is using techniques other than brute force to attempt to uncover a key. This is also referred to as academic or knowledge-based code breaking. In some cases, cryptographic techniques are used to test the efficacy of a cryptographic algorithm. Such techniques are frequently used to test hash algorithms for collisions. Any attempt to crack a nontrivial cryptographic algorithm is simply an attempt. There is no guarantee of any method working. And whether it works or not, it will probably be a long and tedious process. If cracking encryption were a trivial process, then encryption would be useless.

Frequency Analysis

This is the basic tool for breaking most classical ciphers. In natural languages, certain letters of the alphabet appear more frequently than others. By examining those frequencies, you can derive some information about the key that was used. This method is very effective against classic ciphers like Caesar, Vigenère, and so on. It is not effective against modern methods of cryptography. Remember, in English, the words *the* and *and* are the two most common three-letter words. The most common single-letter words are *a* and *I*. If you see two of the same letters together in a word, it is most likely *ee* or *oo*.

Kasiski Examination

Kasiski examination was developed by Friedrich Kasiski in 1863. It is a method of attacking polyalphabetic substitution ciphers, such as the Vigenère cipher. This method can be used to deduce the length of the keyword used in a polyalphabetic substitution cipher. Once the length of the keyword is discovered, the ciphertext is lined up in *n* columns, where *n* is the length of the keyword. Then, each column can be treated as a monoalphabetic substitution cipher and each column can be cracked with simple frequency analysis. The method simply involves looking for repeated strings in the ciphertext. The longer the ciphertext, the more effective this method will be. This is sometimes also called Kasiski's test or Kasiski's method.

Modern Methods

Cracking modern cryptographic methods is a nontrivial task. In fact, the most likely outcome is failure. However, with enough time and resources (i.e., computational power, sample cipher/plaintexts, etc.), it is possible. Following are some techniques that can be employed in this process:

- **Known plaintext attack**—This method is based on having a sample of known plaintexts and their resulting ciphertexts, and then using this information to try to ascertain something about the key used. It is easier to obtain known plaintext samples than you might think. Consider email. Many people use a standard signature block. If you intercept encrypted emails, you can compare a known signature block with the end of the encrypted email. You would then have a known plaintext and the matching ciphertext to work with.
- **Chosen plaintext attack**—In this attack, the attacker obtains the ciphertexts corresponding to a set of plaintexts of his own choosing. This can allow the attacker to attempt to derive the key used and thus decrypt other messages encrypted with that key. This can be difficult, but it is not impossible.
- **Ciphertext-only**—The attacker only has access to a collection of ciphertexts. This is much more likely than known plaintext, but also the most difficult. The attack is completely successful if the corresponding plaintexts can be deduced, or even better, the key. But obtaining any information at all about the underlying plaintext in this situation is still considered a success.

- **Related-key attack**—This attack is like a chosen plaintext attack, except the attacker can obtain ciphertexts encrypted under two different keys. This is actually a very useful attack if you can obtain the plaintext and matching ciphertext.

There are other methods based on more advanced cryptanalysis techniques—for example, differential and integral cryptanalysis. However, this section should give any forensic examiner a good basic understanding of cryptanalysis.

Tools

A number of tools can aid in cracking passwords and encrypted data. Remember that if the encryption was implemented correctly and is strong, you may not be able to crack it. But passwords can often be cracked (encrypted information less often). It is also possible to obtain keys or copies of information before encryption via a number of nontechnical means that fall in the category of **social engineering**, which includes going through the trash, also known as dumpster diving; lying to a person to obtain the keys, passwords, phrases, or un-encrypted information; or even getting a job at the target company and stealing the desired information.

Rainbow Tables

In 1980, Martin Hellman described a cryptanalytic time-memory tradeoff, which reduces the time of cryptanalysis by using precalculated data stored in memory. Essentially, these types of password crackers work with precalculated hashes of all passwords available within a certain character space, be that a–z or a–zA–z or a–zA–Z0–9, etc. These files are called rainbow tables because they contain every letter combination "under the rainbow." They are particularly useful when trying to crack hashes. Because a hash is a one-way function, the way to break it is to attempt to find a match. The attacker takes the hashed value and searches the rainbow tables seeking a match to the hash. If one is found, then the original text for the hash is found.

Popular hacking tools like Ophcrack depend on rainbow tables. Ophcrack is usually very successful at cracking Windows local machine passwords. The steps are very simple:

1. Download Ophcrack and burn the image to a CD.
2. Put the CD in the target computer and boot through the CD.
3. Wait as it boots as Linux grabs the Windows password file, then uses cracking tools to crack that file and produces a text file with usernames and passwords.

You can see Ophcrack in use in **FIGURE 5-12**. Note that, this is from a live machine, so some information has been redacted. Many forensics tools, such as OSForensics, provide mechanisms for you to create your own smaller, more focused rainbow tables. For example, you can enter every word you believe might be associated with a suspect, and a rainbow table can be generated from those words and variations of them. This makes a much smaller, thus faster, rainbow table.

John the Ripper

John the Ripper is another password cracker that is very popular with both network administrators and hackers. It can be downloaded free of charge from *http://www*

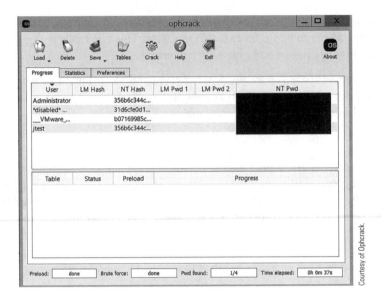

FIGURE 5-12

Ophcrack.

.openwall.com/john/. This product is completely command-line based and has no Windows interface. It enables the user to select text files for word lists to attempt cracking a password. Although John the Ripper is less convenient to use because of its command-line interface, it has been around for a long time and is well regarded by both the security and hacking communities. Interestingly, there is a tool available at *http://www.openwall.com/passwdqc/* that ensures your passwords cannot easily be cracked by John the Ripper.

Quantum Computing and Cryptography

It is beyond the scope of this chapter, or this book, to dive deeply into quantum computing; however, the topic has a substantial impact on cryptography. Therefore, it is necessary that you have at least a generalized knowledge of the topic. In this section, you will be introduced to a very basic general overview of quantum computing and how it will change cryptography.

Quantum computers are simply computers that store data in quantum states rather than in traditional bits. These states can be the polarization of a photon, the energy level of an electron, or other quantum state. This storage is called qubit, as in "quantum bit." While there are numerous news stories about quantum computing, it should be kept in mind that we still do not have a fully working quantum computer. The issue is something called decoherence. Put simply, quantum computers currently can maintain their state for only a short period of time. So processing data on a quantum computer is currently limited to short bursts of work.

What happens once the issues with decoherence (and a few other engineering issues) are addressed? When we have a fully functioning quantum computer, one that can maintain its state, this will have serious ramifications for current widely used asymmetric cryptography algorithms. It has been proven that quantum computers are really good at some tasks. Two relevant examples are factoring large integers into their prime factors and solving discrete logarithm problems. It just so happens that RSA security is based on the difficulty of factoring large integers into their prime factors. Diffie-Hellman (and variations like ElGamal and MQV) security is based on the difficulty of solving the discrete logarithm problem. When we have a fully working quantum computer, these algorithms will no longer be secure. That is a problem, because most online encrypted communication is currently using these algorithms. Fortunately, the National Institute of Standards and Technology (NIST) has been looking for a quantum-resistant cryptographic standard. That process is now in round three, and progressing nicely. You can find out more about the NIST project at *https://csrc.nist.gov/Projects/post-quantum-cryptography /post-quantum-cryptography-standardization.*

CHAPTER SUMMARY

This chapter introduced two complex topics: steganography and cryptography. Steganography is widely utilized to hide data, particularly from forensic examination. As you saw in this chapter, it is easy to implement and has even been used by terrorist organizations for covert communications.

Cryptography is used to systematically scramble information such that it can be unscrambled by use of a key. Scrambled information may be hidden, or hidden information may be scrambled, or steganography or encryption may be used by themselves.

This chapter is meant to provide a general overview of cryptography. Any truly good forensic examiner should be very familiar with the historical methods presented, and at least have a basic understanding of the modern symmetric and asymmetric cryptography algorithms as well as of some of the fundamentals of cryptanalysis.

KEY CONCEPTS AND TERMS

Asymmetric cryptography	Feistel function	Steganography
Block cipher	Kasiski examination	Steganophony
Brute-force attack	Kerckhoffs' principle	Stream cipher
Caesar cipher	Key space	Substitution
Carrier	Least significant bit (LSB)	Symmetric cryptography
Channel	Payload	Transposition
Cryptanalysis	Social engineering	Vigenère cipher
Euler's Totient	Steganalysis	

CHAPTER 5 ASSESSMENT

1. The Caesar cipher is the oldest known encryption method.

   A. True
   B. False

2. An improvement on the Caesar cipher that uses more than one shift is called _____.

   A. DES encryption
   B. multialphabet substitution
   C. IDEA
   D. Triple DES

3. What type of encryption uses a different key to encrypt the message than it uses to decrypt the message?

   A. Private key
   B. Asymmetric
   C. Symmetric
   D. Secure

4. Which of the following is an asymmetric cryptography algorithm invented by three mathematicians in the 1970s?

   A. PGP
   B. DES
   C. DSA
   D. RSA

5. Which of the following encryption algorithms uses three key ciphers in a block system and uses the Rijndael algorithm?

   A. DES
   B. RSA
   C. AES
   D. NSA

6. What is the key length used for DES?

   A. 56
   B. 64
   C. 128
   D. 256

7. Which of the following is an example of a multi-alphabet cipher?

   A. Caesar
   B. Vigenère
   C. Atbash
   D. ROT13

8. How many rounds does DES have?

   A. 64
   B. 56
   C. 16
   D. 4

9. Hiding messages inside another medium is referred to as _____.

   A. cryptography
   B. cryptology
   C. steganalysis
   D. steganography

10. In steganography, the _____ is the data to be covertly communicated. In other words, it is the message you want to hide.

   A. payload
   B. carrier
   C. signal
   D. channel

11. In steganography, the _____ is the stream or file into which the data is hidden.

   A. payload
   B. carrier
   C. signal
   D. channel

12. The most common way steganography is accomplished is via _____.

   A. MSB
   B. ASB
   C. RSB
   D. LSB

References

1. Roy, R. (2020, May 7). Image stenography using Python. *Toward Data Science.* Retrieved from https://towardsdatascience.com/hiding-data-in-an-image-image-steganography -using-python-e491b68b1372 on January 30, 2021.

2. Shankdar, P. (2020, July 8). Best tools to perform steganography [updated 2020]. InfoSec. Retrieved from https://resources.infosecinstitute.com/topic/steganography-and-tools-to -perform-steganography/#gref on January 28, 2021.

3. Nashat, D., & Mamdoah, L. (2019). An efficient steganographic technique for hiding data. *Journal of the Egyptian Mathematical Society, 27.* Retrieved from https://link.springer.com /article/10.1186/s42787-019-0061-6 on January 28, 2021.

4. Security On Demand. (n.d.). Detecting steganography in your SOC [blog post]. Retrieved from https://www.securityondemand.com/news-posts/detecting-steganography-in-your-soc/ on January 28, 2021.

Recovering Data

A COMPUTER USER MAY MAKE AN EFFORT TO DELETE INFORMATION. But the file or remnants of the information may still be available to the forensic examiner. This chapter reviews practical, hands-on steps that you can take to recover deleted data. It discusses undeleting files in Windows, Linux, and Mac OS. However, we will also discuss the computer science facts underlying deleted file recovery.

Chapter 6 Topics

This chapter covers the following topics and concepts:

- How to undelete data
- What you need to know about recovering information from damaged drives

Chapter 6 Goals

When you complete this chapter, you will be able to:

- Recover deleted files in Windows
- Recover deleted files in Linux
- Recover deleted files in Mac OS
- Recover files from damaged drives

Undeleting Data

It is common for people to delete files from their computers. This does not necessarily mean some nefarious intent; it can be simply deleting files that are no longer needed. It is a trivially easy task—and criminals who are not very technically savvy think that deleting a file will keep authorities from discovering it. So you should expect that evidence will frequently be deleted from computers you examine. For this reason, one of the most fundamental tasks a forensic examiner will conduct is retrieving deleted data.

This chapter does not dive into the specifics of the three major operating systems—Windows, Linux, and Mac OS. Instead, the focus is simply on recovering files from them. Just enough information about each operating system's file system as it relates to file deletion and recovery is covered.

File Systems and Hard Drives

Let us begin by discussing traditional hard drives. These are drives that use platters to magnetically store data. While solid-state drives are becoming more and more common, traditional hard drives are still found in personal computers and servers. They are less common in laptops, and not used at all in tablets. Hard drives store data as a sector. For many years, a typical sector has been 512 bytes; however, modern hard drives use what is called the Advanced Format, which has 4,096-byte sectors. A sector is basically an area of one of the disk platters defined by two radii. Sectors are contiguous on a disk, and are defined by two radii on the platter. The hard drive views data in sectors; however, file systems look at clusters, not sectors. A cluster can be from 1 to 128 sectors. The clusters need not be contiguous sectors, as illustrated in **FIGURE 6-1**. For example, a 10-sector cluster may have the sectors in different locations.

> **NOTE**
>
> The formal description of a group of sectors was changed from cluster to allocation unit; however, in most technical literature, the term cluster is still used.

Windows

Windows is a very common operating system. In fact, it would be quite a challenge to find any office that did not have any computers running Windows. PCs running Windows also account for the overwhelming majority of home computers. So recovering deleted Windows files is the first skill you learn in this chapter.

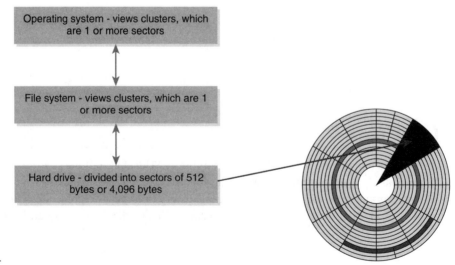

Operating system - views clusters, which are 1 or more sectors

File system - views clusters, which are 1 or more sectors

Hard drive - divided into sectors of 512 bytes or 4,096 bytes

FIGURE 6-1

Clusters and sectors.

You can recover deleted files from the Windows operating system because of the way the file system works. Older versions of Windows use FAT (either FAT16 or FAT32), and newer versions (since Windows 2000) use NTFS. This section explores FAT and NTFS file systems in relationship to recovering deleted files. In both file systems, a table is used to map files to specific clusters where they are stored on the disk. Even today, with Windows 10, NTFS is the file system used in Microsoft Windows.

FAT

In FAT16 and FAT32, the table used to store cluster/file information is the file allocation table (FAT)—thus the name of the file system. The file allocation table is really a list of entries that map to each cluster on the disk partition. Each entry records one of five things:

1. The cluster number of the next cluster for this file is recorded.
2. If this cluster is the end of a chain, then it has a special end of cluster chain (EOC) entry.
3. Bad clusters have a special entry in the file allocation table.
4. Reserved clusters have a special entry in the file allocation table.
5. Open or available clusters are also marked in the file allocation table.

> Marks bad, reserved, or opened clusters.

When a file is deleted, the data is not actually removed from the drive. Rather, the FAT is updated to reflect that those clusters are no longer in use. If new information is saved to the drive, it may be saved to those clusters, overwriting the old information. What this means from a forensic point of view is that the more recently a file was deleted, the more likely it is that you will be able to recover the file. Over time, it becomes more likely that those clusters have had other information saved in them. In fact, the cluster may have been deleted and saved over several times. Because of this, recovering a deleted file is not always an all-or-nothing procedure. It is possible to recover just a portion of a file.

NTFS

NFTS is an acronym for New Technology File System. Starting with Windows 2000, NTFS has been the preferred file system for Windows operating systems. From a forensic point of view, two fundamental files that are part of NTFS are of most interest. These are the Master File Table (MFT), which some sources call the Meta File Table, and the cluster bitmap. The MFT describes all files on the volume, including filenames, time stamps, security identifiers, and file attributes, such as read-only, compressed, encrypted, and so on. This file contains one base file record for each file and directory on an NTFS volume. It serves the same purpose as the file allocation table does in FAT and FAT32. The cluster bitmap file is a map of all the clusters on the hard drive. This is an array of bit entries where each bit indicates whether its corresponding cluster is allocated/used or free/unused.

When files are deleted from an NTFS system, the process is similar to what occurs in FAT. However, there is one difference: Before the cluster is marked as available, it is first marked as "deleted," which effectively moves it to the Recycle Bin. Note that *not a single bit* is actually deleted—the clusters are simply noted as being in the Recycle Bin. Before Windows Vista, the Recycle Bin resided in a hidden directory called RECYCLER. In Vista and beyond, the name of the directory was changed to $Recycle.bin. Only when a user empties the Recycle Bin is the cluster marked as fully available. However, even at this point, nothing is actually deleted. The filename in the MFT is simply updated with a special character to signify to the computer that the file has been deleted. This means that at this point, one can completely recover the entire file. There are any number of file recovery utilities available for this purpose. Just as with FAT systems, clusters in an NTFS system are more likely to be overwritten as more time elapses after deletion.

With older versions of Windows (2000 and before), the recycle bin's activities were structured in a very specific manner. The default Recycle Bin configuration for a Windows computer is to move deleted files to a folder named \Recycler\%SID%\, where %SID% is the SID (Security Identifier) of the currently logged-on user. Every user on the system will have such a directory created the first time that the Recycle Bin is used. As well, each user will have a hidden file called INFO2 created the first time the Recycle Bin is used; its purpose is to keep track of the original location of deleted file(s)/folder(s), as well as file size and deletion time. This makes it possible to relate deleted files to specific users.

When you delete a file, the INFO2 list looks like this:

D%DriveLetter%_%IndexNumber%_%FileExtension%

The "D" stands for Drive.

%DriveLetter% is the drive that the file was on before it was deleted.

%IndexNumber% is an index number that is assigned to each file or folder that is sent to the Recycle Bin, indicating the order of deletion.

%FileExtension% is the original file extension; if the deleted item is a folder, there will be no extension.

Starting with Windows 7 and on through Windows 10, Microsoft did away with the INFO2 file. Starting with Vista, the Recycle Bin is located in a hidden directory named \$Recycle.Bin\%SID%, where %SID% is the SID of the user who performed the deletion. When files are moved into the Recycle Bin, the original file is renamed to $R followed by a set of random characters, but maintaining the original file extension. Also, a new file beginning with $I, followed by the same set of random characters given to the $R file and the same extension, is created; this file contains the original filename/path, original file size, and the date and time that the file was moved to the Recycle Bin. Note that all of the $I files are exactly 544 bytes long. In Windows 7 and beyond, The I$ structure is as follows:

- Bytes 0–7: $I File header—always set to 01 followed by seven sets of 00.
- Bytes 8–15: Original file size—stored in hex, in little-endian format.
- Bytes 16–23: Deleted date/time stamp—represented in number of seconds since midnight, January 1, 1601. Use a program such as Decode, available at *http://www.digital-detective. co.uk/freetools/decode.asp*, to assist with figuring out the exact date/time, if you don't want to do the math.
- Bytes 24–543: Original file path/name.

File systems view a cluster as entirely utilized if even one bit is used. To illustrate this, assume that a system has a sector size of 4,096 bytes. Then further assume that it is using a cluster size of 10 sectors. This means each cluster has a total of 40,960 bytes of storage. If the user saves a file that is 42,000 bytes in size, the file system will need to utilize two

Cluster 1   Cluster 1

FIGURE 6-2

Windows clusters.

clusters. All 10 sectors of the first cluster are used, but only one sector of the second cluster is used. From the file system's point of view, and thus the operating system's point of view, both clusters are completely used. This is illustrated in **FIGURE 6-2**.

Windows Tools

There are a number of mechanisms for recovering deleted files. Many forensics books discuss this process in some detail. In *The Official EnCE: EnCase Certified Examiner Study Guide*, Chapter 2 discusses file systems at length, and discusses how to recover deleted files using EnCase.[1] In the book *Computer Forensics: Hard Disk and Operating Systems: 2*, Chapter 1 deals with file systems and discusses how to recover deleted files.[2] Chapter 2 of the book *The Basics of Digital Forensics: The Primer for Getting Started in Digital Forensics* discusses the recovery of deleted files.[3]

A number of tools are available to recover deleted files from Windows computers. This section introduces a few of these tools. You should definitely take the time to explore the various tools available and select the one you prefer. Simply using your favorite search engine to look for "how to recover deleted Windows files" will result in a number of tools you can try. Many are free, and those that are not usually have a trial version with which you can experiment.

DiskDigger

DiskDigger (*http://diskdigger.org/*) is an easy-to-use tool. It can be downloaded free of charge and is fully functional. But when recovering files in the free version, you have to recover them one at a time. If you pay for the commercial version, you can recover as many files at one time as you want. The interface is very easy to use. When you launch the program, you see a screen like the one shown in **FIGURE 6-3**.

Then you select the drive you want to examine, and choose Dig Deep or Dig Deeper, as shown in **FIGURE 6-4**. The difference is the use of file carving.

Once recovery is done, you will see a screen like the one shown in **FIGURE 6-5**. You can select any file and recover it. On your screen the files will be in color. For files in green, you should get the entire file back. Gray indicates a partial file, and red indicates very little of the file is left.

Forensically Scrubbing a File or Folder

Many web pages report that the Department of Defense operating manual DOD 5220.22-M recommends that data be overwritten with random characters seven times to ensure it is completely wiped . That is accurate, but incomplete. There is actually a matrix of how to sanitize different types of media as described in **TABLE 6-1**, which is based on the 2001 DOD 5220.22-M ECE recommendations.

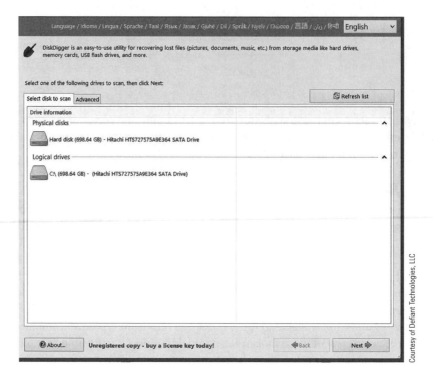

FIGURE 6-3

DiskDigger.

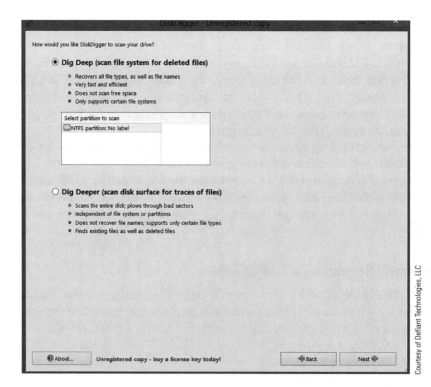

FIGURE 6-4

DiskDigger starting data recovery.

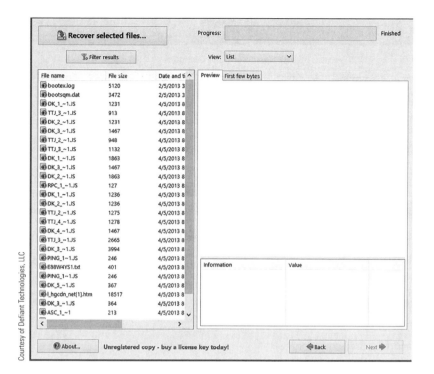

Courtesy of Defiant Technologies, LLC

FIGURE 6-5

Recovering an individual file using DiskDigger.

TABLE 6-1 Forensically scrubbing a file or folder.

MEDIA	CLEAR	SANITIZE
MAGNETIC TAPE1		
Type I	a or b	a, b, or m
Type II	a or b	b or m
Type III	a or b	m
MAGNETIC DISK		
Bernoullis	a, b, or c	m
Floppies	a, b, or c	m
Nonremovable rigid disk	c	a, b, d, or m
Removable rigid disk	a, b, or c	a, b, d, or m
OPTICAL DISC		
Read many, write many	c	m

(Continues)

TABLE 6-1 Forensically scrubbing a file or folder. (*Continued*)		
Read-only		m, n
Write once, read many (Worm)		m, n
MEMORY		
Dynamic random access memory (DRAM)	c or g	c, g, or m
Electronically alterable PROM (EAPROM)	l	j or m
Electronically erasable PROM (EEPROM)	l	h or m
Flash EPROM (FEPROM)	l	c then i, or m
Programmable ROM (PROM)	c	m
Magnetic core memory	c	a, b, e, or m
Magnetic plated wire	c	c and f, or m
Magnetic resistive memory	c	m
Non-volatile RAM (NOVRAM)	c or g	c, g, or m
Read-only memory ROM		m
Static random access memory (SRAM)	c or g	c and f, g, or m
EQUIPMENT		
Cathode ray tube (CRT)	g	q
PRINTERS		
Impact	g	p then g
Laser	g	o then g

a. Degauss with a Type I degausser.
b. Degauss with a Type II degausser.
c. Overwrite all addressable locations with a single character.
d. Overwrite all addressable locations with a character, its complement, and then a random character, and then verify.
e. Overwrite all addressable locations with a character, its complement, and then a random character.
f. Each overwrite must reside in memory for a period longer than the classified data resided.
g. Remove all power, to include battery power.
h. Overwrite all locations with a random pattern, all locations with binary zeros, and all locations with binary ones.
i. Perform a full chip erase as per the manufacturer's data sheets.
j. Perform i, then c, a total of three times.
k. Perform an ultraviolet erase according to the manufacturer's recommendation.
l. Perform k, but increase time by a factor of three.
m. Destroy—disintegrate, incinerate, pulverize, shred, or melt.
n. Destruction required only if classified information is contained.
o. Run five pages of unclassified text (font test acceptable).
p. Ribbons must be destroyed. Platens must be cleaned.
q. Inspect and/or test screen surface for evidence of burned-in information. If present, the cathode ray tube must be destroyed.

WinUndelete

WinUndelete (*http://www.winundelete.com/download.asp*) is another tool that is relatively easy to use. When launched, it starts a wizard that first asks you to select what drive to recover. This is shown in **FIGURE 6-6**.

Step 2 allows you to select the file types you want to recover. This is shown in **FIGURE 6-7**.

The third step is to select a folder to place recovered files in. You can see this in **FIGURE 6-8**.

When WinUndelete has completed running the recovery process, you can go to that folder to see the files.

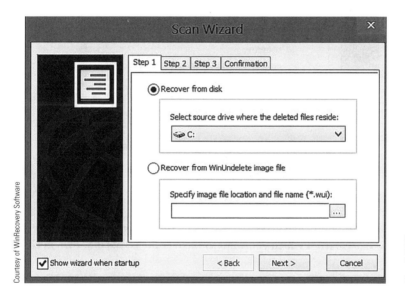

FIGURE 6-6

WinUndelete Wizard Step 1: selecting a drive.

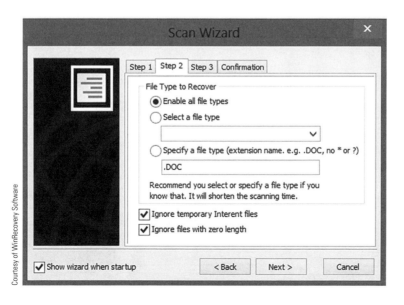

FIGURE 6-7

WinUndelete Step 2: selecting file types.

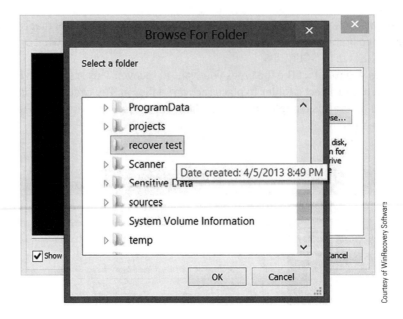

FIGURE 6-8

WinUndelete Step 3: selecting a restore file location.

FreeUndelete

FreeUndelete (*http://www.officerecovery.com/freeundelete/*) is free for personal use. There is a fee for commercial use. When you launch this program, the first screen requires you to select the drive from which you want to recover files. This is shown in **FIGURE 6-9**.

FIGURE 6-9

FreeUndelete selecting a drive.

Then you simply click the Scan button, and any files that can be fully or partially recovered will be listed.

OSForensics

OSForensics is a robust forensics tool. It also provides for undeletion. You can undelete from an image you have mounted, or from the live system. You will find "Deleted Files Search" on the menu on the left-hand side of the main OSForensics screen, as shown in **FIGURE 6-10**.

The search result will display with color coding indicating how likely it is that you can recover a given file. Obviously, some files will be so fragmented that recovery is unlikely. You can see this in **FIGURE 6-11**.

Autopsy

Another interesting tool is Autopsy, available at *https://www.autopsy.com/*. This is a free, open-source digital forensics tool. Like many forensics tools, it includes deleted file recovery. What is most interesting about it is that, when a disk image is loaded, it immediately begins recovering deleted files. This is important because so often evidence is found in deleted files. This can be seen in **FIGURE 6-12**.

FIGURE 6-10

OSForensics deleted files search.

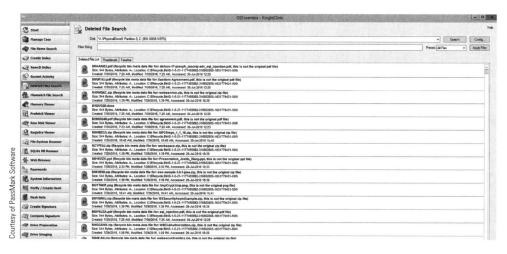

FIGURE 6-11

OSForensics deleted files results.

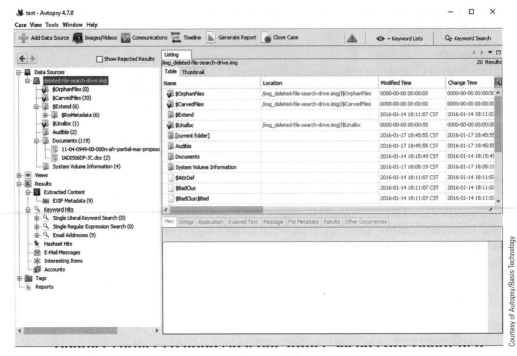

FIGURE 6-12

Autopsy
recovering
deleted files.

Autopsy is an easy-to-use forensics tool. It does not have all the advanced features of some commercial products. However, it is an excellent choice for a second forensic tool to perform validation on your findings. And given that it is open source, it is ideal for students to download and use for experimenting.

There are certainly other tools available for deleted file recovery. Most forensics tools, such as Guidance Software's EnCase and AccessData's Forensic ToolKit (FTK), can recover deleted files.

Linux

With Linux, you have the option of using prepackaged tools or some built-in Linux commands. In this section, you see both, but first you need to understand the extended file system (Ext) it uses. Linux can run on multiple file systems, but Ext is the most common. The most recent version of Ext is Ext4; however, many Linux distributions still use Ext3.

First, consider how Linux stores files. The content of files is stored in contiguous blocks. The exact size of these blocks depends on the parameters used with the command to create that partition (for example, mke2fs can be used to make Ext2 partitions). The size can be 1,024, 2,048, or 4,096 bytes. You can think of these blocks as something similar to the clusters in NTFS, though they are not exactly the same thing, just related conceptually.

Hard drives that run Linux address blocks, or integer multiples of blocks, at a time. The specific block size is stored in the superblock. The entire partition is divided into an integral number of blocks, starting at 0.

Blocks are divided into groups. Each group uses one block as a bitmap to keep track of which block inside that group is allocated (used); thus, there can be at most 32,768

(4,096 × 3 = 32,768) normal blocks per group. Another block is used as a bitmap for the number of allocated inodes. An **inode** is a data structure in the file system that stores all the information about a file except its name and its actual data. Inodes are data structures of 128 bytes that arc stored in a table (4,096 / 128 = 32 inodes per block) in each group.

An inode can refer to a file or a folder/directory. In either case, the inode is really a link to the file. This is important because there are basically two types of links. The first type is the *hard link.* A hard link is an inode that links directly to a specific file. The operating system keeps a count of references to this link. When the reference count reaches zero, the file is deleted. In other words, you can have any number of names referencing a file, but if that number of references reaches zero (i.e., there is *no* name that references that file), then the file is deleted.

The second type of file link is called a *soft link* or *symbolic link.* In this case, the link is not actually a file itself, but rather a pointer to another file or directory. You can think of this as the same thing as a shortcut, such as you might find in Windows.

Because there are at most 32,768 bits in the bitmap, that means that there will be a maximum of 32,768 inodes per group, and thus 1,024 blocks (32,768 / 32 = 1,024) blocks in the inode table of each group. The actual size of the inode table is given by the actual number of inodes per group, which is also stored in the superblock.

The inodes in the inode table of each group contain metadata for each type of data that the file system can store. This type might be a symbolic link, in which case only the inode is sufficient; it might be a directory, a file, and so on. In the case of files and directories, the real data is stored in the file.

Manual Recovery

This method depends on manually recovering deleted files using Linux commands. It does not require external tools. Unfortunately, there are variations between the Linux distributions, so there is no guarantee that this process will work on your specific Linux installation.

The first step is to move the system to single-user mode. If this is a network system, you should probably notify network users first. This can be done with the `wall` command, which sends messages to all logged-in users.

Then, you can move to single-user mode, using the `init` command:

```
init 1
```

The Linux/UNIX command `grep` can be used to search for files, contents of files, and just about anything you may want to search for. The `grep` command is very flexible and quite popular with Linux users. For example, `grep -b 'search-text' /dev/partition > file.txt` will search for `'search-text'` in a given partition and output the results to file.txt.

You can also use this syntax:

```
grep -a -B[size before] -A[size after] 'text' /dev/[your_
partition] > file.txt
```

Linux run levels determine at what level the operating system is running. The `init` command allows you to change the run level (**TABLE 6-2**).

To recover a text file starting with the word *forensics* on /dev/sda2, you can try the following command:

```
# grep -i -a -B10 -A100 'forensics' /dev/sda2 > file.txt
```

TABLE 6-2 Using `init` to change run levels in Linux.

MODE	DIRECTORY	RUN LEVEL DESCRIPTION
0	/etc/rc.d/rc0.d	Halt
1	/etc/rc.d/rc1.d	Single-user mode
2	/etc/rc.d/rc2.d	Not used (user-definable)
3	/etc/rc.d/rc3.d	Full multiuser mode without GUI
4	/etc/rc.d/rc4.d	Not used (user-definable)
5	/etc/rc.d/rc5.d	Full multiuser mode with GUI
6	/etc/rc.d/rc6.d	Reboot

> **NOTE**
>
> If you are unfamiliar with Linux, some of these commands might seem odd to you. It is recommended that if you are unfamiliar with an operating system, you leave forensics for that system to someone who is better qualified. However, given the number of open-source forensic tools that work with Linux, it is advised that you learn at least the fundamentals of Linux.

In this case, `grep` is searching for this phrase, ignoring case, looking through binary files, and essentially looking to find the text, even if the file has a reference count of zero (i.e., has been deleted). Of course, if the file blocks have been overwritten enough times, then it will be unrecoverable.

The `extundelete` Utility

The `extundelete` utility (*http://extundelete.sourceforge.net/*) works with both Ext3 and Ext4 partitions. This product works via shell commands, and they are relatively simple. For example, if you want to restore all deleted files from the sda4 partition, just use this command:

```
extundelete /dev/sda4 --restore-all
```

The website documents all the various options you can utilize with this tool.

> **FYI**
>
> A few `grep` flags of use in these searches:
>
> -`i`—Ignore case distinctions in both the PATTERN and the input files; that is, it matches both uppercase and lowercase characters.
>
> -`a`—Process a binary file as if it were text.
>
> -`B`—Print number lines/size of leading context before matching lines.
>
> -`A`—Print number lines/size of trailing context after matching lines.

Scalpel

This tool works with both Linux and Mac OS, and it is even possible to compile the source code to work in Windows. However, it is easiest to install and work with in Linux. For example, if you are using Ubuntu Linux, this is all it takes to install:

```
sudo apt-get install scalpel
```

Next is some text editing—the configuration file is /etc/scalpel/scalpel.conf. You will find that everything has been commented out—uncomment the specific file format that you want to recover. For example, if you want to recover deleted Zip files, then you need to uncomment the .zip file section in scalpel.conf.

Next, in a terminal, run the following command:

```
sudo scalpel [device/directory/file name] -o [output directory]
```

The output directory, in which you want to store recovered files, should be empty before running Scalpel; otherwise, you will get an error.

Mac OS

Starting with OS X, Mac OS is actually based on FreeBSD, which is a UNIX clone, much like Linux. In fact, if you go to a terminal window in Mac OS, what you actually get is a shell where you can run UNIX shell commands. This means that some of the techniques that work for Linux also work with Mac OS. However, there are also some tools you can use that are made specifically for Mac OS.

You should also be aware that Mac OS has its own file systems. Today, Mac OS uses HFS+, or Hierarchical File System Plus, and APFS, or Apple File System. HFS+ replaced the earliest Macintosh/Mac OS file system called HFS a little over 20 years ago. APFS replaced HFS+ when Apple released its Mac OS High Sierra in 2017. You can get details on HFS and HFS+ at *https://www.techrepublic.com/article/apfs-vs-hfs-which-apple-filesystem-is-better/*.

MacKeeper

MacKeeper (*http://mackeeper.zeobit.com/recover-deleted-files-on-mac*) is a useful tool for recovering deleted files on an Apple computer. There is a free, fully functional trial version. Once you download and install this tool, you can recover files in just a few easy steps:

1. Open the Files Recovery tool. Select the volume where your lost files were and start the scan. This is shown in **FIGURE 6-13**.
2. Then select Undelete, shown in **FIGURE 6-14**.

That is it. This tool is remarkably simple to use.

Courtesy of ZeoBIT

FIGURE 6-13

MacKeeper Step 1.

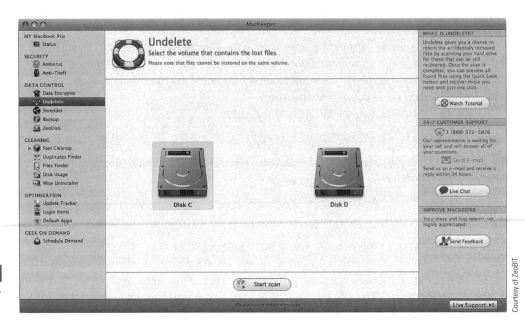

FIGURE 6-14

Files Recovery
tool.

There are certainly other tools that can recover Mac OS deleted files. You should experiment with various tools and find the ones that are most useful for you. As always, you
should be comfortable with a given operating system before attempting forensic analysis of
that operating system.

Recovering Information from Damaged Media

A wide variety of failures cause **physical damage** to storage media. Compact discs (CDs) can
have their metallic substrate or dye layer scratched. Hard disks can suffer any of several
mechanical failures, such as head crashes and failed motors. Tapes can simply break.
Physical damage always causes some data loss, and in many cases, the file system's logical
structures sustain damage as well. This results in logical damage that must be dealt with
before any files can be salvaged from the failed media.

> **FYI**
>
> A **clean room** is an environment that has a controlled level of contamination, such as from dust, microbes,
> and other particles.

End users can't repair most physical damage. Generally, they don't have the hardware
or technical expertise required to make physical repairs. Further, end users' attempts
to repair physical damage often increase the damage. Normally, you shouldn't attempt
to repair physical media. You may try a number of techniques to recover data from
damaged media. However, only organizations with specialized equipment and facilities,
such as clean rooms, should attempt repair or enhanced data recovery.

Physical Damage Recovery Techniques

Recovering data from a hard drive should start with the assumption that, unless the case is visibly damaged, the drive itself is still operable. Today's hard disks are built to be rugged enough to protect against damage. Thus, when presented with a "failed hard drive," use the following techniques to evaluate the drive and retrieve needed data:

1. Remove the drive from the system on which it is installed and connect it to a **test system**—a compatible system that is functional. Make the connection without installing the drive but only connecting the data and power cables.
2. Boot the test system from its own internal drive. Listen to the failed drive to determine whether the internal disks are spinning. If the disks are spinning, it generally means the disk has not experienced a catastrophic failure. Therefore, you can likely recover the data.
3. Determine whether the failed drive is recognized and can be installed as an additional disk on the test system. If the drive installs, copy all directories and files to a hard drive on the test system. If a drive fails on one system but installs on another, the drive may be usable. The drive may have failed because of a power supply failure, corruption of the operating system, malicious software, or some other reason. If you can operate the drive, run a virus check on the recovered data and test for directory and file integrity.
4. If the hard drive is not spinning or the test system does not recognize it, perform limited repair. You may be able to get the hard drive to start, and it may be recognized by the test system. If you can repair the drive, use specialized software to image all data bits from the failed drive to a recovery drive. Use the extracted raw image to reconstruct usable data. Try open-source tools such as DCFLdd (this is an enhanced version of the dd utility) to recover all data except for data in physically damaged sectors.
5. If necessary, send the device to data recovery specialists, who may be able to apply extraordinary recovery techniques.

It is possible that the data is deemed "lost," and there will be no increased loss if you attempt local repair and fail. If so, you can try the following:

1. Remove the printed circuit board and replace it with a matching circuit board from a known healthy drive.
2. Change the read/write head assembly with matching parts from a known healthy drive.
3. Remove the hard disk platters from the original drive and install them into a known healthy drive.

Recovering Data After Logical Damage

Logical damage to a file system is more common than physical damage. Logical damage may prevent the host operating system from mounting or using the file system. Power outages can cause logical damage, preventing file system structures from completely writing information from memory to the storage medium. Even turning off a machine while it is booting or shutting down can lead to logical damage. Errors in hardware controllers—especially RAID (redundant array of inexpensive disks) controllers—and drivers and system crashes can have the same effect.

Logical damage can cause a variety of problems, such as system crashes or actual data loss. It can result in intermittent failures. It can also trigger other strange behavior, such as infinitely recursing directories and drives reporting negative free space remaining. Some programs can correct the inconsistencies that result from logical damage. Most operating systems provide a basic repair tool for their native file systems. Microsoft Windows has chkdsk, for example; Linux comes with the fsck utility; and Mac OS provides Disk Utility. A number of companies have developed products to resolve logical file system errors, such as the Sleuth Kit (*http://www.sleuthkit.org*). Third-party products may be able to recover data even when the operating system's repair utility doesn't recognize the disk. TestDisk (*http://www.cgsecurity.org/wiki/TestDisk*) is one example. It can recover lost partitions and reconstruct corrupted partition tables.

Preventing Logical Damage

Journaling file systems, such as NTFS 5.0 and Ext3, help to reduce the incidence of logical damage. In the event of system failure, you can roll these file systems back to a consistent or stable state. The information most likely to be lost will be in the drive's cache at the time of the system failure.

Using a consistency checker should be a routine part of system maintenance. A consistency checker protects against file system software bugs and storage hardware design incompatibilities. For example, a disk controller may report that file system structures have been saved to disk, but the data is actually still in the write cache. If the computer loses power while this data is in the cache, the file system may be left in an inconsistent or unstable state. To avoid this problem, use hardware that does not report the data as written until it actually is written. Another solution is to use disk controllers with battery backups. When the power is restored after an outage, the pending data is written to disk. For greater protection, use a system battery backup to provide power long enough to shut down the system safely.

Logical Damage Recovery Techniques

Two techniques are common for recovering data after logical damage: consistency checking and zero-knowledge analysis. Use these techniques to either repair or work around most logical damage. However, applying data recovery software doesn't guarantee that no data loss will occur. For example, when two files claim to share the same allocation unit, one of the files is almost certain to lose data.

Consistency Checking

Consistency checking involves scanning a disk's logical structure and ensuring that it is consistent with its specifications. For instance, in most file systems, a directory must have at least two entries: a dot (.) entry that points to itself and a dot-dot (..) entry that points to its parent. A file system repair program reads each directory to ensure that these entries exist and point to the correct directories. If they do not, the program displays an error message, and you can correct the problem. Both chkdsk and fsck work in this fashion. However, consistency checking has two major problems:

- A consistency check can fail if the file system is highly damaged. In this case, the repair program may crash, or it may believe the drive has an invalid file system.

- The chkdsk utility might automatically delete data files if the files are out of place or unexplainable. The utility does this to ensure that the operating system can run properly. However, the deleted files may be important and irreplaceable user files.

The same type of problem occurs with system restore disks that restore the operating system by removing the previous installation. Avoid this problem by installing the operating system on a separate partition from the user data.

Zero-Knowledge Analysis

Zero-knowledge analysis is the second technique for file system repair. With zero-knowledge analysis, few assumptions are made about the state of the file system. The file system is rebuilt from scratch using knowledge of an undamaged file system structure. In this process, scan the drive of the affected computer, noting all file system structures and possible file boundaries. Then match the results to the specifications of a working file system.

Zero-knowledge analysis is usually much slower than consistency checking. You can use it, however, to recover data even when the logical structures are almost completely destroyed. This technique generally does not repair the damaged file system but allows you to extract the data to another storage device.

File Carving

When a file is only partially recovered, regardless of the file system, you can use file carving to attempt to recover the file. One popular file carving tool is Scalpel, which was discussed previously in this chapter. File carving, sometimes just called "carving," is often used to recover data from a disk where there has been some damage or where the file itself is corrupt. Regardless of the name used, the purpose is to extract the data from a single file from the larger set of data—that is, the entire disk or partition. This is a common method of data recovery, particularly when the file metadata has been damaged.

Most file carving utilities operate by looking for file headers and/or footers, and then pulling out the data that is found between these two boundaries.

We previously discussed Scalpel as a possible file carving tool; another is carver-recovery, which is a free tool that also includes the source code for you to modify if you wish. It contains several utilities. The carver-recovery.exe simply allows you to select a drive image, and it will attempt to recover files. This is a broad-based tool for attempting to recover from an entire drive or partition.

Obviously, to effectively use file carving, one needs to be familiar with file headers and footers. It is beyond the scope of this book to discuss all file headers, but the hexadecimal values for some common files are shown here:

header   footer

	header	footer
JPEG	FF D8	FF D9
BMP	42 4D	
EXE	4D 5A	
GIF	47 49	
MP3	49 44	

PDF	25 50
ZIP	50 4B
PNG	89 50
WAV	52 49
AVI	52 49

CHAPTER SUMMARY

In this chapter, you learned the essentials of file recovery in the three major operating systems as well as different storage media. The most attention was given to Windows due to how widely it is used. It is important that you be comfortable with these undeletion techniques. You should also be familiar with how to utilize any undeletion functionality in your preferred forensic toolkit (such as EnCase or Forensic Toolkit).

KEY CONCEPTS AND TERMS

Clean room	Inode	Test system
Consistency checking	Logical damage	Zero-knowledge analysis
grep	Physical damage	

CHAPTER 6 ASSESSMENT

1. Which of the following is the Linux equivalent of a shortcut?

A. Hard link
B. Symbolic link
C. Partial link
D. Faux link

2. What file system does Windows 10 use?

A. FAT
B. FAT32
C. NTFS
D. HPFS

3. What file system does Mac OS use?

A. HPFS
B. HFS+
C. NTFS
D. EXT3

4. Why can you undelete files in Windows 7?

A. Nothing is deleted; it is just removed from MFT.
B. Nothing is deleted; it is just removed from FAT.
C. Fragments might exist, even though the file is deleted.
D. You cannot.

References

1. Bunting, S. (2012). *EnCE: EnCAse Computer Forensics: The Official EnCase Certified Examiner Study Guide*, 3rd ed. Indianapolis, IN: John Wiley & Sons.

2. International Council of Electronic Commerce Consultants (EC-Council). (2009). *Computer Forensics: Hard Disk and Operating Systems*. Boston, MA: Cengage Learning.

3. Sammons, J. (2012). *The Basics of Digital Forensics: The Primer for Getting Started in Digital Forensics*. Rockland, MA: Syngress Publishing.

Incident Response

I N THIS CHAPTER, you will learn about the relationship between incident response and forensics. When an incident occurs, be it a disaster or an intrusion, forensics may be the best method to discover what went wrong, and thus work to avoid it recurring. Forensics techniques also provide methods for recovering data in the event of a disaster. And it is always possible that the disaster was caused by a criminal act, leading to criminal prosecution, or an act of negligence that would warrant civil litigation.

It is common today to refer to digital forensics as digital forensics and incident response (DFIR). Consider a virus outbreak on a corporate network. It is quite possible that the actual creator of the virus will never be identified and prosecuted. However, it is important to know the extent of the virus's damage and how it entered the network. As an example, as early as 2015, there was a variant of the ransomware CryptoWall that not only encrypted files for ransom, but also placed spyware on the infected machine. Any incident response team that simply focused on getting the files unencrypted but did not perform forensic analysis of at least a few infected machines would not have been aware of the spyware. If any incident response does not include any forensics, it is entirely possible that you won't discover the secondary effect of any incident.

Some might object to using disaster recovery and incident response together. However, this is perfectly reasonable. Consider, what is a disaster? What is an incident? An incident is any negative event. Whether or not it is a disaster is a function of both how extensive the incident is and the perspective of the person involved. As an example, suppose you own a jewelry store. All of your business takes place in person. But you do have a website for marketing purposes. If that website is down for an entire day, it is an incident, but you probably don't consider it a disaster. However, imagine that instead you run an online sports memorabilia website. Your website is down for one full day, and it is a week before Christmas. That same incident, in a different context, has become a disaster. Differentiating between *incident* and *disaster* is really an argument over semantics. You will approach any incident the same way you might approach a disaster; you just may abbreviate some steps.

Chapter 7 Topics

This chapter covers the following concepts and topics:

- Understanding disaster recovery
- Preserving evidence
- Adding forensics to the disaster recovery plan

Chapter 7 Goals

When you complete this chapter, you will be able to:

- Understand key disaster recovery terms such as BIA, MTD, BCP, and DRP
- Understand the phases of incident response
- Be able to integrate forensics into an incident response plan

Disaster Recovery

Disaster recovery, business continuity, and forensics have become closely related topics. You may think forensics only applies to criminal activities, and it often does. However, after an information technology–related disaster, forensic techniques may be the best method for determining what caused the disaster and avoiding it in the future. It is also possible that a disaster was instigated by the commission of a cybercrime, in which case the need for forensics is clear.

The forensics process really begins once an incident has been discovered, but it does not get fully under way until after the disaster or incident is contained. However, before you examine the forensic process for disasters, it would be a good idea to start with a basic understanding of disaster recovery. Containment is always the first priority in incident response. However, one must be careful not to damage any potential forensic evidence.

All organizations must plan for the possibility of some disaster occurring that disrupts normal operations. When narrowing the focus to just computer-related operations, there are a number of possibilities to consider. They include equipment failure, computer viruses, malicious hacking, insider data theft, and more. Of course, the usual disasters still apply, such as:

- Fire
- Flood
- Hurricane
- Tornado

However, those typically do not involve computer forensics. So for the purposes of this chapter, we will narrow our focus to only computer disasters, such as:

- Hard drive failure
- Network outage
- Malware infection
- Data theft or deletion
- Intrusion

Each of these activities can disrupt normal operations for the organization's computer systems, and therefore constitute a disaster. As was mentioned in the introduction, how you view the severity each of these will depend greatly on context. There are actually two plans most organizations have for responding to such disaster: the **Business Continuity Plan (BCP)** and the **Disaster Recovery Plan (DRP)**. A BCP is focused on keeping the organization functioning as well as possible until a full recovery can be made. A DRP is focused on executing a full recovery to normal operations. For example, consider a scenario where a virus takes the main web server offline. A BCP would be concerned about what can be done to get minimal operations going until such time as the organization can be returned to full functionality—perhaps temporarily using an old server, one that may not be as robust but could provide minimal functionality. A DRP is focused on actually returning the organization to full functionality. In the scenario just described, this would be a full web server, equivalent to the failed server, back online and running at full capacity.

There are some federal standards for BCPs.

ISO 27001

ISO 27001 outlines requirements for information security management systems. This standard was first released in 2005 and revised in 2014. There was an update for Europe only in 2017 to meet the European Union's General Data Protection Regulation requirements. ISO 27001 is a very broad standard covering information security management in general. Section 14 addresses business continuity management.

NIST 800-34

This standard is entitled *Contingency Planning Guide for Information Technology Systems*—thus it is clearly related to business continuity and disaster recovery. This plan introduces some additional acronyms such as continuity of operations plan (COOP), critical infrastructure protection (CIP), and information system contingency plan (ISCP). COOP is focused solely on identifying mission-essential functions (MEF) and being able to sustain those for 30 days. NIST 800-34 defines CIP as "critical infrastructure and key resources (CIKR) [which] are those components of the national infrastructure that are deemed so vital that their loss would have a debilitating effect on the safety, security, economy, and/or health of the United States."[1] ICSP is concerned with assessment and recovery of a system following some disruption. The plan includes a seven-step process for BCP and DRP projects. Those seven steps are:

1. **Develop the contingency planning policy statement**. A formal policy provides the authority and guidance necessary to develop an effective contingency plan.
2. **Conduct the business impact analysis (BIA)**. The BIA is used to identify and prioritize information systems and components critical to supporting the organization's mission/business functions.
3. **Identify preventive controls**. Measures taken to reduce the effects of system disruptions can increase system availability and reduce contingency life-cycle costs.
4. **Create contingency strategies**. Thorough strategies ensure that the system may be recovered quickly and effectively following a disruption.
5. **Develop an information system contingency plan**. The contingency plan should contain detailed guidance and procedures for restoring a system based the system's security impact level and recovery requirements.
6. **Plan testing and training**. Ensure the BCP and DRP are tested and staff are trained in these plans.
7. **Plan maintenance**. The plan should updated frequently to remain current with system and organizational changes.

NFPA 1600

This is formally titled *Standard on Disaster/Emergency Management and Business Continuity Programs.* It was created by the U.S. National Fire Protection Association. The focus is clearly on responding to fire-related incidents. These typically won't involve digital forensics.

These standards provide a good overview of what should be covered in any BCP, and some (like NIST 800-34) are also applicable to DRPs. You should certainly consider reviewing these standards at some point in your career. For the purposes of forensic examination, you don't need to be an expert in disaster recovery; just a basic overview of the process is sufficient. The essential steps are outlined here.

Business Impact Analysis

Business impact analysis (BIA) is a process whereby the disaster recovery team contemplates likely disasters and what the impact each would have on the organization. For example, a company that ships goods to retail stores but does not sell directly to the public might be slightly impacted if its web server was down for a day. A company that sells directly to the public both in-store and online would be moderately impacted by such an outage. But a completely e-commerce company, one that only sells products online, would be severely impacted.

Usually, some sort of table is created listing the various disasters being planned for and the impact they would have on the organization. In more complex scenarios, the organization may be broken down into subsections, and the impact of each disaster on each piece of the organization is rated. Whether a plan goes into great detail or not, one item that must be considered is the **maximum tolerable downtime (MTD)**. That is how long can the system(s) be down before it is impossible for the organization to recover. Imagine your favorite e-commerce site goes down. You may be a loyal customer and wait for it to come back up. But as time goes on, fewer and fewer customers wait, and more money is lost, until it may reach a point that the company simply cannot recover. If the disaster recovery team knows the MTD for the organization as well as for portions of the organization, they can then prioritize the recovery plan.

Two other terms are related to maximum tolerable downtime. One is **mean time to repair (MTTR)**, which is sometimes called *mean time to recover*. This is the average time it takes to repair an item. The second term is **mean time to failure (MTTF)**. How long, on average, is it before a given device is likely to fail through normal use? These are important questions to answer when performing a BIA. If an organization cannot be without a given piece of equipment more than 14 days and still recover (that is, the MTD = 14 days), yet the MTTR is 7 days, that means you have only 7 days after a disaster to initiate repairs or the organization will be unable to recover.

MTD simply means how long a given system can be down without causing substantial long-term harm to the organization. With some disasters or incidents, MTD won't be an issue. For example, a hard drive failing on a server that is part of a cluster is unlikely to include the issue of MTD. The cluster has data duplicated, and one hard drive failing won't dramatically affect the organization. However, with respect to determining a computer MTD, there are a number of factors to take into account. One is the importance of that system to the organization. There are also some related numbers that need to be calculated. One of those is the **recovery point objective (RPO)**. That refers to how much data will be lost. Let's assume you do a backup of a critical database every hour. The most data that could be lost in a database failure is 59 minutes' worth. Is that a risk your organization can accept? Or is that too much? This is clearly related to the MTD. Another number is **recovery time objective (RTO)**. When a system is down, what is the target time to have it back up and running? Clearly, that RTO must be less than the MTD.

There are a few calculations commonly used in BIAs. The first is **single loss expectency (SLE)**. This is calculated by multiplying the asset value times the exposure factor. This will make more sense with an example. Let us assume you have an e-commerce site that generates $10,000 per week. That is the asset value. Now, assume that if it is hit by a denial-of-service (DoS) attack, you can expect it to be down one full day (I am using easy numbers to make the math simple). Well, that is an exposure factor of 1/7, or about 0.142. So the calculation becomes:

$$SLE = AV * EF$$

or

$$SLE = \$10,000 * 0.142$$

$$SLE = \$1,428.57$$

Next, you need to determine the **annualized loss expectancy (ALE)**. Let's suppose that, based on past incident reports and statistics for businesses similar to yours, you expect three DoS attacks per year. That would be the **annual rate of occurrence (ARO)**, so your formula is now:

ALE = ARO * SLE

or

ALE = 3 * $1,428.57

ALE = $4,285.71

These numbers are used to calculate how much you should spend on mitigating the attack. Let us further assume that a vendor has a product that is guaranteed to reduce DoS attacks by 90%. That should roughly make your ALE only 10% of what it has been, or $428.57. That sounds like a wonderful deal. But what if the product costs $5,000 per year to license? That is more than your ALE. You can see how SLE and ALE help you to quantify loss and then how to allocate resources to mitigate losses.

Describing the Incident

It is necessary to describe any incident in order to analyze it. The description is not an ad hoc or subjective process. There are specific measurements that will help to describe any incident and will facilitate your forensic analysis.

Common Vulnerability Scoring System

A common method for scoring system vulnerabilities is the Common Vulnerability Scoring System (CVSS). The CVSS is widely used to classify vulnerabilities. This is an open industry standard that allows for the scoring of vulnerabilities based on severity. When responding to an incident, it is very helpful to describe the vulnerabilities that lead to the incident. When using CVSS, there are three groups of metrics: base, temporal, and environmental. The base group describes the basic characteristics of the vulnerability that are not determined by time (temporal) or environment. The metrics in this group are Attack Vector, Attack Complexity, Privileges Required, User Interaction, Scope, Confidentiality Impact, Integrity Impact, and Availability Impact.

The Attack Vector metric can be Network (N), Adjacent (A), Local (L), or Physical (P). Attack Complexity can be None (N), Low (L), or High (H). User Interaction can be None (N) or Required (R). The Scope metric captures whether a vulnerability in one vulnerable component impacts resources in components beyond its security scope. Its values can be Unchanged (U) or Changed (C). The Impact metrics (Confidentiality, Availability, or Integrity) are all rated as High (H), Low (L), or None (N). This allows you to understand the nature of vulnerabilities that facilitated the incident in question. It should be noted that CVSS v3.x introduced a new level, that of Critical, so the options are now Low, Medium, High, and Critical.

The Temporal Metric Group has three metrics: Exploit Code Maturity, Remediation Level, and Report Confidence. The Environmental Metric Group has four metrics: Modified Base Metrics, Confidentiality Requirement, Integrity Requirement, and Availability Requirement.

Exploit Code Maturity measures the likelihood of the vulnerability being attacked and is typically based on the current state of exploit techniques, exploit code availability, or active, "in-the-wild" exploitation. The possible ratings are Not Defined (X), High (H), Functional (F),

Proof of Concept (P), and Unproven (U). The Remediation Level metric can be Not Defined (X), Unavailable (U), Workaround (W), Temporary Fix (T), or Official Fix (O). The Report Confidence metric indicates how confident we are in the details of the vulnerability. Its value can be Not Defined (X), Confirmed (C), Reasonable (R), or Unknown (U).

The values for the various metrics are summarized in **TABLE 7-1**.

CVSS scoring is often represented as a string such as:

```
CVSS:3.1/S:U/AV:N/AC:L/PR:H/UI:N/C:L/I:L/A:N/E:F/RL:X
```

TABLE 7-1 CVSS.

METRIC GROUP	METRIC NAME (AND ABBREVIATED FORM)	POSSIBLE VALUES	MANDATORY?
Base	Attack Vector (AV)	[N, A, L, P]	Yes
	Attack Complexity (AC)	[L, H]	Yes
	Privileges Required (PR)	[N, L, H]	Yes
	User Interaction (UI)	[N, R]	Yes
	Scope (S)	[U, C]	Yes
	Confidentiality (C)	[H, L, N]	Yes
	Integrity (I)	[H, L, N]	Yes
	Availability (A)	[H, L, N]	Yes
Temporal	Exploit Code Maturity (E)	[X, H, F, P, U]	No
	Remediation Level (RL)	[X, U, W, T, O]	No
	Report Confidence (RC)	[X, C, R, U]	No
Environmental	Confidentiality Requirement (CR)	[X, H, M, L]	No
	Integrity Requirement (IR)	[X, H, M, L]	No
	Availability Requirement (AR)	[X, H, M, L]	No
	Modified Attack Vector (MAV)	[X, N, A, L, P]	No
	Modified Attack Complexity (MAC)	[X, L, H]	No
	Modified Privileges Required (MPR)	[X, N, L, H]	No
	Modified User Interaction (MUI)	[X, N, R]	No
	Modified Scope (MS)	[X, U, C]	No
	Modified Confidentiality (MC)	[X, N, L, H]	No
	Modified Integrity (MI)	[X, N, L, H]	No
	Modified Availability (MA)	[X, N, L, H]	No

Understanding the vulnerabilities that a network faces and quantifying the threat they pose is important for incident response. CVSS is often used before an attack, to rank vulnerabilities in risk assessment. But it is also useful in the later stages of incident response to quantify what has occurred.

DREAD

DREAD is an acronym for Damage Potential, Reproducibility, Exploitability, Affected Users, and Discoverability. It is a mnemonic for risk rating using five categories. How much damage would an attack cause? In the case of incident response, the question is, how much damage *did* the attack cause? How easy is it for an attacker to reproduce this attack? How much effort is required to execute the attack? How many users will be impacted? And finally, how easy is it to discover the threat? DREAD asks what the likelihood of an attack is and what damage it would cause. DREAD is an effective model for evaluating the impact of an attack.

RMON

The Remote Network MONitoring (RMON) was developed by the Internet Engineering Task Force (IETF) in order to support network monitoring and protocol analysis. This might not seem like a useful tool for incident response, but it can be. It provides a standardized method of classifying network traffic. RMON is a standard monitoring specification that allows various network monitors to exchange network monitoring data.

The original version of RMON had 10 groups:

1. **Statistics**: real-time LAN statistics, e.g., utilization, collisions, CRC errors
2. **History**: history of selected statistics
3. **Alarm**: definitions for RMON SNMP traps to be set when statistics exceed defined thresholds
4. **Hosts**: host-specific LAN statistics, e.g., bytes sent/received, frames sent/received
5. **Hosts top N**: record of N most active connections over a given time period
6. **Matrix**: the sent–received traffic matrix between systems
7. **Filter**: defines packet data patterns of interest, e.g., MAC address or TCP port
8. **Capture**: collect and forward packets matching the Filter
9. **Event**: send alerts (SNMP traps) for the Alarm group
10. **Token Ring**: extensions specific to Token Ring

The original RMON was defined by RFC 2819. RMON2 was defined in RFC 4502. There have been modifications of RMON for specialized networks. For example, Remote Network Monitoring Management Information Base for High Capacity Networks, or HCRMON, was defined in RFC 3272. Remote Network Monitoring MIB Extensions for Switched Network, or SIMON, was defined in RFC 2613. Using this technique allows you to perform a "postmortem" analysis on network logs to determine when an attack began—and perhaps identify its source.

Mean Squared Deviation

The mean squared deviation (MSD) formula is relatively simple and provides insight into how any system deviates from expectations. This is sometimes referred to as the *mean squared error*. It essentially takes the square of the errors or deviations from expected/desired outcomes. This formula is shown in **FIGURE 7-1**.

In Figure 7-1, y_i is the actual value and T is the target value. This is commonly used in many engineering disciplines. The metric is a positive integer. Interpreting it is quite simple: The closer to zero the MSD is, the more reliable the system in question is. It is sometimes the case that one takes the square root of the mean squared error, yielding the root mean squared deviation (or root mean squared error). This formula can also be used to provide a metric of the impact an incident had on a given system. How far did the system deviate from norm?

Mean Percentage Error

Closely related to the MSD is the mean percentage error (MPE) formula. The MPE is the arithmetic mean of errors from modeling. This metric compares expected values to actual values and calculates mean error. An error is defined as any deviation from the planned or expected value. This is critical in modeling, as it can be used to evaluate the efficacy of the model itself. The MPE formula is shown in **FIGURE 7-2**.

In Figure 7-2, *n* is the number of different times for which the variable is forecast; *at* is the actual value of the quantity being forecast; and *ft* is the forecast.

Essentially, this metric is describing the difference between expected values and the actual value. This is an effective way to measure the impact of an incident.

Ishikawa Diagram

Ishikawa diagrams are a commonly used engineering tool in failure mode and effects analysis (FMEA) in engineering. These are sometimes called "fish diagrams" because the defect is the fish's head and the issues leading to the defect are branches or fish bones. A generic example of how to create an Ishikawa diagram is shown in **FIGURE 7-3**.

This can be effective in tracing the root cause of an incident. Root cause analysis is an important aspect of incident response.

$$MSD = \frac{1}{n} \sum_{i=2}^{n} (y_i - T)^2$$

FIGURE 7-1

Mean square deviation formula.

FIGURE 7-2

Mean percentage error
formula.

$$MPE = \frac{100\%}{n} \sum_{t=1}^{n} \frac{a_t - f_t}{a_t}$$

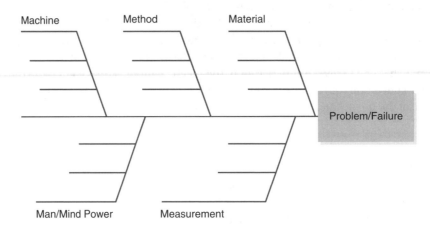

FIGURE 7-3

Ishikawa diagram.

The Recovery Plan

The recovery plan consists of two parts. The ultimate goal is a complete recovery, and this is outlined in the disaster recovery plan. But unless that DRP is going to get the organization back up to full capacity within 24 hours or less, there will also be a need for a BCP, a plan for how to get at least minimal functionality until full recovery is accomplished. Both plans are based on the priorities that were established during the BIA phase.

Even though the DRP and the BCP don't have exactly the same goals, they do require the same questions to be asked:

- Do you have alternate equipment identified?
- If needed, do you have alternate facilities identified?
- Is there a mechanism in place for contacting employees, vendors, customers, etc., even if the primary means of communication are down?
- Is there offsite backup of the data?
- Can that backup be readily retrieved and restored?

When considering backups, and restoring backups, you need to think about what type of backups you have. While database administrators may use a number of different types of data backups, from a security point of view, there are three primary backup types we are concerned with:

Types of backups

- **Full**—all changes
- **Differential**—all changes since last full backup
- **Incremental**—all changes since last backup of any type

If you did a full backup, then just restore the last backup. However, if the backup strategy includes differential or incremental backups, and it probably will, then there will be additional backup data to restore.

There is another type of backup that is becoming more popular, called hierarchical storage management (HSM). HSM provides continuous online backup by using optical or tape "jukeboxes." It appears as an infinite disk to the system, and can be configured to provide the closest version of an available real-time backup.

> **NOTE**
>
> Even though more organizations are going to electronic backups, it is important to consider backup media rotation. Even with electronic backup, you don't have infinite storage and will eventually have to overwrite something. This necessitates overwriting and reusing media. There are two main approaches to this. One is the Tower of Hanoi, which is fairly complicated and thus rarely used. The more common approach is the Grandfather–Father–Son. To illustrate this, consider a server using traditional tape backup, which is backed up daily. Each daily backup is the son. At the end of the week, a weekly backup is made. That weekly backup is the father. Now the daily backups begin to be reused. At the end of the month, there is a monthly backup made. That is the grandfather, and then the weekly backups can begin to be reused. This is a simple and widely used system to reuse backup media.

The Post Recovery Follow-Up

Different disaster recovery textbooks will label this differently, but the content is the same: Now that the disaster is over and the organization has recovered, you have to find out what happened and why. This is where forensics comes into play. This phase is not necessarily about assigning blame; it is about discovering if the disaster was caused by some weakness in the system. That could be an act of negligence by an individual, or it could be a gap in policy. But if the root cause is not discovered and addressed, the chances of it occurring again are significant.

Incident Response

When an incident occurs, even if it does not rise to the level of a disaster, there needs to be an organized response. For example, if a single workstation is infected with a virus, this probably does not constitute a disaster. But if it is not responded to quickly, it may grow into a disaster as the virus spreads, so proper incident response is important.

There are some key steps that every incident response plan must include. These are outlined in this section. You will also find some sources refer to the six phases of incident response; others will list five or seven phases. The issue is not how finely you break out the steps, but that all necessary steps are done, and done at the appropriate time.

Detection

Obviously, you have to detect the incident before you can respond. However, at this initial stage, you don't have time to conduct a detailed analysis. You need to simply detect there is an incident, its basic nature, and what systems are affected, then go to containment. As an example, if you detect malware, then your initial goal is just to determine affected systems and contain them. Then you can go back and discover more details such as the type of malware, the damage it caused, how it got on the network, etc. This does not mean you won't do analysis. You absolutely will. But if you spend time here on analysis, the incident is still ongoing. If it is malware, the malware is still spreading.

Containment

The first step in the response is always to limit the incident. This means keeping it from impacting more systems. In the case of a virus, the goal is clear: Keep the virus from spreading. It is probably a good idea to have a policy in place that instructs users to disconnect their computer from the network, then call tech support, if they suspect they have a virus. This contains the virus and prevents it from spreading further.

Other incidents may not have such a clear containment path. For example, if there is an intruder getting into the web server, how is that contained? First, the web server itself is isolated from the rest of the network. Then you seek to prevent further intrusion. This can be done by changing passwords throughout the organization, on the assumption that the intruder might have compromised passwords.

While the specifics of containment might vary, the goal does not: Limit the spread of whatever the incident is, as much as possible. And this phase must occur before any others. It is vital that the incident's effects not spread further. This must be addressed before you attempt to eradicate the threat.

Eradication

Once the incident is contained, the next step is to eradicate the problem. In the case of malware, the issue is to remove the malware. In some cases, anti-malware tools such as Norton, Bit Defender, McAfee, Kapersky, Windows Defender, or AVG can remove the malware. In other cases, the IT staff will need to manually remove the malware.

Other attacks are not so clear. For example, if the incident is an intruder infiltrating the network via an SQL injection, what does eradication entail? The first step is to fix whatever vulnerability allowed the intruder to infiltrate the network. In the case of SQL injection, it would involve correcting the flaws in the web page that allowed this attack to occur.

Regardless of the particular incident, eradication needs to be thorough. That means a comprehensive examination of what occurred and how far it reached. It is imperative to ensure that the issue is completely addressed.

This is the stage at which forensics must begin. If the incident is simply eradicated, it is likely that evidence will be eradicated. It is imperative that you begin collecting evidence prior to eradicating the incident. This may involve performing the forensic investigation prior to any eradication steps taking place. In some cases, it is just not possible to perform a full forensic investigation while keeping the systems on hold. In that case, simply image the drives involved so that a forensic investigation can be conducted at a later time.

Recovery

Recovery involves returning the affected systems to normal status. In the case of malware, that means ensuring the system is back in full working order with absolutely no presence of the malware. In many cases, this will involve restoring software and data from a backup source that has been verified to be free from the malware infection.

Follow-Up

The follow-up phase is another stage at which forensics plays a critical role. The IT team must determine how this incident occurred and what steps can be taken to keep this type of incident from reoccurring. Clearly, those decisions cannot be made without the input from the forensic examination. This is when we return to the analysis that we only briefly touched on in the detection phase. Now we have the time to carefully analyze and learn from the incident.

One part of the follow-up is classifying the incident. There are several standards that require the incidents be reported to some authority, and those reports require some description and classification. As an example, the payment card industry requires its merchants to report security incidents involving cardholder data. This report should be issued whenever a breach is detected that violates the Payment Card Industry Data Security Standard (PCI DSS). The following are examples of the sorts of things that PCI identifies as methods to gain unauthorized access to systems and sensitive information:

> **NOTE**
>
> This is one reason why corporations are becoming more interested in their IT security team including personnel with forensics training. Even if the goal is not to collect evidence for legal proceedings, the same forensics techniques can be utilized to determine the exact cause and extent of a computer security breach. And that information is absolutely essential for preventing future incidents.

- **SQL injection**—A technique that inserts modified SQL (Structured Query Language) into a website. This attack depends on the website allowing unfiltered input.
- **Malicious code or malware**—Programs (such as viruses, worms, Trojan horses, back doors, and spyware) added to a system without a user's knowledge. These programs can damage systems, delete files, encrypt files and demand ransom, or exfiltrate confidential data.
- **Insecure remote access**—Attacks gaining access through remote services. These vulnerabilities can allow an attacker to gain access to your network.
- **Insecure wireless**—Attacks accessing the network through wireless points of entry. Insecure wireless can allow an attacker to compromise servers, workstations, wireless security cameras, and even IoT devices.

Another example is the Federal Information Security Management Act (FISMA). The federal government uses the National Institute of Standards and Technology (NIST) Special Publication 800-61. This publication classifies incidents into the following events on a system or network:

- **Malicious code**—This is a broad category for all code that causes some harm, including computer viruses, Trojan horses, and spyware.
- **Denial of service**—An attacker crafting packets to cause networks and/or computers to crash.
- **Unauthorized access**—An exploit to gain access.
- **Inappropriate usage**—Any use of the computer that violates company policies. This can also facilitate other attacks. For example, visiting websites that are not allowed or inserting portable USB storage that is not approved can lead to malware getting onto the system.

It is important that during the follow-up phase of incident response, you accurately and completely document the nature of the attack. This will be useful in investigation as well as in taking steps to mitigate this threat in the future.

Preserving Evidence

An event is any observable occurrence within a system or network. This includes any activity on the network, such as when a user accesses files on a server or when a firewall blocks network traffic. Adverse events are events with a negative result or negative consequences. Attacks on systems are adverse events. Adverse events in this book are events that are computer security–related. They are not events caused by factors such as natural disasters and power failures.

A computer security incident is any event that violates an organization's security policies. This includes computer security policies, acceptable use policies, and standard security practices. The following are examples of computer security incidents:

- **Denial-of-service (DoS) attacks**—A DoS attack could result from an attacker sending specially crafted packets to a web server that cause it to crash. It could also result from an attacker directing hundreds of external compromised workstations to send many Internet Control Message Protocol (ICMP) requests to an organization's network. When the attack is from multiple sources, you refer to it as a distributed DoS (DDoS) attack.
- **Malicious code**—Malicious software, or malware, is any malicious code, such as viruses, worms, and Trojans. For example, a worm uses open file shares to quickly infect hundreds of systems in an organization. Employees may innocently introduce viruses into a network from their home computer on USB thumb drives. When they plug the USB drive into the work computer, the virus infects it.
- **Unauthorized access**—This includes any time someone accesses files they shouldn't be able to access. The access can be from someone within the organization, such as an employee, or from an external attacker. If you don't lock down shared files with appropriate permissions, users may stumble upon data they shouldn't see. If you don't secure databases used by web servers, attackers may be able to access sensitive customer data, such as credit card information, from anywhere on the internet.
- **Inappropriate usage**—Inappropriate usage could take a number of forms. For example, a user might provide illegal copies of software to others through peer-to-peer (P2P) file-sharing services. This same P2P software could cause data leakage resulting in private

Matching on test

data from the user's computer being shared on the internet to anyone else using the same P2P software. Or a person might threaten another person through email.

Regardless of the specifics of the incident, it is critical that the evidence be preserved. Throughout this book, evidence preservation has been discussed. However, this topic takes on a new perspective in the case of incident response. The usual emphasis for corporate disaster recovery is simply a return to normal operations as soon as possible. Frequently, this is done at the expense of preserving forensic evidence. This can lead to many problems.

First and foremost, failure to preserve forensic information will prevent the IT team from effectively evaluating the cause of the incident and adjusting company policies and procedures to reduce the risk of such an incident being repeated. Even if the incident does not involve a crime, or the company simply does not wish to prosecute, forensic data plays an integral part in preventing future incidents.

There are also situations where the organization may not have initially thought a crime was committed, but further investigation reveals that a criminal act occurred. For example, a hard drive crash might initially be thought to be a normal failure of the device, but further examination uncovers malware that caused the hard drive to fail much sooner than it should have. If proper forensic procedures have not been followed, it may be impossible to prosecute or pursue civil litigation.

> **NOTE**
>
> The issue of preserving evidence is very much the same as with non-computer crimes. Imagine that a person was murdered in a hotel room. What if the hotel focused only on returning the room to normal use, and immediately thoroughly cleaned the room and rented it to a new guest? This would destroy all physical evidence and make identifying and prosecuting the murderer extremely difficult. Unfortunately, an analogous situation frequently occurs with IT systems after a computer breach. In the haste to restore the systems to normal operations, the evidence is often destroyed.

Adding Forensics to Incident Response

Realizing the importance of forensics in incident response is an important first step. But this realization still leaves the question of how to implement proper forensics procedures. There are specific steps that an IT department can take to intertwine forensic techniques with the company's incident response policies.

Forensic Resources

The first step is to identify forensic resources that the organization can utilize in case of an incident. No amount of policy changes will be effective if the company does not have access to forensically trained individuals. One approach an organization can take is to get basic forensics training for its own IT security staff. Many college computer-related degrees now include forensics courses, and most security-related degrees include at least an introductory forensics course. If no one on the company's IT security staff has had such training, it may be helpful to send staff members to be trained in computer forensics, perhaps to obtain one of the major forensics certifications.

Another option the organization can pursue is to identify an outside party that can respond to incidents with forensically trained personnel. In this case, part of incident planning would involve ensuring there is an agreement in place with a reliable forensics company or individual consultant. If this is the option an organization wishes to pursue, it is critical to ensure that the organization identified has both an appropriate level of competency and the necessary resources to respond to incidents.

Forensics and Policy

Once appropriate forensic resources have been identified, forensic methodology must be interwoven into the incident response policy for the organization. This means that all policies regarding disaster recovery and incident response will need to be updated.

The purpose of updating policies is to ensure that evidence is not destroyed in the process of recovering from an incident or disaster. For example, the policy regarding how to handle a malware infection would be modified so that as soon as the infection was contained, at least one infected machine would be imaged for forensic evidence, prior to the eradication of the malware. In the case of external intrusions, the policies would be changed to preserve all logs prior to full recovery.

It is likely that even if the IT security staff are not trained specifically in forensics, they have some basic knowledge of the field. The reason is that many security textbooks now include at least a chapter on basic forensics. Most of the general computer security certifications such as CompTIA Security+ and CISSP also include sections on basic forensics. Even if your staff lack the appropriate training to perform a forensic investigation, they should be trained well enough to know how to preserve evidence and avoid any alteration of the evidence.

CHAPTER SUMMARY

In this chapter, you learned about the fundamentals of disaster recovery, as well as how that process is impacted by computer forensics. The most important lesson from this chapter is that every organization must intertwine forensic evidence gathering with its disaster recovery and incident response policies. As soon as an incident is contained, and before it is eradicated, it is important to preserve the evidence. This evidence will be useful in gaining a better understanding of the causes of the incident, thus leading to better planning to avoid similar incidents in the future.

KEY CONCEPTS AND TERMS

Annualized loss expectancy (ALE)

Annual rate of occurrence (ARO)

Business Continuity Plan (BCP)

Business impact analysis (BIA)

Disaster Recovery Plan (DRP)

Hierarchical storage management (HSM)

Maximum tolerable downtime (MTD)

Mean time to failure (MTTF)

Mean time to recovery (MTTR)

Recovery point objective (RPO)

Recovery time objective (RTO)

Single loss expectancy (SLE)

CHAPTER 7 ASSESSMENT

1. What assesses potential loss that could be caused by a disaster?

  A. Business Assessment (BA)
  B. Business Impact Analysis (BIA)
  C. Risk Assessment (RA)
  D. Business Continuity Plan (BCP)

2. Which of the following focuses on sustaining an organization's business functions during and after a disruption?

  A. Business Continuity Plan
  B. Business Recovery Plan
  C. Continuity of Operations Plan
  D. Disaster Recovery Plan

3. Once an intrusion into your organization's information system has been detected, which of the following actions should be performed first?

  A. Eliminate all means of intruder access.
  B. Contain the intrusion.
  C. Determine to what extent systems and data are compromised.
  D. Communicate with relevant parties.

4. Business Continuity Plan development depends most on:

  A. directives from senior management.
  B. the Business Impact Analysis (BIA).
  C. scope and plan initiation.
  D. the skills of the BCP committee.

Reference

1. Swanson, M., Bowen, P., Phillips, A. W., Gallup, D., & Lynes, D. (2010). *Contingency Planning Guide for Federal Information Systems.* National Institute of Standards and Technology Special Publication 800-34. Gaithersburg, MD: NIST.

PART III

Branches of Digital Forensics

Windows Forensics

MICROSOFT WINDOWS IS A UBIQUITOUS operating system. It is difficult to imagine you working in digital forensics and not routinely encountering Windows machines. Therefore, it is important that you be very familiar with conducting forensics on Windows machines. In this chapter, you will learn how to perform forensic examination of a Windows computer. That includes examining the Registry, the index.dat, the swap file, and more.

Chapter 8 Topics

This chapter covers the following topics and concepts:

- The details of Windows
- Evidence in volatile data
- The Windows swap file
- Windows logs
- Windows directories
- Data stored in index.dat
- Windows Registry

Chapter 8 Goals

When you complete this chapter, you will be able to:

- Understand the workings of the Windows operating system
- Gather evidence from the Registry
- Retrieve evidence from logs
- Examine directories for evidence
- Check the index.dat file for evidence

Windows Details

Before delving deeply into Windows forensics, it is a good idea to get a better idea of the operating system itself. In this section, you learn about the history of Windows and its structure. This gives you a context within which to learn Windows forensics. For deeper coverage of Windows internals, refer to the book *Windows Sysinternals Administrator's Reference* by Mark E. Russinovich and Aaron Margosis.

Windows History

The first version of Windows to gain widespread use was version 3.1, released in 1992. It was then that the Windows system became widely popular. At that time, Windows was a **graphical user interface (GUI)**, and not really an operating system. The operating system was **Disk Operating System (DOS)**. Windows provided a visual interface for interacting with the operating system by means of mouse clicks, rather than typing in DOS commands.

During the early 1990s, you could use other, non-Microsoft user interfaces to work with DOS. You could also install Windows on systems running some non-Microsoft operating systems, such as Dr. DOS (an alternative to DOS). There were also several competing operating systems for PCs, including OS2 and OS2 Warp from IBM.

For servers and serious professionals, Microsoft had Windows NT Versions 3.1, 3.51, and 4.0, which were widely used. Each version had both workstation and server editions. The NT version of Windows was widely considered more stable and more secure than Windows 3.1.

The release of Windows 95 in 1995 marked a change in Windows. At this point, the underlying operating system and the GUI—a point-and-click user interface—were fused into one single, coherent product. This meant that you could not choose some non-Windows GUI. Shortly after the release of Windows 95, Windows NT 4.0 was released. Many consider Windows 98 just an intermediate step, an improvement on Windows 95. The interface looked very much the same as Windows 95, but the performance was vastly improved. Windows 95 and 98 used the FAT32 file system.

Windows 2000 was widely considered a major improvement in the Windows line. Essentially, the days of separate NT and Windows lines were over. Now there would simply be different editions of Windows 2000. There were editions for home users, for professional users, and for servers. The differences among the editions were primarily in the features available and the capacity, such as how much random access memory (RAM) could be addressed. Windows 2000 was also the version of Windows wherein Microsoft began to recommend NTFS over FAT32 as a file system.

Windows XP was the next milestone for Microsoft, and Windows Server 2003 was released the same year. This marked a return to the approach of having a separate server and desktop system (unlike Windows 2000). The interface was not very different, but there were structural improvements.

Windows Vista and Windows 7 did not have significantly different user interfaces from XP. There were feature changes and additional capabilities, but essentially the interface was moderately tweaked with each version. The same can be said of the relationship between

A Brief History of Windows

1985 Windows 1.0 opened

1990 Windows 3.0

1992 Windows 3.1

1995 Windows 95

1996 Windows NT 4.0

1998 Windows 98

2000 Windows 2000

2001 Windows XP (first 64-bit version)

2003 Windows XP with Windows Server 2003

2007 general release of Windows Vista

2008 Windows Vista Home Basic, Home Premium, Business, and Ultimate; Windows Server 2008

2009 Windows 7 and Windows Server 2008 R2

2012 Windows 8 and Windows Server 2012

2013 Windows Server 2012 R1

2015 Windows 10

2016 Windows Server 2016

2018 Windows Server 2019

8

Windows
Forensics

Windows Server 2008 and Windows Server 2003. Someone comfortable with Windows Server 2003 would have no problem working with Windows Server 2008.

Windows 8 was a radical change. The operating system is meant to be more like that of a tablet. You can get to a desktop that looks much like Windows 7, but the default behavior of Windows 8 is tablet-like. Microsoft also released Windows Server 2012 during the same general time frame.

Windows 10 was another dramatic change for Windows. New features like Cortana and the Edge browser changed the way users interacted with the Windows operating system, and in some cases changed forensics. Windows Server continued on to Windows Server 2016, and then 2019.

Not all the differences in Windows versions are pertinent to forensics. However, certain issues are, which requires you to ask questions such as the following:

- Does the Windows version in question support 64-bit processing?
- Does it have a firewall—XP was the first Windows version to have one—and if so, is the firewall automatically on, as in Windows XP Service Pack 1?
- Does the version of Windows support the Encrypted File System (EFS), which allows the user to encrypt specific files and folders? This was first introduced with Windows 2000, but starting with Vista, this feature is available only on professional/business or higher editions.

64-Bit Processing

What exactly does 64-bit processing mean? Why is it so important?

First of all, the term refers to how the central processing unit (CPU) and the operating system process information. A 32-bit system can address up to 4,294,967,295 bytes, with each byte having its own address. That is why 32-bit systems were limited to 4 gigabytes (GB) of RAM. But 64-bit systems can use 64-bit addressing to address up to 18,446,744,073,709,551,616 bytes—literally millions of billions of bytes. This is a huge number. So, you can clearly see that a 64-bit processor and a 64-bit operating system have significant advantages over a 32-bit system.

Just as important to forensics is how Windows handles 32-bit programs. You can install 32-bit programs on a 64-bit system. However, they usually are installed into the Program Files (x86) directory. Windows uses x86 to refer to 32-bit versions of programs, files, and so on.

The Boot Process

A forensic examiner needs to understand the Windows boot process for many reasons. A virus might infect a suspect drive at a specific point in the boot process. It is also the case that hard drive encryption programs operate during the boot process of the system. The following is a summary of the basic process. There may be some variation depending on the version of Windows being used:

1. The BIOS conducts the **power-on self-test (POST)**. This is when the system's **basic input/output system (BIOS)** checks to see if the drives, keyboard, and other key items are present and working. This occurs before any operating system components are loaded.
2. The computer reads the **master boot record (MBR)** and partition table.
3. The MBR locates the boot partition. This is the partition that has the operating system on it.
4. The MBR passes control to the boot sector on the boot partition.
5. The boot sector loads NTLDR. NTLDR is the NT loader; it is the first part of the Windows operating system and is responsible for preparing and loading the rest of the operating system.
6. Note that if instead of being shut down, Windows has been put in the hibernation state, the contents of *hiberfil.sys* are loaded into memory and the system resumes at the previous state.
7. NTLDR switches from real mode to 32-bit memory or 64-bit memory depending on the system. Real mode is the default for x86 systems. It provides no support for memory protection, multitasking, or code privilege levels.
8. NTLDR starts minimal file system drivers (FAT, FAT32, NTFS).
9. NTLDR reads boot.ini and displays the boot loader menu. If there are multiple operating systems, they will be displayed.
10. NTLDR loads NTOSKRNL and passes hardware information. The NTOSKRNL is the actual kernel for the Windows operating system. This is the end of the *boot phase* and the beginning of the *load phase*.

[handwritten annotations in margin: "BIOS" bracketing items 1–2; "Boot Loader" bracketing items 5–7; "Boot Files" bracketing items 8–10]

11. NTLDR loads hal.dll (hardware abstraction layer).
12. NTLDR loads the system hive (i.e., the Registry) and reads in settings from it.
13. Kernel initialization begins (the screen turns blue).
14. The services load phase begins.
15. The Win32 subsystem start phase begins.
16. The user logs on.

Knowing the boot order can allow you to diagnose issues that might prevent booting the system, understand when encryption is implemented, and more. Some viruses infect the boot sector, so they are loaded when the system loads and can affect how the system loads. These are all good reasons to understand the boot order, at least in a general way.

Important Files

Windows has a number of files. If you look at the Task Manager, you will see many processes/programs running. Clever virus and spyware writers give their malware a name that is similar to these system processes. This makes a casual observer think these are part of the operating system. A few of the more important Windows files are listed here:

- **Ntdetect.com**—A program that queries the computer for basic device/config data like time/date from CMOS, system bus types, disk drives, ports, and so on
- **Ntbootdd.sys**—A storage controller device driver
- **Ntoskrnl.exe**—The core of the operating system
- **Hal.dll**—An interface for hardware
- **Smss.exe**—A program that handles services on your system
- **Winlogon.exe**—The program that logs you on
- **Lsass.exe**—The program that handles security and logon policies
- **Explorer.exe**—The interface the user interacts with, such as the desktop, Windows Explorer, and so on
- **Crss.exe**—The program that handles tasks like creating threads, console windows, and so forth

Of particular interest in forensics are those programs that are named similarly to the system processes. If you see a running process with a similar name (for example, Lsassx.exe), that could indicate the presence of malware.

A list of files that are part of the actual NTFS file system is given in **FIGURE 8-1A**. Some of these files may contain data when a forensically sophisticated perpetrator has attempted to erase evidence. For example, the $logfile might indicate actions taken. The $mftmirr may have recoverable data.

Windows NTFS has changed over the years. There are new properties with new versions of NTFS. You can easily find out what version of NTFS is being used. Open a command prompt as the administrator and type in `fsutil fsinfo ntfsinfo <volume>` (in place of <volume>, insert your volume letter). You will retrieve a great deal of information about the system in question. This is shown in **FIGURE 8-1B**.

File Name	Description
$attrdef	Contains definitions of all system and user-defined attributes of the volume
$badclus	Contains all the bad clusters
$bitmap	Contains bitmap for the entire volume
$boot	Contains the volume's bootstrap
$logfile	Used for recovery purposes
$mft	Contains a record for every file
$mftmirr	Mirror of the MFT used for recovering files
$quota	Indicates disk quota for each user
$upcase	Converts characters into uppercase Unicode
$volume	Contains volume name and version number

FIGURE 8-1A

NTFS file system.

```
Administrator: Command Prompt

Microsoft Windows [Version 10.0.19041.630]
(c) 2020 Microsoft Corporation. All rights reserved.

C:\WINDOWS\system32>fsutil fsinfo ntfsinfo c:
NTFS Volume Serial Number :        0xe4b42c91b42c686e
NTFS Version       :               3.1
LFS Version        :               2.0
Total Sectors      :               1,950,406,539  (930.0 GB)
Total Clusters     :                 243,800,817  (930.0 GB)
Free Clusters      :                  30,245,241  (115.4 GB)
Total Reserved Clusters :               37,630  (147.0 MB)
Reserved For Storage Reserve :               0  (  0.0 KB)
Bytes Per Sector   :               512
Bytes Per Physical Sector :        4096
Bytes Per Cluster  :               4096
Bytes Per FileRecord Segment    :  1024
Clusters Per FileRecord Segment :  0
Mft Valid Data Length :            2.42 GB
Mft Start Lcn  :                   0x00000000000c0000
Mft2 Start Lcn :                   0x0000000000000002
Mft Zone Start :                   0x000000000c4d6880
Mft Zone End   :                   0x000000000c4e30a0
MFT Zone Size  :                   200.13 MB
Max Device Trim Extent Count :     0
Max Device Trim Byte Count :       0
Max Volume Trim Extent Count :     62
Max Volume Trim Byte Count :       0x40000000
Resource Manager Identifier :      4A5B0201-EA8B-11E5-876A-DB6F8E671AD2

C:\WINDOWS\system32>_
```

FIGURE 8-1B

The `fsutil` command.

The `fsutil` command performs tasks and provides information about the file system. For it to run, you must first use PowerShell to enable the Windows Subsystem for Linux. That process is shown in **FIGURE 8-1C**. Note that you must run PowerShell as an administrator for this to work.

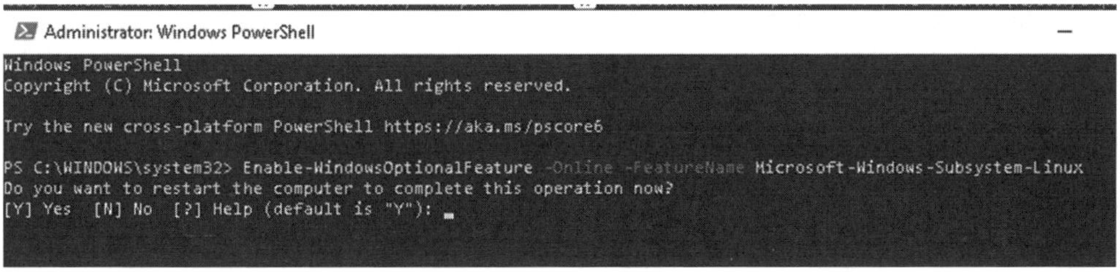

FIGURE 8-1C

Enable Windows
Subsystem for
Linux.

You can find out more about `fsutil` at *https://docs.microsoft.com/en-us/windows-server /administration/windows-commands/fsutil*. We will also discuss PowerShell more later in this chapter.

Volatile Data

Volatile memory analysis is a live-system forensic technique in which you collect a memory dump and perform analysis in an isolated environment. Volatile memory analysis is similar to live response in that you must first establish a trusted command shell. Next, you establish a data collection system and a method for transmitting the data. However, you would only acquire a physical memory dump of the compromised system and transmit it to the data collection system for analysis. In this case, VMware allows you to simply suspend the virtual machine and use the .vmem file as a memory image.

As in other forensic investigations, you would also compute the hash after you complete the memory capture. Unlike with traditional hard drive forensics, you don't need to calculate a hash before data acquisition. Due to the volatile nature of running memory, the imaging process involves taking a snapshot of a "moving target."

The primary difference between this approach and live response is that you don't need any additional evidence from the compromised system. Therefore, you can analyze the evidence on the collection system.

To produce digital data from a live system as evidence in court, it is essential to justify the validity of the acquired memory data. One common approach is to acquire volatile memory data in a dump file for offline examination. A **dump** is a complete copy of every bit of memory or cache recorded in permanent storage or printed on paper. You can then analyze the dump electronically or manually in its static state.

Programmers have developed a number of toolkits to collect volatile memory data. These automated programs run on live systems and collect transient memory data. These tools suffer from one critical drawback: If run on a compromised system, such a tool heavily relies on the underlying operating system. This could affect the collected data's reliability. Some response tools may even substantially alter the digital environment of the original system and cause an adverse impact on the dumped memory data.

As a result, you may have to study those changes to determine whether the alterations have affected the acquired data. Data in memory is not consistently maintained during system operation. This issue poses a challenge for computer forensics.

Maintaining **data consistency** is a problem with live-system forensics in which data is not acquired at a unified moment and is thus inconsistent. If a system is running, it is impossible to freeze the machine states in the course of data acquisition. Even the most efficient method introduces a time difference between the moment you acquire the first bit and the moment you acquire the last bit. For example, the program may execute Function A at the beginning of the memory dump and execute Function B at the end.

The data in the dump may correspond to different execution steps somewhere between Function A and Function B. Because you didn't acquire the data at a unified moment, data inconsistency is inevitable in the memory dump.

When dumping memory, it is useful for the forensic examiner to be aware of the fact that there are actually two types of memory:

- **Stack (S)**—Memory in the **stack (S)** segment is allocated to local variables and parameters within each function. This memory is allocated based on the last-in, first-out (LIFO) principle. When the program is running, program variables use the memory allocated to the stack area again and again. This segment is the most dynamic area of the memory process. The data within this segment is discrepant and influenced by the program's various function calls.

- **Heap (H)**—Dynamic memory for a program comes from the **heap (H)** segment. A process may use a memory allocator such as malloc to request dynamic memory. When this happens, the address space of the process expands. The data in the heap area can exist between function calls. The memory allocator may reuse memory that has been released by the process. Therefore, heap data is less stable than the data in the data segment.

When a program is running, the code, data, and heap segments are usually placed in a single contiguous area. The stack segment is separated from the other segments. It expands within the memory allocated space. Indeed, the memory comprises a number of processes of the operating system or the applications it is supporting. Memory can be viewed as a large array that contains many segments for different processes. In a live system, process memory grows and shrinks, depending on system usage and user activities.

This growth and shrinking of memory is related to either the growth of heap data or the expansion and release of stack data. The data in the code segment is static and remains intact at all times for a particular program or program segment. Data in the growing heap segment and stack segment causes inconsistency in the data contained in memory as a whole. The stack data has a greater effect than the heap data. Nevertheless, the code segment contains consistent data. Consistent data is usually dormant and not affected when a process is running in memory. When you obtain a process dump of a running program, data in the code segment remains unchanged.

Tools

A number of tools and even some Windows utilities are available that can help you to analyze live data on a Windows system. Also, many forensics tools will allow you to mount a Windows image as a virtual machine. Then you can examine the images just as you would a live system. This section looks at some of the more widely used tools and utilities.

PsList

Use PsList to view process and thread statistics on a system. Running PsList lists all running processes on the system. However, it does not reveal the presence of the rootkit or the other processes that the rootkit has hidden. PsList is a part of a suite of tools, PsTools, available as a free download from *http://technet.microsoft.com/en-us/sysinternals/bb896682.aspx*. You can see this tool used in **FIGURE 8-2**.

PsInfo

This tool is also from the PsTools suite. It can tell you system uptime (time since last reboot), operating system details, and other general information about the system. This is good background information to put into your forensic report. This tool is shown in **FIGURE 8-3**.

ListDLLs

ListDLLs allows you to view the currently loaded dynamic-link libraries (DLLs) for a process. Running ListDLLs lists the DLLs loaded by all running processes. However, ListDLLs cannot show the DLLs loaded for hidden processes. Using a Trojan horse to compromise a program or system DLL, however, is a common attack vector. So this tool can be important to your forensic investigation. This tool is also available online for free. You can download it from *http://technet.microsoft.com/en-us/sysinternals/bb896656.aspx*. You can see this utility in use in **FIGURE 8-4**.

```
                    C:\Windows\system32\cmd.exe                    _  □  ×
Copyright (C) 2000-2012 Mark Russinovich
Sysinternals - www.sysinternals.com

Process information for CHUCKSLAPTOP:

Name                  Pid Pri Thd  Hnd   Priv       CPU Time      Elapsed Time
Idle                    0   0   8    0      0  333:07:39.906       0:00:00.000
System                  4   8 150 1070    144    4:10:51.781      53:01:22.315
smss                  340  11   2   36    288    0:00:00.125      53:01:22.190
csrss                 512  13  10  586   2544    0:00:04.531      53:01:12.477
csrss                 652  13  13  539   4032    0:02:58.328      53:01:10.491
wininit               660  13   2   71    928    0:00:00.109      53:01:10.476
winlogon              716  13   3  141   1436    0:00:00.703      53:01:09.366
services              760   9  14  427   8152    0:00:13.718      53:01:08.585
lsass                 768   9   8 1276  10696    0:01:54.015      53:01:08.319
svchost               872   8   7  398   4280    0:00:02.046      53:01:03.007
nvvsvc                908   8   4  140   2044    0:00:00.140      53:01:02.679
svchost               948   8   9  785   8836    0:00:18.921      53:01:02.163
svchost              1000   8  26  878  22080    0:00:24.468      53:01:01.694
dwm                   356  13   5  254  28940    0:51:45.265      53:01:01.413
svchost               384   8  43 1187 140972    0:37:10.203      53:01:01.288
svchost               524   8  56 2192 269672    0:25:43.718      53:01:01.288
svchost               500   8  27  857  23852    0:00:23.781      53:01:00.678
nvxdsync             1076   8   9  303   6288    0:00:01.703      53:00:59.491
nvvsvc               1096   8   4  191   4960    0:00:00.406      53:00:59.428
svchost              1192   8  18  649  15920    0:00:56.390      53:00:57.866
spoolsv              1572   8  25  541  10804    0:00:06.218      53:00:51.902
svchost              1600   8  21  506  29540    0:00:57.046      53:00:51.746
AppleMobileDeviceService 1740  8  9  228  2940  0:00:32.421    53:00:49.542
mDNSResponder        1972   8   4  125   1816    0:00:01.968      53:00:41.542
EvtEng               2032   8  20  274   5704    0:00:02.187      53:00:41.292
dasHost              1048   8  11  374   5928    0:00:01.781      53:00:41.073
HeciServer            848   8   3  100   1296    0:00:00.015      53:00:40.636
Jhi_service          1556   8   3   75   1176    0:00:00.015      53:00:40.464
mfevtps              1892   8   4  176   1448    0:00:00.031      53:00:39.589
MsDtsSrvr            2076   8  14  358  97824    0:00:01.281      53:00:38.901
```

FIGURE 8-2
PsList.

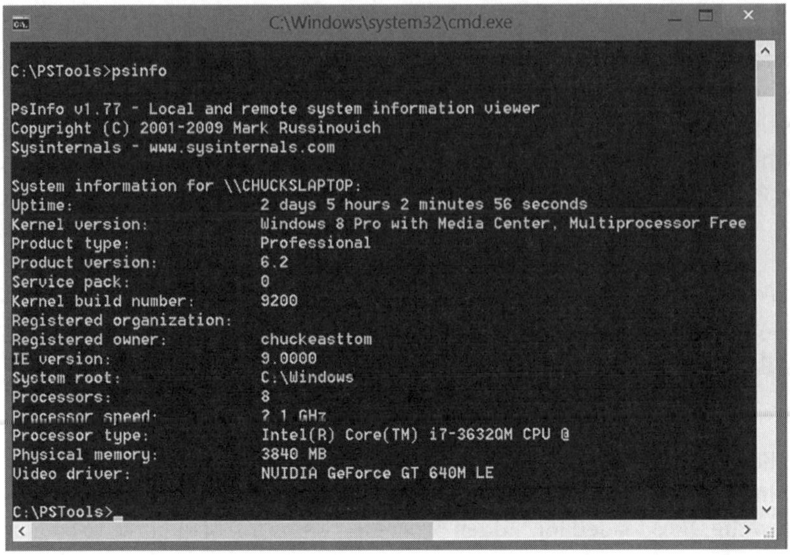

Used with permission from Microsoft

FIGURE 8-3
PsInfo.

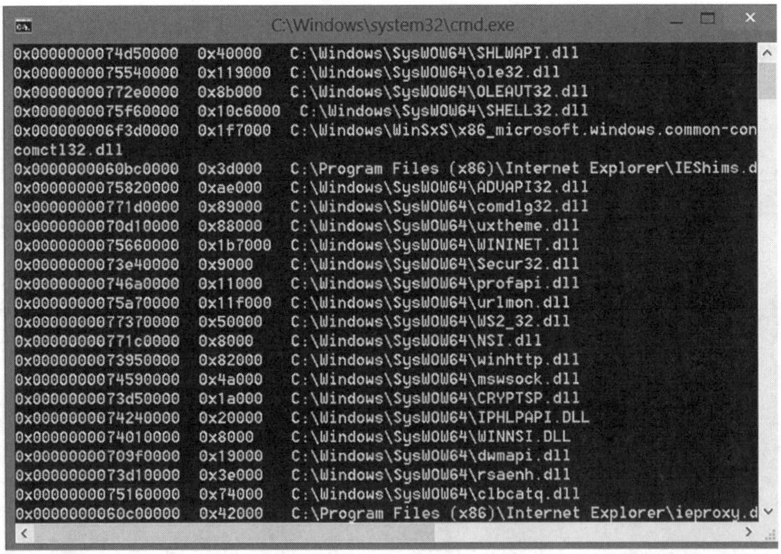

Used with permission from Microsoft

FIGURE 8-4
ListDLLs.

PsLoggedOn

PsLoggedOn helps you discover users who have logged on both locally and remotely. Of most importance, it tells you who is logged on to shares on the current machine. This is also part of the PsTools suite available from Microsoft TechNet. This utility is shown in **FIGURE 8-5**.

Using `netstat`

Port 4444 is a common reverse shell port

This utility is important in the context of checking live system data. Remember that `netstat` is a command-line tool that displays both incoming and outgoing network

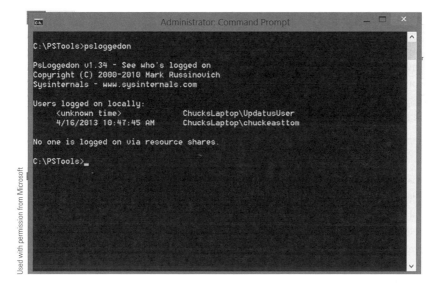

FIGURE 8-5

PsLoggedOn.

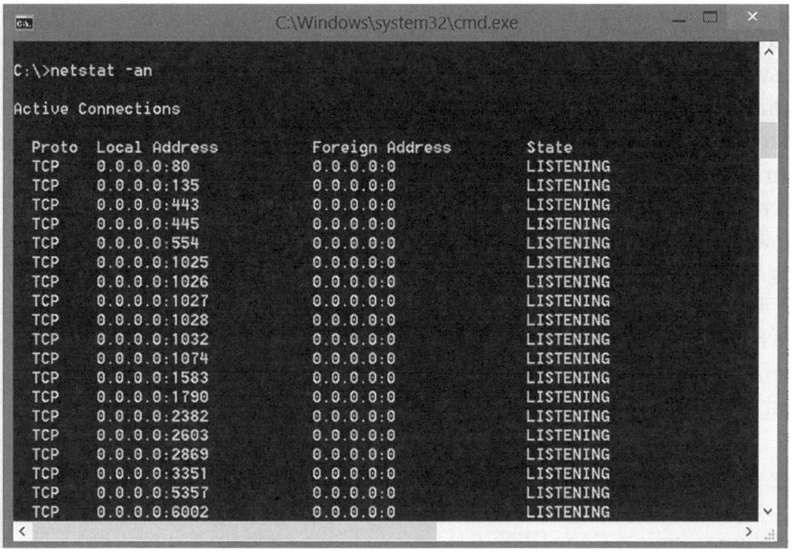

FIGURE 8-6

The `netstat` utility.

connections. It also displays routing tables and a number of network interface statistics. It is available on Unix, Unix-like, and Windows-based operating systems.

Use the `netstat` utility to view the network connections of a running machine. Running `netstat` with the `-an` option will show all ports, list what they are doing (listening or sending), and list them in numerical order. This can be useful information in your forensic analysis, particularly if the suspected crime uses spyware or a botnet. You can see `netstat` in **FIGURE 8-6**.

Windows Swap File

The Windows swap file is used to augment the RAM. Essentially, it is a special place on the hard drive where items from memory can be temporarily stored for fast retrieval. For example, you might have five programs open at one time, but you are only using one at a time. If the system is running low on RAM, it can take the program or file that has been inactive the longest and move it to the swap file.

FYI

A common situation you may encounter during a live forensic investigation is the use of virtual environments. A virtual machine is a software program that appears to be a physical computer and executes programs as if it were a physical computer. You commonly use a virtual machine when you need to run an operating system on another computer. For example, you can run one or more Linux virtual machines on a computer running a Microsoft Windows operating system. Virtual machines are popular in organizations that want to save IT costs by running several virtual machines on a single physical computer. Two of the most popular software packages that implement virtual machines are VMware and VirtualBox.

The Windows swap file used to end in a .swp extension; since Windows XP, however, it ends in pagefile.sys. It is typically found in the Windows root directory. The swap file is a binary file. Given that the swap file is used to augment RAM, it is often referred to as virtual memory.

Related to the swap file is the hiberfil.sys. Hiberfil.sys is a memory file that can be converted to an image file and processed with volatility or even simple string searches. Within this file, there may be password artifacts from applications that were recently run.

Starting with Windows 8, and moving on to Window 10, there have been some changes in hyberfil.sys, swapfile.sys, and pagefile.sys.

Starting with Windows 8, the pagefile.sys is there all the time, but the hiberfil.sys is only there if you have fast startup enabled in Windows 8. Also, by default, Windows 8 uses a hybrid shutdown that causes a hyberfil.sys to be generated, but it only has the kernel and files needed to boot, so it will be smaller.

Volume Shadow Copy – records all file system changes

Windows Volume Shadow Copy (VSS) is a service in which state changes in blocks of data are compared daily and changed blocks are copied to a volume shadow. The VSS service runs once per day and stores change data as 16-KB blocks of data. In differential copies of VSS, only the changes are backed up, on a cluster-by-cluster basis. For a full copy or clone, entire files are backed up.

Windows Logs

All versions of Windows support logging. However, the method to get to the log can vary from one version to another. With Windows 7 and Windows Server 2008, you find the logs by clicking on the Start button in the lower-left corner of the desktop and then clicking

Control Panel. You then select Administrative Tools and then Event Viewer. You would check for the following logs:

gh
+1s r
~vi2

- **Security log**—This is probably the <u>most important log</u> from a forensics point of view. It has both successful and unsuccessful login events.
- **Application log**—This log contains various events logged by applications or programs. Many applications record their errors here in the Application log.
- **System log**—The System log contains events logged by Windows system components. This includes events like driver failures. This particular log is not as interesting from a forensics perspective as the other logs are.
- **ForwardedEvents log**—The ForwardedEvents log is used to store events collected from remote computers. This has data in it only if event forwarding has been configured.
- **Applications and Services logs**—This log is used to store events from a single application or component rather than events that might have systemwide impact.

You can view logs, as shown in **FIGURE 8-7**.

Windows servers have similar logs. However, it is also possible that the logs will be empty. For example, the tool auditpol.exe can turn logging on and off. Savvy criminals might turn the logging off while they do their misdeeds, then turn it back on. In addition, the tool WinZapper allows you to selectively erase individual records in the log. So it is possible that the logs will yield no evidence, even if a crime did take place.

Another type of tool that is often used on PCs, servers, routers, switches, and other devices is Tripwire, which you can find at *http://www.tripwire.com*. A newer tool is CimTrak, which you can find at *http://www.fileintegritymonitoring.com/cimtrak-home*, and related software. These programs store a secure hash of files and the static part of device memory and monitor for changes to the files and/or memory. Security practitioners can use the

8

Windows
Forensics

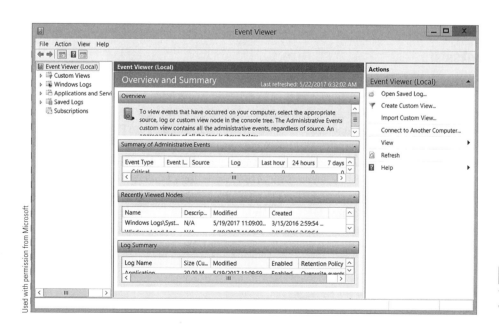

Used with permission from Microsoft

FIGURE 8-7

Viewing
Windows logs.

tools to harden their defenses and make their systems "aware" of attacks when they occur. They can also allow files or memory to be checkpointed and restored to a preattack condition. This class of tools can also be very important to the forensic examiner, as a large amount of information is made available due to different generations of files as well as multiple log files.

Windows Directories

There are certain directories in Windows that are more likely than others to contain evidence. Obviously, a technically savvy criminal can erase evidence. However, not all criminals are technically savvy, and even those who are might have missed something. Or the computer might have been seized before they could erase the incriminating evidence. Although there are many directories on a computer, the following are the most forensically interesting:

Old
- **C:\Windows documents and settings**—This folder is the default location to save documents. A criminal can save documents anywhere on the computer; however, it is a good idea to check this folder.
- **C:\users**—This is where you will find user profile information, documents, pictures, and more for all users, not just the one currently logged on.
- **C:\Program Files**—By default, programs are installed in subdirectories of this directory.
- **C:\Program Files (x86)**—In 64-bit systems, 32-bit programs are installed here.
- **C:\Users\username\Documents**—The current user's Documents folder. This is a very important place to look.

And, of course, you should do a general search of the entire suspect drive—not just these specific folders and directories.

UserAssist

UserAssist is a feature of Windows 2000 and later. Its purpose was to help programs launch faster. For this reason, it maintains a record of programs that have been launched. By examining the appropriate Registry key for UserAssist, one can view all the programs that have been executed on that machine. This information is stored in the Registry (HKEY_CURRENT_USER\Software\Microsoft\Windows\CurrentVersion\ Explorer\UserAssist), but it's encrypted, so you'll need something like the free UserAssist tool to find out more.

You can get the UserAssist tool free from *http://www.downloadcrew.com/article/23805 -userassist*. An example of this tool is shown in **FIGURE 8-8**. As you can see, this gives a lot of information as to what programs were run, and when.

Most major forensics tools, including Guidance Software's EnCase, AccessData's FTK, and Passmark's OSForensics, will retrieve the UserAssist entries, as well as other entries for you.

Unallocated/Slack Space

You will need to search the entire disk to locate all relevant documents, logs, emails, and more in most of your cases. At times, though, you may want to find relevant data only in the

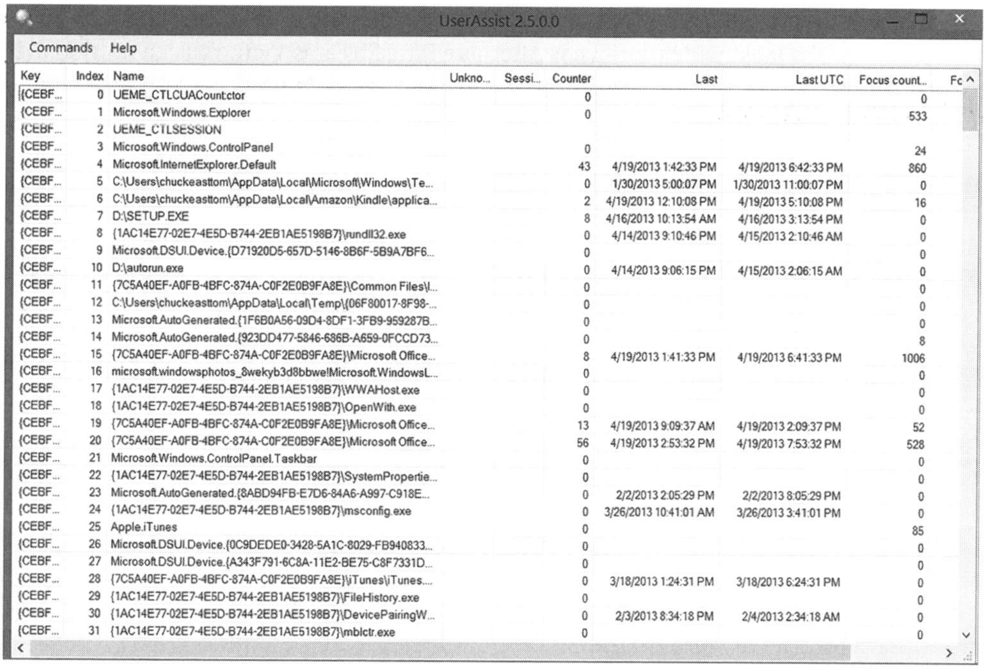

UserAssist 2.5.0.0

Commands   Help

Key	Index	Name	Unkno...	Sessi...	Counter	Last	Last UTC	Focus count...	Fc
{CEBF...	0	UEME_CTLCUACount.ctor			0			0	
{CEBF...	1	Microsoft.Windows.Explorer			0			533	
{CEBF...	2	UEME_CTLSESSION							
{CEBF...	3	Microsoft.Windows.ControlPanel			0			24	
{CEBF...	4	Microsoft.InternetExplorer.Default			43	4/19/2013 1:42:33 PM	4/19/2013 6:42:33 PM	860	
{CEBF...	5	C:\Users\chuckeasttom\AppData\Local\Microsoft\Windows\Te...			0	1/30/2013 5:00:07 PM	1/30/2013 11:00:07 PM	0	
{CEBF...	6	C:\Users\chuckeasttom\AppData\Local\Amazon\Kindle\applica...			2	4/19/2013 12:10:08 PM	4/19/2013 5:10:08 PM	16	
{CEBF...	7	D:\SETUP.EXE			8	4/16/2013 10:13:54 AM	4/16/2013 3:13:54 PM	0	
{CEBF...	8	{1AC14E77-02E7-4E5D-B744-2EB1AE5198B7}\rundll32.exe			0	4/14/2013 9:10:46 PM	4/15/2013 2:10:46 AM	0	
{CEBF...	9	Microsoft.DSUI.Device.{D71920D5-657D-5146-8B6F-5B9A7BF6...			0			0	
{CEBF...	10	D:\autorun.exe			0	4/14/2013 9:06:15 PM	4/15/2013 2:06:15 AM	0	
{CEBF...	11	{7C5A40EF-A0FB-4BFC-874A-C0F2E0B9FA8E}\Common Files\I...			0			0	
{CEBF...	12	C:\Users\chuckeasttom\AppData\Local\Temp\{06F80017-8F98-...			0			0	
{CEBF...	13	Microsoft.AutoGenerated.{1F6B0A56-09D4-8DF1-3FB9-959287B...			0			0	
{CEBF...	14	Microsoft.AutoGenerated.{923DD477-5846-686B-A659-0FCCD73...			0			8	
{CEBF...	15	{7C5A40EF-A0FB-4BFC-874A-C0F2E0B9FA8E}\Microsoft Office...			8	4/19/2013 1:41:33 PM	4/19/2013 6:41:33 PM	1006	
{CEBF...	16	microsoft.windowsphotos_8wekyb3d8bbwe!Microsoft.WindowsL...			0			0	
{CEBF...	17	{1AC14E77-02E7-4E5D-B744-2EB1AE5198B7}\WWAHost.exe			0			0	
{CEBF...	18	{1AC14E77-02E7-4E5D-B744-2EB1AE5198B7}\OpenWith.exe			0			0	
{CEBF...	19	{7C5A40EF-A0FB-4BFC-874A-C0F2E0B9FA8E}\Microsoft Office...			13	4/19/2013 9:09:37 AM	4/19/2013 2:09:37 PM	52	
{CEBF...	20	{7C5A40EF-A0FB-4BFC-874A-C0F2E0B9FA8E}\Microsoft Office...			56	4/19/2013 2:53:32 PM	4/19/2013 7:53:32 PM	528	
{CEBF...	21	Microsoft.Windows.ControlPanel.Taskbar			0			0	
{CEBF...	22	{1AC14E77-02E7-4E5D-B744-2EB1AE5198B7}\SystemPropertie...			0			0	
{CEBF...	23	Microsoft.AutoGenerated.{8ABD94FB-E7D6-84A6-A997-C918E...			0	2/2/2013 2:05:29 PM	2/2/2013 8:05:29 PM	0	
{CEBF...	24	{1AC14E77-02E7-4E5D-B744-2EB1AE5198B7}\msconfig.exe			0	3/26/2013 10:41:01 AM	3/26/2013 3:41:01 PM	0	
{CEBF...	25	Apple.iTunes			0			85	
{CEBF...	26	Microsoft.DSUI.Device.{0C9DEDE0-3428-5A1C-8029-FB940833...			0			0	
{CEBF...	27	Microsoft.DSUI.Device.{A343F791-6C8A-11E2-BE75-C8F7331D...			0			0	
{CEBF...	28	{7C5A40EF-A0FB-4BFC-874A-C0F2E0B9FA8E}\iTunes\iTunes....			0	3/18/2013 1:24:31 PM	3/18/2013 6:24:31 PM	0	
{CEBF...	29	{1AC14E77-02E7-4E5D-B744-2EB1AE5198B7}\FileHistory.exe			0			0	
{CEBF...	30	{1AC14E77-02E7-4E5D-B744-2EB1AE5198B7}\DevicePairingW...			0	2/3/2013 8:34:18 PM	2/4/2013 2:34:18 AM	0	
{CEBF...	31	{1AC14E77-02E7-4E5D-B744-2EB1AE5198B7}\mblctr.exe			0			0	

Used with permission from Microsoft

FIGURE 8-8

UserAssist.

8

Windows Forensics

unallocated space. To do so, you would search the unallocated space for keywords. Tools such as AccessData's Forensic Toolkit (FTK) allow an investigator to take an entire image and try to identify all of the documents in the file system, including the unallocated space. If you want to search the entire disk many times over, tools such as FTK can help you build a full-text index. Full-text indexing allows you to build a binary tree-based dictionary of all the words that exist in an image, and you can search the entire image for those words in seconds.

Alternate Data Streams

This is a clever way that a criminal can hide things on the target computer. Alternate data streams are essentially a method of attaching one file to another file, using the NTFS file system. According to Irongeek.com,[1]

> Alternative Data Stream support was added to NTFS (Windows NT, Windows 2000 and Windows XP) to help support Macintosh Hierarchical File System (HFS), which uses resource forks to store icons and other information for a file. While this is the intended use (as well as a few Windows internal functions) there are other uses for Alternative Data Streams that should concern system administrators and security professionals. Using Alternative Data Streams a user can easily hide files that can go undetected unless closely inspected.

For example, if a criminal wants to attach a script to a text file, the following command will attach that script using alternate data streams:

```
type somescript.vbs> ADSFile.txt:somescript.vbs
```

A number of tools are available that will detect whether files are attached via alternate data streams. One of the most widely known is Alternate Data Streams View. You can download it free from *https://www.nirsoft.net/utils/alternate_data_streams.html*.

or list alternate data steams

Index.dat

The browser can be a source of both direct evidence and circumstantial or supporting evidence. Obviously, in cases of child pornography, the browser might contain direct evidence of the specific crime. You may also find direct evidence in the case of cyberstalking. However, if you suspect someone of creating a virus that infected a network, you would probably find only indirect evidence, such as evidence of the suspect having searched virus creation or programming-related topics.

Even if the suspect's browsing history has been erased, it is still possible to retrieve it if he or she was using Microsoft Internet Explorer. Index.dat is a file used by Internet Explorer to store web addresses, search queries, and recently opened files. So if a file is on a universal serial bus (USB) device but was opened on the suspect machine, index.dat would contain a record of that file.

You can download a number of tools from the internet that will allow you to retrieve and review the index.dat file. Here are a few:

- *http://www.eusing.com/Window_Washer/Index_dat.htm*
- *http://www.acesoft.net/index.dat%20viewer/index.dat_viewer.htm*
- *http://download.cnet.com/Index-dat-Analyzer/3000-2144_4-10564321.html*

You can see Window Washer in **FIGURE 8-9**.

Whatever tool you choose to use, the index.dat is a fantastic source of forensic information that cannot be overlooked in your forensic investigation.

This has been supplanted in later versions of Internet Explorer. Since version 10, Internet Explorer has kept history in C:\user\username\AppData\Local\Microsoft\Windows\WebCache\WebcacheV01.dat.

Other browsers use their own locations. For example, Mozilla Firefox keeps history in a file named history.dat that is analogous to index.dat. It is located in one of two locations:

C:\Documents and Settings\user\Application Data\Mozilla\Firefox\Profiles\<random text>\history.dat
C:\Documents and Settings\user\Application Data\Mozilla\Profiles\<profile name>\<random text>\history.dat

There are three types of files in this directory:

- A cache map file
- Three cache block files
- Separate cache data files

Fortunately, you won't have to examine these files and extract data manually. All the major forensics software packages extract internet history for you. This includes AccessData's FTK, Guidance's EnCase, and PassMark's OSForensics.

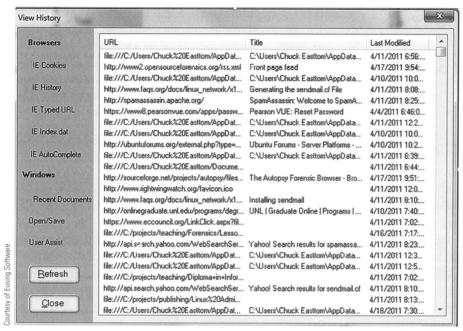

FIGURE 8-9

Window Washer.

8

Windows
Forensics

Windows Files and Permissions

File permissions can change when moving a file. How they change depends on whether this is a copy-and-paste or a cut-and-paste, and whether the operation is within the same partition or not. Copy/paste on the same partition means that files/folders will inherit the rights of the folder the file is being copied to. Cut/paste (move) means that files/folders will retain the original permissions if the new location is on the same partition. This is because when the files/folders are on the same partition, they don't actually move; rather, the pointers to their locations get updated. With copying or cutting to a different partition, the file will inherit rights of the destination folder.

MAC Mandatory Access Control

In the context of Windows files, MAC refers to three critical properties: Modified, Accessed, Created.

File Created: This is the date the file was "created" on the volume. This does not change when working normally with a file, such as opening, closing, saving, or modifying the file.

File Accessed: This is the date the file was last accessed. An access can be a move, an open, or any other simple access. It can also be tripped by antivirus scanners or Windows system processes.

File Modified: This date as shown by Windows indicates that there has been a change to the file itself.

Clearly, these date/time stamps can be important forensically. For example, if the modified date for an image is later than the created date, then that image has been edited.

The Registry

What is the Registry? It is a repository of all the information on a Windows system. When you install a new program, its configuration settings are stored in the Registry. When you change the desktop background, that is also stored in the Registry.

According to a Microsoft TechNet article,[2]

> The *Microsoft Computer Dictionary*, Fifth Edition, defines the Registry as: A central hierarchical database used in Windows 98, Windows CE, Windows NT, and Windows 2000 used to store information that is necessary to configure the system for one or more users, applications, and hardware devices.
>
> The Registry contains information that Windows continually references during operation, such as profiles for each user, the applications installed on the computer and the types of documents that each can create, property sheet settings for folders and application icons, what hardware exists on the system, and the ports that are being used.
>
> The Registry replaces most of the text-based .ini files that are used in Windows 3.x and MS-DOS configuration files, such as the Autoexec.bat and Config.sys. Although the Registry is common to several Windows operating systems, there are some differences among them. A Registry hive is a group of keys, subkeys, and values in the Registry that has a set of supporting files that contain backups of its data. The supporting files for all hives except HKEY_CURRENT_USER are in the %SystemRoot%\System32\Config folder on Windows NT 4.0, Windows 2000, Windows XP, Windows Server 2003, and Windows Vista. The supporting files for HKEY_CURRENT_USER are in the %SystemRoot%\Profiles\Username folder. The filename extensions of the files in these folders indicate the type of data that they contain. Also, the lack of an extension may sometimes indicate the type of data that they contain. See **TABLE 8-1**.

TABLE 8-1 Description of the Registry.

REGISTRY HIVE	SUPPORTING FILES
HKEY_LOCAL_MACHINE\SAM	Sam, Sam.log, Sam.sav
HKEY_LOCAL_MACHINE\Security	Security, Security.log, Security.sav
HKEY_LOCAL_MACHINE\Software	Software, Software.log, Software.sav
HKEY_LOCAL_MACHINE\System	System, System.alt, System.log, System.sav
HKEY_CURRENT_CONFIG	System, System.alt, System.log, System.sav, Ntuser.dat, Ntuser.dat.log
HKEY_USERS\DEFAULT	Default, Default.log, Default.sav

As you see in this section, there is a great deal of forensic information you can gather from the Registry, which is why it is important to have a thorough understanding of Registry forensics. But, first, how do you get to the Registry? The usual path is through the tool regedit. In Windows 7 and Server 2008, you select Start, then Run, then type in `regedit`. In Windows 8, you need to go to the applications list, select All Apps, and then find regedit. With Windows 10, you can click on the search button (it looks like a magnifying class) and type in `regedit`.

The Registry is organized into five sections referred to as **hives**. Each of these sections contains specific information that can be useful to you. The five hives are described here:

1. **HKEY_CLASSES_ROOT (HKCR)**—This hive stores information about drag-and-drop rules, program shortcuts, the user interface, and related items.
2. **HKEY_CURRENT_USER (HKCU)**—This hive is very important to any forensic investigation. It stores information about the currently logged-on user, including desktop settings, user folders, and so forth.
3. **HKEY_LOCAL_MACHINE (HKLM)**—This hive can also be important to a forensic investigation. It contains those settings common to the entire machine, regardless of the individual user.
4. **HKEY_USERS (HKU)**—This hive is very critical to forensic investigations. It has profiles for all the users, including their settings.
5. **HKEY_CURRENT_CONFIG (HCU)**—This hive contains the current system configuration. This might also prove useful in your forensic examinations.

You can see these five hives in **FIGURE 8-10**. As you move forward in this section and learn where to find certain critical values in the Registry, keep in mind the specific hive names.

All Registry keys contain a value associated with them called LastWriteTime. You can think of this like the modification time on a file or folder. Looking at the LastWriteTime tells you when this Registry value was last changed. Rather than be a standard date/time, this value is stored as a FILETIME structure. A FILETIME structure represents the number of 100-nanosecond intervals since January 1, 1601.

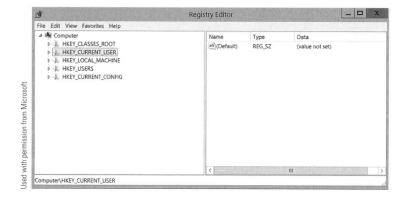

Used with permission from Microsoft

The Windows Registry.

Before you learn about specific evidence found in the Registry, consider a few general settings that can be useful. Auto-run locations are Registry keys that launch programs automatically during boot-up. It is common for viruses and spyware to be automatically run at startup. Another setting to look at is the MRU, or most recently used. These are program specific. For example, Microsoft Word might have an MRU describing the most recently used documents.

A typical Registry key may contain up to four sub-entries, labeled a "control set".[3] The four you may encounter are listed here:

\ControlSet001	ControlSet001 is the last control set you booted with.
\ControlSet002	ControlSet002 is the last known good control set, or the control set that last successfully booted Windows. If all went well at boot-up, then ControlSet001 and ControlSet002 should be identical.
\CurrentControlSet	The CurrentControlSet subkey is just a pointer to either ControlSet001 or ControlSet002 keys.
\Clone	Clone is a clone of CurrentControlSet, and is created each time you boot your computer.

In an ideal situation, all of these will contain identical information. Any discrepancy should be noted and investigated.

USB Information

One important thing you can find is any USB devices that have been connected to the machine.

The Registry key HKEY_LOCAL_MACHINE\System\ControlSet\Enum\USBTOR lists USB devices that have been connected to the machine. It is often the case that a criminal will move evidence or exfiltrate other information to an external device and take it with him or her. This could indicate to you that there are devices you need to find and examine. Often, criminals attempt to move files offline onto an external drive. This Registry setting tells you about the external drives that have been connected to this system.

There are other keys related to USBSTOR that provide related information. For example, SYSTEM\MountedDevices allows investigators to match the serial number to a given drive letter or volume that was mounted when the USB device was inserted. This information should be combined with the information from USBSTOR in order to get a more complete picture of USB-related activities.

The Registry key \Software\Microsoft\Windows\CurrentVersion\Explorer\MountPoints2 will indicate what user was logged onto the system when the USB device was connected. This allows the investigator to associate a specific user with a particular USB device.

Wireless Networks

Think, for just a moment, about connecting to a Wi-Fi network. You probably had to enter some passphrase. But you did not have to enter that passphrase the next time you connected to that Wi-Fi, did you? That information is stored somewhere on the computer, but where? It is stored in the Registry.

When an individual connects to a wireless network, the service set identifier (SSID) is logged as a preferred network connection. This information can be found in the Registry in the HKEY_LOCAL_MACHINE \SOFTWARE\Microsoft\WZCSVC\Parameters\ Interfaces key.

The Registry key HKLM\SOFTWARE\Microsoft\Windows NT\CurrentVersion\ NetworkList\Profiles\ gives you a list of all the Wi-Fi networks to which this network interface has connected. The SSID of the network is contained within the Description key. When the computer first connected to the network is recorded in the DateCreated field.

The Registry key HKLM\SOFTWARE\Microsoft\WindowsNT\CurrentVersion\NetworkList\Signatures\Unmanaged \{ProfileGUID} stores the MAC address of the wireless access point to which it was connected.

Tracking Word Documents in the Registry

Many versions of Word store a PID_GUID value in the Registry—for example, something like { 1 2 3 A 8 B 2 2 - 6 2 2 B - 1 4 C 4 - 8 4 A D - 0 0 D 1 B 6 1 B 0 3 A 4 }. The string 0 0 D 1 B 6 1 B 0 3 A 4 is the MAC address of the machine on which this document was created. In cases involving theft of intellectual property, espionage, and similar crimes, tracking the origin of a document can be very important. This is a rather obscure aspect of the Windows Registry that is not well known, even among forensic analysts.

Malware in the Registry

If you search the Registry and find HKLM\SOFTWARE\Microsoft\Windows NT\CurrentVersion\Winlogon, it has a value named Shell with default data Explorer.exe. Basically, it tells the system to launch Windows Explorer when the login is completed. Some malware appends the malware executable file to the default values data, so that the malware will load every time the system launches. It is important to check this Registry setting if you suspect malware is an issue.

The key HKLM\SYSTEM\CurrentControlSet\Services\ lists system services. There are several examples of malware that installs as a service, particularly backdoor software. So again, check this key if you suspect malware is an issue.

Uninstalled Software

Uninstalled software is a very important Registry key for any forensic examination. An intruder who breaks into a computer might install software on that computer for various purposes such as recovering deleted files or creating a back door. He will then, most likely, delete the software he used. It is also possible that an employee who is stealing data might install steganography software so he can hide the data. He will subsequently uninstall that software. This key lets you see all the software that has been uninstalled from this machine:

HKLM\SOFTWARE\Microsoft\Windows\CurrentVersion\Uninstall

Passwords

If the user tells Internet Explorer to remember passwords, then those passwords are stored in the Registry, and you can retrieve them.[4] The following key holds these values:

HKCU\Software\Microsoft\Internet Explorer\IntelliForms\SPW

In some versions of Windows, this key will be \IntelliForms\Storage 1.

Any source of passwords is particularly interesting. It is not uncommon for people to re-use passwords. Therefore, if you are able to obtain passwords used in one context, they may be the same passwords used in other contexts.

ShellBag

This entry can be found at HKCU\Software\Microsoft\Shell\Bags. ShellBag entries indicate a given folder was accessed, not a specific file.[5] This Windows Registry key is of particular interest in child pornography investigations. It is common for defendants to claim they were not aware those files were on the computer in question. The ShellBag entries can confirm or refute that claim.

A good resource for more information on the Windows Registry can be found at the SANS Institute online Reading Room, which you can find at *http://www.sans.org/reading_room /whitepapers/auditing/wireless-networks-windows-registry-computer-been_33659.*

The forensics tool OSForensics brings together many different Windows Registry values into a single screen named "User Activity." This is shown in **FIGURE 8-11**. Note that actual

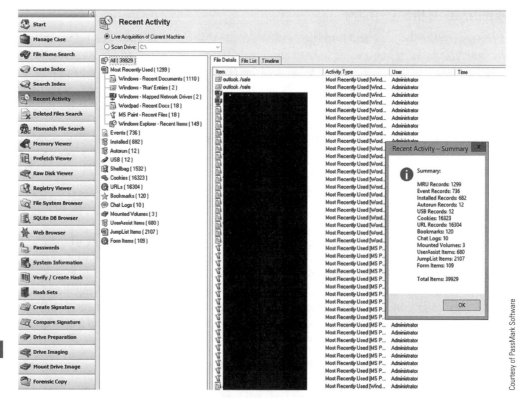

FIGURE 8-11

OSForensics User Activity.

filenames are redacted, as this image was taken from my own computer. However, you can see that this tool provides the forensic examiner with a very easy-to-view output showing ShellBags, internet history, UserAssist, USB devices, and other important information from the Windows Registry.

Shimcache

Also known as AppCompatCache, this is found at Registry Key HKLM\SYSTEM\CurrentControlSet\Control\SessionManager\AppCompatCache\AppCompatCache. This is shown in **FIGURE 8-12**.

The Windows Shimcache was created by Microsoft beginning in Windows XP to track compatibility issues with executed programs. The cache stores various file metadata depending on the operating system, such as:

File Full Path
File Size
$Standard_Information (SI) Last Modified time
Shimcache Last Updated time
Process Execution Flag

Similar to a log file, the Shimcache also uses a queue, meaning that the oldest data is replaced by new entries. The amount of data retained varies by operating system. Forensically speaking, this Registry entry is another way to find out what programs have been executed on a given Windows computer. There are two actions that can cause the Shimcache to record an entry:

* A file is executed. This is recorded on all versions of Windows beginning with XP.
* On Windows 8, 10, Server 2012, and Server 2016, the Application Experience Lookup Service may record Shimcache entries for files in a directory that a user interactively browses. For example, if a directory contains the files "file1.txt" and "file2.exe," a Windows10 system may record entries for these two files in the Shimcache.

Amcache

Amcache is yet another Registry key that stores information about executed applications. Especially interesting is that this entry records a hash of the file. This allows one to search sources such as Virus Total (*https://www.virustotal.com/gui/*) to see if this is a known

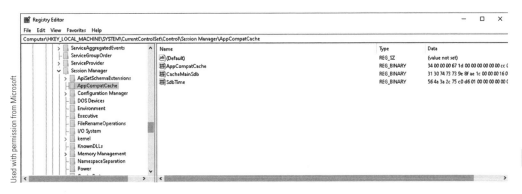

FIGURE 8-12

Shimcache.

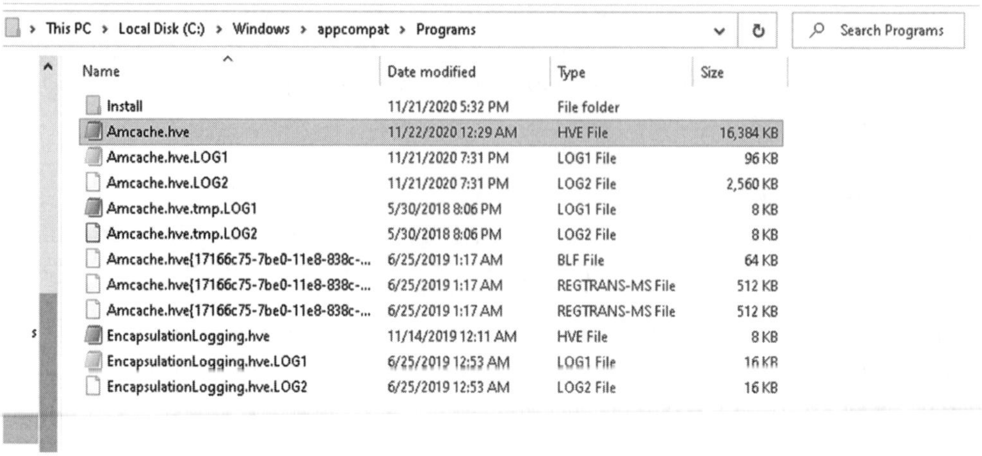

FIGURE 8-13

Amcache.

malware. Amcache was introduced with Windows 8 and Amcache.hve replaces Recent-FileCache.bcf. This file is actually found at C:\Windows\appcompat\Programs. Most modern Windows forensics software will pull this data for you; however, if you wish to view it manually, you simply navigate to that folder. You cannot open the files on a running system, because the Windows process is using the files. You can see the folder in **FIGURE 8-13**.

Prefetch

This is found at Registry key HKEY_LOCAL_MACHINE\SYSTEM\CurrentControlSet\Control\Session Manager\Memory Management\PrefetchParameter. Prefetch files contain the name of the executable, a Unicode list of DLLs used by that executable, a count of how many times the executable has been run, and a time stamp indicating the last time the program was run. This also lets you know when an executable was run on the system. Notice that there are multiple ways to determine what programs have been executed. This is one of the benefits of examining a Windows computer: It stores related data in multiple places. That makes it difficult for even a forensically sophisticated perpetrator to erase all the entries.

Windows Prefetch files, introduced in Windows XP, are designed to speed up the application startup process. Windows will maintain 128 Prefetch files (.pf) in the folder %windir%\Prefetch. Starting with Windows Vista, the technology was expanded upon and renamed SuperFetch. Windows has used different names for essentially the same feature, such as SuperFetch and ReadyBoot.

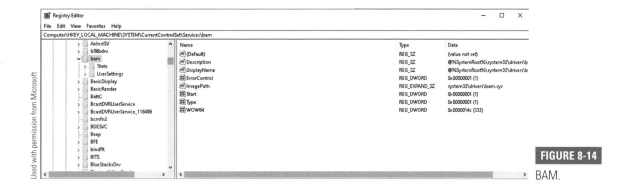

FIGURE 8-14

BAM.

SRUM

The System Resource Usage Monitor (SRUM) database collects data on executables. The data is stored in Microsoft's database format Extensible Storage Engine (ESE). This was first introduced with Windows 8. It allows one to trace resource utilization, including network activity. For network activity, SRUM tracks the network interface, the network profile, the time connection was established, and the length of the connection. In addition to the fact that many commercial tools will capture SRUM information, there is an open-source tool you can download from *https://github.com/MarkBaggett/srum-dump*. The SRUM database is normally found at \Windows\system32\sru\SRUDB.dat.

BAM and DAM

Windows Background Activity Monitor and Desktop Activity Monitor can yield information about application usage. BAM provides the full path of the executable file that was run on the system and the last execution date/time. It is located in this Registry path: HKLM\SYSTEM\CurrentControlSet\Services\bam\UserSettings\{SID}. BAM is shown in **FIGURE 8-14**.

As you may surmise, DAM is in a very similar location in the Windows Registry: HKLM\SYSTEM\CurrentControlSet\Services\dam.

Recycle Bin

Let us start with an older Recycle Bin, the one found in Windows 2000 and Windows XP. The reason to cover older versions is that you may very well encounter older systems in digital forensics.

The default Recycle Bin configuration for a Windows computer is to move deleted files to a folder named \Recycler\%SID%\, where %SID% is the SID (Security Identifier) of the currently logged on user. Every user on the system will have such a directory created the first time that the Recycle Bin is used. As well, each user will have a hidden file called INFO2 that is created the first time the Recycle Bin is used—its purpose is to keep track of the deleted file(s)/folder(s) original location(s), as well as file size and deletion time. This makes it possible to relate deleted files with specific users.

When you delete a file, the INFO2 list looks like this:

D%DriveLetter%_%IndexNumber%_%FileExtension%.

The "D" stands for Drive.

%DriveLetter%: This is the drive that the file was on before it was deleted.

%IndexNumber%: An index number is assigned to each file or file that is sent to the Recycle Bin, and indicates the order of deletion.

%FileExtension%: This is the original file extension; if it is a folder, there will be no extension.

Starting with Windows 7 and beyond, Microsoft discontinued the INFO2 file. Now, the Recycle Bin is located in a hidden directory named \$Recycle.Bin\%SID%, where %SID% is the SID of the user who performed the deletion. When files are moved into the Recycle Bin, the original file is renamed to $R followed by a set of random characters, but maintaining the original file extension. Also, a new file beginning with $I, followed by the same set of random characters given to the $R file and the same extension, is created; this file contains the original filename/ path, original file size, and the date and time that the file was moved to the Recycle Bin. Note that all of the $I files are exactly 544 bytes long. The I$ structure is as follows:

Bytes 0–7: $I File header—always set to 01 followed by seven sets of 00.

Bytes 8–15: Original file size—stored in hex, in little-endian.

Bytes 16–23: Deleted date/time stamp—represented in number of seconds since midnight, January 1, 1601. Use a program such as Decode to assist with figuring out the exact date/time, if you don't want to do the math.

Bytes 24–543: Original file path/name.

You can recover a corrupted Recycle Bin with the following steps:

1. Open an elevated Command Prompt window. To open an elevated Command Prompt, click Start, click All Programs, click Accessories, right-click Command Prompt, and then click Run as administrator.

2. Type the following command and press ENTER:

```
rd /s /q C:\$Recycle.bin
```

Note that this process clears out the $Recycle.bin folder for the C:\ drive.

3. Type exit to close the Command Prompt window.

The $I30 Attribute

The NTFS file system maintains an index of all files/directories that belong to a directory called the $I30 attribute. Every directory in the file system contains a $I30 attribute that must be maintained whenever there are changes to the directory's contents. When files or folders are removed from the directory, the $I30 index records are rearranged accordingly. However, rearranging of the index records may leave remnants of the deleted file/folder entry within the slack space. This can be useful in forensics analysis for identifying files that may have existed on the drive.

The $I30 is the "file" name given to NTFS MFT attributes containing filename indexes for directories. NTFS stores the filename contents of the directory in several places, depending on the number of files in the directory.

PowerShell Forensics

Earlier in this chapter you were introduced to one PowerShell command. In this section, we will dive a bit deeper. Windows PowerShell is an extensible automation engine from Microsoft, consisting of a command-line shell and associated scripting language. Windows PowerShell is based on the .Net framework. In Windows 10, just use the search and type `PowerShell`. For many of the most interesting commands, you will need to run PowerShell as the administrator. PowerShell offers a number of commands that are useful in forensic examinations, particularly in triage of live machines.

There are a host of forensically useful commands. A few are listed here:

`Get-LocalUser`: This has a number of options, such as `Get-LocalUser` | where `Enabled -eq $True`. This commands illustrates the basics of PowerShell. Each command is actually a cmdlet (command let). You can also pipe in additional commands to refine the command, using the | symbol. It is easy to see that = is represented with `-eq`.

You can also view specific Registry keys. This example will search for some uninstalled program:

`Get-ItemProperty`

"HKLM:\Software\Wow6432Node\Microsoft\Windows\CurrentVersion \Uninstall\" | where DisplayName -Like "spy" | Select-Object DisplayName, DisplayVersion, InstallDate, Publisher

Of course, if that program has not been uninstalled, your results will be nothing.

The command `Get-Service` can retrieve all services running on this machine. The syntax is:

`Get-Service` | Select-Object Name, DisplayName, Status, StartType

You can see the results in **FIGURE 8-15**.

A list of active connections can be found with the PowerShell command:

`Get-NetTCPConnection –State Established`

This is shown in **FIGURE 8-16**.

You can get more details on PowerShell at *https://docs.microsoft.com/en-us /powershell/*.

```
Administrator: Windows PowerShell
PS C:\WINDOWS\system32> Get-Service | Select-Object Name, DisplayName, Status, StartType

Name                                    DisplayName
----                                    -----------
AarSvc_116498                           Agent Activation Runtime_116498
AdobeARMservice                         Adobe Acrobat Update Service
AdobeFlashPlayerUpdateSvc               Adobe Flash Player Update Service
AGMService                              Adobe Genuine Monitor Service
AGSService                              Adobe Genuine Software Integrity Service
AJRouter                                AllJoyn Router Service
ALG                                     Application Layer Gateway Service
AppIDSvc                                Application Identity
Appinfo                                 Application Information
Apple Mobile Device Service             Apple Mobile Device Service
AppMgmt                                 Application Management
AppReadiness                            App Readiness
AppVClient                              Microsoft App-V Client
AppXSvc                                 AppX Deployment Service (AppXSVC)
aspnet_state                            ASP.NET State Service
AssignedAccessManagerSvc                AssignedAccessManager Service
AudioEndpointBuilder                    Windows Audio Endpoint Builder
Audiosrv                                Windows Audio
autotimesvc                             Cellular Time
AxInstSV                                ActiveX Installer (AxInstSV)
BcastDVRUserService_116498              GameDVR and Broadcast User Service_116498
BDESVC                                  BitLocker Drive Encryption Service
BFE                                     Base Filtering Engine
BITS                                    Background Intelligent Transfer Service
BluetoothUserService_116498             Bluetooth User Support Service_116498
Bonjour Service                         Bonjour Service
BrokerInfrastructure                    Background Tasks Infrastructure Service
Browser                                 Computer Browser
BTAGService                             Bluetooth Audio Gateway Service
BthAvctpSvc                             AVCTP service
bthserv                                 Bluetooth Support Service
c2wts                                   Claims to Windows Token Service
camsvc                                  Capability Access Manager Service
CaptureService_116498                   CaptureService_116498
cbdhsvc_116498                          Clipboard User Service_116498
CDPSvc                                  Connected Devices Platform Service
CDPUserSvc_116498                       Connected Devices Platform User Service_116498
CertPropSvc                             Certificate Propagation
ClickToRunSvc                           Microsoft Office Click-to-Run Service
ClipSVC                                 Client License Service (ClipSVC)
CodeMeter.exe                           CodeMeter Runtime Server
COMSysApp                               COM+ System Application
```

Used with permission from Microsoft

FIGURE 8-15
Get-Service.

```
Administrator: Windows PowerShell
PS C:\WINDOWS\system32>  Get-NetTCPConnection -State Established

LocalAddress                          LocalPort RemoteAddress                        RemotePort State       AppliedSettin
------------                          --------- -------------                        ---------- -----       -------------
2603:8081:1800:75e6:6d52:f3cb:cc... 2102      2606:4700::6810:f8f9                 443        Established Internet
2603:8081:1800:75e6:6d52:f3cb:cc... 1621      2001:4998:20:800::1000               443        Established Internet
2603:8081:1800:75e6:6d52:f3cb:cc... 1405      2606:4700:3031::ac43:d208            443        Established Internet
2603:8081:1800:75e6:6d52:f3cb:cc... 1395      2a03:2880:f034:112:face:b00c:0:2     443        Established Internet
2603:8081:1800:75e6:6d52:f3cb:cc... 1394      2a03:2880:f034:112:face:b00c:0:2     443        Established Internet
2603:8081:1800:75e6:6d52:f3cb:cc... 1385      2600:1404:6400:5::172f:302e          80         Established Internet
2603:8081:1800:75e6:6d52:f3cb:cc... 1379      2a03:2880:f134:183:face:b00c:0:25de  443        Established Internet
2603:8081:1800:75e6:6d52:f3cb:cc... 1378      2620:109:c002::6cae:a0e              443        Established Internet
2603:8081:1800:75e6:6d52:f3cb:cc... 1366      2620:1ec:21::14                      443        Established Internet
2603:8081:1800:75e6:6d52:f3cb:cc... 1360      2600:1402:9800:3b7::25ea             443        Established Internet
2603:8081:1800:75e6:6d52:f3cb:cc... 1358      2607:f8b0:4000:812::2008             443        Established Internet
2603:8081:1800:75e6:6d52:f3cb:cc... 1345      2607:f8b0:4000:80c::2008             443        Established Internet
2603:8081:1800:75e6:6d52:f3cb:cc... 1342      2606:4700::6812:e134                 443        Established Internet
2603:8081:1800:75e6:6d52:f3cb:cc... 1341      2606:4700:3036::ac43:b992            443        Established Internet
2603:8081:1800:75e6:6d52:f3cb:cc... 1339      2606:2800:21f:edfc:49f9:c096:a5a...  443        Established Internet
2603:8081:1800:75e6:6d52:f3cb:cc... 1337      2606:2800:220:de:468:2285:c1:4a3     443        Established Internet
2603:8081:1800:75e6:6d52:f3cb:cc... 1336      2607:f8b0:4000:80c::200a             443        Established Internet
2603:8081:1800:75e6:6d52:f3cb:cc... 1329      2606:4700::6812:14e2                 80         Established Internet
2603:8081:1800:75e6:6d52:f3cb:cc... 1326      2620:1ec:c::11                       443        Established Internet
2603:8081:1800:75e6:6d52:f3cb:cc... 1311      2606:2800:220:de:468:2285:c1:4a3     443        Established Internet
2603:8081:1800:75e6:6d52:f3cb:cc... 1310      2a03:2880:f034:11a:face:b00c:0:3     443        Established Internet
2603:8081:1800:75e6:6d52:f3cb:cc... 1309      2a03:2880:f034:11a:face:b00c:0:3     443        Established Internet
2603:8081:1800:75e6:6d52:f3cb:cc... 1308      2606:2800:220:de:468:2285:c1:4a3     80         Established Internet
2603:8081:1800:75e6:6d52:f3cb:cc... 1301      2600:3c03::f03c:91ff:feb0:f4a8       80         Established Internet
2603:8081:1800:75e6:6d52:f3cb:cc... 1300      2600:3c03::f03c:91ff:feb0:f4a8       80         Established Internet
2603:8081:1800:75e6:6d52:f3cb:cc... 1299      2600:3c03::f03c:91ff:feb0:f4a8       80         Established Internet
2603:8081:1800:75e6:6d52:f3cb:cc... 1298      2600:3c03::f03c:91ff:feb0:f4a8       80         Established Internet
2603:8081:1800:75e6:6d52:f3cb:cc... 1297      2607:f8b0:4003:c02::9b               443        Established Internet
2603:8081:1800:75e6:6d52:f3cb:cc... 1294      2607:f8b0:4000:80d::200e             443        Established Internet
2603:8081:1800:75e6:6d52:f3cb:cc... 1292      2606:4700:10::ac43:2794              443        Established Internet
2603:8081:1800:75e6:6d52:f3cb:cc... 1259      2607:f8b0:4000:813::200a             443        Established Internet
```

Used with permission from Microsoft

FIGURE 8-16
Get-Net TCP Connection.

CHAPTER SUMMARY

This chapter introduced you to the details of forensic analysis of a Microsoft Windows system. You should pay particular attention to the Registry and the forensic data you can extract from it. Also important to your forensic investigation is the index.dat file. These two are the most important items to learn in this chapter.

Additional topics in this chapter, such as examining the swap file and extracting data from a live system, are also important to any forensic examination of a Windows computer. But they may not yield quite as much information as examining index.dat and the Registry.

KEY CONCEPTS AND TERMS

Basic input/output system (BIOS)	Dump	Master boot record (MBR)
Data consistency	Graphical user interface (GUI)	Power-on self-test (POST)
Disk Operating System (DOS)	Heap (H)	Slurred image
	Hives	Stack (S)

CHAPTER 8 ASSESSMENT

1. What was the first Windows operating system to support FAT32?

A. Windows 2000
B. Windows 98
C. Windows 95
D. Windows 3.1

2. How many hives are in the Windows Registry?

A. 1
B. 2
C. 5
D. 8

3. Stack memory is stored in a first-in, last-out format.

A. True
B. False

4. In Windows 10, the swap file ends with what extension?

A. .sys
B. .swp
C. .swap
D. .vmem

References

1. Crenshaw, A. (n.d.). Practical guide to alternative data streams in NTFS. Irongeek.com [blog]. Retrieved from https://www.irongeek.com/i.php?page=security/altds on February 8, 2021.

2. No authors listed. (2020, September 8). Windows registry information for advanced users. Retrieved from https://docs.microsoft.com/en-us/troubleshoot/windows-server/performance/windows-registry-advanced-users#references on February 8, 2021.

3. Russinovich, M., Ionescu, A., & Solomon, D. (2012). *Windows Internals, Sixth Edition*. Microsoft Press.

4. Easttom, C. (2014). *System Forensics, Investigation, and Response*. Burlington, MA: Jones & Bartlett Learning.

5. Carvey, H. (2011). *Investigating Windows Systems*. Academic Press.

Linux Forensics

I N THIS CHAPTER, YOU WILL LEARN ABOUT forensics on a Linux system. Assuming you may not have a good working knowledge of Linux, this chapter spends a significant amount of time giving you the basic background in Linux required to do forensics. Then, you will learn about specific shell commands, directories, and logs that are important to a forensic investigation of a Linux system.

Chapter 9 Topics

This chapter covers the following topics and concepts:

- The Linux operating system
- Linux file systems
- What to look for in the system logs
- Forensically interesting directories
- Important shell commands
- How to undelete files from Linux

Chapter 9 Goals

When you complete this chapter, you will be able to:

- Understand the Linux operating system
- Retrieve logs from Linux
- Utilize important shell commands
- Understand what directories are important in a Linux forensic investigation
- Undelete files from Linux

Linux and Forensics

Linux is a very important topic for anyone studying forensics. The first and most obvious reason is that one might need to examine a Linux machine in the course of a forensic investigation. Linux is quite popular in certain areas of the computing community, particularly in web servers. If you should need to investigate a web breach, there is a reasonable chance that it could include a Linux machine.

Another reason to study Linux is that it is the operating system that Android is based on. In Chapter 11 we will look at Android and other mobile devices. The more you understand about Linux itself, the more you will understand Android phones and tablets. Obviously, this single chapter cannot make you an expert in Linux, but it can give you a start.

A third reason to study Linux is due to Kali Linux. Kali Linux is a Linux distribution that is replete with security-related tools. It has gained a great deal of attention due to its hacking/penetration testing tools like Metasploit, and it also has a number of forensics tools. We will look at some of these later in this chapter.

Linux Basics

Before you can conduct forensics on a Linux machine, you need to have a basic understanding of how Linux works. If you do have a good working knowledge of Linux, feel free to skim over this section anyway, as it provides a common background knowledge level for all learners.

Linux History

A good way to get an overview of Linux is to begin by studying the history of Linux. And the first, most important thing to know about the history of Linux is that it is actually a clone of Unix. That means that the history of Linux includes the history of Unix. So that is where this examination of Linux history begins: with the birth of Unix.

The Unix operating system was created at Bell Laboratories. Bell Labs is famous for a number of major scientific discoveries. It was there that the first evidence of the Big Bang was found, and it was there that the C programming language was born. So innovation is nothing new for Bell Labs.

By the 1960s, computing was spreading, but there was no widely available operating system. Bell Labs had been involved in a project called Multics (Multiplexed Information and Computing Service). Multics was a combined effort of Massachusetts Institute of Technology, Bell Labs, and General Electric to create an operating system with wide general applicability. Due to significant problems with the Multics project, Bell Labs decided to pull out. A team at Bell Labs, consisting of Ken Thompson, Dennis Ritchie, Brian Kernighan, Douglas McElroy, and Joe Ossanna, decided to create a new operating system that might have wide usage. They wanted to create an operating system that would run on a range of types of hardware. The culmination of their project was the release of the Unix operating system in 1972. Even though that was more than 40 years ago, Unix is still considered a very stable, secure operating system today. That should be an indication of how successful they were.

The original name of the project was Unics, a play on the term Multics. Originally, Unix was a side project for the team, as Bell Labs was not providing financial support for the project. However, that changed once the team added functionality that could be used on other Bell computers. Then the company began to enthusiastically support the project. In 1972, after the C programming language was created, Unix was rewritten entirely in C. Before this time, all operating systems were written in assembly language.

In 1983, Richard Stallman, one of the fathers of the open-source movement, began working on a Unix clone. He called this operating system GNU (an acronym for "GNU's Not Unix"). His goal was simply to create an open-source version of Unix. He wanted it to be as much like Unix as possible, despite the name of GNU's Not Unix. However, Stallman's open-source Unix variant did not achieve widespread popularity, and it was soon replaced by other, more robust variants.

In 1987, a university professor named Andrew S. Tanenbaum created another Unix variant, this one called Minix. Minix was a fairly stable, functional, and reasonably good Unix clone. Minix was completely written in C by Tanenbaum. He created it primarily as a teaching tool for his students. He wanted them to learn operating systems by being able to study the actual source code for an operating system. The source code for Minix was included in his book *Operating Systems: Design and Implementation*. Placing the source code in a textbook that was widely used meant a large number of computer science students would be exposed to this source code.

Though Minix failed to gain the popularity of some other Unix variants, it was an inspiration for the creator of Linux. The story of the Linux operating system is really the story of Linus Torvalds. He began his work on Linux when he was a graduate student working toward his PhD in computer science. Linus decided to create his own Unix clone. The name derives from his name (Linus) combined with the word Unix. Linus had extensive exposure to both Unix and Minix, which made creating a good Unix clone more achievable for him.

Linux Shells

Now that you have a grasp of the essential history of Linux, the next step is to look at what is arguably the most important part of Linux: the shell. Many Linux administrators work entirely in the shell without ever using a graphical user interface (GUI). Linux offers many different shells. Each shell is designed for a different purpose. The following list details the most common shells:

- **Bourne shell (sh)**—This was the original default shell for Unix. It was first released in 1977.
- **Bourne-again shell (Bash)**—This is the most commonly used shell in Linux. It was released in 1989.
- **C shell (csh)**—This shell derives its name from the fact that it uses very C-like syntax. Linux users who are familiar with C will like this shell. It was first released for Unix in 1978.
- **Korn shell (ksh)**—This is a popular shell developed by David Korn in the 1980s. The Korn shell is meant to be compatible with the Bourne shell, but also incorporates true programming language capabilities.

There are other shells, but these are the most common. And of these, Bash is the most widely used. Most Linux distributions ship with Bash.

You do not have to be a master of Linux in order to perform some basic Linux forensics. However, there are some essential shell commands you should know, which are shown in

TABLE 9-1. Note that all commands have flags that can be applied to alter their behavior. Some common flags for select commands are also shown in Table 9-1.

If you need more training on Linux shell commands, the following websites could be helpful:

- *https://www.geeksforgeeks.org/basic-shell-commands-in-linux/*
- *http://lowfatlinux.com/linux-basics.html*
- *http://www.cyberciti.biz/tips/linux-unix-commands-cheat-sheets.html*

TABLE 9-1 Basic Linux shell commands.

LINUX COMMAND	EXPLANATION AND EXAMPLE
`ls`	The `ls` command lists the contents of the current directory. Example: `ls` Common Flags `ls -l` displays file or directory, size, modified date and time, file or folder name and owner of file, and its permission. `ls -a` shows even hidden files. `ls -ls` shows the files in order of size.
`cp`	The `cp` command copies one file to another directory. Example: `cp filename.txt directoryname` `cp -R` is used if you are copying two directories rather than files and want all the contents to be copied as well.
`mkdir`	The `mkdir` command creates a new directory. Example: `mkdir directoryname` `mkdir -p` will create parent directories as needed. Example: `mkdir -p /directory1/directorytwo/directory3`
`cd`	The `cd` command is used to change directories. Example: `cd directory name` `cd ..` will go up one level in the directory tree. `cd /` goes directly to the root directory. `cd ~` moves to the home directory of the current user.
`rm`	The `rm` command is used to delete or remove a file. Example: `rm filename` `rm-i` will prompt before any removal. `-r` removes directories and contents recursively.
`rmdir`	The `rmdir` command is used to remove or delete entire directories. Example: `rmdir directoryname`
`mv`	The `mv` command is used to move a file. Example: `mv myfile.txt myfolder`

(Continues)

TABLE 9-1 Basic Linux shell commands. (*Continued*)

`diff`	The `diff` command performs a byte-by-byte comparison of two files and tells you what is different about them. Example: `diff myfile.txt myfile2.txt`
`cmp`	The `cmp` command performs a textual comparison of two files and tells you the difference between the two. Example: `cmp myfile.txt myfile2.txt`
`>`	This is the redirect command. Instead of displaying the output of a command like `ls` to the screen, it redirects it to a file. Example: `ls > file1.txt`
`ps`	The `ps` command lists all currently running processes that the user has started. Any program or daemon is a process. Example: `ps` `ps-a` lists all processes for all users, not just the current user. `ps -aux` provides details for each process, such as process ID, percentage of memory used, etc.
`Pstree`	The `pstree` command shows all processes (whether started by the current user or not) in a tree format, clearly showing which process started which other processes. This is definitely of interest forensically.
`top`	The `top` command lists all currently running processes, whether the user started them or not. It also lists more detail on the processes. Example: `top`
`fsck`	This is a file system check. The `fsck` command can check to see whether a given partition is in good working condition. Example: `fsck /dev/hda1`
`fdisk`	The `fdisk` command lists the various partitions. Example: `fdisk-1`
`mount`	The `mount` command mounts a partition, allowing you to work with it. Example: `mount /dev/fd0 /mnt/floppy`
`lsof`	This command lists open files. This is helpful in forensics to see not only what files are open but also the processes which opened them.
`lsattr`	This command lists file attributes on a Linux second extended file system.
`env`	The `env` command prints all environmental variables.

It is a good idea to become comfortable working with shell commands. In the next section, you will be briefly introduced to the GUIs that are available in Linux. You will find that these interfaces are fairly intuitive and not that dissimilar to Windows. However, many forensic commands and utilities work primarily from the shell. You might recall that you can make a forensic copy of a disk using the dd command. That is a shell command, and only one of many you will want to be familiar with.

9

Linux
Forensics

Graphical User Interface

Although Linux aficionados prefer the shell, and a great deal of forensics can be done from the shell, Linux does have a GUI. In fact, there are several you can choose from. The most widely used are GNOME and KDE.

GNU Network Object Model Environment (GNOME)

The name GNOME is an acronym of GNU Network Object Model Environment. There is no doubt that GNOME (*http://www.gnome.org/*) is one of the two most popular GUIs for Linux. Many Linux distributions include GNOME, or a choice between GNOME and some other desktop environment. In fact, the popular Ubuntu distribution ships only with GNOME. GNOME, which is built on GTK+, is a cross-platform toolkit for creating GUIs. You can see the GNOME desktop in **FIGURE 9-1**. Currently, GNOME 3 is the most widely used, even though it was released in 2011. GNOME 3 is used in Fedora, Debian, SUSE, CentOS, and other Linux distributions.

K Desktop Environment (KDE)

KDE (*http://www.kde.org/*) is the other of the two most popular Linux GUIs available. Historically this was just called the KDE desktop. However, now there is the KDE Plasma Desktop. As of this writing, the current version of Plasma is KDE Plasma 5. Version 5.19 was released in June 2020, and version 5.20 was released in October 2020. KDE Plasma uses the X Windows System for windowing functions. There is also Plasma Mobile for phones. Plasma Mobile is used on the Nexus 5 and related models. Some of the features of KDE Plasma 5 include:

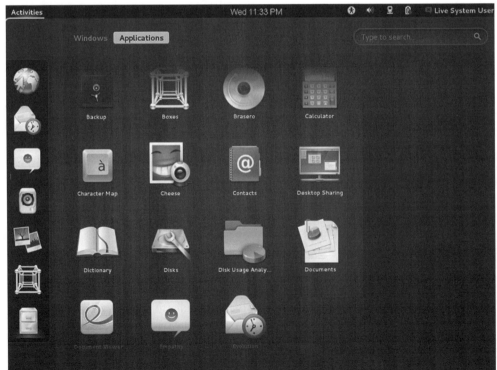

FIGURE 9-1

GNOME.

- KRunner: A search tool that allows for additional plugins
- Dolphin: A file manager
- Spectacle: A screenshot tool

Most Linux distributions ship with either KDE or GNOME, or both. For example, the Kbuntu distribution is essentially Ubuntu with KDE. KDE was founded in 1996 by Matthias Ettrich. At the time of KDE's creation, Ettrich was, like Linus Torvalds, a computer science student. The name KDE was intended as a word play on the Common Desktop Environment (CDE) available for Unix systems.

KDE is built on the Qt framework. Qt is a multiplatform GUI framework written in C++. KDE Plasma is shown in **FIGURE 9-2**.

Although KDE and GNOME are the most widely known and used GUIs for Linux, there are certainly others. A couple of the more widely used are listed and briefly described here:

- **Common Desktop Environment (CDE)**—The CDE (*http://www.opengroup.org/cde/*) was originally developed in 1994 for Unix systems. At one time it was the default desktop for Sun Solaris systems. CDE is based on Hewlett-Packard's Visual User Environment (VUE). It was originally proprietary but was released under GNU Lesser General Public License in 2012.
- **Enlightenment**—This desktop was first released in 1997 and is meant specifically for graphics developers. You can learn more at *http://www.enlightenment.org/*.
- **Cinnamon**—This desktop is based on GNOME. This desktop is frequently seen in Linux Mint. Cinnamon is known to be quite easy to learn and use.
- **LXDE (Lightweight X11 Desktop Environment)** —As the name suggests, this is a lightweight (i.e., low resource utilization) desktop. LXDE is the default desktop environment for LXLE Linux, Artix, and Knoppix.

Linux Boot Process

It is important to understand the Linux boot process because some crimes, including malware attacks, can affect the boot process.

Linux is often used on embedded systems, even smartphones. In such cases, when the system is first powered on, the first step is to load the bootstrap environment. The **bootstrap environment** is a special program, such as U-Boot or RedBoot, that is stored in

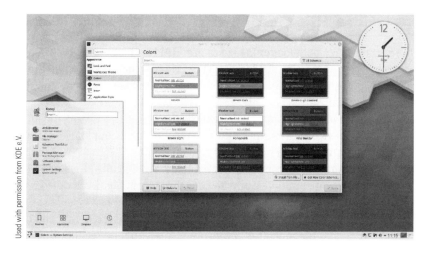

Used with permission from KDE e.V.

FIGURE 9-2
KDE Plasma.

a special section of flash memory. On a PC, booting Linux begins in the BIOS (basic input/output system) at address 0xFFFF0. Note that, modern systems use Unified Extensible Firmware Interface (UEFI), which, while being a substantial improvement over BIOS, accomplishes essentially the same goal.

Just as with Windows, the first sector on any disk is called the boot sector. It contains executable code that is used in the boot process. A boot sector also has the hex value 0xaa55 in the final two bytes. Also, as in Windows, after the BIOS has been loaded and the power-on self-test (POST) has completed, the BIOS/UEFI locates the master boot record (MBR) and passes control to it. The MBR is located on the first sector of the bootable disk (/dev/hda or /dev sda). Passing the control from the BIOS/UEFI to MBR marks the end of the first stage of the boot process.

The MBR then loads up a boot loader program, such as **LILO (Linux Loader)** or **GRUB (Grand Unified Bootloader)**. GRUB is the more modern and much more widely used boot loader. GRUB version 2 works with either BIOS or UEFI systems. Unless you are working with a very old system, it is most likely a GRUB version 2 working with UEFI. Often boot loaders are larger than a single sector, so they are loaded in stages. When a bootable device is found, the first-stage boot loader is loaded into random access memory (RAM) and executed.

In Linux, there are actually two boot loaders. The first boot loader is rather small, only 512 bytes in length (a single sector). The first 446 bytes are the primary boot loader, which contains both executable code and error message text. The next 64 bytes are the partition table, which contains a record for each of four partitions. Each is just 16 bytes. The first boot loader is terminated with 2 bytes that are defined as the magic number (0xAA55). This boot loader's job is to load the second-stage boot loader. The second boot loader is responsible for loading the Linux kernel.

FYI

You can view what is in the MBR. Just type the following two lines in the shell of your choice:

```
# dd if=/dev/hda of=mbr.bin bs=512 count=1
# od -xa mbr.bin
```

When forensically examining a Linux machine, you may want to examine the master boot record to see if it has been altered.

When the second-stage boot loader is loaded into RAM and executing, a splash screen is commonly displayed. At this point, the Linux image is loaded into RAM. When the images are loaded, the second-stage boot loader passes control to the kernel image and the kernel is decompressed and initialized.

At this point, the second-stage boot loader checks the system hardware and any attached peripherals. Once the devices are enumerated, the second-stage boot loader can attempt to mount the root device and load the necessary kernel modules.

The second-stage boot loader loads the kernel image. This is called the kernel stage of the boot process. The kernel must initialize any devices the system has. Even devices that have been initialized by the BIOS must be reinitialized. The system then switches the CPU from real mode to protected mode. The system now loads the compressed kernel and calls the decompress_kernel() function. It is at this point that you may see the "Uncompressing

TABLE 9-2 Typical default active services.

MODE	DIRECTORY	RUN LEVEL DESCRIPTION
0	/etc/rc.d/rc0.d	Halt
1	/etc/rc.d/rc1.d	Single-user mode
2	/etc/rc.d/rc2.d	Not used (user-definable)
3	/etc/rc.d/rc3.d	Full multiuser mode without GUI
4	/etc/rc.d/rc4.d	Not used (user-definable)
5	/etc/rc.d/rc5.d	Full multiuser mode with GUI
6	/etc/rc.d/rc6.d	Reboot

Linux..." message displayed on the screen. Now the `start_kernel()` function is called, and the uncompressed kernel displays a large number of messages on the screen as it initializes the various hardware items and processes such as the scheduler.

Once the kernel is initialized, the first user program starts. In PC-based Linux systems, that first process is called init. The `kernel_thread()` function is called next to start init. The kernel goes into an idle loop and becomes an idle thread with process ID 0. The process init() begins high-level system initialization. Note that unlike PC systems, embedded systems have a simpler first user process than init.

The boot process then inspects the /etc/inittab file to determine the appropriate run level. As a reference, the Linux run levels are listed in **TABLE 9-2**.

Based on the run level, the init process then executes the appropriate startup script. Those scripts are located in subdirectories of the /etc/rc.d directory. Scripts used for run levels 0 to 6 are located in subdirectories /etc/rc.d/rc0.d through /etc/rc.d /rc6.d, respectively. The default boot run level is set in the file /etc/inittab with the initdefault variable. At this point, the boot process is over, and Linux is up and running!

> **NOTE**
>
> Unlike in Windows, the boot messages are displayed on the screen and you can see everything. However, this often happens too fast to follow. After the system is booted up, you can use the `dmesg` command from the shell to see what boot messages were displayed.

Logical Volume Management

Logical Volume Manager (LVM) is an abstraction layer that provides volume management for the Linux Kernel. The technology has many purposes, but on a single system (like a single desktop or server) its primary role is to allow the resizing of partitions, and the ability to create backups by taking snapshots of the logical volumes.

With LVM, the first megabyte of the physical drive or volume (called a PV) contains a structure called the LVM header. The PV for a drive contains that drive/volumes layout. The Scientific Working Group on Digital Evidence (SWDGE) describes LVM as follows:

Some Linux installations use LVM, a logical volume manager for the Linux kernel that manages disk drives and similar mass-storage devices, providing an abstraction layer on top of traditional partitions and block devices. LVM provides a more flexible configuration of storage on block devices by virtualizing the partitions and allowing them to be split, combined, and or arrayed across independent physical disks or physical partitions. In order to parse on-disk structures properly, forensic tools must be LVM aware. Acquisition of an LVM volume must consider the logical configuration of the storage.[1]

Linux Distributions

Linux is open source. That means the source code is available for anyone who wants to modify, repackage, and distribute it. Therefore a lot of different distributions are available. They are all Linux, and they all have the same Linux shells, but each has some differences. For example, some use KDE by default, whereas others use GNOME. Some ship with lots of additional open-source tools, whereas others don't have quite as many tools, or have different tools. A few of the more common distributions include the following:

- **Ubuntu**—Very popular with beginners
- **Red Hat Enterprise Linux (RHEL)**—Often used with large-scale servers
- **OpenSuse**—A popular, general-purpose Linux distribution
- **Debian**—Another popular, general-purpose Linux distribution
- **Mint**—Very popular in 2020
- **Fedora**—Essentially a client version of Red Hat, and very popular
- **CentOS**—This distribution has been around for quite some time and is often in the top 30 on *www.distrowatch.com*.

Kali Linux is the one most interesting to forensic analysts. Kali is replete with tools for hacking, security, and forensics. It is a very good idea to become at least basically familiar with Kali. There are some great tutorials for Kali at *https://www.kali.org/category/tutorials/*.

The website *http://www.DistroWatch.com* has a list of 100 best-selling distributions.

> **NOTE**
>
> All operating systems must connect to a device or partition and assign it some designation, such as a drive letter, so it can be accessed by the user. Linux and all Unix-like operating systems assign a device name to each device. This usually happens automatically but Linux has a mount command that allows you to manually mount devices and partitions.

Linux File Systems

This section provides details about Linux file systems.

Ext

Although there are other file systems, the Extended File System (Ext) is the one most commonly used with Linux. The current version is Ext4. The Ext4 file system can support volumes with sizes up to 1 exabyte (10^{18} bytes or 1 billion gigabytes) and single files with sizes up to 16 terabytes. These sizes are extremely large, indicating that there will not be a need for an update to Ext anytime soon.

The first two versions of Ext did not support journaling. Ext3 was the first to support journaling. Ext3 and Ext4 support three specific types of journaling. The most secure and safe level is called *journal*. With the journal level, metadata and file contents are written to the journal before being written to the main file system. The next level, slightly less secure than journal, is called *ordered*. With the ordered level only metadata is written to the journal; however, changes to files are not journaled until they have been committed to the disk. Finally, the least secure level is *writeback*. With the writeback level, only metadata is written to the journal, and it might be written to the journal before or after it is actually committed. Ext4 added checksums in the journal to prevent errors.

The Reiser File System

The Reiser File System (ReiserFS) was first introduced as a part of the Linux kernel version 2.4.1. ReiserFS has always supported journaling. ReiserFS performs very well when the hard drive has a large number of smaller files. In fact, tests have shown that when you are dealing with files that are under 4 KB in size, ReiserFS outperforms Ext2 and Ext3.

The Berkeley Fast File System

The Berkeley Fast File System is also known as the Unix File System. It was developed at University of California, Berkeley specifically for use with Linux. Berkeley uses a bitmap to track free clusters, indicating which clusters are available and which are not.

Linux Logs

Like Windows, Linux has a number of logs that can be very interesting for a forensic investigation. This section provides a brief description of each of the major Linux logs and the forensic relevance of that log.

The /var/log/faillog Log

This log file contains failed user logins. This can be very important when tracking attempts to crack into the system. Usually, a normal user might occasionally have one or two failed login attempts. Numerous failed login attempts, or even frequent failed login attempts that occur at diverse times, can be an indicator of someone trying to compromise access to the system. It is also worth noting the times of failed login attempts. If an employee normally works from 8:00 a.m. to 5:00 p.m. and there are failed login attempts at 11:00 p.m., that may be a warning sign.

The /var/log/kern.log Log

This log file is used for messages from the operating system's kernel. This log is less interesting forensically. It is more likely to show systemwide problems. However, it is entirely possible for someone to mistake system issues for some intrusion or malware. If you have odd behavior on a target system and find related messages in the kern.log, it may allow you to rule out malware.

The /var/log/lpr.log Log

This is the printer log. It can give you a record of any items that have been printed from this machine. That can be useful in many cases. To begin with, corporate espionage cases often involve the criminal printing out sensitive documents. Having a record of exactly what was printed when, and which user printed it, can be very useful.

The /var/log/mail.* Log

This is the mail server log and can be very useful in any computer crime investigation. Email can be useful in many different criminal investigations. It is obviously very useful in cyber-stalking cases, as well as many civil litigation cases.

The /var/log/mysql.* Log

This log records activities related to the MySQL database server. These are of most interest in crimes involving database attacks. For example, SQL injection attacks might leave a record in the database log.

The /var/log/apache2/* Log

If this machine is running the Apache web server, then this log shows related activity. This can be very useful in tracking attempts to hack into the web server. You can examine the log to see attempts at buffer overflow attacks, denial-of-service attacks, and a variety of other attacks.

FYI

Snort is an open-source **intrusion detection system (IDS)**. Intrusion detection systems monitor network traffic looking for suspicious activity. There are two types of intrusion detection systems: passive and active.

A passive IDS will simply log suspicious activity and perhaps notify a network administrator. Active IDSs (also called intrusion prevention systems [IPSs]) also log the activity, but then shut down the suspected attack. The problem is that all systems get false positives—traffic that appears to be an attack but is not. For example, suppose Jane usually works from 8:00 a.m. to 5:00 p.m. and uses no more than 50 megabytes of bandwidth per hour. Suddenly, the system shows Jane logged on at 11:00 p.m. and is using 300 megabytes of bandwidth per hour. The active IDS assumes this is an attack and blocks the traffic. However, in reality, Jane is working late on an important presentation that is due tomorrow.

The issue of active versus passive is one for the organization's security administrator to deal with. From a forensic point of view, the IDS log is the important issue. If an organization is using an IDS, any IDS, you should absolutely view those logs.

The /var/log/lighttpd/* Log

If this machine is running the Lighttpd web server, then this log shows related activity. This can be very useful in tracking attempts to hack into the web server.

The /var/log/apport.log Log

This log records application crashes. Sometimes these can reveal attempts to compromise the system or the presence of malware. Of course, it can also simply reveal a buggy application. That is the real challenge with computer forensics: determining what is evidence of an actual crime.

Other Logs

Any other applications running on the Linux computer that store logs can be useful in your forensic examination. For example, if you are using an IDS such as Snort, it keeps logs of all suspicious traffic. That can be very useful in your investigation.

Viewing Logs

With Linux, you can use a variety of shell commands to view a log. You can also simply use your favorite text editor within your preferred GUI. Using the Linux dmesg command is the preferred way to view logs from the shell. It works like this:

```
dmesg | lpr
```

Or, you can use any of these methods as well:

```
# tail -f /var/log/lpr.log
# less /var/log/ lpr.log
# more -f /var/log/ lpr.log
```

As you can see, there are a number of methods for viewing logs in Linux. Beyond simply viewing the logs, you can search for specific things. For example, a log with binary data in it may mean malware is hidden in the log. You can search for that with this command:

```
grep [[:cntrl:]] /var/log/*.log
```

It will also be important to find any logs that have nothing in them. That might indicate someone wiped the log. You can do that with this command:

```
ls -al /var/log/*
```

Linux Directories

In any operating system, there are key directories that are important to the functioning of that operating system. In Linux, these directories are important places to seek out evidence. Knowing the general purpose of the major directories, as well as their potential forensic importance, is useful in conducting a forensic analysis of a Linux system.

The /root Directory

The /root directory is the home directory for the root user. The root in Linux is the same as the administrator in Windows. This directory is where any data for the administrator will be located.

The /bin Directory

The /bin directory holds binary or compiled files. This means programs, including some malware, may be found here. You absolutely should examine this directory. You can see an example of this directory in **FIGURE 9-3**.

9

Linux
Forensics

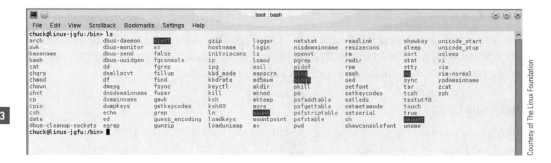

FIGURE 9-3

The /bin
directory.

The /sbin Directory

This directory is similar to /bin, but it contains binary files that are not intended for the average computer user. For example, the `mke2fs` command, a file system utility that is usually utilized by administrators, is in this directory.

The /etc Folder

The /etc folder contains configuration files. Most applications require some configuration when they start up. The web servers, boot loaders (LILO and GRUB), and many other applications have configuration files. Obviously, an intruder into a system may want to change how a given application behaves. Web server, boot loader, and security software configuration files would be attractive targets for any hacker.

The /etc/inittab File

This is where the boot-up process and operation are set. For example, the init level for the system on startup is set in this file. Again, a sophisticated attacker might want to change the inittab to change the behavior of the system. Even some advanced malware might alter your inittab.

The inittab has a number of entries. Each is defined by four fields separated by colons. Those fields include the following:

- **label**—A unique identification label of up to four characters.
- **run_level**—The init level at which the entry is executed.
- **action:a**—A keyword indicating the action that init is to take on the process.
- **process**—The process init executes upon entering the specified run level.
- **boot**—Starts the process and continues to the next entry without waiting for the process to complete. When the process dies, init does not restart the process.
- **bootwait**—Starts the process once and waits for it to terminate before going on to the next inittab entry.
- **initdefault**—Determines which run level to enter initially, using the highest number in the run_level field. If there is no initdefault entry in inittab, then init requests an initial run level from the user at boot time.
- **sysinit**—Starts the process the first time init reads the table and waits for it to terminate before going on to the next inittab entry.

The /dev Directory

This directory contains device files. Device files are really interfaces to devices, including drives. Storage devices, sound devices, and, in fact, all of your devices should have a device file located in this directory. Some naming conventions can help you navigate this directory. For example, all hard drives start with hd, floppy drives start with fd, and CD drives start with cd. So, the main hard drive might be named /dev/hd0. The floppy drive would be called /dev/fd0.

The /mnt Directory

Many devices, such as floppy and CD-ROM drives, are mounted in the /mnt directory. Any drive must be mounted prior to its use. The process of mounting a drive simply involves the operating system accessing it and loading it into memory. Modern Linux distributions do this for you. From a forensic perspective, checking this directory lets you know what things are currently mounted on the system.

The /boot Directory

The boot directory contains those files critical for booting. Your boot loader (whether it is LILO or GRUB) looks in this directory. It is a common practice to keep kernel images in this directory.

The /usr Directory

This directory contains the subdirectories for individual users. In cases of suspected corporate espionage, these directories might contain valuable evidence.

The /tmp Directory

As the name suggests, this directory primarily contains files that are needed temporarily. However, you may find data regarding what has been happening most recently on the system. This directory contains necessary files that are temporarily required by the system as well as other software and applications running on the machine. The files that are stored in the /tmp directory get removed immediately on system reboot. That means the /tmp directory must be searched live.

The /var Directory

The /var directory contains a great many logs, as you have already seen from previous sections. This is the place to look for any logs. There are also some interesting subdirectories, such as /var/tmp, /var/backups, and /var/spool.

/var/tmp

The /var/tmp directory is made available for programs that require temporary files or directories that are preserved between system reboots. Therefore, data stored in /var/tmp is more persistent than data in /tmp. By default, all the files and data that get stored in /var/tmp stay there for up to 30 days.

/var/backups

This subdirectory contains backups of various system files such as /etc/shadow/ and /etc /inetd.conf. The files are normally named either with a .bak extension or with a number such as .0, .1, etc.

/var/spool

This directory contains the print queue, so it can be very important to see if something is currently in the print queue. Also, even though the "spool" directory is obviously for printers, this directory has a history of being a favorite place for hackers to hide files and communications for each other.

The /proc Directory

The /proc directory is created in memory and keeps information about currently running processes. It is different from any other directory in that it is not really stored on your hard disk. If you have a live Linux system and you want to see what is running on that system before powering it down, the contents of this directory can be very useful. You can see an example of the contents of a /proc directory in **FIGURE 9-4**.

This directory also has subdirectories that can be used to recover files and evidence. Consider this scenario: Assume that an intruder has downloaded a password cracker and is attempting to crack system passwords. The tool is attempting a number of passwords in a text file called pass. The intruder subsequently deletes both the executable and the text file, but the process is still running in memory. You can use `ps` or `pstree` to find the running processes and get the process ID. Assume the process ID is 3201. Now in the /proc directory, you can find /proc/3201. If you simply copy the executable from /proc to some other directory, it recovers that deleted executable. Of course, this works only on a live system, prior to shutting it down.

The /run Directory

This directory has information about run-time variable data. It will be cleared during the boot process. Some of what is found in this directory was formerly in /var/run. In fact, in some distributions /var/run is simlinked to /run.

The /run directory can be seen in **FIGURE 9-5**.

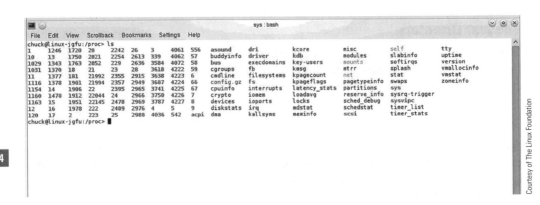

FIGURE 9-4

The /proc directory.

Courtesy of The Linux Foundation

FIGURE 9-5

The /run directory.

Tmpfs

Tmpfs (temporary file system) is a Linux file system whose contents reside only in memory. This means that files and directories inside of tmpfs mounts are never written to the local disk, so that once a tmpfs mount is unmounted, the entire file system is wiped. This may have interesting data if you can capture it before the system is shut down.

On some Linux distributions, the /tmp is mounted directly as tmpfs, so only by capturing tmpfs will you be able to get what was in /tmp. Linux also uses tmpfs to implement shared memory through /dev/shm. More sophisticated attackers can use tmpfs to download malicious files and use tmpfs as a staging area.

You can find out more about tmpfs at:

https://www.kernel.org/doc/html/latest/filesystems/tmpfs.html

The tmpfs is normally captured using memory capture, which is discussed elsewhere. The specific command is

```
volatility --profile=Linuxthisx86 -f /root/lime-tmpfs
linux_tmpfs
```

Shell Commands for Forensics

There are hundreds of shell commands, and earlier in this chapter you were given a few links to some shell tutorials. Many of those commands are basic file/directory navigation, network administration, and general commands. In this section, you are introduced to a few Linux shell commands that can be very useful in your forensic investigations.

The dmesg Command

When your system boots up, you see a lot of information telling you what processes are starting, what processes failed, what hardware is being initialized, and more. This can be invaluable information to a forensic investigation. You can use the dmesg command to view all the messages that were displayed during the boot process.

The command dmesg displays the messages for you. However, it does tend to fill up multiple screens. It is recommended that you simply pipe the output to some file (for example, dmesg>myfile.txt) and then search that file. You can see some sample output of dmesg in **FIGURE 9-6**.

The fsck Command

Hard drives eventually age and begin to encounter problems. It is also possible that a suspect hard drive may have some issues preventing a full forensic analysis. You can use fsck (file system check) to help with that. There are several related commands, such as e2fsck.

9

Linux
Forensics

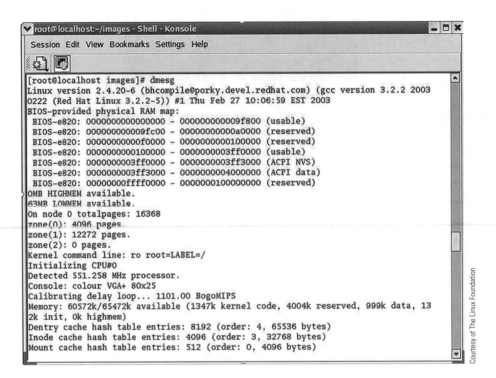

FIGURE 9-6

The dmesg command.

Be aware, however, that you should try all other forensic methods before using any file system utility. It is possible that a file system utility will erase some data and lose some evidence—particularly evidence hidden in slack space.

The `grep` Command

This is the single most popular search command for Linux. It allows you to search for a wide range of parameters. For example, you might use `dmesg>myfile.txt`, then `grep myfile.txt` for specific data. Here are some specific examples of using `grep`:

- Find all instances of the word *corrupt* in a file named somefile:

    `grep "corrupt" somefile`

- Look for the same data in the same file, but ignore case:

    `grep -i "corrupt" somefile`

- Look for words beginning with *c* and ending with *e* in file somefile:

    `grep "c..e" somefile`

- Count the number of accounts that have /bin/false as the shell:

    `grep -c false /etc/passwd`

As you can see, this can be very useful in searching both files and directories. As you gain more experience with Linux, you will most likely find yourself using grep very regularly. There are some great tutorials on the web to help you learn about grep and about variants of grep, such as those in the following list:

* *https://www.opensourceforu.com/2012/06/beginners-guide-gnu-grep-basics/*
* *https://www.tutorialspoint.com/unix_commands/grep.htm*
* *https://danielmiessler.com/study/grep/*

The first tutorial in the preceding list is ideal for people who are new to Linux. You can also find tutorials about other Linux commands on that site.

The history Command

The history command allows you to see the commands that have previously been entered. By default, this command returns the last 500 shell commands. This command can be very useful on a live system. When you first locate a Linux machine that is suspect, this is one of the commands you might want to run and record the results of before powering down the system. This can provide a wealth of forensic information. For example, if the command touch was run, that would be worth noting, as that command can alter the date/time stamps of files. You may also want to find the history files for specific users. You can do this with the following command:

```
find / -name .*history
```

The mount Command

The mount command is used to mount a new file system. When you add drives, they must be mounted. You will use this command frequently, specifically when you have a suspect drive you want to mount on your forensic workstation. Most of the commercial forensic tools like Forensic Toolkit (FTK) and EnCase can mount drives for you; however, many forensic analysts work completely with open-source tools. In that case, you will need to mount the drives yourself.

The ps Command

The ps command shows the currently running processes for the current user. By default, ps selects all processes with the same user ID as the current user and associated with the same terminal as the invoker. It displays the process ID (PID), the terminal associated with the process (TTY), the accumulated CPU time in dd-hh:mm:ss format, and the executable name. There are flags you can add to this command to get more details about processes. Here are a few examples:

```
ps -aux
```

Display more info:

```
ps -ef
```

This is another command you will want to run on the live suspect system before powering it down.

The `pstree` Command

The `pstree` command is very similar to the `ps` command, except it shows all the processes in the form of a tree structure. The tree format gives more information particular to a given forensic investigation. Not only will you know what processes are running, but also what process initiated those processes. You can see an example of **FIGURE 9-7**.

The `pgrep` Command

The `pgrep` command takes the name you provide it and returns the PID for that process. It can even work with partial names. This is useful as many other commands require the PID, so `pgrep` can help you retrieve that if you know the name of a process.

The `top` Command

The `top` command is similar to the `ps` command, except it lists the processes in the order of how much CPU time the process is utilizing. When examining a drive for the presence of malware, this can be a useful command. A virus or worm may be using an excessive amount of CPU time, thus slowing down the infected machine.

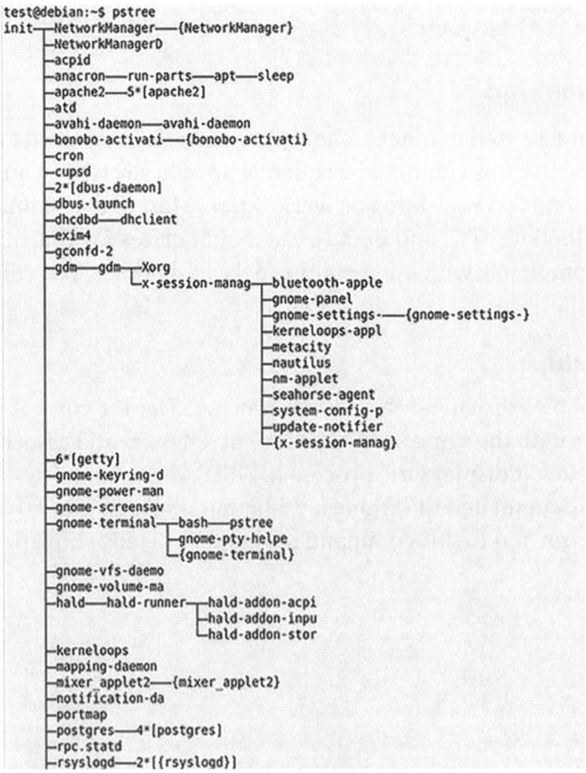

```
test@debian:~$ pstree
init─┬─NetworkManager───{NetworkManager}
     ├─NetworkManagerD
     ├─acpid
     ├─anacron───run-parts───apt───sleep
     ├─apache2───5*[apache2]
     ├─atd
     ├─avahi-daemon───avahi-daemon
     ├─bonobo-activati───{bonobo-activati}
     ├─cron
     ├─cupsd
     ├─2*[dbus-daemon]
     ├─dbus-launch
     ├─dhcdbd───dhclient
     ├─exim4
     ├─gconfd-2
     ├─gdm───gdm─┬─Xorg
     │           └─x-session-manag─┬─bluetooth-apple
     │                             ├─gnome-panel
     │                             ├─gnome-settings-───{gnome-settings-}
     │                             ├─kerneloops-appl
     │                             ├─metacity
     │                             ├─nautilus
     │                             ├─nm-applet
     │                             ├─seahorse-agent
     │                             ├─system-config-p
     │                             ├─update-notifier
     │                             └─{x-session-manag}
     ├─6*[getty]
     ├─gnome-keyring-d
     ├─gnome-power-man
     ├─gnome-screensav
     ├─gnome-terminal─┬─bash───pstree
     │                ├─gnome-pty-helpe
     │                └─{gnome-terminal}
     ├─gnome-vfs-daemo
     ├─gnome-volume-ma
     ├─hald───hald-runner─┬─hald-addon-acpi
     │                    ├─hald-addon-inpu
     │                    └─hald-addon-stor
     ├─kerneloops
     ├─mapping-daemon
     ├─mixer_applet2───{mixer_applet2}
     ├─notification-da
     ├─portmap
     ├─postgres───4*[postgres]
     ├─rpc.statd
     └─rsyslogd───2*[{rsyslogd}]
```

FIGURE 9-7

The `pstree` command.

The `kill` Command

The `kill` command is perhaps the simplest command of all. You simply type in the word *kill* followed by the PID to halt a running process. An example is as follows:

```
kill 1045
```

The `file` Command

The `file` command can tell you exactly what a file is regardless of whether or not it has been renamed or had its extension changed. This can be very important in a forensic investigation. The criminal may have changed the file extension to make the file appear to be something other than what it is. The `file` command will help you with this. An example of the `file` command is shown in **FIGURE 9-8**.

The `su` Command

At times, you may be at a Linux machine where someone has logged in, and you need to perform some task that requires the privileges of the root user. Logging out, then logging back in as the root, can be tedious. Fortunately, you don't have to do that. You can simply invoke the super-user mode. If you type in `su` at the shell, you are asked for the root password. If you can successfully supply it, you will then have root privileges.

The `who` Command

The `who` command tells you all the users currently logged in to the system. This is useful only if you run it on the live suspect machine prior to shutting it down.

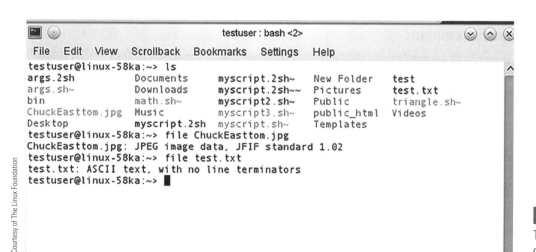

Courtesy of The Linux Foundation

FIGURE 9-8

The `file` command.

The `finger` Command

The `finger` command is used to get back information regarding a specific user. This is often useful for a system administrator. For example, if you run `top`, and see that one specific user is spawning several processes on your server, and those processes are consuming resources, then you may want to find out about that user. This is great to use along with `who`. After you know who is on your system, you can find out specific information about that user.

The `dd` Command

The `dd` command can be used to make a forensic copy of a suspect drive. But that is not all `dd` can do for you. You can use `dd` to make a physical image of what is live in memory. Linux physical memory is accessible via two files, the /dev/mem file and the /proc/kcore file. The following command is one example of making an image of memory:

```
dd if=/dev/mem of=/evidence/image.memory1
```

This command takes whatever is in /dev/mem and sends it to the evidence partition, creating an image of it.

The `ls` Command

The command `ls` is a simple file management command. It lists the contents of the current directory. But `ls` can also be used to quickly catalog a suspect drive. For example, if you want to create a text file that has a listing of all directories and subdirectories, then try this command:

```
ls -R > directories.txt
```

The -R flag causes a recursive listing of all subdirectories. The `>` `directories.txt` writes the output of `ls` to the directories.txt file.

Find Executables

Obviously, an executable could be malware of some type. It is not practical to search every single directory. Linux uses the ELF file format for executables. This allows you to combine that information with the `find` command to find executables in places they should not be, such as the /tmp directory.

```
find / -type f -exec file -p '{}' \; | grep ELF
find /tmp -type f -exec file -p '{}' \; | grep ELF
```

Checking Scheduled Tasks

Someone attacking a machine could schedule tasks to occur. It is important to know what has been scheduled. That can be done with:

```
crontab -latqsystemctl list-timers --all
```

Finding Oddities

Odd items in odd places can indicate someone has tampered with the machine. We previously discussed looking for logs that have nothing in them, or binary files in the /tmp directory. There are several commands used to find oddities. Here are some common commands:

Files or directories that have no user or group:

```
find / \( -nouser -o -nogroup \) -exec ls -lg {} \;
```

Files modified or created in the last day:

```
find / -mtime -1
```

List any hidden directories:

```
find / -type d -name ".*"
```

Can You Undelete in Linux?

This section expands on the details of Linux files and discusses a method for recovering deleted files.

Whenever you refer to a file by name, the operating system uses the filename to look up the corresponding inode, which then enables the system to obtain the information it needs about the file to perform further operations. An inode is a data structure in the file system that stores all the information about a file except its name and its actual data. Inodes can refer to either files or directories.

> **NOTE**
>
> When you use the ls command with the −i option, you get the inode number for the files that are listed.

From the operating system's perspective, a filename is really just an entry in a table with inode numbers. The name is not directly associated with the file. The name is just a human-readable method of locating the inode number.

The inode is really a link to the file. The operating system keeps a count of references to this link. When the reference count reaches zero, the file is deleted. This is why deleted files can sometimes be recovered.

Manual Method

In Linux, a file is deleted when its internal inode link count reaches zero. Just follow these steps to retrieve the deleted file:

1. Move the system to single-user mode. The init command can be used for this purpose.
2. Once you have moved to single user mode, there are several methods you might use. The following is a rather traditional Unix/Linux method using the grep command. Use the following grep syntax:

```
grep -b 'search-text' /dev/partition > file.txt
```

or

```
grep -a -B[size before] -A[size after] 'text' /dev/[your_
partition] > file.txt
```

The flags used are defined as follows:

- -i—Ignore case distinctions in both the PATTERN and the input files; that is, match both uppercase and lowercase characters.
- -a—Process a binary file as if it were text.
- -B—Print number lines/size of leading context before matching lines.
- -A—Print number lines/size of trailing context after matching lines.

For example, to recover a text file starting with "criminalevidence" on /dev/sda1, you can try the following command:

```
# grep -i -a -B10 -A100 'criminalevidence' /dev/sda1 > file.txt
```

3. Next, use any command-line text editor you like to see file.txt. You can then save that file.

This is only one of many methods for recovering deleted files in Linux.

Kali Linux Forensics

As was mentioned earlier in this chapter, the Kali Linux distribution has a number of forensics tools. Even if you have a commercial tool that you are satisfied with, such as OSForensics, FTK, or EnCase, it is often a very good idea to ensure quality control by repeating certain tests with a second tool. Note that different versions of Kali may have different tools. For this section, we are using Kali Linux 2020b. Having an open-source tool is certainly a cost-effective way to do this. You can see the tools available to you in **FIGURE 9-9**.

Autopsy launches as a command line; however, that just gives you a web address to enter into your browser. The reason for this is that Autopsy is a web-based GUI for the command-line tool Sleuth Kit. Both Autopsy and Sleuth Kit are very well-known and widely respected open-source tools. You can see the command-line window in **FIGURE 9-10**.

The default browser for Kali Linux was formerly IceWeasel, which is meant as a bit of a parody of Mozilla Firefox. Later versions of IceWeasel are referred to as IceCat. As of 2020b, Kali uses several browsers; Firefox ESR is commonly used. You can see Autopsy in IceWeasel in **FIGURE 9-11**.

The first step is to create a new case. This can be seen in **FIGURE 9-12**. Like most commercial tools, Autopsy allows you to enter information about the case and the investigators working on the case. This is useful, albeit very basic, information.

The next step is to add a host. This is the computer you are investigating. You can see this in **FIGURE 9-13**.

The next step is critical. Now we add an image to examine. This is a forensic image that was captured previously. You can use tools such as FTK Imager or any forensic imaging tool

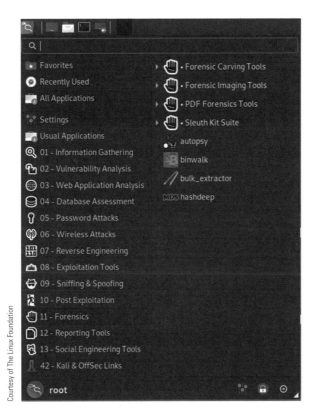

Courtesy of The Linux Foundation

FIGURE 9-9

Kali forensics
tools.

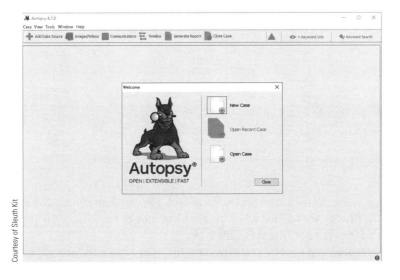

Courtesy of Sleuth Kit

FIGURE 9-10

Autopsy
command
window.

9

Linux
Forensics

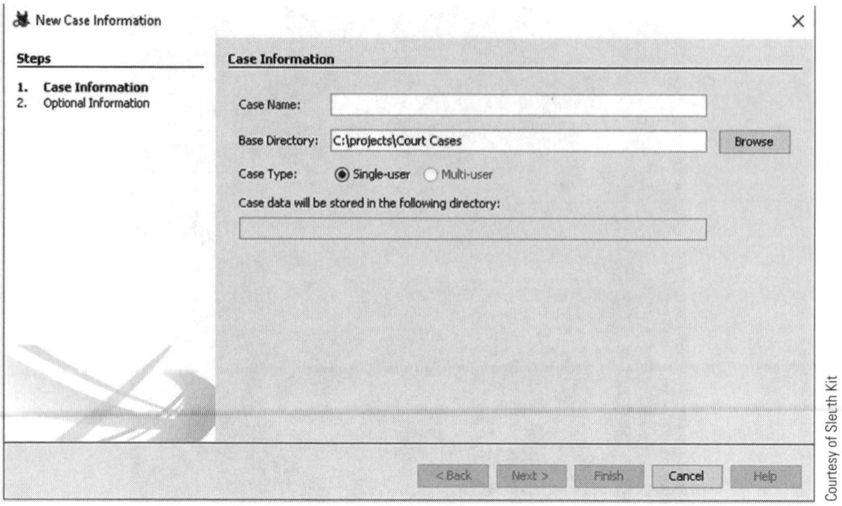

FIGURE 9-11

Autopsy web interface.

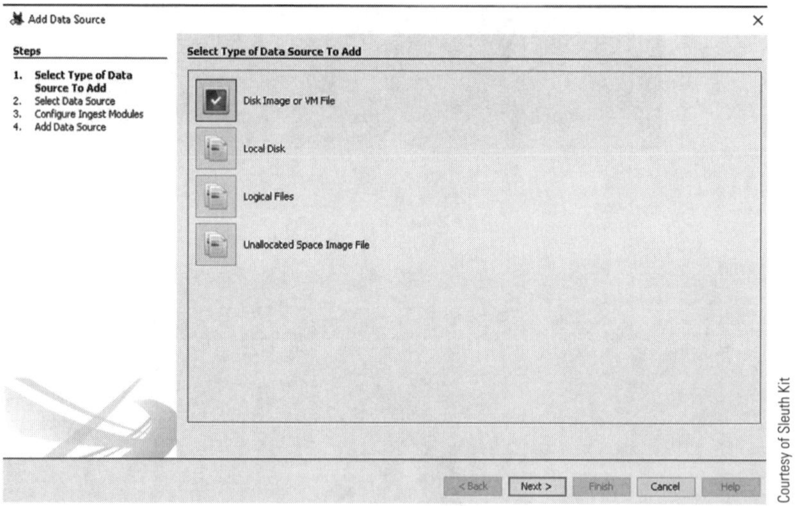

FIGURE 9-12

Autopsy new case.

you like, but you must have a forensic image to add. You can then choose to hash this image or not. Usually images are hashed when created, but they can also have the hash verified when mounted. You can see this in **FIGURE 9-14**.

After a few more simple steps, you now have the image mounted and in your case, as you see in **FIGURE 9-15**. You can now analyze the image.

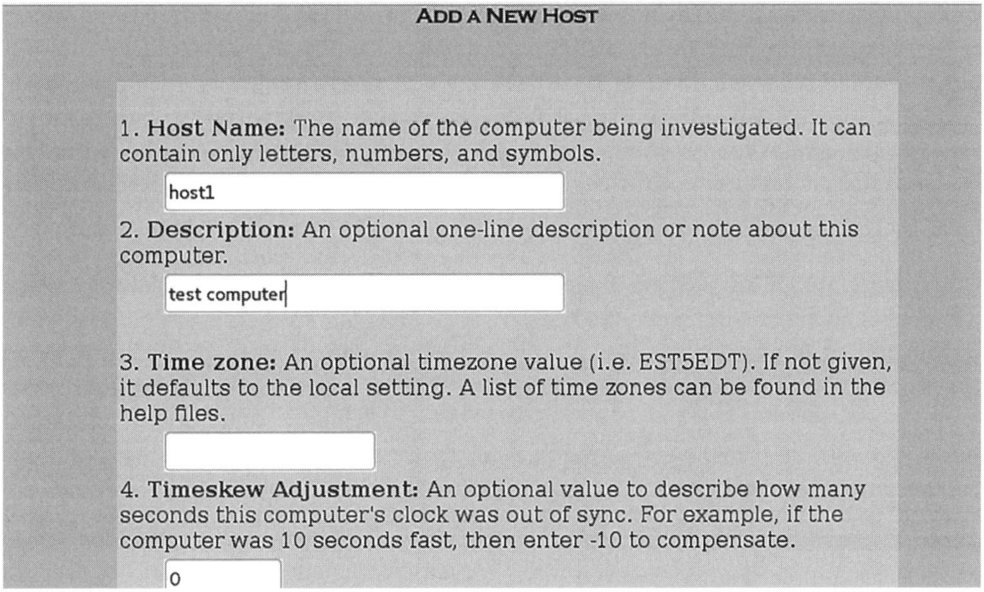

ADD A NEW HOST

1. **Host Name:** The name of the computer being investigated. It can contain only letters, numbers, and symbols.

host1

2. **Description:** An optional one-line description or note about this computer.

test computer

3. **Time zone:** An optional timezone value (i.e. EST5EDT). If not given, it defaults to the local setting. A list of time zones can be found in the help files.

4. **Timeskew Adjustment:** An optional value to describe how many seconds this computer's clock was out of sync. For example, if the computer was 10 seconds fast, then enter -10 to compensate.

0

Courtesy of Sleuth Kit

FIGURE 9-13

Autopsy new host.

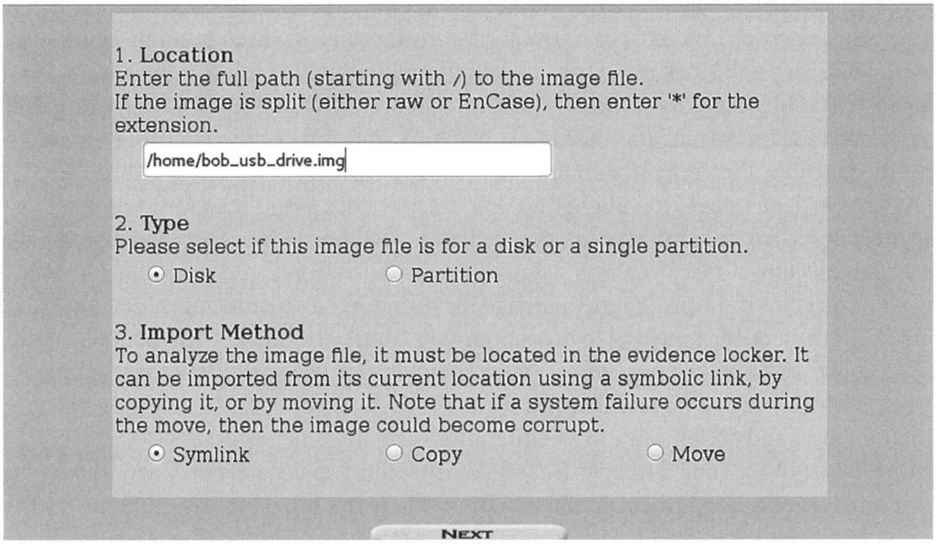

1. **Location**
Enter the full path (starting with /) to the image file.
If the image is split (either raw or EnCase), then enter '*' for the extension.

/home/bob_usb_drive.img

2. **Type**
Please select if this image file is for a disk or a single partition.
   ⊙ Disk   ○ Partition

3. **Import Method**
To analyze the image file, it must be located in the evidence locker. It can be imported from its current location using a symbolic link, by copying it, or by moving it. Note that if a system failure occurs during the move, then the image could become corrupt.
   ⊙ Symlink   ○ Copy   ○ Move

NEXT

Courtesy of Sleuth Kit

FIGURE 9-14

Autopsy verify the hash.

9

Linux Forensics

There are several options in the analysis. For example, you can do keyword searches, use `grep`, etc. This tool does not have anywhere close to the analysis tools that commercial products like FTK, EnCase, and OSForensics have; however, it can be a good secondary test tool for confirming findings.

Kali offers other forensics tools, but Autopsy is the most widely known and recognized.

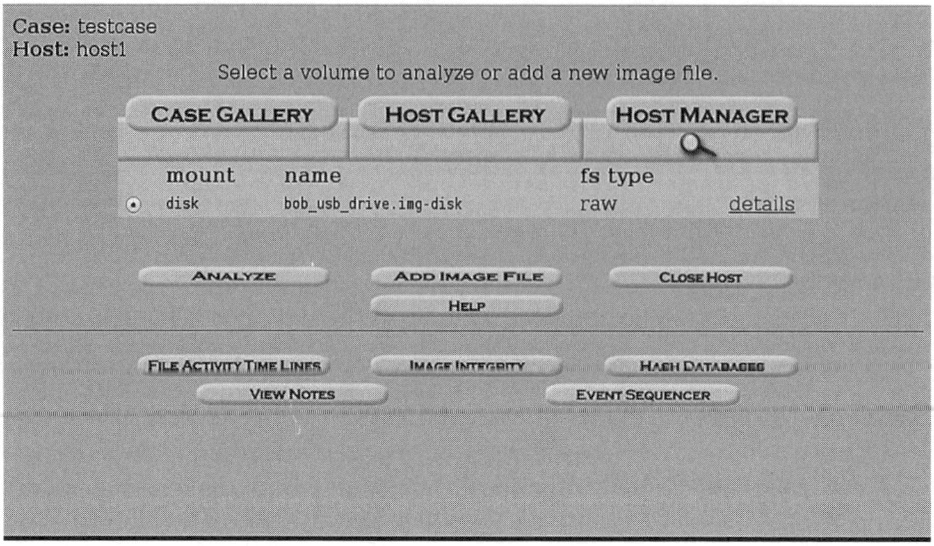

Case: testcase
Host: host1

Select a volume to analyze or add a new image file.

| CASE GALLERY | HOST GALLERY | HOST MANAGER |

| mount | name | fs type |
| disk | bob_usb_drive.img-disk | raw | details |

| ANALYZE | ADD IMAGE FILE | CLOSE HOST |
| HELP |

| FILE ACTIVITY TIME LINES | IMAGE INTEGRITY | HASH DATABASES |
| VIEW NOTES | EVENT SEQUENCER |

Courtesy of Sleuth Kit

FIGURE 9-15

Autopsy image is added.

Forensics Tools for Linux

You will quickly discover that most of the major forensics tools meant to examine Windows machines, while they will work on a Linux disk image, will provide far less information. For this reason, it may be necessary to examine the image directly. Now, I am not suggesting that you simply start poking around on a live Linux machine. You still need to create a forensic image of the machine and verify that image using an appropriate hashing algorithm. But once you have such an image, you might find that the forensics tools you have used don't provide much information. At that point, the next step would be to mount that image as if it were a virtual machine.

However, you cannot simply mount an image file as if it were a virtual machine—that just won't work. You will need some tool to do that for you. There are various instructions on the internet to convert a forensic image into a virtual machine for use with VMWare Workstation, Oracle Virtual Box, or other similar products. However, some of these methods are somewhat tedious, and not all work in all situations.

The forensic tool ForensicExplorer (*http://www.forensicexplorer.com/*) will allow you to mount any forensic image as a virtual machine. Then you log on to the machine and interact with it as you would a live machine with one major exception: This is a read-only forensic image. Now you can navigate to the folders and logs we mentioned earlier in this chapter. You can also execute shell commands and gather information on the target system. This will frequently be the best approach to forensically examine a Linux machine.

More Linux Forensics

The previous sections of this chapter should have given you a solid working knowledge of Linux and Linux forensics. In this section, we will explore some additional Linux forensics techniques you should consider.

Documenting

As you know by now, it is important to thoroughly document your forensic examination. Doing so requires gathering a great deal of data. So it will be important to know Linux commands that give you the information about a system you need to know. A good place to start is with the `cat` command. There are many variations of this command:

```
cat /etc/os-release
cat /etc/hostname
cat /etc/timezone
```

Each of these commands will provide you with basic system information.

Advanced Commands

There are several advanced Linux commands you may find useful when performing forensics on a Linux machine. However, you must keep in mind that not all Linux distributions support all of these commands. Here are a few:

`dcat`—Displays the contents of a disk block.

`dls`—Lists contents of deleted disk blocks.

`dcalc`—Maps between `dd` images and `dls` results.

`dstat`—Lists statistics associated with specific disk blocks.

`mmls`—Displays list of partitions in a disk image.

`locate`—This command is similar to `find`. The `-i flag` makes it case insensitive. The asterisk lets you combine words—for example, `locate -i finance*data.`

`xargs`—The `xargs` command in Linux is a shell command for building an execution pipeline from standard input. While tools like `grep` can accept standard input as a parameter, many other tools cannot. Using `xargs` allows tools like `echo`, `rm`, and `mkdir` to accept standard input as arguments. Here is an example where you wish to copy all png images to an external drive:

```
ls *.png | xargs -n1 -i cp {} /external-hard-drive/directory
```

9

Linux
Forensics

CHAPTER SUMMARY

In this chapter, you were given a general introduction to the Linux operating system, along with basic forensics. You learned which logs to look at for specific types of evidence and how to retrieve those logs. You also learned about specific directories and shell commands that are useful in a forensic investigation. Furthermore, you were introduced to recovering data from a file system. You may also want to check out specific websites devoted to Linux forensics. A great one is *http://www.linux-forensics.com/*.

KEY CONCEPTS AND TERMS

Bootstrap environment
Grand Unified Bootloader (GRUB)

Intrusion detection system (IDS)
Linux Loader (LILO)

CHAPTER 9 ASSESSMENT

1. Where are the startup scripts defined?

A. etc/init.d

B. /etc/scripts

C. /etc/start

D. /etc/inittab

2. Which of the following file systems *cannot* be mounted by using the `mount` command?

A. Ext2

B. Swap

C. FAT

D. ReiserFS

3. Which of the following is a file system that provides system statistics? It doesn't contain real files but provides an interface to run-time system information.

A. /proc

B. /var

C. /home

D. /boot

4. _____ is a commonly used name for a command-line utility that provides disk partitioning functions in an operating system. It can list the partitions on a Linux system.

A. `mkfs`

B. `parted`

C. `fdisk`

D. `format`

5. What single shell command will tell you the home directory, current user, and current history size?

A. `who`

B. `whois`

C. `env`

D. `logname`

6. Use the _____ command to see running processes as a tree.

7. The `dmesg` command can be used to see the Linux boot messages.

A. True

B. False

8. John is investigating a Linux web server. It is suspected that someone executed an SQL injection attack on this server, and John wants to look for evidence of this. To do this he wants to start by examining the web server log. Which of the following directories should he look in to find the web server logs?

A. /etc

B. /dev

C. /var

D. /sys

Reference

1. Scientific Working Group on Digital Evidence. (2016, February 8). SWDGE Linux Tech Notes, version 1.0. Retrieved from https://www.swgde.org/documents/published on February 9, 2021.

Mac OS Forensics

APPLE COMPUTERS MAY NOT BE AS UBIQUITOUS AS MICROSOFT-BASED PCs, but they represent a significant portion of personal computers. For this reason, it is important that you have at least a basic understanding of the Mac OS operating system and how to conduct forensics on it. In this chapter, you will learn some history of the Mac operating system as well as some operating system basics. You will also learn some basic forensic techniques to use on an Apple device running Mac OS.

Chapter 10 Topics

This chapter covers the following topics and concepts:

- Basic knowledge about Mac OS
- Where to find the logs in Mac OS
- Forensically interesting directories
- Forensic techniques for Mac OS
- How to undelete files in Mac OS

Chapter 10 Goals

When you complete this chapter, you will be able to:

- Understand the basics of Mac OS and its history
- Know where to find logs in a Mac OS system
- Be able to examine the virtual memory of a Mac OS
- Be able to undelete Mac OS files

Mac Basics

It is important that you have a working understanding of the Mac OS operating system before attempting forensics. As with Linux, however, it is common for forensic examiners *not* to have a good working knowledge of Mac OS systems. The reason for this is simple: Most people have more exposure to Windows than to Mac OS. In fact, it is not uncommon to have a forensic examiner who may have never even used an Apple device. So this section first shows you the history of the Mac OS and then discusses the operating system fundamentals. This will establish a baseline of knowledge to help you understand Apple systems.

Apple History

Apple began with Steve Wozniak and Steve Jobs collaborating while working from their homes. In 1975, they finished the prototype of the first Apple computer. Steve Wozniak worked for Hewlett-Packard, and his employment contract required him to give his employer first right of refusal on any new inventions he came up with. However, Hewlett-Packard was not interested and released the technology to Steve Wozniak. This led to the formation of Apple Computer in April 1976. The company's three founders were Steve Jobs, Steve Wozniak, and Ronald Wayne.

The first computer was the Apple I, created by Wozniak. That computer had an 8-bit microprocessor running at just below 1 MHz. The Apple I had a built-in video terminal, sockets for 8 kilobytes of onboard random access memory (RAM), a keyboard, and a cassette board meant to work with regular cassette recorders.

Apple II

It wasn't long before the team came up with the Apple II. This computer was based on the same microprocessor but came in a plastic case with the keyboard built in. It was also the first personal computer with color graphics. This was followed by a series of enhancements to the Apple II: Apple II+, IIe, IIc, IIc+, IIe Enhanced, and IIe Platinum. In 1986, the Apple IIGS was released; this computer was 16-bit rather than 8-bit.

There were multiple operating systems for the Apple II, including the following:

- **Apple DOS (Disk Operating System)**—The first edition was released as Apple DOS 3.1 in 1978. It had no relationship to Microsoft DOS.
- **Apple Pascal**—This was based on the p-system, an operating system developed at the University of California, San Diego. It was basically a virtual machine running p-code, and Pascal was the most popular language for it. Apple Pascal was a similar design released in 1979.
- **Apple SOS**—This operating system was developed for the Apple III. The acronym stands for Sophisticated Operating System. Every program that used SOS loaded the operating system into memory as well. A SOS application disk consisted of a kernel (SOS.kernel), an interpreter (SOS.Interp), which was often the application itself, and a set of drivers (SOS. Driver).
- **ProDOS**—This was meant as a replacement for Apple DOS 3.3 and was based on SOS. It had more support for programming, including assembly and BASIC. Eventually, this led to a 16-bit version called ProDOS 16.

- **Lisa OS**—This operating system had a full graphical user interface with a file browser that was navigated with mouse clicks. It also came with some basic office programs.

Beyond the Apple II

After the Apple II, the company changed the brand name to Macintosh and took a new direction with its computers. The main points in that evolution are as follows:

- **The Macintosh**—Although today many people may think of Apple and Macintosh as synonymous, the Macintosh was actually released by Apple in January 1984. It had an 8-MHz Motorola processor, a black-and-white monitor, and a 3.5-inch floppy drive. The operating system for Macintosh was System 1. This eventually led to the Macintosh II running System 7.
- **System 7**—This system allowed text dragging between applications, viewing and switching applications from a menu, a control panel, and cooperative multitasking.
- **Mac OS for PowerPC**—This Mac introduced the System 7.1.2 operating system.
- **AIX for PowerPC**—In 1996, Apple had a product called Apple Network Server that used a variation of the IBM AIX system. It also used the Common Desktop Environment, a graphical user interface that is popular in the Unix world. This product did not do well in the market and was discontinued in 1997.

Mac OS X

The next major change was the introduction of Mac OS X, which is still used in Mac OS computers today, although it was later renamed simply "OSX" and is now branded as "macOS." The public beta version of the product was named Kodiak. The real change with Mac OS X was that the operating system was based on FreeBSD, a Unix clone. When using Mac OS, you can navigate to a shell and run Unix/Linux shell commands. The initial release of OS X was followed by periodic improvements, each with an animal name:

- Mac OS X v10.0, named Cheetah, was released in March 2001.
- Mac OS X v10.1 was released the same year and was named Puma.
- The next release was Mac OS X v10.2 in 2002, called Jaguar. This release included improved graphics and iChat messaging.
- In 2003, Apple released Mac OS X v10.3, named Panther.
- Mac OS X v10.4, named Tiger, was released in 2005. This release had built-in support for FireWire, and it had a new dashboard and updated mail program.
- Mac OS X v10.5, called Leopard, was released in 2007. It had over 300 new features, support for Intel x86 chips, and support for the G5 processor.
- In 2009, Apple released Mac OS X v10.6, Snow Leopard. Most of the changes in this release were performance enhancements, rather than new features. For example, Snow Leopard had support for multicore processors.
- Mac OS X 10.7 was released in 2011 and code-named Lion. The major interface change with this release was to make it more like the iOS interfaces used on iPhone and iPad.
- Mac OS X 10.8, named Mountain Lion, was released in 2012. This release had built-in support for iCloud, to support cloud computing. This was the last of the animal-named

OS versions; it was also after this that Apple called its operating system versions simply "OSX" rather than "Mac OS X".

- OSX 10.10, named Yosemite, was released by Apple in October 2014. The most important part of this release, from a forensics standpoint, is that it allowed users who had iPhones with iOS 8.1 or later to pass certain tasks to their Mac OS computer. For example, they could complete unfinished iPhone emails on the Mac OS computer. This functionality is called Handoff. This is important forensically, because you may find evidence connected to a mobile device on the Mac OS computer.
- When version 10.12, called Sierra, was released in September 2016, Apple changed the operating system brand name to macOS. It was meant to be more in sync with the style of other Apple systems such as iOS and watchOS.
- Mac OS 11.0, Big Sur, was announced in June 2020 and publicly released November 12, 2020. This is the 17th major release of Mac OS. Big Sur supports file-level encryption, unlike previous versions, which only supported drive-level encryption. Big Sur introduces a lot of new technology support, which helps Apple ease the transition to the Apple silicon processor architecture.

Though not directly related to operating systems, in 2020 Apple announced its computers were moving to its own Apple Silicon chips. These use an ARM64 architecture. This is a System on a Chip (SoC). The first versions of these chips have a quad core design with rather large cache sizes, but use approximately a quarter of the power of the previous chips.

The Mac OS desktop is shown in **FIGURE 10-1**.

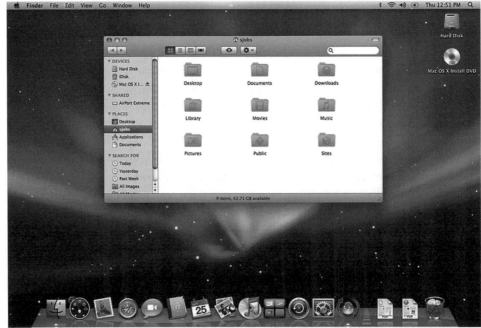

FIGURE 10-1

Mac OS Desktop.

When performing forensics on an Apple system, you are most likely to encounter Mac OS, as it is the most widely used Apple operating system today. In fact, it is the only operating system still supported by Apple.

Mac File Systems

In this section, you will learn details about the Hierarchical File System (HFS) and other file systems used by Mac OS operating systems.

Macintosh File System

Macintosh File System (MFS) is an older Apple technology that has not been used in over 15 years. You are unlikely to encounter it. It has long since been replaced, first with HFS, then with HFS+. It shipped with the first Macintosh in 1984.

Hierarchical File System

The HFS was used on the Macintosh Plus. But with Mac OS 8.1, it was replaced by HFS+. Because HFS was the standard for Mac OS, it became known as *HFS Standard*, while HFS+ became known as *HFS Extended*. Apple introduced this file system in 1985 specifically to support its new Apple hard drive. HFS replaced the earlier Macintosh File System.

HFS used concepts from the earlier SOS operating system that had been designed for the Apple III. HFS was able to support filenames as long as 255 characters, which was not available in FAT (used by DOS).

Hierarchical File System Plus

HFS+ is an enhancement of the HFS file system. HFS+ was the preferred file system on Mac OS for quite some time. Most important, it supports journaling. Journaling is basically the process whereby the file system keeps a record of what file transactions take place so that in the event of a hard drive crash, the files can be recovered. Journaling file systems are fault tolerant because the file system logs all changes to files, directories, or file structures. The log in which changes are recorded is referred to as the file system's journal—thus, the term journaling file systems.

HFS+ also supports disk quotas. That allows the administrator to limit the amount of disk space a given user can use, keeping that user from taking up all the space. HFS+ also has hard and soft links. There are basically two types of links. The first type is the hard link. A hard link is an inode that links directly to a specific file. A soft link or symbolic link is essentially a shortcut.

HFS+ is architecturally similar to HFS, which is not surprising, as it is an enhancement to HFS. However, there are some key differences. One such difference is that HFS+ uses 32 bits for allocation blocks, rather than 16 bits. HFS+ also supports long filenames, up to 255 characters. Furthermore, HFS+ uses **Unicode**, which is the international standard for information encoding (for file naming), rather than **ASCII (American Standard Code for Information Interchange)**, which is a set of codes defining all the various keystrokes you could make, including letters, numbers, characters, and even the spacebar and return keys.

For forensic examinations, one of the more important differences in HFS+ to keep in mind is aliases. Aliases are like symbolic links; they allow you to have multiple references to a single file or directory. HFS+ also has a very interesting optimization scheme. It essentially does defragmentation on a per-file basis. The following conditions are checked, and if met, the file is defragmented when it is opened:

- The file is less than 20 megabytes in size.
- The file is not already in use.
- The file is not read-only.
- The file is fragmented.
- The system uptime is at least three minutes.

This means an HFS+ volume is routinely defragmenting itself. This is a significant advantage over some other file systems such as NFTS and FAT.

With an HFS+ volume, the first two sectors (sectors 0 and 1) are the boot blocks and are identical to the boot blocks used in HFS. The third sector (sector 2) has the volume header. It has a great deal of pertinent forensic information such as the size of allocation blocks and a time stamp that describes when the volume was created.

The allocation file is important for forensics. It keeps track of which allocation blocks are free and which are not. A 0 indicates the block is free, while a 1 indicates the block is in use. The catalog file contains the records for all the files/directories on that volume. It uses a B-tree structure to hold the data. Each record in the catalog file is 8 kilobytes in size.

Of particular interest is the command prompt. The command prompt in Mac OS is a BASH shell so you can execute Linux commands. This means the commands we discussed in Chapter 9 can be used—for example, `lsof`, `pstree`, and others.

Because HFS+ was the preferred file system for quite some time for Mac OS, it is one you will likely encounter when doing forensic examinations of Apple computers. However, it has since been supplanted.

Apple File System

Apple File System, also called APFS, was created for MacOS 10.13 (High Sierra) and tvOS 10.2 and later versions. It is also used by iOS 10.3 and later. APFS was designed explicitly to correct some issues with HFS+. APFS is specifically optimized to work with flash drives and solid-state drives. APFS was first announced at the Apple Developer Conference in 2016.

APFS still uses iNodes; they are 64 bit, which allows for more addresses, and thus larger storage. APFS supports creating snapshots of the system at specific points in time. It also supports full disk encryption. You are likely to encounter APFS on newer Apple devices.

ISO9660

ISO9660 is the file system used by compact discs (CDs). ISO9660 is not Mac OS–specific, but Apple does have its own set of ISO9660 extensions. Although a CD may be readable on either a PC—Windows or Linux—or an Apple computer, the files on that CD may require a specific operating system in order to be read.

Microsoft Disk Operating System

Mac OS includes support for Microsoft Disk Operating System (MS-DOS) file systems FAT12, FAT16, and FAT32. This allows a Mac OS machine to read floppy disks (FAT12) as well as files created with DOS/Windows 3.1.

New Technology File System

Mac OS includes read-only support for the New Technology File System (NTFS). This means if you have a portable drive that is NTFS, Mac OS can read that partition. But like ISO9660, the files on that drive may be operating system–specific.

Universal Disk Format

Universal Disk Format (UDF) is the file system used by DVD-ROM discs (both video and audio). Like ISO9660, this only guarantees that Mac OS can read the partition or drive; it does not guarantee that Mac OS can read the files.

Unix File System

Unix File System (UFS) is the file system used by FreeBSD and many other Unix variants. Being based on FreeBSD, Mac OS can read UFS volumes.

Partition Types

Partition types are referred to in Apple documents as "partition schemes." The partition type determines how the partition is organized on the drive. Apple directly supports three different partition schemes: the GUID (GUID stands for "globally unique identifier"), the Partition Table, the Apple Partition Map, and the master boot record. The partition types are described in this section.

It should be noted that if the system is using APFS, then it is recommended that you do not partition the drive, but rather create multiple APFS partitions in a single partition. Furthermore, if you are creating a partition so that you can support a dual boot with Windows, Apple recommends that you not create a separate partition, but rather use Boot Camp Assistant.

GUID Partition Table

The GUID Partition Table is used primarily with computers that have an Intel-based processor. It requires OS X v10.4 or later. Intel-based Mac OS machines can boot only from drives that use the GUID Partition Table.

Apple Partition Map

The Apple Partition Map is used with any PowerPC-based Mac. Intel-based Macs can mount and use a drive formatted with the Apple Partition Map, but cannot boot from the device. PowerPC-based Macs can both mount and use a drive formatted with the Apple Partition Map, and can also use it as a startup device.

Master Boot Record

The master boot record (MBR), contained in the boot sector, is used when DOS- or Windows-based computers start up. The MBR contains important information such as a partition table, bootstrap code, and other information.

Boot Camp Assistant

This utility was mentioned in the previous section. It is designed to allow one to install additional operating systems on the same machine, alongside Mac OS. It does perform boot partitioning, but does it for the user in a non-destructive manner. Boot Camp Assistant was first introduced with Mac OS X 10.5 (Leopard). As of Boot Camp version 10 (released in 2015), there is support for Windows 10. When conducting forensics on an Apple computer, it is important to be aware of whether Boot Camp is also in use. That would require you to also analyze the Windows system that is hosted in Boot Camp.

Mac OS Logs

One of the first steps in any forensic examination should be to check the logs. Remember that logs are very important when examining a Windows or a Linux computer. They are just as important when examining an Apple computer. This section examines the Mac OS logs and what is contained in them.

The /var/log Log

The name of this log should suggest that it is a general repository for a lot of information. The naming structure should also seem familiar. Remember that Mac OS is based on Free-BSD, so seeing file structures similar to Linux should be no surprise.

This directory has many logs in it. The /var/log/daily.out contains data on all mounted volumes, including the dates they were mounted. This is very important in cases involving stolen data. You can see what devices have been attached and get data from them. This folder includes data on removable media, including serial numbers.

The /var/spool/cups Folder

In this folder, you will also find information about printed documents. If you need to know what documents have been printed from this Apple device, this folder can give you that information. This includes the name of the document printed and the user who printed it.

The /private/var/audit Logs

As the name suggests, these are logs of system audits. This includes things like user login. Obviously, this can be very interesting forensically. These audits are often not in a human-readable format. However, Guidance software makes an audit log parser for Mac OS audit logs, which can be found at *https://www.guidancesoftware.com/app /Mac-OS-X-OpenBSM-Audit-Log-Parser*.

The /private/var/VM Folder

This folder contains swap and sleep image files. If you hibernate your Mac, this directory will usually occupy more than 5 gigabytes of disk space. This can be a source of important forensic data.

The /Library/Receipts Folder

This folder contains information about system and software updates. It is less useful for a forensic investigation than some of the other folders; however, it can be useful to know if a given patch was applied and when it was applied. This might be of some interest in investigating malware crimes.

/Library/Mobile Documents

This folder is what syncs with iCloud. This is where you will find items that have been saved to iCloud. It should be quite clear that this can be very interesting forensically.

The /Users/<user>/.bash_history Log

As you know, Mac OS is based on FreeBSD, a Unix variant. When you launch the terminal window, what you actually get is a BASH shell. So this particular log can be very interesting. It will show you a variety of commands. You might look for commands such as rm, which would be removing or deleting something, or commands like dd, indicating the user might have tried to make an image of the drive.

The var/vm Folder

In this folder, you will find a subfolder named app profile. This will contain lists of recently opened applications as well as temporary data used by applications. Both of these can be very interesting in a forensic examination.

The /Users/ Directory

This is where various users' files are stored. It is always a good idea to check in this directory to find out if users have saved data here that could be used as evidence.

The /Users/<user>/Library/Preferences Folder

As you probably suspect, this folder contains user preferences. This might not seem that interesting for a forensic investigation, except for one small issue. This folder even maintains the preferences of programs that have been deleted. This could be a very valuable place to get clues about programs that have been deleted from the system.

Directories

Like Windows and Linux, Mac OS has a number of directories. Some are more important than others. You must know the ones in the following sections in order to do an effective forensic examination of an Apple machine.

The /Volumes Directory

This directory contains information about mounted devices. You will find data here regarding hard disks, external disks, CDs, digital video discs (DVDs), and even virtual machines. This is a very important directory in your forensic examination.

The /Users Directory

This directory contains all the user accounts and associated files. This is clearly critical to your investigation of a machine running Mac OS.

The /Applications Directory

This directory is where all applications are stored. Particularly in cases of malware, this is a critical directory to check.

The /Network Directory

This directory contains information about servers, network libraries, and network properties.

The /etc Directory

Just as in Linux, this is where configuration files are located. Obviously, configuration files can be quite interesting in a forensic investigation. It is often true that cybercriminals like to adjust the system's configuration. Sometimes this is done in order to facilitate the criminal's return to the system later.

The /Library/Preferences/SystemConfiguration/ dom.apple.preferences.plist File

This file contains the network configuration data for each network card. This is important information to document before beginning your search for evidence.

Mac OS Forensic Techniques

This section covers some general forensic techniques to use on Mac OS systems. In the preceding sections, you learned about the Mac OS operating system, and you learned where to look for important logs, which is a valuable step in any forensic investigation. Now, you will learn a variety of forensic techniques.

Target Disk Mode

One of the most fundamental steps in forensics is to create a bit-level copy of the suspect drive. If the suspect drive is a Mac OS, all the techniques you know from Linux or Windows can still be used. You can utilize the dd command along with netcat to make a forensic copy. You can also use the imaging tools within EnCase or Forensic Toolkit. However, Mac OS provides another way to make a forensically sound copy of a drive. You begin by placing the suspect computer into Target Disk Mode. When you put the computer in that mode, it cannot be written to, so there is no chance of altering the source disk. Then simply connect to the suspect computer with universal serial bus (USB) or FireWire and image the disk.

Also, Target Disk Mode allows you to preview the computer on-site. This allows investigators to do a quick inspection before disconnecting and transporting the computer to a

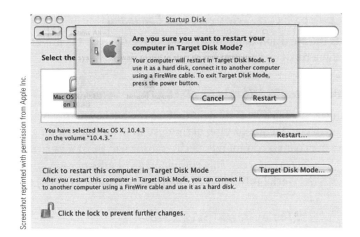

Screenshot reprinted with permission from Apple Inc.

FIGURE 10-2

Target Disk Mode.

forensic lab. This is important because, just like with Windows or Linux, you will want to check running systems' processes before shutting the machine down. You simply have to reboot the machine in Target Disk Mode, as shown in **FIGURE 10-2**.

Searching Virtual Memory

Checking virtual memory is just as important with a Mac OS as it is with a Windows or Linux computer. With Mac OS, the swap file/virtual memory is located in the folder /var/vm/. You can check it with simple Linux commands like ls (for listing files). A good option is ls —al, which gives you a listing of all the files in virtual memory as well as of who launched the program and when. The best news is that you can use the grep search tool to search in the virtual memory folder.

> **NOTE**
>
> Because Mac OS is based on FreeBSD, Linux commands can be used here. So before shutting the suspect Mac OS down, you will want to run netstat to see any connections the system has. You may also want to run ps, pstree, and top to check running processes.

Shell Commands

Because Mac OS is based on FreeBSD, you can use shell commands to extract information. A number of commands can be quite useful in your forensic examination. Some additional commands are available that are specific to Mac OS.

The date Command

The date command returns the current date and time zone. It is good for documenting when exactly you begin your forensic examination. If you need the date in Coordinated Universal Time (UTC), then use the date —u version of the command.

The ls/dev/disk? Command

This command lists the current device files that are in use. You should document this information before shutting the system down for transport to the forensic lab.

The `/hdiutil partition /dev/disk0` Command

This command lists the partition table for the boot drive. Clearly, it is important to know the partitions the machine recognizes upon boot-up.

The `system_profiler SPHardwareDataType` Command

This command returns the hardware information for the host system. This provides information useful for the basic documentation of the system prior to beginning your forensic examination. There are related commands, such as `system_profiler SPSerialATA-DataType`. This command gives information on all the attached Serial Advanced Technology Attachment (SATA) devices.

> ■ **NOTE**
>
> There is an interesting trick you can do to circumvent passwords in Mac OS. If you change the amount of physical memory, the firmware password is automatically reset. So simply add or remove RAM, then reboot.

The `system_profiler SPSoftwareDataType` Command

Related to `system_profiler SPHardwareDataType`, this command returns information about the operating system. This is also important for documenting the system prior to starting the forensic examination.

How to Examine an Apple Device

Many forensics tools do a wonderful job of extracting data from Windows machines, but are less effective in Mac OS. OSForensics version 4.0 will include Mac OS artifacts in its "recent history." But to examine the directories mentioned in this chapter, or to execute the BASH commands, you may need more than these tools can provide.

One technique is to create a copy of the forensic image and to mount it as a read-only virtual machine (VM). It is critical that you mount it as read-only. There are various instructions that can be found on the internet for converting a forensic image to a VM (such as a VMWare or Oracle Virtual box VM). However, the forensic tool Forensic Explorer (*http://www.forensic explorer.com/*) will mount forensic images as read-only VMs, using the VM of your choice. OSForensics version 4 (*http://www.osforensics.com/*) will also allow you to create a VM from a forensic image.

MacQuisition

Blacklight forensics produces a product called MacQuisition. Note that Blacklight has been bought by Cellebrite, so it is now technically Cellebrite MacQuisition. It is a tool for imaging Mac OS systems. This is a commercial tool, and current pricing should be requested from the manufacturer (*https://www.blackbagtech.com/macquisition-quick-start-guide*).

You can either run MacQuisition on an Apple device that is already booted, or boot to MacQuisition. When the system displays MacQuisition, it will display several different partitions; it is the Application partition that has the MacQuisition application you are launching. You will need a second external drive to copy the image to.

Reading Apple Drives

Obviously, if you have an Apple machine for your forensics workstation, you will have no problem reading Apple drives. However, the majority of forensic workstations are running Windows, with a percentage also running Linux. There are several utilities that allow one to connect and view an Apple drive on a Windows computer. One of those is MacDrive 10 pro (*https://www.macdrive.com/*). This is shown in **FIGURE 10-3**.

　　Another, similar tool is APFS for Windows by Paragon software (*https://www.paragon -software.com/us/home/apfs-windows/#*). When the software is launched, if it does not detect any APFS volumes, you will be prompted to connect one. This is shown in **FIGURE 10-4**.

Screenshot reprinted with permission from Apple Inc.

FIGURE 10-3

MacDrive 10 pro.

Used with permission from Paragon Technologie GmbH

FIGURE 10-4

APFS for Windows.

As you can see, there are multiple options for examining an Apple drive on a Windows workstation, if you need to.

Can You Undelete in Mac OS?

Recall that in Windows systems, deleting actually just removes a file from the master file table (MFT) or file allocation table (FAT) and marks those clusters as available. The file's data is still there and can be recovered. What happens when a file is deleted on an HFS or HFS+ volume? Although the details are a bit different, a similar thing occurs. The references to the file are gone and the clusters might be used and overwritten. But, depending on how soon after the deletion you attempt to recover data, you may be able to recover some or all of the data. Even if the data is overwritten, data may still exist in unallocated space and in index nodes. When a file is deleted in Mac OS, it is moved to the Trash folder—much like the Recycle Bin in Windows. The Trash is represented on the file system as a hidden folder, .Trash, on the root directory of the file system. You can list the contents with a shell command, as shown here:

```
$/.Trash ls -al
total 764
drwx------ 7 pc pc 306 Oct 30 15:05 .
drwxr-xr-x 30 pc pc 1054 Oct 30 12:44 ..
-rw------- 1 pc pc 6148 Oct 30 14:38 .DS_Store
-rw-r--r-- 1 pc pc 187500 Oct 27 15:41 Resume.pdf
-rw-r--r-- 1 pc pc 108382 Oct 27 15:43 VacationPIC.jpg
-rw-r--r-- 1 pc pc 108382 Oct 27 15:43 Report.pdf
```

Now files in the Trash directory can be recovered just by copying or moving them to any other location.

Note that the Trash (.Trash folder) contains four files, each of which can be recovered by simply copying or moving it to an alternate location. There are tools that will recover files, even after the Trash bin has been emptied.

One such tool is Disk Drill (*https://www.cleverfiles.com/disk-drill-win.html*). This is rather easy-to-use software that allows you to recover deleted files from a Mac OS system. This is shown in **FIGURE 10-5**.

Another similar product is Mac Undelete from Remo Software (*http://www.macundelete.com/*). A screenshot is provided in **FIGURE 10-6**.

A few additional tools are given here:

- Mac Undelete at *http://www.macundelete.com/*
- Free Undelete Mac at *http://www.freeundeletemac.com/*

Any of these tools can aid you in recovering deleted Mac OS files.

FIGURE 10-5

Disk Drill.

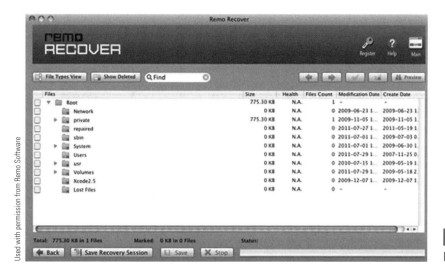

FIGURE 10-6

Mac Undelete.

10

Mac OS
Forensics

Mac OS Password Recovery

It may be the case that you need to examine an Apple device, such as a MacBook, running Mac OS but do not have the password. It should first be remembered that accessing a computer device, without legal authorization, is a crime. So this should only be attempted if you do, indeed, have legal authorization.

The first step is to enter Recovery mode. The MacBook must be fully powered off. Press the power and the Command + R keys simultaneously to restart the device in Recovery mode. When the Apple logo appears, let go of the Command + R. You should see something similar to **FIGURE 10-7**.

Choose Disk Utility. If the MacBook requests a password, it means the firmware is protected and configured to prevent Recovery mode attacks. That means this technique won't work. However, if a firmware password is not set (and that password must be intentionally set by the user), you can proceed. If the firmware password is not set, you can get a terminal window, as seen in **FIGURE 10-8**.

Depending on the Apple device, you have a few options. One is simply to type reset-password (yes, all one word). You then close the terminal and a list of the accounts on that Apple device will be displayed. Set a new password for one or more accounts.

For later versions of Mac OS, it won't be that easy. There are files called plist files that contain passwords, and you cannot change them. So you will need a USB drive. It can be FAT32 or APFS formatted, but not NTFS. Now, from the terminal, we are going to use some commands. These will look like Linux commands, which is because Mac OS is based on FreeBSD, a Unix clone.

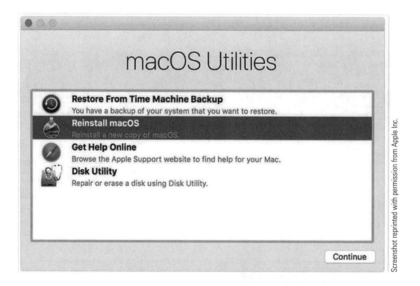

macOS Utilities

Restore From Time Machine Backup
You have a backup of your system that you want to restore.

Reinstall macOS
Reinstall a new copy of macOS.

Get Help Online
Browse the Apple Support website to find help for your Mac.

Disk Utility
Repair or erase a disk using Disk Utility.

Continue

Screenshot reprinted with permission from Apple Inc.

FIGURE 10-7

Mac OS Recovery.

Screenshot reprinted with permission from Apple Inc.

FIGURE 10-8

Mac OS Recovery
Terminal Window.

First, find out if there is System Integrity Protection (SIP) that needs to be turned off:

```
ls -R /Volumes/<hard drive name>/var/db/dslocal/nodes/Default/
```

This will list all files in the directory and output files. If you get an error message, "Operation not permitted," that means SIP is turned on, and you need to turn it off:

```
csrutil disable
```

You will then restart the computer. Boot into Recovery mode again, and again start the terminal. Now insert your USB drive and copy out the plist we need:

```
cp /Volumes/<hard drive name>/var/db/dslocal/nodes/Default/
users/<username>.plist /Volumes/<usb name>/
```

That is all on the Apple device. Now you take that plist file to your computer and convert it to input for the Hashcat tool (*https://hashcat.net/hashcat/*). You can get that Python script from

*https://github.com/EmpireProject/Empire/blob/e37fb2eef8ff8f5a0a689f1589f424906fe
13055/lib/modules/python/collection/osx/hashdump.py*

```
chmod +x hashdump.py
sudo python hashdump.py
```

You will then get a hash output that you can save to a text file. That text file can be fed into Hashcat.

CHAPTER SUMMARY

In this chapter, you learned the fundamentals of the Mac OS operating system. It is important to have a working understanding of any operating system before attempting forensics on that system. You also learned where to look for log files and what is contained in those logs.

The shell commands that you learned in this chapter are critical. It is important that you remember those and be able to use them on Apple computers you examine. It is also important that you understand imaging a suspect Apple computer and recovering deleted files.

KEY CONCEPTS AND TERMS

American Standard Code for
Information Interchange
(ASCII)

ISO9660
Unicode

Universal Disk Format (UDF)

CHAPTER 10 ASSESSMENT

1. Which partition type is used to boot Intel-based Apple machines?

   A. GUID
   B. APM
   C. MBR
   D. HFS

2. John has been working in forensics for five years, but primarily focusing on Windows computers. He wants to start training to prepare for working on Apple computers. What file system is used in most modern Mac OS systems?

   A. FAT32
   B. EXT3
   C. HFS+
   D. NTFS

3. Where would you look for configuration files on an Apple computer?

   A. /etc
   B. /var
   C. /tmp
   D. /cfg

4. You can undelete files in Mac OS.

   A. True
   B. False

5. What was the most important forensic feature in OSX 10.10?

   A. Handoff
   B. Support for BASH commands
   C. Support for FireWire
   D. Larger filenames.

Email Forensics

A GREAT MANY COMPUTER CRIMES involve email. In fact, many noncomputer crimes, and even civil litigation, can require extracting evidence from email. Electronic communication is so ubiquitous that email communications can often shed light on issues. In civil lawsuits, subpoenas for all email correspondence are common. But it is also possible to spoof email addresses and hide the real sender. It is important to be able to track and appropriately analyze emails.

Chapter 11 Topics

This chapter covers the following topics and concepts:

- How email clients and servers work
- Email headers
- How to trace emails
- Email server forensic examination
- Laws relevant to email forensics

Chapter 11 Goals

When you complete this chapter, you will be able to:

- Understand the functionality of email and email protocols
- Obtain the full email headers for a variety of email clients
- Read and understand the contents of email headers
- Trace email to its origin
- Work with email servers
- Understand the laws related to email investigations

How Email Works

You might already have a strong working knowledge of how email works. If you don't, this section provides a common base of knowledge, which allows you to get the most from this chapter. As with most aspects of digital forensics, it is very difficult to perform forensics without a basic knowledge of the underlying technologies.

Different types of devices and methods generate emails. Most commonly, a user composes a message on his or her computer or perhaps a tablet or phone, and then sends it to his or her mail server. At this point, the user's computer is finished with the job, but the mail server still has to deliver the message. A mail server is like an electronic post office—it sends and receives electronic mail. Most of the time, the mail server is separate from the computer where the mail was composed.

The sender's mail server forwards the message through the organization's network and/ or the internet to the recipient's mail server. The message then resides on that second mail server and is available to the recipient. The software program used to compose and read email messages is the email client.

Depending on how the recipient's email client is configured, copies of the message may exist in a number of places. The recipient's and sender's computers, another electronic device such as a smartphone or a tablet, and the mail server or servers and their backups may all hold copies of the message. In addition, any of the servers that relay the message from the sender to the recipient may retain a copy of the email message. This is shown in **FIGURE 11-1**.

The number of relay "hops" may be only one if the sender and recipient are on the same network. Transmitting a message to a remotely located recipient might require many hops.

A forensic investigation of email might reveal information such as the following:

- Email messages related to the investigation
- Email addresses related to the investigation
- Sender and recipient information
- Information about those copied on the email
- Content of the communications
- Internet Protocol (IP) addresses
- Date and time information
- User information
- Attachments
- Passwords
- Application logs that show evidence of spoofing

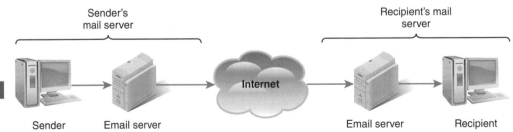

FIGURE 11-1

Delivering email.

FYI

Consider in how many places an email might be saved. It could be saved on the sender's machine, on the recipient's machine, on either the sender's or recipient's email server, or both, and on backup media for either server. If you consider the many places an email could reside, that should indicate to you that it is rare that an email is ever truly deleted. It may be quite hard to find, but it probably exists somewhere. This is one reason why email forensics is so important.

It is also important to keep in mind that the content of email can be very important even in non–computer crime cases. Given how common email communications are, it should not surprise you to find that criminals often communicate via email. Some crimes, like cyberstalking, usually include an email element. Other crimes, such as drug trafficking and terrorism, can also utilize email communication.

In financial crimes, such as insider trading, as well as in discrimination lawsuits, email is often a critical piece of evidence. Keep in mind that the sender and perhaps even the recipient may have deleted the email. But it could still reside on an email server or in the backup media for that server.

Today it is also common for people to utilize completely web-based email services. This can include Gmail, Hotmail, and similar services. When that is the situation, there may not be any local storage of email files. One will need to log into the email service in order to analyze emails. Gmail and similar services do not provide any mechanism to retrieve an email if it has been deleted from the trash folder. At that point, it is unrecoverable from the mailbox. In some cases a subpoena may be issued to the service provider, and it may search backups for the missing email.

Email Protocols

The **Simple Mail Transfer Protocol (SMTP)** is a protocol used to send email. SMTP typically operates on port 25. For many years, **Post Office Protocol version 3 (POP3)** was the only means for retrieving email. POP3 operates on port 110. However, POP3 has been largely replaced by the **Internet Message Access Protocol (IMAP)**. IMAP operates on port 143. One advantage of IMAP over POP3 is it allows the client to download only the email headers to the machine, so that the user can choose which messages are to be downloaded completely. This is particularly useful for smartphones and any wireless devices where bandwidth may be at a premium. Another advantage is that the emails stay on the server, allowing the user to check email from multiple devices. IMAP is defined by the standard RFC 3501. IMAP was designed to permit management of an email box by multiple email clients.

[handwritten margin note: POP3 deletes email off the server]

Each of these email protocols also has a secure version that is encrypted with the Transport Layer Security (TLS) Protocol. For SMTP, the secure alternative is SMTPS on port 465. For POP3, the secure version functions on port 995. And for IMAP, the secure version operates on port 993.

Faking Email

Criminals may send fake email messages. Some of them use email programs that strip the message header from the message before delivering it to the recipient. Or they may bury the message header within the email program. In other cases, the "From:" line in a message header is fake.

In addition to manipulating the email header, perpetrators may simply set up a temporary, bogus email account. For example, free email accounts, as offered by Yahoo!, Gmail, and Hotmail, are easy to set up, and you can use any desired and available name.

Spoofing

Spoofing involves making an email message appear to come from someone or someplace other than the real sender or location. The email sender uses a software tool that is readily available on the internet to cut out his or her IP address and replace it with someone else's IP address. However, the first machine to receive the spoofed message records the machine's real IP address. Thus, the header contains both the faked IP and the real IP address—unless, of course, the perpetrator is clever enough to have also spoofed his or her actual IP address.

Anonymous Remailing

Anonymous remailing is another attempt to throw tracing or tracking attempts off the trail. A suspect who uses anonymous remailing sends an email message to an anonymizer. An anonymizer is an email server that strips identifying information from an email message before forwarding it with the anonymous mailing computer's IP address.

FYI

The issue of spoofing emails, IP addresses, and similar identifying information brings up the question of the sophistication of computer criminals. Email spoofing is just like any other crime. There are a few very sophisticated criminals—and a host of unsophisticated criminals. The more sophisticated a criminal, the harder it is to find evidence. For example, if you wanted to send an email that you did not want traced to you, you could start by finding a free, public Wi-Fi in an area at least one hour from your home. Then you could spoof both your IP address and your network's media access control (MAC) address. Finally, you could send the email through an anonymous email account set up for that purpose. It is, however, very common for criminals to actually send emails from their own computers without even bothering to spoof their IP address or MAC address. In addition, keep in mind that email address spoofing is only one kind of spoofing. In this section, you also saw MAC and IP spoofing.

NOTE

TOR, *https://www.torproject.org/*, is an anonymous network of proxy servers. You can use the TOR network to send any sort of network traffic, including emails. This makes tracing the traffic back to its source extremely difficult.

To find out who sent remailed email, try to look at any logs maintained by remailer or anonymizer companies. However, these services frequently do not maintain logs. In addition, you can closely analyze the message for embedded information that might give clues to the user or system that sent the message.

There are many websites that let someone send an email and choose any "From" address he or she wants. Here are just a few:

- *http://sendanonymousemail.net/*
- *https://www.5ymail.com/*
- *http://send-email.org/*

Valid Emails   – hacked emails /compromisers

It is also very common for an email to arrive—often from a trusted friend, colleague, or family member—that is valid in every respect except for the content of the message. The email passes all of the normal validity checks, such as header structure and content, and even comes from a known, nonspam email server that is not blacklisted with any of the blacklist services such as SPAM Cop. However, the message is suspect and the website uniform resource locator (URL) pointed to is usually a hacker or phishing site. The message may read something like "Wow! Check out this great website: www.hackersite.com." (Note the www.hackersite.com is a fictitious URL to demonstrate the concept.) These messages usually contain no hidden URLs, pictures, or attachments and are very short. However, clicking the URL can unleash all sorts of malicious software or other negative results.

Email Headers

One of the first things to learn about emails is that they have headers. The header for an email message tells you a great deal about the email. The standard for email format, including headers, is RFC 2822. It is important that all email uses the same format. That is why you can send an email from Outlook on a Windows 8 PC and the recipient can read it from a Hotmail account on an Android phone that runs Linux—because all email programs use the same email format, regardless of what operating system they run on.

Make sure that any email you offer as evidence includes the message, any attachments, and the full email header. The header keeps a record of the message's journey as it travels through the communications network. As the message is routed through one or more mail servers, each server adds its own information to the message header. Each device in a network has an Internet Protocol (IP) address that identifies the device and can be resolved to a location address. A forensic investigator may be able to identify IP addresses from a message header and use this information to determine who sent the message.

Most email programs normally display only a small portion of the email header along with a message. This usually is information that the sender puts in the message, such as the "To" address, subject, and body of the message. You can view and examine the full header record by using tools available in the email client.

An email investigation begins with a review of an email message followed by a detailed examination of the message header information. Look at the header in more detail to find additional information associated with the email message. The message header provides an audit trail of every machine through which the email has passed.

> **NOTE**
>
> RFC 2822 supplements the older RFC 822 with a few notable enhancements. RFC 822 was originally designed for the standard for text messages sent over the ARPANET network, which was the precursor to the modern internet. You can check out *http://tools.ietf.org/html/rfc822* for more details.

Consider the specifications for email format given in RFC 2822:

- The message header <u>must</u> include at least the following fields:
  From—The email address and, optionally, the name of the sender
  Date—The local time and date when the message was written
- The message header <u>should</u> include at least the following fields:
  Message-ID—An automatically generated field
  In-Reply-To—The message-ID of the message that this is a reply to; used to link related messages together

RFC 3864 describes message header field names. Common header fields for email include the following:

- **To**—The email address and, optionally, name of the message's primary recipient(s)
- **Subject**—A brief summary of the topic of the message
- **Cc**—Carbon copy; a copy is sent to secondary recipients
- **Bcc**—Blind carbon copy; a copy is sent to addresses added to the SMTP delivery list while the Bcc address remains invisible to other recipients
- **Content-Type**—Information about how the message is to be displayed, usually a Multi-purpose Internet Mail Extensions (MIME) type
- **Precedence**—Commonly with values "bulk," "junk," or "list"; used to indicate that automated "vacation" or "out of office" responses should not be returned for this mail, for example, to prevent vacation notices from being sent to all other subscribers of a mailing list
- **Received**—Tracking information generated by mail servers that have previously handled a message, in reverse order (last handler first)
- **References**—Message-ID of the message to which this is a reply
- **Reply-To**—Address that should be used to reply to the message
- **Sender**—Address of the actual sender acting on behalf of the author listed in the From field

There is a wealth of information in these headers so examining them is very important.

Getting Headers in Outlook 2019

First, open the email, then select File and then Info, as shown in **FIGURE 11-2**. Then select Properties and you will be able to view the headers, as shown in **FIGURE 11-3**.

It is often helpful to copy the header information and paste it to a text file for analysis. You can see it is relatively easy to view the headers using Outlook. Older versions of Outlook have a different method to get to headers. With Outlook 2007 and 2010, there are two methods:

- **Method #1**—Right-click the message in the folder view, and then choose Options.
- **Method #2**—In an open message, choose View and then Options.

With either method, you'll see the internet headers portion of the Message Options dialog box. Regardless of the version of Outlook you have and the method you use to view the headers, the headers appear similarly to what is shown in **FIGURE 11-4**.

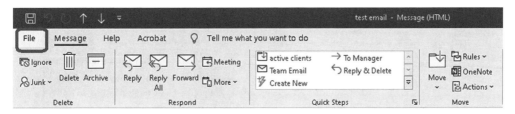

test email

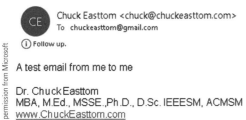

Chuck Easttom <chuck@chuckeasttom.com>
To chuckeasttom@gmail.com

(i) Follow up.

A test email from me to me

Dr. Chuck Easttom
MBA, M.Ed., MSSE.,Ph.D., D.Sc. IEEESM, ACMSM
www.ChuckEasttom.com
chuck@chuckeasttom.com

Used with permission from Microsoft

FIGURE 11-2

Outlook 2019
headers
Step 1.

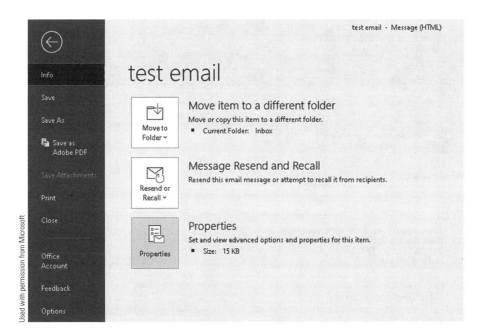

Used with permission from Microsoft

FIGURE 11-3

Outlook 2019
headers
Step 2.

Getting Headers from Yahoo! Email

If you are working with Yahoo! email, then first open the message. On the lower right, there is a link named view raw headers, shown in **FIGURE 11-5**.

If you click on that link, you can see the headers for that email, shown in **FIGURE 11-6**.

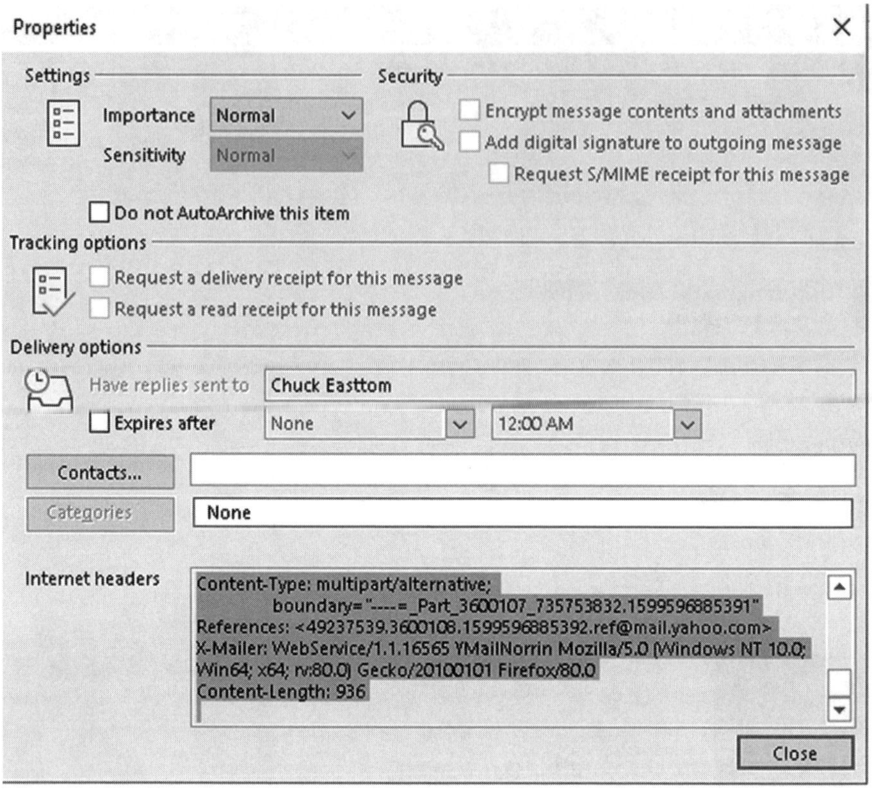

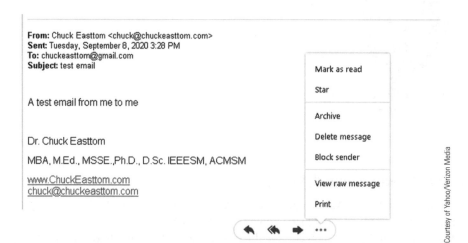

FIGURE 11-4

Outlook headers.

FIGURE 11-5

Finding Yahoo! headers.

```
Received: from 10.201.234.73
  by atlas103.ptnr.mail.bf1.yahoo.com with HTTP; Tue, 8 Sep 2020 20:35:13 +0000
Return-Path: <chuckeasttom@gmail.com>
Received: from 209.85.161.46 (EHLO mail-oo1-f46.google.com)
  by 10.201.234.73 with SMTPs; Tue, 8 Sep 2020 20:35:13 +0000
X-Originating-Ip: [209.85.161.46]
Received-SPF: pass (domain of gmail.com designates 209.85.161.46 as permitted sender)
Authentication-Results: atlas103.ptnr.mail.bf1.yahoo.com;
  dkim=pass header.i=@gmail.com header.s=20161025;
  spf=pass smtp.mailfrom=gmail.com;
  dmarc=success(p=NONE,sp=QUARANTINE) header.from=gmail.com;
X-Apparently-To: chuck@chuckeasttom.com; Tue, 8 Sep 2020 20:35:13 +0000
X-YMailISG: xic9Xw4WLDu8xypveTiDbiiud9vU3O8ghKCVuFz14KpNkae.
  OH26hvwp810APDs1.BT2jZ6OcINeFG58r12YKCoFKrKXdCqVIW6ELbPt5uw1
  Q9OIXqDzOkY43czPeaRZ_hAo2iOrNteb.51aPBTwPaohhRquiX5dCOHJbWXG
  tcGzGHpBUeJfsWRvNXOjVKBV7k1buUquzupjCWXnUOROA2mYDORDQRps.tUB
  ytK7OSeFpKZDtCjop_Nzt.jq6aJonCXusT3kzot8fZ54T3nyq4og71hCzFu5
  X2GDfTzqcoleXVP5EtMu5inUF7uvPHpqFDqku.aNKqHxk25N7WeGGQhPoF1E
  fLKJJP4ONEeZgvv1VL73.1YZmp72KXInxg2G_AO2N4XMzztRSQ.8JW8T9mpM
  bHBbxMh2yOU.9qrvDwt_U_5CdZnf_GOJesiyCNiFoCWmcVsr6xc9MtxBFxGd
  Gwy6H2DbcaYZbov6PBSjA9h65.agDiC7SXAY5oGV3Bs1..yszfWhEzyesK1C
  md2mm_4NIjnulUbNC7Z6925Pk1pfwSNj4gVWszuuJDL7QIy3iZGD_i2Vs8k3
  d1I18N3MzOlu2WHz5GUm4RPSpjExo75FuYgHXjSJ.RtXLYMlitgEzyQjmfb7
  s_dcOdiN5vr4BYSdbJ.hJfOGWxgkXLuNn8PZvHGrP1mV5rxHsO5ODJvpjQl5
  qIhe3I87sYhXv_rbuwlEq8seYi5F2x2.nrGja1h6gKZQu_B59sQSRCnrX_7G
  81BIcwByOYxth9tQvZGlBOyJ2FbI7X8fjiSgmqZlQcDvwt1_zoicwtxoTW6r
  HCkpRyhNYhLFyjAgyz8ut3DiJOqx4UX1hPP1o2dBM_k1Oz2wT36OjipqK95J
  BJxDKBkrceFxBSyHOvX9cDOG2VumEaGlj5u4IXMAcc2VyyB9mQp11pbytMNi
  QtjOAT4WITviHScO139AAcOYMRRRO1VH74LMX.rjsCSTegFGj8vWFNrSQUgv
  1R3pRhq7BX9RiOBNG_C7ex8fh5uakdghhPxKMOOwgMChrvqE8jggYjg1gusD
  t51._OjbNP1W.OU5D4zGOmVIzsg0YLLGdqexmy86HntVBfW.8drQzYmt1PG_
  nPi7CU1kQu4F9Gjgs1qacZeVFROE_5m8KK5_TiZ4WfWCnuGts15DLvwMyOGZ
  5QYKk5yKI78_7Rsw7Lg-
Received: by mail-oo1-f46.google.com with SMTP id r4so61091ooq.7
        for <chuck@chuckeasttom.com>; Tue, 08 Sep 2020 13:35:13 -0700 (PDT)
DKIM-Signature: v=1; a=rsa-sha256; c=relaxed/relaxed;
        d=gmail.com; s=20161025;
        h=from:to:references:in-reply-to:subject:date:message-id:mime-version
        :thread-index:content-language;
        bh=boAGrqPSNJryuOCwUjXpa7cGiMkXG/elwSE6NOjM1us=;
        b=ug8aHS/q3MrPC1aEuV6J/4azqRyMFwaN/q24QKeF5rPLne1D2UjdQnQpaVfTgkmhhw
        RfuHL/q3E1FSGSnqH+rM4nWW3Lc1EGMHqgrr32g6NKXOx55E+GYWGZxtRtaoN7jTApWl
        4qo+JeJNjZaoGhtaBIJ3wPTBJSG7WF6Ih9591ekpLFOvmBO3IW1+5hxsQOM3Hm+cp355
        VAvw8zw8zqt/NBep3kGM3kJDYQzt+2vH6H57z/OCGsKb3zdsxQPqIQ3NmCtvLvFnVO6d
        gYOBVZymtbDdcfIhbiqk/FuXmlioIf+KFUwG66GJ2MgrVVlwNwXKXe4oKEAdk6xtbCtu
        vdUA==
X-Google-DKIM-Signature: v=1; a=rsa-sha256; c=relaxed/relaxed;
        d=1e100.net; s=20161025;
        h=x-gm-message-state:from:to:references:in-reply-to:subject:date
```

FIGURE 11-6

Viewing
Yahoo!
headers.

Getting Headers from Gmail

Viewing email headers in Gmail is fairly simple; just follow these steps:

1. Log on to Gmail.
2. Open the message for which you want to view headers.
3. Look for the ⋮ and click it (**FIGURE 11-7**).
4. Select Show Original.

The headers appear in a separate window and look similar to **FIGURE 11-8**.

FIGURE 11-7

Finding Gmail headers.

```
Delivered-To: chuckeasttom007@gmail.com
Received: by 10.182.25.137 with SMTP id c9csp84759obq;
        Wed, 23 May 2012 13:58:23 -0700 (PDT)
Return-Path: <3b0-9Tw8KD4Ykn6y1n2-xylozv8qyyqvo.mywmr4muok233ywAAHqwksv.myw@scoutcamp.bounces.google.com>
Received-SPF: pass (google.com: domain of 3b0-9Tw8KD4Ykn6y1n2-xylozv8qyyqvo.mywmr4muok233ywAAHqwksv.myw@scoutcamp.bounces.google.com designates 10.50.40
Authentication-Results: mr.google.com; spf=pass (google.com: domain of 3b0-9Tw8KD4Ykn6y1n2-xylozv8qyyqvo.mywmr4muok233ywAAHqwksv.myw@scoutcamp.bounces.go
Received: from mr.google.com ([10.50.40.230])
        by 10.50.40.230 with SMTP id a6mr20555688igl.2.1337806703082 (num_hops = 1);
        Wed, 23 May 2012 13:58:23 -0700 (PDT)
DKIM-Signature: v=1; a=rsa-sha256; c=relaxed/relaxed;
        d=google.com; s=20120113;
        h=date:from:to:cc:subject:reply-to:x-google-ads-sender:message-id
        :x-trak-extra-language:mime-version:content-type;
        bh=XekTgcS1iYSkFAHQTAJcm7aGSzICw8DGRTeLhcUe8M8=;
        b=H6rb7OD+xtuyUTc1NCDwh+e3H1JphFiN1BO431WP2SkZuYqn3BT/2XJ2muJslF+7A0
        g716xr4Q/a+pquw01yOQyMCfRQVBZFxThD90f6HdYHje/9GiMdu/YS+LrDbYh1WmgKqJ
        nV9CMQyjAj1cOFkAqAOcd9EIDqJ8elnTGan8U+rl8OUrKtL83R4rauiXIObnpdBrDF3t
        ykwzmC42LXMELs53FCjM+Abn/geyxEB4wKmAfmvpxBbOOUC8S1bzs6PgqURKjl12V1Xb
        rcvDOazwpdqhL1PRND8a9PfFv2RHzWtPn13thYQd1jmkB1/vEIvVV9XMHGbe1j9StGy6
        1PNA==
Date: Wed, 23 May 2012 20:58:23 +0000
Received: by 10.50.40.230 with SMTP id a6mrl1939917igl.2.1337806703051;
        Wed, 23 May 2012 13:58:23 -0700 (PDT)
From: Google AdWords <adwords-noreply@google.com>
To: chuckeasttom007@gmail.com
Cc:
Subject: =?utf-8?q?Only_days_left_to_get_=24100_=26_tips_from_Google_AdWords=2E_En?=
        =?utf-8?q?ds_May_31=2E?=
Reply-To: adwords-noreply@google.com
X-Google-Ads-Sender: auto_adsense_emails
Message-ID: <29060e2c.1337806701.000000.53518.1.EN_US.2f59020b@google.com>
X-Trak-Extra-Language: EN_US
MIME-Version: 1.0
Content-Type: multipart/alternative; boundary="================0825779531=="
```

FIGURE 11-8

Viewing Gmail headers.

Other Email Clients

A vast number of email clients are available for people to use. It is not beneficial to you to go through each and every one separately. By now, you should be noticing some similarities in the processes. However, you can see the basic steps for many of these clients in this section.

Hotmail

Hotmail is similar to Gmail:

1. Select Inbox from the menu on the left.
2. Right-click the message for which you want to view headers and select View Message Source.
3. The full headers will appear in a new window.

Apple Mail

Apple Mail is pretty straightforward:

1. Open Apple Mail.
2. Click on the message for which you want to view headers.
3. Go to the View menu.
4. Select Message, then Long Headers.
5. The full headers will appear in the window below your Inbox.

You can get a list of other email clients from Google Support at *http://support.google.com /mail/answer/22454?hl=en.*

Of course, you can always use your favorite search engine to search for the email client you are using. It is usually quite easy to find out how to view headers.

Email Files

Local storage archives are any archives that have an independent archive format from a mail server. Examples of these types of archives include the following:

- .pst (Outlook)
- .ost (Offline Outlook Storage)
- .mbx or .dbx (Outlook Express)
- .mbx (Eudora)
- .emi (common to several email clients)

You need to know how to find these files and how to view them. For example, in Outlook, a clever criminal might have a second .pst file containing email messages that he loads only when committing his nefarious activities. If his computer is seized and you simply look in Microsoft Outlook, you won't see any incriminating evidence. If you search the suspect drive and find an additional .pst file, you can easily mount it in Outlook by selecting File, Open, and Open Outlook Data File, as shown in **FIGURE 11-9.**

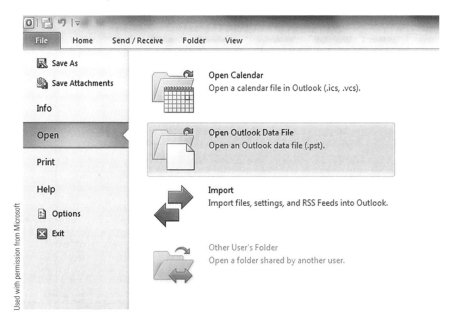

Used with permission from Microsoft

FIGURE 11-9

Opening a .pst file in Outlook.

There are tools that allow you to convert from one email file format to another. For example, the accused's email file could be an EML file, but you use Outlook. It would be helpful to translate that file into an Outlook .pst format. Transend Migrator (*http://www.transend.com/*) is a tool that will do this for you.

In addition, a number of forensic tools can examine the email files for you. A few examples include the following:

- **Paraben's Email Examiner**—This tool is meant specifically to analyze email. It is available at *https://paraben.com/email-forensics/.*
- **Guidance Software's EnCase**—This is a general-purpose forensic tool. You can find more information about EnCase at *http://www.guidancesoftware.com.*
- **AccessData's Forensic Toolkit (FTK)**—This is another general-purpose forensic tool. You can find more details about FTK at *https://accessdata.com/products-services/forensic-toolkit-ftk.*
- **PassMark's OSForensics** is a general-purpose forensics tool that can find and examine emails on a suspect drive image. You can learn more at *http://www.osforensics.com/.*
- **LibPST package**—This is an open source tool. You can get this tool from *http://www.five-ten-sg.com/libpst/.*

Paraben's Email Examiner

Although there are many tools available that may be used with email forensics, this tool is exclusively for email forensics, so it merits a closer look. Paraben works like the more complete forensic suites (Forensic Toolkit and EnCase) in that evidence is grouped by case. When you first start Paraben, you select New and then create a new case, as shown in **FIGURE 11-10**.

Paraben will also associate information about the investigator with the case information. This is shown in **FIGURE 11-11**.

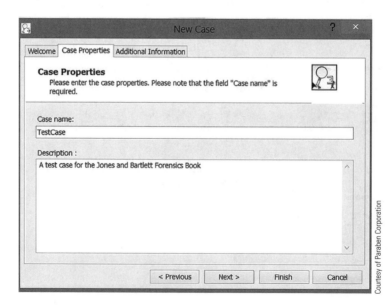

FIGURE 11-10

A new Paraben case.

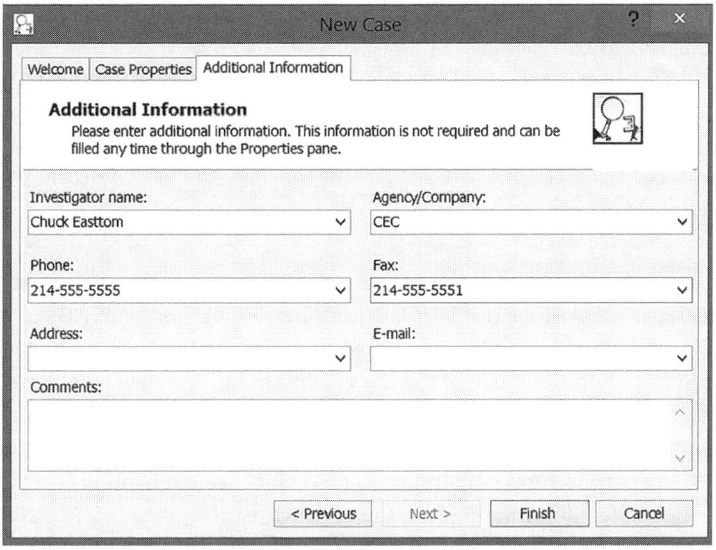

Courtesy of Paraben Corporation.

FIGURE 11-11 The investigator.

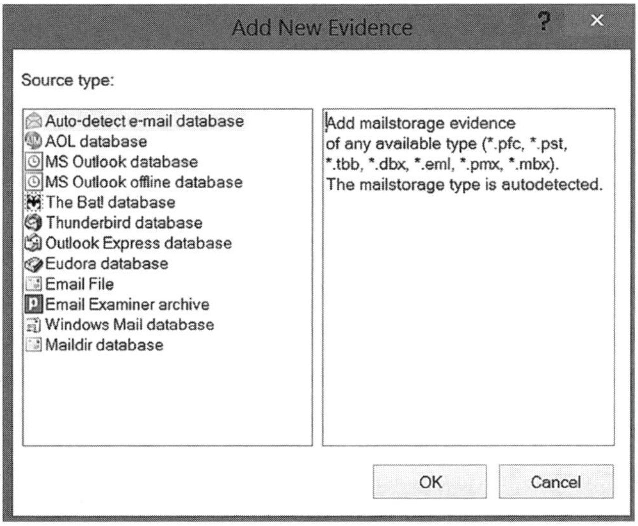

Courtesy of Paraben Corporation.

FIGURE 11-12 Select your email database.

Next, you select the type of email database you are going to be working with. The major email clients are all represented, as you can see in **FIGURE 11-12**.

At this point, you select the database you want to work with, and it is added to the case. From within Paraben, you can sort, search, scan, and otherwise work with the email data. Paraben can also generate reports of the data showing whatever data is most relevant to your case—or all the email data, if you prefer.

ReadPST

ReadPST is a program made available as part of the libPST package. You can find the ReadPST main page at *https://linux.die.net/man/1/readpst*. You will need to download and compile it because it is not available in precompiled format. Once you have done so, you can run it and use it to examine PST files.

ReadPST will first convert the PST into RFC-compliant Unix mail. You can access the extracted mail and attachments with any standard Unix mail client. If you have access to Microsoft Outlook, there is no need to use ReadPST.

Tracing Email

Email tracing involves examining email header information to look for clues about where a message has been. This will be one of your more frequent responsibilities as a forensic investigator. You will often use audits or paper trails of email traffic as evidence in court. Many investigators recommend use of the tracert command. However, because of the dynamic nature of the internet, tracert does not provide reliable, consistent, or accurate routing information for an email. To prove this, you can simply compare the routing from the email header to the results shown by tracert. The results are likely different, and the greater the distance between sender and receiver, the bigger the difference between the theoretical tracert results and the results determined from the actual routing information embedded in the header.

It may be useful to determine the ownership of the source email server for a message. If you need to manually find out to whom a given IP address is registered, a number of WHOIS databases are available on the web. Here are just a few:

- *http://www.whois.net*
- *http://www.networksolutions.com/whois/index.jsp*
- *http://www.who.is*
- *http://www.internic.net/whois.html*
- *http://cqcounter.com/whois/*

After a suspect comes to the authorities' attention, your organization may ask you to monitor that person's traffic. For example, administrators might request security checks on an employee who appears to be disgruntled or who has access to sensitive information. This employee's email logs and network usage may, for example, show him or her sending innocent family photos to a Hotmail account, but no traffic coming back from that Hotmail account. These seemingly innocent photos might carry steganographically hidden messages, and so provide evidence of the employee's part in corporate espionage.

Forensic email tracing is similar to traditional gumshoe detective work. It involves looking at each point through which an email passed. You work step by step back to the originating computer and, eventually, the perpetrator.

Email Server Forensics

At some point, you need to check the email server. Both the sender and the recipient could have deleted the relevant emails, but there is a good chance a copy is still on the email server. Many servers have a retention policy, which may be governed by law in certain industries. When you examine an email server, be aware that there are a variety of email server programs that could be in use. Microsoft Exchange is a very common server. Lotus Notes and Novell GroupWise are also popular email server products.

The file extensions associated with the most widely used email server software are listed here:

- Exchange Server (.edb)
- Exchange Public Folders (pub.edb)
- Exchange Private Folders (priv.edb)
- Streaming Data (priv.stm)
- Lotus Notes (.nsf)
- GroupWise (.db)
- GroupWise Post Office Database (wphost.db)
- GroupWise User Databases (userxxx.db)
- Linux Email Server Logs/var/log/mail.*

Obviously, tools like Forensic Toolkit and EnCase allow you to add these files to a case and to work with them. You can also manually examine these files provided that you have access to the relevant software (for example, Exchange or Lotus Notes).

Email and the Law

There are specific laws in the United States that are applicable to email investigations. It is critical that you be aware of the relevant laws. Failure to adhere to the legal guidelines can render evidence inadmissible.

The Fourth Amendment to the U.S. Constitution

If an email message resides on a sender's or recipient's computer or other device, the Fourth Amendment to the U.S. Constitution and state requirements govern the seizure and collection of the message. Determine whether the person on whose computer the evidence resides has a reasonable expectation of privacy on that computer. The Fourth Amendment requires a search warrant or one of the recognized exceptions to the search warrant requirements, such as consent from the device owner.

The Electronic Communications Privacy Act

If an internet service provider (ISP) or any other communications network stores an email, retrieval of that evidence must be analyzed under the Electronic Communications Privacy Act (ECPA). The ECPA creates statutory restrictions on government access to such evidence from ISPs or other electronic communications service providers.

The ECPA requires different legal processes to obtain specific types of information:

- **Basic subscriber information**—This information includes name, address, billing information including a credit card number, telephone toll billing records, subscriber's telephone number, type of service, and length of service. An investigator can obtain this type of information with a subpoena, court order, or search warrant.

- **Transactional information**—This information includes websites visited, email addresses of others with whom the subscriber exchanged email, and buddy lists. An investigator can obtain this type of information with a court order or search warrant.
- **Content information**—An investigator who has a search warrant can obtain content information from retrieved email messages and also acquire unretrieved stored emails.
- **Real-time access**—To intercept traffic as it is sent or received, an investigator needs to obtain a wiretap order.

The CAN-SPAM Act

The CAN-SPAM Act of 2003 was the first law meant to curtail unsolicited email, often referred to as *spam*. However, the law has many loopholes. For example, you do not need permission before sending an email. This means that unsolicited email—what most people consider spam to be—is not prohibited. The second issue is that it applies only to commercial emails—messages that are trying to sell some product or service. Therefore, mass emailings for political, religious, or ideological purposes are not covered by the CAN-SPAM Act.

The only requirement of CAN-SPAM is that the sender must provide some mechanism whereby the receiver can opt out of future emails and that method cannot require the receiver to pay in order to opt out.

The law defines commercial email as "any electronic mail message the primary purpose of which is the commercial advertisement or promotion of a commercial product or service (including content on an Internet website operated for a commercial purpose)." This means that any mass emails that have no commercial purpose are not covered by this law.

All commercial email is required to offer ways for the recipient to opt out. Those methods must meet the following guidelines:

- A visible and operable unsubscribe mechanism is present in all emails.
- Consumer opt-out requests are honored within 10 days.
- Opt-out lists, also known as suppression lists, can be used only for compliance purposes, and cannot be sold to other vendors/senders.

There are also restrictions on how the sender can acquire the recipient's email address and how the sender can actually transmit the email. Those requirements are as follows:

- A message cannot be sent through an open relay.
- A message cannot be sent to a harvested email address.
- A message cannot contain a false header.

This is important because these are the methods often used by people who send spam email. Spam is one crime that obviously lends itself to email forensics. Tracking down the original sender of the email is the first step in investigating spam. Unfortunately, the email is sometimes sent from offshore sites or relayed through an innocent third party's servers. This makes prosecuting spam very difficult, and even if a judgment is obtained, in most cases it is impossible to enforce.

18 U.S.C. 2252B

You might be at least somewhat familiar with the laws already discussed in this chapter. However, this law is less well known. To begin, read the actual law. *Findlaw.com* (2013) provides details of the law as follows:

(a) Whoever knowingly uses a misleading domain name on the Internet with the intent to deceive a person into viewing material constituting obscenity shall be fined under this title or imprisoned not more than 2 years, or both.

(b) Whoever knowingly uses a misleading domain name on the Internet with the intent to deceive a minor into viewing material that is harmful to minors on the Internet shall be fined under this title or imprisoned not more than 4 years, or both.

(c) For the purposes of this section, a domain name that includes a word or words to indicate the sexual content of the site, such as "sex" or "porn," is not misleading.

(d) For the purposes of this section, the term "material that is harmful to minors" means any communication, consisting of nudity, sex, or excretion, that, taken as a whole and with reference to its context—

  (1) predominantly appeals to a prurient interest of minors;

  (2) is patently offensive to prevailing standards in the adult community as a whole with respect to what is suitable material for minors; and

  (3) lacks serious literary, artistic, political, or scientific value for minors.

(e) For the purposes of subsection (d), the term "sex" means acts of masturbation, sexual intercourse, or physical contact with a person's genitals, or the condition of human male or female genitals when in a state of sexual stimulation or arousal.

This law is about perpetrators who attempt to hide the pornographic nature of their website, often to make it more accessible to minors. This is a very serious concern, and one that sometimes arises in child predator cases.

The Communication Assistance to Law Enforcement Act

The Communication Assistance to Law Enforcement Act (CALEA), not to be confused with the law enforcement standards certification of the same name, is a U.S. wiretapping law passed in 1994.

CALEA's purpose is to allow law enforcement and intelligence agencies to lawfully conduct electronic surveillance. It requires that telecommunications carriers and manufacturers of telecommunications equipment modify and design their equipment, facilities, and services to ensure that they have built-in surveillance capabilities, allowing federal agencies to monitor all telephone, broadband internet, and VoIP traffic in real time. CALEA is widely used, and a basic awareness of CALEA should be a part of every forensic investigator's base knowledge.

The Foreign Intelligence Surveillance Act

The **Foreign Intelligence Surveillance Act (FISA)** of 1978 is a U.S. law that prescribes procedures for the physical and electronic surveillance and collection of "foreign intelligence information" between foreign powers and agents of foreign powers, which may include American citizens and permanent residents suspected of espionage or terrorism. The law does not apply outside the United States but may be encountered by a forensic investigator in researching intelligence even if it does not specifically regard espionage or terrorism. The law is an important part of many agencies' approaches to information gathering. It has been amended frequently, so it is important to stay current on the latest revisions and court cases.

The USA PATRIOT Act

The **USA PATRIOT Act** of 2001 incorporates in its name a 10-letter acronym standing for **U**niting (and) **S**trengthening **A**merica (by) **P**roviding **A**ppropriate **T**ools **R**equired (to) **I**ntercept (and) **O**bstruct **T**errorism. The act was passed into law as a response to the terrorist attacks of September 11, 2001. It significantly reduced restrictions on law enforcement agencies' gathering of intelligence within the United States; expanded the Secretary of the Treasury's authority to regulate financial transactions, particularly those involving foreign individuals and entities; and broadened the discretion of law enforcement and immigration authorities in detaining and/or deporting immigrants suspected of terrorism and related acts. The law also expanded the definition of terrorism to include domestic terrorism, thus enlarging the number of activities to which the USA PATRIOT Act's expanded law enforcement powers can be applied.

In May 2011, President Barack Obama signed the PATRIOT Sunsets Extension Act of 2011, which is a four-year extension of three key provisions in the USA PATRIOT Act: roving wiretaps, searches of business records, and conducting surveillance of individuals suspected of terrorist-related activities who are not linked to terrorist groups, and so are known as lone wolves. The USA PATRIOT Act gives law enforcement dramatically enhanced powers for information gathering and should be a part of a comprehensive knowledge base for any forensic investigator.

CHAPTER SUMMARY

In this chapter, you learned the process of email forensics. You examined email headers, learned about file formats, and worked with a few email tools. You also learned about laws relevant to email forensics. You should be very comfortable with the material in this chapter because email evidence is common to many cases.

KEY CONCEPTS AND TERMS

Anonymous remailing
Foreign Intelligence Surveillance
  Act (FISA)
Internet Message Access
  Protocol (IMAP)

Post Office Protocol version 3
  (POP3)
Simple Mail Transfer Protocol
  (SMTP)

Spoofing
USA PATRIOT Act

CHAPTER 11 ASSESSMENT

1. What is the file format .edb used with?

   A. GroupWise
   B. Microsoft Exchange
   C. Microsoft Outlook
   D. Linux email

2. IMAP uses port 143.

   A. True
   B. False

3. Which of the following types of mass emails are *not* covered by the CAN-SPAM Act?

   A. Emails advertising products
   B. Emails advertising legal services
   C. Emails advertising a church event
   D. Emails advertising stock prices

4. What is the .ost file format used for?

   A. Microsoft Outlook mailbox
   B. Microsoft Outlook offline storage
   C. Microsoft Lotus Notes
   D. Microsoft Outlook Express

5. Lotus Notes uses the following file format.

   A. mbx
   B. pst
   C. ost
   D. nsf

Mobile Forensics

MOBILE DEVICES OF ALL TYPES are ubiquitous in our modern world. It is almost guaranteed that everyone reading this has a smartphone. It is also quite probable that many readers have a tablet of some type. It is a fact that mobile devices are a central part of our modern life. This means they are an important topic for forensics. Mobile devices can be a veritable treasure trove of forensic evidence. Even in non-computer crimes, mobile devices can reveal locations, messages, emails, and many other relevant pieces of information. There are numerous real-world cases wherein mobile device evidence has either convicted or exonerated a suspect. Many digital forensics practitioners find that they spend more time examining mobile devices than they do PCs and laptops. In this chapter, you will learn the basics of mobile devices and how to extract evidence from them.

Chapter 12 Topics

This chapter covers the following topics and concepts:

- Cellular device concepts
- Evidence you can obtain from a mobile device
- How to seize evidence from a mobile device

Chapter 12 Goals

When you complete this chapter, you will be able to:

- Understand cellular concepts and terminology
- Understand what evidence to look for on mobile devices
- Seize evidence from an iPhone, iPod, or iPad
- Seize evidence from an Android phone

Cellular Device Concepts

As with the Windows, Linux, and Mac OS operating systems, it is important that you fully understand the technology of cell phones and other devices before you explore the forensic analysis of the devices. In this section, you will learn the essential concepts and technologies used in mobile devices. This section introduces you to some basic concepts that you need to understand in order to be able to conduct forensics on cellular devices.

Terms

The first place to start is with terminology. This section introduces a number of terms—along with brief definitions—that are relevant to mobile technology. It is important that you be comfortable with the terms in this section.

Mobile Switching Center

A **mobile switching center (MSC)** is the switching system for the cellular network. MSCs are used in 1G, 2G, 3G, and **Global System for Mobile (GSM) communications networks**. You will learn about 3G and GSM networks later in this section. The MSC processes all the connections between mobile devices and between mobile devices and landline phones. The MSC is also responsible for routing calls between base stations and the public switched telephone network (PSTN).

Base Transceiver Station

The **base transceiver station (BTS)** is the part of the cellular network responsible for communications between the mobile phone and the network switching system. The base station system (BSS) is a set of radio transceiver equipment that communicates with cellular devices. It consists of a BTS and a base station controller (BSC). The BSC is a central controller coordinating the other pieces of the BSS.

Home Location Register

The **home location register (HLR)** is a database used by the MSC that contains subscriber data and service information. It is related to the **visitor location register (VLR)**, which is used for roaming phones.

Subscriber Identity Module

The **subscriber identity module (SIM)** is a memory chip that stores the International Mobile Subscriber Identity (IMSI). It is intended to be unique for each phone and is what you use to identify the phone. Many modern phones have removable SIMs, which means you could change out the SIM and essentially have a different phone with a different number. A SIM card contains its unique serial number—the ICCID—as well as the IMSI, security authentication, and ciphering information. The SIM will also usually have network information, services the user has access to, and two passwords. Those passwords are the **personal identification number (PIN)** and the personal unlocking code (PUK).

> **NOTE**
>
> SIM cloning occurs when a SIM card's identifying information is copied to a different SIM card. That card can then be used in a new phone, but that phone will operate as if it were the original phone. SIM cloning is illegal, but it happens frequently and is done fairly easily with a minimum of technical knowledge and very little specialized equipment.

Electronic Serial Number

Electronic serial numbers (ESNs) are unique identification numbers developed by the U.S. Federal Communications Commission (FCC) to identify cell phones. They are now used only in code division multiple access (CDMA) phones, whereas GSM and later phones use the **International Mobile Equipment Identity (IMEI) number**. The IMEI is a number, usually unique, that is assigned to identify modern mobile phones. It is usually found printed inside the battery compartment of the phone, but can also be displayed on-screen on most phones by entering *#06# on the dial pad, or alongside other system information in the settings menu on smartphone operating systems.

Personal Unlocking Code

The **personal unlocking code (PUK)** is a code used to reset a forgotten PIN. Using the code returns the phone to its original state, causing loss of most forensic data. If the code is entered incorrectly 10 times in a row, the device becomes permanently blocked and unrecoverable.

Integrated Circuit Card Identifier

Each SIM is identified by its **integrated circuit card identifier (ICCID)**. These numbers are engraved on the SIM during manufacturing. This number has subsections that are very important for forensics. This number starts with the issuer identification number (IIN), which is a seven-digit number that identifies the country code and issuer, followed by a variable-length individual account identification number to identify the specific phone, and a check digit. The ICCID has some interesting information. From ForensicWiki,[1] in the example 89 91 10 1200 00 320451 0:

> The first two digits (89 in the example) refer to the Major Industry Identifier.
> The next two digits (91 in the example) refer to the country code (91-India).
> The next two digits (10 in the example) refer to the issuer identifier number.
> The next four digits (1200 in the example) refer to the month and year of manufacturing.
> The next two digits (00 in the example) refer to the switch configuration code.
> The next six digits (320451 in the example) refer to the SIM number.
> The last digit, which is separated from the rest, is called the checksum digit.

3GPP

This is actually a group of related standards organizations. The acronym stands for 3rd-Generation Partnership Project (3GPP). Standards for GSM, UMTS, LTE, and 5G are all managed by 3GPP. This group has a core membership of seven national/regional telecommunication standards organizations and other associate members.

Networks

Although this section covers terms as well, they are terms specific to networks. Therefore, they are listed separately. Knowing the types of networks used may be the most fundamental part of understanding mobile devices. The network-specific terms are as follows:

- **Global System for Mobile (GSM) communications**—GSM communications is a standard developed by the European Telecommunications Standards Institute (ETSI). Basically, GSM is the 2G network.
- **Enhanced Data Rates for GSM Evolution (EDGE)—Enhanced Data Rates for GSM Evolution (EDGE)** does not fit neatly into the 2G-3G-4G continuum. It is technically considered 2G+, but was an improvement on GSM (2G), so it can be considered a bridge between 2G and 3G technologies.
- **Universal Mobile Telecommunications System (UMTS)—Universal Mobile Telecommunications System (UMTS)** is a 3G standard based on GSM. It is essentially an improvement of GSM.
- **Long Term Evolution (LTE)—Long Term Evolution (LTE)** is a standard for wireless communication of high-speed data for mobile devices. This is what is commonly called 4G.
- **5G**—5th-Generation Wireless Systems (abbreviated 5G) meets ITU IMT-2020 requirements and 3GPP Release 15 Peak Data Rate 20 Gbit/s Expected User Data Rate 100 Mbit/s. Due to the increased bandwidth, it is expected that 5G networks will not just serve cell phones like existing cellular networks, but also be used as general internet service providers, competing with existing ISPs such as cable internet and providing connection for wireless sensors that are part of the Internet of Things (IoT).

> **NOTE**
>
> The real differentiator between 3G and 4G is speed. To be considered 4G, a wireless communication technology must have a speed of 100 megabits per second (Mbps) for mobile communications (such as when you are in a car) and 1 gigabit per second (Gbps) for stationary users.

- **Wireless fidelity (Wi-Fi)**—Most cellular phones and other mobile devices today are able to connect to Wi-Fi networks. Wireless networking has become the norm, and free Wi-Fi hotspots can be found in restaurants, coffee shops, hotels, homes, and many other locations.

Operating Systems

Today's mobile devices are complex computer systems. Whether you prefer an Android, Windows, or Apple phone, the phone will have an operating system. The same is true for tablets. Therefore, it is important to have some basic understanding of the major operating systems used on mobile devices.

iOS

The iOS operating system is used by iPhone, iPod, and iPad. It was originally released in 2007 for the iPod Touch and the iPhone. The user interface is based all on touching the icons directly. It supports what Apple calls gestures: swipe, drag, pinch, tap, and so on. The iOS operating system is derived from OS X.

The iOS kernel is the XNU kernel of Darwin. The original iPhone OS (1.0) up to iPhone OS 3.1.3 used Darwin 9.0.0d1. iOS 4 was based on Darwin 10. iOS 5 was based on Darwin 11. iOS 6 was based on Darwin 13. iOS 7 and iOS 8 are based on Darwin 14. iOS 9 is based on Darwin 15. iOS 10 is based on Darwin 16. iOS 11 is based on Darwin 17. iOS 12 is based on Darwin 18.

Darwin is an open-source Unix code first released by Apple in 2000. Darwin is the core for OS X, iOS, watchOS, tvOS, etc. The iOS operating system uses 256-bit encryption, so the device encryption is quite secure.

As of this writing, iOS 14 is the current version; it was released in June 2020. This version does have interesting security enhancements. A good example is that with iOS 14, a recording indicator is displayed whenever an app has access to the microphone or camera.

There are four layers to iOS. The first is the Core OS layer. This is the heart of the operating system. Next is the Core Services layer. The Core Services layer is how applications interact with the iOS. Next is the Media layer, which is responsible for music, video, and so on. Finally, there is the Cocoa Touch layer, which responds to the aforementioned gestures.

The file system for iOS has a similar structure to Unix. The root directory is called root and is denoted by simply /. Usually, a user cannot access this. Under the root, there are system data and user data. Fortunately, criminals also cannot access system data; thus only accessing user data is not prohibitive for iOS forensics.

Since iOS 10.3, iOS has used the Apple File System (AFS). This is the same file system used on Mac OS 10.13 and later, as well as tvOS 10.2 and watchOS 3.2. It is a replacement for the older HFS+. AFS supports full disk and file encryption. It also supports read-only snapshots of the file system at a point in time. AFS supports 64-bit inode numbers, allowing a much larger number of files to be stored. This file system also uses checksums to ensure metadata data integrity.

The iOS contains several elements in the data partition:

- Calendar entries
- Contacts entries
- Note entries
- iPod_control directory (this directory is hidden)
- Apple media apps configuration
- Apple Music app in Mac OS and iTunes on Windows

This exact list can vary from model to model. In **FIGURE 12-1**, you can see the user portion of the file system on an iPhone 11. Some information in Figure 12-1 has been redacted because this image was taken from an actual phone.

Of particular interest to forensic investigation is the folder iPod_control\device\sysinfo. This folder contains two very important pieces of information:

- Model number
- Serial number

The iOS runs on iPhones, iPods, and iPads. This means that once you are comfortable with the operating system on one Apple device, you should be comfortable with any Apple device. This applies not just to the features that users interact with, but also to the operating system fundamentals. Thus, if you have experience with forensics on an iPhone, you will have no problem conducting a forensic analysis of an iPad.

If you are unable to access the iPhone, it is possible to get much of the data from the suspect's iCloud account. As of 2018, 850 million customers were backing up their data to the cloud. Information stored in the iCloud can be retrieved by anyone without having access to a physical device, provided that the original Apple ID and password are known. Often, the user name and password can be extracted from the user's computer.

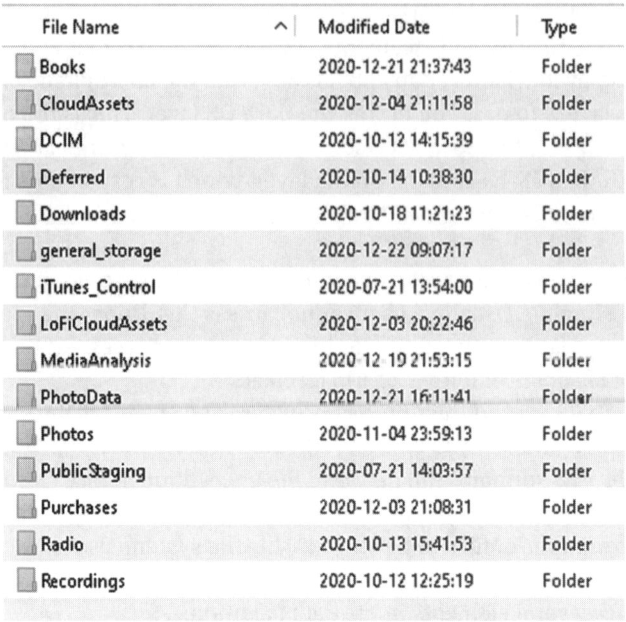

File Name	^	Modified Date	Type
Books		2020-12-21 21:37:43	Folder
CloudAssets		2020-12-04 21:11:58	Folder
DCIM		2020-10-12 14:15:39	Folder
Deferred		2020-10-14 10:38:30	Folder
Downloads		2020-10-18 11:21:23	Folder
general_storage		2020-12-22 09:07:17	Folder
iTunes_Control		2020-07-21 13:54:00	Folder
LoFiCloudAssets		2020-12-03 20:22:46	Folder
MediaAnalysis		2020-12-19 21:53:15	Folder
PhotoData		2020-12-21 16:11:41	Folder
Photos		2020-11-04 23:59:13	Folder
PublicStaging		2020-07-21 14:03:57	Folder
Purchases		2020-12-03 21:08:31	Folder
Radio		2020-10-13 15:41:53	Folder
Recordings		2020-10-12 12:25:19	Folder

Screenshot reprinted with permission from Apple Inc.

FIGURE 12-1

User File System,
iPhone 11.

Later in this chapter, we will briefly describe some commercial tools. However, there are free tools for iOS forensics you can use. The tool 3uTools is downloadable for free from *http://www.3u.com/.*

3uTools immediately displays a great deal of important information such as IMEI, iOS version, SPU, etc. You can also get a full listing of apps on the phone as well as music, photos, and other data. You have to jailbreak the iPhone to extract call and message history.

Android

The Android operating system is a Linux-based operating system, and it is completely open source. If you have a programming and operating systems background, you may find it useful to examine the Android source code from *http://source.android.com/.*

Android was first released in 2003 and is the creation of Rich Miner, Andy Rubin, and Nick Sears. Google acquired Android in 2005, but still keeps the code open source. The versions of Android have been named after sweets:

- Version 1.5 Cupcake
- Version 1.6 Donut
- Version 2.0–2.1 Éclair
- Version 2.2 Froyo
- Version 2.3 Gingerbread
- Version 3.1–3.2 Honeycomb
- Version 4.0 Ice Cream Sandwich
- Version 4.1–4.2 Jellybean
- Version 4.3 Kitkat
- Version 5.0 Lollipop released November 3, 2014

- Version 6.0 Marshmallow released October 2015
- Version 7.0 Nougat was released August 2016
- Version 8.0 Oreo released August 2017
- Version 9.0 Pie released August 6, 2018
- Android 10. This was called Q during beta testing, and it marks a departure from using the names of desserts. This was released in September 2019.
- Android 11 released February 2020

The differences from version to version usually involve adding new features, not a radical change to the operating system. This means that if you are comfortable with version 7.0 (Nougat), you will be able to do forensic examination on version 9.0 (Pie). While the Android source code is open source, each vendor may make modifications. This means even the partition layout can vary. However, there are common partitions that are present on most Android devices (phones or tablets).

- The boot loader partition is necessary for hardware initialization and loading the Android kernel. This is unlikely to have forensically important data.
- The boot partition has the information needed to boot up. Again, this is unlikely to have forensically important data.
- The recovery partition is used to boot the phone into a recovery console. While the partition may not have forensically relevant data, sometimes you may need to boot into recovery mode.
- The user data partition is the one most relevant to forensic investigations. Here you will find the majority of user data, including all the data for apps.
- The cache partition stores frequently accessed data and recovery logs. This can be very important for forensic investigations.
- The system partition is not usually important for forensic examinations.

Remember that Android is Linux based; if you have an image of an Android phone, you may be able to execute at least some Linux commands on it. For example, using `cat proc/partitions` will reveal to you the partitions that exist on the specific phone you are examining.

In addition to these partitions, there are specific directories that may yield forensic evidence.

- The acct directory is the mount point for the control group and provides user accounting.
- The cache directory stores frequently accessed data. This will almost always be interesting forensically.
- The data directory has data for each app. This is clearly critical for forensic examinations.
- The mnt directory is a mount point for all file systems and can indicate internal and external storage such as SD cards. If you have an Android image, the Linux `ls` command used on this directory will show you the various storage devices.

To extract data from an Android phone or tablet, it must be in developer mode. How you get there has changed with different versions; where to access developer mode is given here (note that some models might have slightly different steps):

Settings > General > About and tap the Build Number 7 times.
After tapping the Build Number 7 times, you will see the message "You are now a developer!"
Return to the main Settings menu and now you'll be able to see Developer Options.
Tap on Developer options and mark the box in front of USB Debugging to enable it.
To disable USB Debugging mode later, you can uncheck the box before the option.
To enable Developer Options, go to Settings > Developer options and tap on the ON/
    OFF slider at the top of the page.

It should also be noted that there are numerous bits of information you can get from the keypad of an Android phone. There are numerous "secret" codes that will retrieve information. Do keep in mind that these won't work on all models.

Diagnostic configuration *#9090#
Battery status *#0228#
System dump mode *#9900#
Testing menu *#*#4636#*#*
Display information about the device *#*#4636#*#*
Factory restore *#*#7780#*#*
Camera information *#*#34971539#*#*
Completely wipe device, install stock firmware *2767*3855#
Quick GPS test *#*#1472365#*#*
Wi-Fi MAC address *#*#232338#*#*
RAM version *#*#3264#*#*
Bluetooth test *#*#232331#*#*
Display IMEI number *#06#
Remove Google account setting *#*#7780#*#*

> **NOTE**
>
> Many cell phone manufacturers take the base Android code that is publicly available and add their own items to it. This means that even if you are well versed in the public Android code, you may not know every nuance of the code actually running on a given Android phone.

These are just a sample of codes. You can search the internet for something like "secret codes for Motorola phones" to get information on codes for that specific phone model.

Android Debugging Bridge

With Android phones, you have another option for forensics other than the commercial tools we will discuss later in this chapter. That tool is the Android Debugging Bridge. You can download this free tool from *https://developer.android.com/studio/command-line/adb*. The Android Debugging Bridge was developed to aid programmers who are developing apps for Android devices and enable them to interact with a test device for debugging purposes. However, it does allow for the extraction of forensic data. This provides an additional tool for forensic analysts. There have been some limited studies of using Android Debugging Bridge for forensics.[2,3] Commonly called ADB, the Android Debugging Bridge has three components:

- A client, which sends commands. The client runs on the development machine. The investigator can invoke a client from a command-line terminal by issuing an adb command.
- A daemon (adbd), which runs commands on a device. The daemon runs as a background process on each device.
- A server, which manages communication between the client and the daemon. The server runs as a background process on your development machine.

As with all mobile device forensic tools, the phone must be in debugger mode to interact with it. These specific steps are not described in this chapter as they are common knowledge to mobile device forensic practitioners and are documented in most digital forensics textbooks.

When you start an ADB client, the client first checks whether there is an ADB server process already running. If there isn't, it starts the server process. When the server starts, it binds to local TCP port 5037 and listens for commands sent from ADB clients—all ADB clients use port 5037 to communicate with the ADB server. When a device is connected to a computer that has ADB, the first step is to list all connected devices. This is shown in **FIGURE 12-2**.

There are several commands that are of interest when using ADB. The `adb shell` command enters a shell on the Android, from which the user can utilize standard Linux commands. This is shown in **FIGURE 12-3**.

Common commands done from within the ADB shell include `pstree`, to list all the processes on the target device in a tree format. Other standard Linux commands such as `ps`, `ls`, `netstat`, and `lsof` can also be useful. To see all the Linux commands available on a given device, from within the ADB shell, you can type `ls /system/bin`. This will show all the system binary files (i.e., executables).

Aside from issuing Linux commands from within the ADB shell, there are also ADB-specific commands that can be useful in a forensic examination. Common ADB commands are summarized in **TABLE 12-1**.

Rooting Android

Unfortunately, there is some data you cannot get to without rooting the Android phone. The term *root* is the Linux term for the administrator. In Linux, you simply type `su` (super-user or switch user) and enter the root password. However, Android phones don't allow you to do

FIGURE 12-2

ADB devices.

Google and the Google logo are trademarks of Google LLC.

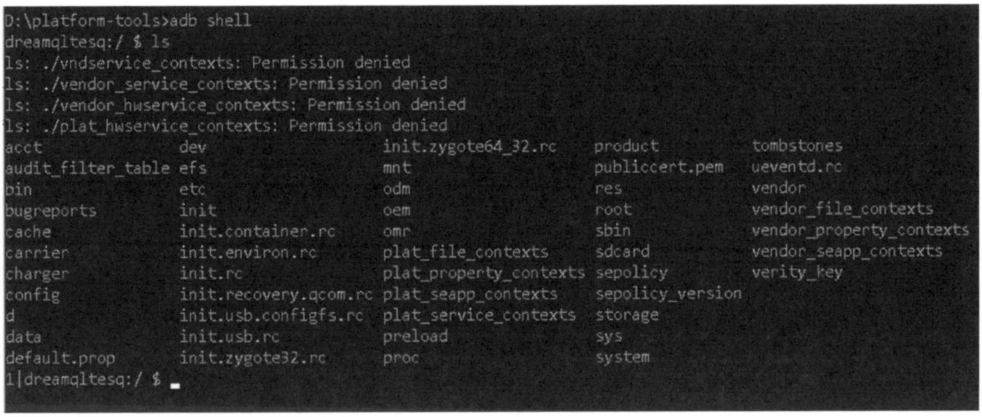

FIGURE 12-3

ADB shell.

Google and the Google logo are trademarks of Google LLC.

TABLE 12-1 ADB commands.	
COMMAND	**PURPOSE**
`adb pull`	Pulls a single file or entire directory from the device to the connected computer.
`adb restore <archive name>`	Creates a backup of the device.

`adb reboot`	Causes the phone to reboot. There are several modes:
	`adb reboot`
	`adb reboot recovery`
	`adb reboot bootloader`

`dumpsys`	This is a very versatile command with several options: adb shell `dumpsys package com.android.chrome` will dump all the data for a given package. adb shell `dumpsys activity` provides information about Activity Manager, activities, providers, services, broadcasts, etc.
`pm list packages`	Lists all packages on the device. There are a number of options for this command, including: `pm list packages -f` See their associated files `pm list packages -d` Filter to only show disabled packages `pm list packages -e` Filter to only show enabled packages `pm list packages -i` See the installer for the packages `pm list packages -u` Also include uninstalled packages
`dumpstate`	adb shell `dumpstate` will dump a great deal of information. It is probably best to output this to a file—for example: `adb shell dumpstate >state.txt`

that. Rooting a phone gives you complete root access to all aspects of the phone. However, that will also void any warranty.

In the past, rooting was not terribly difficult. There were even apps you could get that would root the phone for you. Having worked with many different Android models, I can attest to you that none of the apps I have encountered work on current models. However, there are some methods that might work, depending on a number of variables. For example, the model you have, the version of Android, etc. will affect whether or not you will be successful.

Before you can root a phone, it must first be Original Equipment Manufacturer (OEM) unlocked. And it so happens that before you can OEM unlock a phone, you must first unlock it from the carrier. The only consistently effective method for carrier unlocking is to contact the carrier, assuming the contract is paid off, and request a carrier unlock. After that you have several options for OEM unlock, again depending on what manufacturer and model you are working with. If the phone has "OEM Unlock" enabled and visible under developer settings, then you have the option to use ADB (discussed in the previous section) and move to what is called fastboot mode. For most phones, this is done by using ADB and typing in `adb reboot bootloader`. At that point you can try `fastboot oem unlock`. If that does not work, then your model requires you to get an unlock code and send it to the vendor to get OEM unlock. This is shown in **FIGURE 12-4**.

You will know if your phone is OEM unlocked. Once the phone is OEM unlocked, you can then root the phone. But be aware that for many phones, getting to the OEM unlock might be very difficult. Type

```
adb reboot bootloader
```

followed by

```
fastboot oem device-info
```

You will then see the device's OEM unlock status, as shown in **FIGURE 12-5**.

Once it is OEM unlocked, you can use free tools such as Magisk to install a new image that is rooted. One you have installed Magisk, you can update your system. But you need to push the image; onto the system for Magisk to be able to find it. That can be done with `adb push`. Also, new images take up a lot of space; make sure you have enough space for the image.

Once you have the phone OEM unlocked, rooting is not that difficult. You will need a TWRP image; those can be found at *https://twrp.me/Devices/*. The process once you have OEM unlocked is as follows:

- Place the TWRP recovery image in the "ADB and Fastboot" folder.
- Open fastboot.

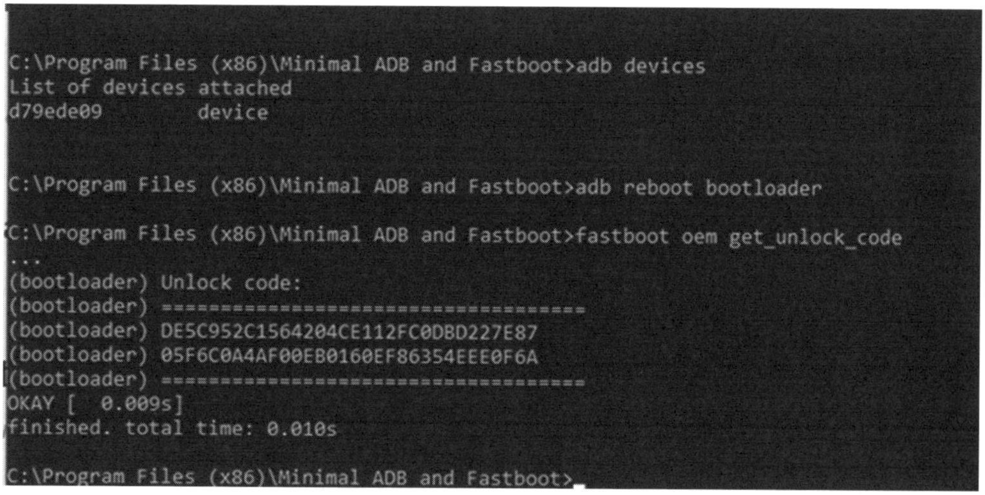

```
C:\Program Files (x86)\Minimal ADB and Fastboot>adb devices
List of devices attached
d79ede09        device


C:\Program Files (x86)\Minimal ADB and Fastboot>adb reboot bootloader

C:\Program Files (x86)\Minimal ADB and Fastboot>fastboot oem get_unlock_code
...
(bootloader) Unlock code:
(bootloader) =======================================
(bootloader) DE5C952C1564204CE112FC0DBD227E87
(bootloader) 05F6C0A4AF00EB0160EF86354EEE0F6A
(bootloader) =======================================
OKAY [  0.009s]
finished. total time: 0.010s

C:\Program Files (x86)\Minimal ADB and Fastboot>
```

FIGURE 12-4

OEM unlock.

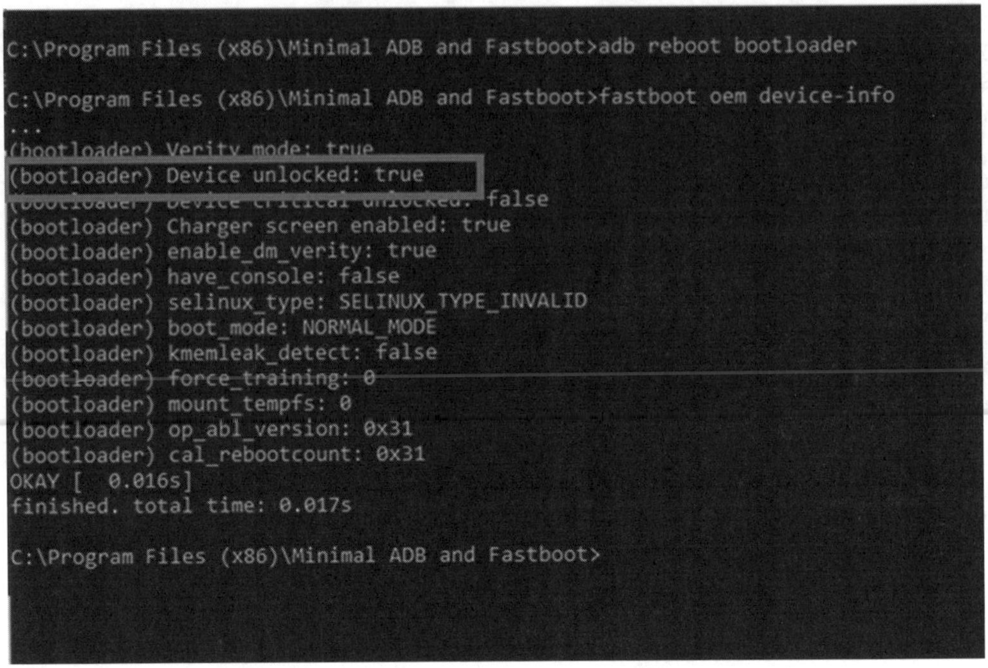

```
C:\Program Files (x86)\Minimal ADB and Fastboot>adb reboot bootloader

C:\Program Files (x86)\Minimal ADB and Fastboot>fastboot oem device-info
...
(bootloader) Verity mode: true
(bootloader) Device unlocked: true
(bootloader) Device critical unlocked: false
(bootloader) Charger screen enabled: true
(bootloader) enable_dm_verity: true
(bootloader) have_console: false
(bootloader) selinux_type: SELINUX_TYPE_INVALID
(bootloader) boot_mode: NORMAL_MODE
(bootloader) kmemleak_detect: false
(bootloader) force_training: 0
(bootloader) mount_tempfs: 0
(bootloader) op_abl_version: 0x31
(bootloader) cal_rebootcount: 0x31
OKAY [  0.016s]
finished. total time: 0.017s

C:\Program Files (x86)\Minimal ADB and Fastboot>
```

FIGURE 12-5

OEM unlock status.

- Check to make sure the device is connected with ADB devices.
- Reboot in boot loader mode by typing adb reboot bootloader.
- Use the phone screen to select Apply UPdate from ADB Sideload, or a similar entry.
- Type fastboot flash recovery twrp.img.

Note that the twrp.img is whatever image you intend to put on the phone, and it must be in the fastboot directory.

Do keep in mind that with newer phone models, any one of these steps may fail. Rooting modern phones is a difficult task and frequently fails.

Android Free Tools

Given the open-source nature of Android, it should not be surprising that there are many free tools on the internet to automate your interactions with an Android phone. Many of these simply automate the ADB processes, making them much easier. One such tool is a free download, Android Tools, that can be obtained from *https://sourceforge.net/p/android-tools/wiki/Home/*. This tool is shown in **FIGURE 12-6**.

This tool is one of those that basically automates ADB. Once you are comfortable with ADB, it is possible to use tools such as this one to automate the process of ADB commands. The Android All in One Tool is another free tool that automates ADB commands. This tool is available at *https://toolaio.tk/*. You can see this tool in **FIGURE 12-7**.

These free tools expand what you can do with Android forensics.

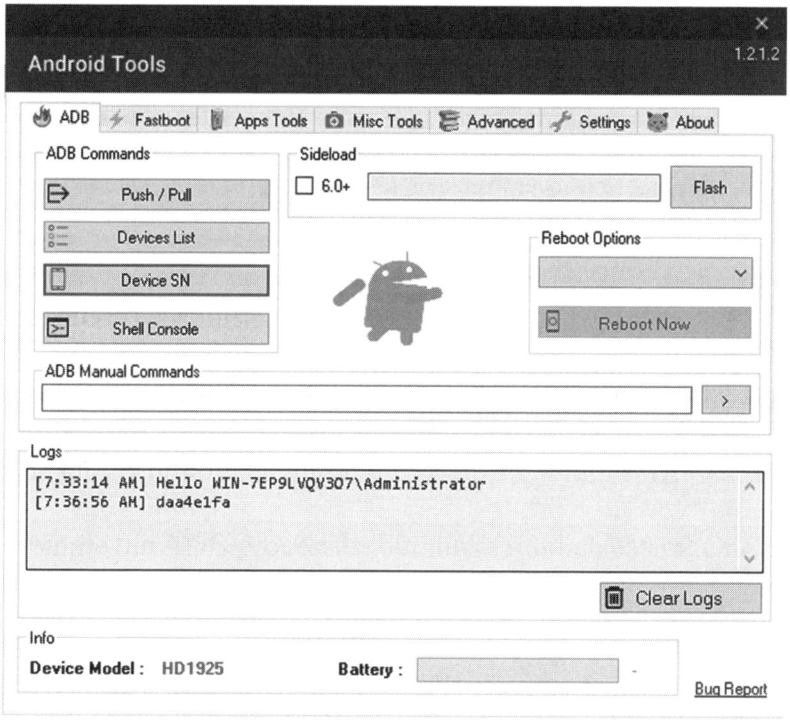

Courtesy of Android Tools/Ravhi Rizaldi.

FIGURE 12-6

Android Tools.

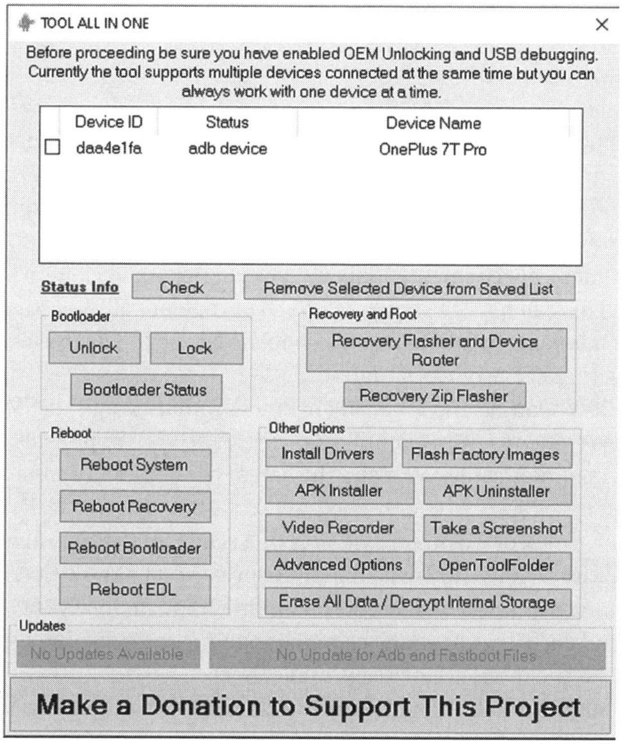

Courtesy of Tool All In One.

FIGURE 12-7

All in One
Android tool.

12

Mobile
Forensics

Evidence You Can Get from a Cell Phone

A cell phone or tablet can be a treasure trove of forensic information. This is one area of digital forensics that definitely extends well beyond the scope of computer crimes. With mobile devices, the evidence found can be relevant to any crime.

Items you should attempt to recover from a mobile device include the following:

- Call history
- Emails, texts, and/or other messages
- Photos and video
- Phone information
- Global positioning system (GPS) information
- Network information

The call history lets you know who the user has spoken to and for how long. Yes, this is easily erasable, but many users don't erase their call history. Or perhaps the suspect intended to delete this data and simply did not get to it yet. In either case, call history does not provide direct evidence of a crime—with the exception of cyberstalking cases. In a cyberstalking case, the call history can show a pattern of contact with the victim. However, in other cases, it provides only circumstantial evidence. For example, if John Smith is suspected of drug dealing and his call history shows a pattern of regular calls to a known drug supplier, by itself this is not adequate evidence of any crime. However, it aids the investigators in getting an accurate picture of the entire situation.

Many phones allow sending and receiving of emails and messages in SMS or other formats. Gathering this evidence from a mobile device can be very important. Both the parties that the suspect is communicating with and the actual content of the communications are very important.

Photos and video can provide direct evidence of a crime. In the case of child pornography cases, the relevance is obvious. However, it may surprise you to know that it is not uncommon for some criminals to actually photograph or videotape themselves committing serious crimes. This is particularly true of young criminals conducting unplanned crimes or conducting crimes under the influence of drugs or alcohol.

Information about the phone should be one of the first things you document in your investigation. This will include the model number, serial number of the SIM card, operating system, and other similar information. The more detailed, descriptive information you can document, the better.

Global positioning system information has become increasingly important in a variety of cases. So many individuals have devices with GPS enabled, that it would seem negligent for a forensic analyst not to retrieve this information. GPS information has begun to play a significant role in contentious divorces, for instance. If someone suspects a spouse of being unfaithful, determining that the spouse's phone and his or her car were at a specific motel when he or she claimed to be at work can be important.

It should be noted that until recently, many cell phones did not provide true GPS. Rather than use GPS satellites to determine location (which is the most reliable method), they instead would use triangulation of signal strength with various cell towers. This could lead to inaccuracies of up to 50 to 100 feet. However, this situation has changed. Many modern phones and/or the apps on the phone use true GPS for much more accurate data.

The use of Wi-Fi along with GPS will improve the accuracy of GPS. The reason for this is that various organizations, including Google, track the Basic Service Set Identifier (BSSID) used by wireless routers, and correlate it with physical addresses. The BSSID is a unique address that identifies the access point/router that creates the wireless network. To identify access points and their clients, the access point's MAC address is used. This means that if your phone connects to a wireless access point, then even with no other data, the phone's location can be pinpointed to within 100 yards or so of that access point. Network information is also important. What Wi-Fi networks does the phone recognize? This might give you an indication of where the phone has been. For example, if the phone belongs to someone suspected of stalking a victim, and the suspect's phone network records show he or she has frequently been using Wi-Fi networks in close proximity to the victim's home, this can be important evidence.

SWGDE Guidelines

The Scientific Working Group on Digital Evidence (*https://www.swgde.org/*) provides guidance on many digital forensics topics. Related to mobile device forensics, SWGDE provides a general overview of the types of phone forensic investigations:

Mobile Forensics Pyramid—The level of extraction and analysis required depends on the request and the specifics of the investigation. Higher levels require a more comprehensive examination and additional skills and may not be applicable or possible for every phone or situation. Each level of the Mobile Forensics Pyramid has its own corresponding skill set. The levels are:

1. Manual—A process that involves the manual operation of the keypad and handset display to document data present in the phone's internal memory.
2. Logical—A process that extracts a portion of the file system.
3. File System—A process that provides access to the file system.
4. Physical (Noninvasive)—A process that provides physical acquisition of a phone's data without requiring opening the case of the phone.
5. Physical (Invasive)—A process that provides physical acquisition of a phone's data and requires disassembly of the phone to access the circuit board (e.g., JTAG).

6. Chip-Off—A process that involves the removal and reading of a memory chip to conduct analysis.

7. MicroRead—A process that involves the use of a high-power microscope to provide a physical view of memory cells.[4]

Types of Investigations

It is important to keep in mind that cell phone forensics extends beyond traditional cyber-crime. In fact, few crimes today do not involve at least some aspect of cyber forensics of the phones of the suspects. The aforementioned GPS information can be important in drug cases, burglaries, homicides, and a variety of other crimes. A few examples are given here:

● Adam Howe took a "selfie" photo of himself at the scene of a church burglary. This evidence led to a search of the suspect's property, which turned up the stolen goods from the church.

● In 2013, cell phone pictures led to an arrest in a burglary of a jewelry store. The alleged thief discarded clothing and accidently dropped his cell phone behind a nearby 7-Eleven store. The cell phone photos positively identified him.

Types of Information

The National Institute of Standards and Technology (NIST) guidelines at *http://csrc.nist .gov/publications/nistpubs/800-72/sp800-72.pdf* list four different states a mobile device can be in when you extract data:

● **Nascent State**—Devices are in the nascent state when received from the manufacturer; the device contains no user data and has its original factory configuration settings.

● **Active State**—Devices that are in the active state are powered on, performing tasks, and able to be customized by the user and have their file systems populated with data.

● **Quiescent State**—The quiescent state is a dormant mode that conserves battery life while maintaining user data and performing other background functions. Context information for the device is preserved in memory to allow a quick resumption of processing when returning to the active state.

● **Semi-Active State**—The semi-active state is a state partway between active and quiescent. The state is reached by a timer, which is triggered after a period of inactivity, allowing battery life to be preserved by dimming the display and taking other appropriate actions.

You should document what state the device is in when you conduct your investigation and analysis. If you change state—for example, by turning on the device—that should also be documented.

Seizing Evidence from a Mobile Device

Once you are ready to seize evidence from the mobile device, remember the following rules:

● If you are going to plug the phone into a computer, make sure the phone does not synchronize with the computer. This is particularly important with the iPhone, which routinely auto-syncs.

- Follow the same advice you follow for PCs. Make sure you touch the evidence as little as possible, and document what you do to the device.

One of the most important things to do is to make sure you don't accidentally write data to the mobile device. For example, if you plug an iPhone into your forensic workstation, you want to make sure you don't accidentally write information from your workstation to the iPhone.

If the forensic workstation is a Windows machine, you can use the Windows Registry to prevent the workstation from writing to the mobile device. Before connecting to a Windows machine, find the Registry key (HKEY_LOCAL_MACHINE\System\CurrentControlset\StorageDevicePolicies), set the value to 0x00000001, and then restart the computer. This prevents that computer from writing to mobile devices that are connected to it.

Although Forensic Toolkit and EnCase can both image a phone for you, there are other products made specifically for phone forensics:

- **Oxygen Forensics**—This is a full forensic tool capable of imaging and examining iPhones and Android phones. It provides a number of user-friendly tools for extracting specific data such as contacts, social media data, etc.
- **Cellebrite**—This is probably the most widely known phone forensics tool. It is used heavily by federal law enforcement. It is a very robust and effective tool. The only downside to Cellebrite that I am aware of is its high cost. It is the most expensive phone forensics tool on the market.
- **MobileEdit**—There are several variations of this product. MobileEdit Lite is the most forensically advanced version of MobileEdit. This is a very easy-to-use tool that can aid a forensic examiner in extracting data from cell phones.
- **Data Doctor**—This product recovers all Inbox and Outbox data and all contacts data, and has an easy-to-use interface. Most important, it has a free trial version, but there is a cost for the full version. It is available from *http://www.simrestore.com/*.
- **Device Seizure**—This is available from Paraben Software at *http://www.paraben.com/*. There is a license fee associated with this product. Paraben makes a number of forensic products.
- **Forensic SIM Cloner**—This tool is used to clone SIM cards, allowing you to perform forensic analysis of the SIM card.

Forensics for a Windows 10 phone is done in much the same way as forensics for a Windows 10 PC or laptop is done. The only issue is to make certain the phone does not synchronize with the forensic workstation. A similar issue arises with the Android. Because it is based on Linux, many of the same forensic techniques can be applied. Keep in mind that a handheld portable device probably will not have all the same logs that a PC or server has, but if the operating system is the same, then the forensics will be largely the same.

Regardless of the tool you choose, you should ensure that it is adequate for your forensic needs. The NIST-sponsored Computer Forensics Tool Testing Program (CFTT; *http://www.cftt.nist.gov/*) provides a measure of assurance that the tools used in the investigations of computer-related crimes produce valid results. Testing includes a set of core requirements as well as optional requirements. It is a good idea to refer to these standards when selecting a tool.

12

Mobile
Forensics

NIST also provides general guidelines on how to write a mobile device forensic report. The guidelines regarding what to include are as follows:

- Descriptive list of items submitted for examination, including serial number, make, and model
- Identity and signature of the examiner
- The equipment and setup used in the examination
- Brief description of steps taken during examination, such as string searches, graphics image searches, and recovering erased files
- Supporting materials, such as printouts of particular items of evidence, digital copies of evidence, and chain of custody documentation
- Details of findings:
  - Specific files related to the request
  - Other files, including deleted files, that support the findings
  - String searches, keyword searches, and text string searches
  - Internet-related evidence, such as website traffic analysis, chat logs, cache files, email, and news group activity
  - Graphic image analysis
  - Indicators of ownership, which could include program registration data
  - Data analysis
  - Description of relevant programs on the examined items
  - Techniques used to hide or mask data, such as encryption, steganography, hidden attributes, hidden partitions, and file name anomalies
- Report conclusions

SQLite

Both iPhone and Android make use of SQLite databases. These normally end in a .db extension. D. Richard Hipp designed SQLite in the spring of 2000 while working for General Dynamics on contract with the U.S. Navy. SQLite is not a client–server database engine. Rather, it is embedded into the end program.

SQLite is a popular choice as embedded database software for local/client storage in application software such as web browsers.

SQLite stores the entire database (definitions, tables, indices, and the data itself) as a single cross-platform file on a host machine. It implements this simple design by locking the entire database file during writing. SQLite read operations can be multitasked, though writes can only be performed sequentially.

The SQLite data types are:

NULL: Null value
INTEGER: Signed integer, stored in 1, 2, 3, 4, 6, or 8 bytes depending on the magnitude of the value
REAL: A floating-point value; an 8-byte IEEE floating-point number
TEXT: Text string, stored using the database encoding (UTF-8, UTF-16BE, or UTF-16LE)
BLOB: A blob of data, stored exactly as it was input

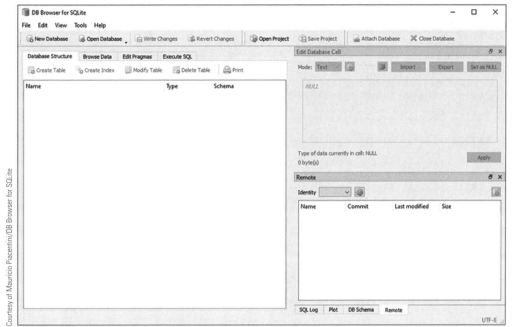

FIGURE 12-8
SQLite browser.

If you are able to find SQLite databases on a phone and can copy them to your forensics machine, you will need an SQLite viewer. You may download an SQLite browser for free from *https://sqlitebrowser.org/.* This is shown in **FIGURE 12-8**.

The iPhone

There are automated processes for breaking an iPhone passcode. XRY is one such tool, which can be found at *https://www.msab.com/products/xry/.* Keep in mind that older iPhones had only a four-digit PIN, which means there are 10,000 possible combinations of the digits 0–9. Now iPhone has a six-digit PIN, allowing for 1 million combinations.[5]

If you are using a forensic workstation with the Apple Music app (on Mac OS) or iTunes (on Windows), you can simply plug the iPhone (or iPad/iPod) into the workstation and use the Apple Music app or iTunes to extract a great deal of information about the phone. This is shown in **FIGURE 12-9**.

You can immediately notice three important items to document:

1. The iOS version number
2. The phone number
3. The serial number

Notice you can also see where the phone is backed up. That can indicate yet another place you should search during your forensic investigation.

If you have imaged the iPhone and you then search for information, you may have to look more closely to find some data.

For example, Library_CallHistory_call_history.db has the entire call history. If you cannot view that directly on the iPhone itself, the database file has all call information. Starting with

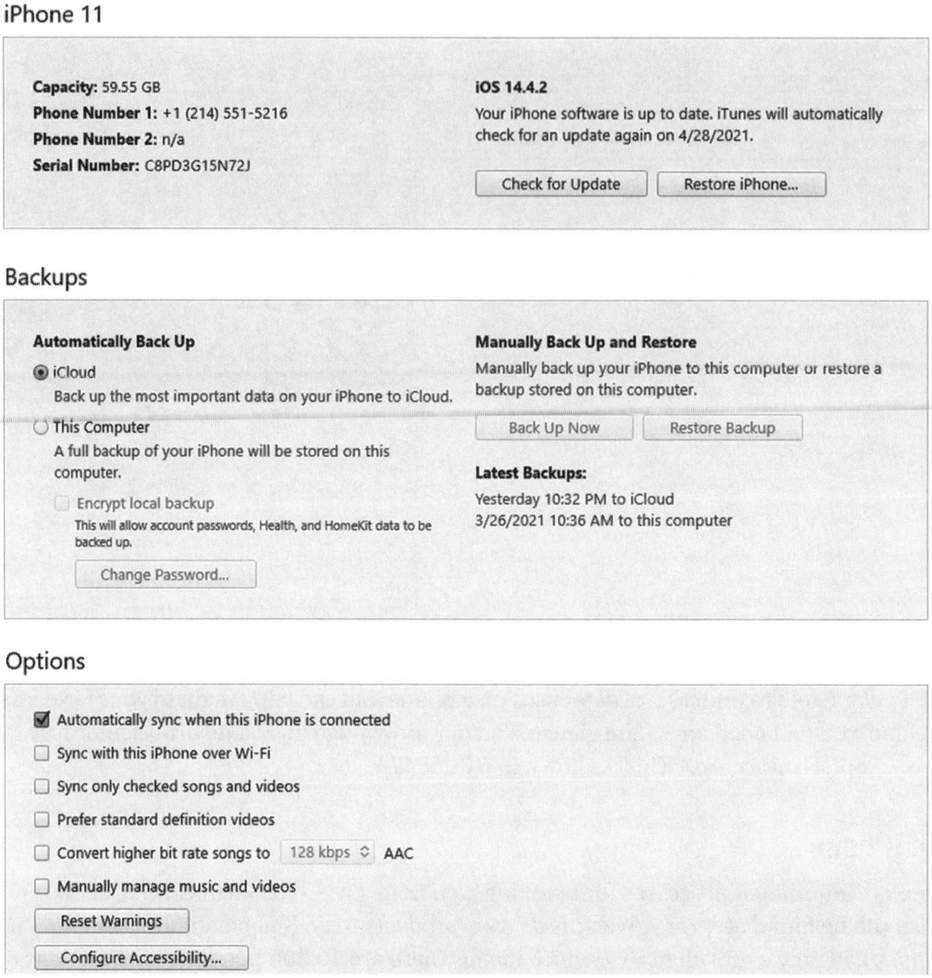

iPhone 11

Capacity: 59.55 GB
Phone Number 1: +1 (214) 551-5216
Phone Number 2: n/a
Serial Number: C8PD3G15N72J

iOS 14.4.2
Your iPhone software is up to date. iTunes will automatically check for an update again on 4/28/2021.

[Check for Update]   [Restore iPhone...]

Backups

Automatically Back Up

○ iCloud
Back up the most important data on your iPhone to iCloud.

○ This Computer
A full backup of your iPhone will be stored on this computer.

☐ Encrypt local backup
This will allow account passwords, Health, and HomeKit data to be backed up.

[Change Password...]

Manually Back Up and Restore

Manually back up your iPhone to this computer or restore a backup stored on this computer.

[Back Up Now]   [Restore Backup]

Latest Backups:
Yesterday 10:32 PM to iCloud
3/26/2021 10:36 AM to this computer

Options

☑ Automatically sync when this iPhone is connected
☐ Sync with this iPhone over Wi-Fi
☐ Sync only checked songs and videos
☐ Prefer standard definition videos
☐ Convert higher bit rate songs to [128 kbps ◇] AAC
☐ Manually manage music and videos
[Reset Warnings]
[Configure Accessibility...]

FIGURE 12-9

Apple iPhone Music app/ iTunes display.

Screenshot reprinted with permission from Apple Inc.

iOS 8.0, this was changed to CallHistory.storedata, but that is still an SQLite database. Cookies can be found in the file Library_Cookies_Cookies.plist. This can give you a history of the phone user's internet activities. These and other files are actually copied to a PC during synchronization. Here are a few of those files:

- Library_Preferences_com.apple.mobileipod.plist
- Library_Preferences_com.apple.mobileemail.plist
- Library_Preferences_com.apple.mobilevpn.plist

The mobileemail.plist file has obvious forensic evidence. It will give you information about email sent and received from the phone. The mobilevpn.plist file can also be interesting. If the user has utilized the phone to communicate over a virtual private network (VPN), this file will have information about that.

The plist files are very important. Plist means property list. These files are used to store data for a wide range of purposes, including for various apps. The format for plists was originally a binary format, but now XML is more widely used. XML is something you can view directly and understand.

Deleted Files

When a file is deleted on the iPhone, iPad, or iPod, it is actually moved to the .Trashes\501 folder. Essentially, the data is still there until it is overwritten, so recently deleted files can be retrieved.

Tools

There are tools specifically for the iOS devices. These can be a useful addition to your forensic toolset. Here are few widely used tools:

- **Pwnage**—This utility allows you to unlock a locked iPod Touch and is available from *https://pwnage.com/.*
- **Recover My iPod**—This utility allows you to recover files deleted from an iPod and is available from *http://www.recovermyipod.com/.*
- **APowerSoft**—This is a general deleted file utility for iPhone and related devices, available at *https://www.apowersoft.com/recover-deleted-files-on-iphone.html.*
- **iMyPhone** makes a number of utilities for data recovery for iPhone and related devices, found at *https://www.imyfone.com.*
- **iPhone Analyzer**—This is a free Java program used to analyze iPhone backups; the tool is available from *https://sourceforge.net/projects/iphoneanalyzer/.*

CHAPTER SUMMARY

In this chapter, you were introduced to fundamental mobile terms and concepts. It is important that you fully understand these and commit them to memory. You were also shown mobile device forensic concepts. This chapter also gave you a look at each of the major phones, and you learned how to extract data from those devices.

Of at least as much importance, you learned what data is important and how phone forensics can provide a treasure trove of data.

KEY CONCEPTS AND TERMS

Base transceiver station (BTS)

Electronic Serial Number (ESN)

Enhanced Data Rates for GSM Evolution (EDGE)

Global System for Mobile (GSM) communications

Home location register (HLR)

Integrated circuit card identifier (ICCID)

International Mobile Equipment Identity (IMEI) number

Long Term Evolution (LTE)

Mobile switching center (MSC)

Personal identification number (PIN)

Personal unlocking code (PUK)

Subscriber identity module (SIM)

Universal Mobile Telecommunications System (UMTS)

Visitor location register (VLR)

CHAPTER 12 ASSESSMENT

1. It is important to write-block a phone before doing forensic analysis to make certain data is not copied to the phone.

   A. True
   B. False

2. Which of the following is a 4G standard?

   A. EDGE
   B. GSM
   C. LTE
   D. GSM4

3. Where is the data for roaming phones stored?

   A. VLR
   B. HLR
   C. BTS
   D. GSM

4. All devices are in the following state when received from the manufacturer.

   A. dormant
   B. nascent

   C. quiescent
   D. normal

5. You are performing a forensic analysis on a cell phone. You have tried entering the PUK 6 times, all incorrectly. What does this mean for John's investigation?

   A. The phone is now restored to factory conditions and data cannot be recovered.
   B. Nothing; you can keep trying the PUK as many times as needed.
   C. Nothing; you can try the PUK 9 times before the phone is restored to factory conditions on the 10th attempt.
   D. The phone is now wiped forensically.

References

1. SIM Cards. (2014, September 25). *Forensics Wiki*. Retrieved from https://forensicswiki.xyz/wiki/index.php?title=SIM_Cards&oldid=9306 on February 13, 2021.

2. Easttom, C., & Sanders W. (2019). On the efficacy of using Android Debugging Bridge for Android device forensics. *2019 IEEE 10th Annual Ubiquitous Computing, Electronics & Mobile Communication Conference (UEMCON)*, New York, NY, 2019, pp. 0730–0735, doi: 10.1109/UEMCON47517.2019.8992948.

3. Lessard, J., & Kessler, G. (2010). *Android Forensics: Simplifying Cell Phone Examinations.*

4. Scientific Working Group on Digital Evidence. (2013, February 13). *SWGDE Best Practices for Mobile Phone Forensics.* Retrieved from https://www.swgde.org/documents/published on February 14, 2021.

5. Benson, T. Your phone's PIN code is probably so bad anyone could guess it, study finds. *Inverse.* Retrieved from https://www.inverse.com/innovation/study-finds-people-can-probably-guess-your-phones-pin-code on February 13, 2021.

Network Forensics

I N THIS CHAPTER, you will learn about network forensics. The main topic is network packet analysis. However, you will also explore network traffic analysis, router forensics, and firewall forensics. Unlike other areas of forensics, some of these tasks will be performed on live systems. For example, network analysis is done, at least in part, on a live network with actual traffic. Router forensics is usually done on an active router.

Chapter 13 Topics

This chapter covers the following topics and concepts:

- Network packet structure
- Network packet capture

Chapter 13 Goals

When you complete this chapter, you will be able to:

- Understand network packets
- Perform network analysis
- Analyze routers for forensic evidence
- Examine firewall logs for evidence

Network Basics

You won't be effective at analyzing network traffic without some basic understanding of network technology and terminology. So this first section will provide a brief review of some networking basics.

IP Addresses and MAC Addresses

The most common Internet Protocol (IP) addressing scheme is still IP version 4 (IPv4). An IPv4 address appears as a series of four decimal numbers. (An example would be 107.22.98.198.) You might occasionally see an address that seems to have fewer than three digits, such as 172.10.20.14. Technically speaking, there are leading zeros that just are not shown. Each of the three-digit numbers must be between 0 and 255; thus, an address of 107.22.98.466 would not be a valid one. These addresses are actually four binary numbers; they are displayed in decimal format so that humans can readily read them. Since each of these numbers is really just a decimal representation of 8 bits, they are often referred to as octets. So there are four octets in an IPv4 address. Recall that a byte is 8 bits (1s and 0s), and an 8-bit binary number converted to decimal format will be between 0 and 255. Given that an IPv4 address is 32 bits long (in binary), that means there are 2^{32} possible IPv4 addresses. That is a total of over 4.2 billion possible IP addresses. Soon we'll discuss why 4.2 billion public addresses are not enough and haven't been for over 10 years.

For readers who are not familiar with converting decimal to binary, there are several methods to accomplish this. We will explore one such method here:

Divide repeatedly by 2, using "remainders" rather than decimal places, until you get down to 1. For example, convert decimal 25 to binary:

25/2 = 12 Remainder 1
12/2 = 6 Remainder 0
6/2 = 3 Remainder 0
3/2 = 1 Remainder 1
1/2 = 0 Remainder 1

Now read the remainders from bottom to top: The binary equivalent is 11001.

Earlier, it was mentioned that we have already run out of IPv4 addresses. The issue is rather simple to grasp. There are more than 7.5 billion people on the planet. Certainly, there are people in remote areas with no computers, and thus no IP address. But consider the average person in a modern society. Consider you own a home. You probably have more than one computer, set-top boxes for television, smartphones, game stations, etc., that all have IP addresses. Then consider every computer in every business. Now add to that the myriad servers. And we still have not talked about all the switches and routers. All of these devices have IP addresses.

The first method to solve this issue was using public and private IP addresses. The public IP addresses are for computers connected to the internet. No two public IP addresses can be the same. However, a private IP address, such as one on a private company network, only has to be unique in that network. It does not matter if other computers in the world have the same IP address because this computer is never connected to those other worldwide computers. Network administrators use private IP addresses. There are specific ranges of IP addresses that are set aside for private use. We will discuss those later in this chapter.

It should also be pointed out that often an internet service provider (ISP) will buy a pool of public IP addresses and assign them to you when you log on. An ISP might own multiple public IP address, but that number is likely to be far smaller than its customer base. So ISPs also use network address translation (NAT). That is why if a packet is traced to an ISP, then a subpoena needs to be issued to determine which customer had that IP at that time. Because all 10,000 customers will not be online at the same time, the ISP simply assigns an IP address to a customer when they log on, and the ISP unassigns the IP address when the customer logs off.

The address of a computer tells you a lot about that computer. The first byte (or the first decimal number) in an address tells you to what class of network that machine belongs. **TABLE 13-1** summarizes the three network classes. These three classes of networks will become more important later in this book (or should you decide to study networking on a deeper level).

You may have noticed that the 127.x.x.x byte was skipped—Class A ends at 126.x.x.x and Class B starts at 128.x.x.x. This omission is because that 127.x.x.x byte range is reserved for testing. The IP address of 127.0.0.1 designates the machine you are on, regardless of that machine's assigned IP address. This address is often referred to as the *loopback address*. That address will be used often in testing your machine and your network interface card (NIC), which we'll discuss later in this chapter. We will also examine the loopback address a bit later in this chapter in the section on network utilities.

These particular network classes are important because they tell you what part of the address represents the network and what part represents the node. For example, in a Class A address, the first octet represents the network, and the remaining three represent the node. In a Class B address, the first two octets represent the network, and the second two represent the node. And finally, in a Class C address, the first three octets represent the network, and the last represents the node.

There are also some very specific IP addresses and IP address ranges you should be aware of. The first, as previously mentioned, is 127.0.0.1, or the loopback address. It is another way of referring to the NIC of the machine you are on.

As previously mentioned, there are specific IP addresses set aside as private. These IP addresses cannot be routed over the internet. They can only be used on private networks. Those IP addresses are:

10.0.0.10 to 10.255.255.255
172.16.0.0 to 172.31.255.255
192.168.0.0 to 192.168.255.255

TABLE 13-1 Network classes.

CLASS	IP RANGE FOR THE FIRST BYTE	USE
A	0–126	Extremely large networks. No Class A network IP addresses are left. All have been used.
B	128–191	Large corporate and government networks. All Class B IP addresses have been used.
C	192–223	The most common group of IP addresses. Your ISP probably has a Class C address.

You can communicate within your network using private IP addresses, but to communicate with any computer outside your network, you must use public IP addresses. One of the roles of a gateway router is to perform what is called network address translation (NAT). That takes the private IP address on outgoing packets and replaces it with the public IP address of the gateway router so that the packet can be routed through the internet.

Subnetting and CIDR

We have already discussed IPv4 network addresses; now let's turn our attention to subnetting. This topic tends to confuse those new to networking, so you might need to read it more than once. Let us begin by defining the concept. **Subnetting** is simply dividing a network into smaller portions. Recall the classes of IP addresses. Those are pre-made subnets. Class A has the first octet define the network, and the next three octets define individual nodes. But what if you don't want specific classes, but something in between? What if, rather than a Class C with three octets defining the network and one octet defining the nodes, you only want part of the last octet defining nodes? You can do this with subnetting.

In fact, the specific classes of IP addresses are rarely used today. Instead, people use a **Variable Length Subnet Mask (VLSM)** to define what part of the IP address represents the network.

More technically, the subnet mask is a 32-bit number that is assigned to each host to divide the 32-bit binary IP address into network and node portions. You also cannot just put in any number you want. The first value of a subnet mask must be 255; the remaining three values can be 255, 254, 252, 248, 240, or 224. Essentially, when you convert the decimal number to binary, once you hit a zero the rest are all zeros. That is shown in **TABLE 13-2**.

The part of the address covered with 1s is reserved for the network; the remaining part is available for nodes. For example, 255.255.255.224 converted to binary is 11111111.11 111111.11111111.11100000. The first 27 bits are 1s, so those 27 bits are used to define the network, and the remaining five are for individual nodes. Today we have used Classless Inter Domain Routing (CIDR), and write it with the IP address followed by a "/n," where n is the number of bits for the network. Here is an example: 192.168.2.3/27. Your computer

TABLE 13-2 Subnetting.

BINARY	DECIMAL	EXAMPLE
1000 0000	128	255.255.255.128
1100 0000	192	255.255.255.192
1110 0000	224	255.255.255.224
1111 0000	240	255.255.255.240
1111 1000	248	255.255.255.248
1111 1100	252	255.255.255.252
1111 1110	254	255.255.255.254

will take your network IP address and the subnet mask and use a binary AND operation to combine them.

The last thing about IPv4 we will cover is **Automatic Private IP Addresses (APIPA)**. Many workstations are configured to use dynamic IP addresses. This means they don't get their private IP address until they boot up, and then the network assigns that machine an IP address. A protocol named **Dynamic Host Configuration Protocol (DHCP)** is used to handle this. When the computer boots up, it first assigns itself a random APIPA address, which will be in the range 169.254.X.X; then it will request from the DHCP server a private IP address (like 192.168.X.X). If, for some reason, that DHCP server cannot be found, then the machine will retain the APIPA address. Thus, if a machine has an APIPA address, that means it is not really capable of communicating with the network.

IPv6

As was previously mentioned, IPv4 uses public and private IP addresses to prevent running out of IP addresses. The newer solution is to use IP version 6 (IPv6). IPv6 utilizes a 128-bit address (instead of 32 bits), so there is no chance of running out of IP addresses in the foreseeable future. IPv6 also utilizes a hex-numbering method in order to avoid long addresses, such as 132.64.34.26.64.156.143.57.1.3.7.44.122.111.201.5. The hex address format will appear in the form of 3FFE:B00:800:2::C, for example. IPv6 also uses the CIDE format for subnetting, as in these examples:

/48
/64

There is a loopback address for IPv6, which can be written as ::/128.

IPV6 *link/machine-local* is the equivalent of the IPv4 APIPA address. The link/machine local IP addresses all start with fe80::. So if your computer has this address, that means it could not get to a DHCP server and therefore made up its own generic IP address.

The IPv6 version of the IPv4 private address is called *site/network-local*. In other words, these are real IP addresses, but they only work on this local network. They are not routable on the internet.

All site/network-local IP addresses begin with FE and have C to F for the third hexadecimal digit: FEC, FED, FEE, or FEF. DHCPv6 uses the Managed Address Configuration flag (M flag). When set to 1, the device should use DHCPV6 to obtain a stateful IPv6 address.

Other stateful configuration flag (O flag)

When set to 1, the device should use DHCPv6 to obtain other TCP/IP configuration settings. In other words, it should use the DHCP server to set things like the IP address of the gateway and DNS servers.

M flag

This indicates that the machine should use DHCPv6 to retrieve an IP address.

This is the essence of IPv6. You still have all the same utilities you used with IPv4. However, the number 6 appears after the `ping` or `traceroute`. So, if your computer has IPv6 enabled, you can use the following:

```
ping6 www.yahoo.com
```

Open Systems Interconnection Model

The Open Systems Interconnection (OSI) model is a description of how networks communicate. It describes the various protocols and activities, and it tells how the protocols and activities relate to each other. This model is divided into seven layers, as shown in **TABLE 13-3**, and was originally developed by the International Standards Organization (ISO) in the 1980s.

Often network forensics involves web traffic. There are a number of details about web traffic that you will need to know. First, despite the detailed and involved websites you find today, all web traffic comes down to a few Hypertext Transfer Protocol (HTTP) messages. These are shown in **TABLE 13-4**.

The most common are GET, HEAD, PUT, and POST. In fact, you might see only those four during most of your analysis of web traffic.

The response codes are just as important. You have probably seen Error 404: file not found. But, there are a host of messages going back and forth, most of which you don't see. These messages are shown in **TABLE 13-5**.

> ### ● NOTE
>
> There is sometimes some confusion over HTTP GET and POST commands. The HTML specifications define the difference between GET and POST so that GET means that form data is to be encoded by a browser into a URL, while POST indicates that the form data is to appear inside a message body. They both actually send data to the server. Neither is getting data from the server. There are some great articles on the web that describe the technical nuances of these two commands, one of which is *http://www.diffen.com/difference/Get_vs_Post.*

TABLE 13-3 The OSI model.			
LAYER NUMBER	**LAYER**	**DESCRIPTION**	**PROTOCOLS**
7	Application	This layer interfaces directly to the application and performs common application services for the application processes.	POP, SMTP, DNS, FTP, and so on
6	Presentation	The presentation layer relieves the application layer of concern regarding syntactical differences in data representation within the end-user systems.	
5	Session	The session layer provides the mechanism for managing the dialogue between end-user application processes.	NetBIOS

(Continues)

TABLE 13-3 The OSI model. (*Continued*)

LAYER NUMBER	LAYER	DESCRIPTION	PROTOCOLS
4	Transport	This layer provides end-to-end communication control.	TCP, UDP
3	Network	This layer routes the information in the network.	IP, Address Resolution Protocol, Internet Control Message Protocol
2	Data Link	This layer describes the logical organization of data bits transmitted on a particular medium. Data link is divided into two sublayers: the media access control layer (MAC) and the logical link control layer (LLC).	Serial Line Internet Protocol, Point-to-Point Protocol
1	Physical	This layer describes the physical properties of the various communications media, as well as the electrical properties and interpretation of the exchanged signals. In other words, the physical layer is the actual NIC, Ethernet cable, and so forth. This layer is where bits are translated into voltages, and vice versa.	802.11 (Wi-Fi) Ethernet (this is really both data link and physical)

13

Network
Forensics

This section provides the bare minimum network knowledge you need to have to perform network analysis. The more you know, the better you will be able to conduct such analysis. Thus, you should consider the information in this section as just a starting point. It will allow you to follow the rest of the chapter and perform basic network forensics. But if this is all new information to you, then you should seriously consider learning more. The equivalent of the CompTIA Network+ certification knowledge base would be a good idea.

TABLE 13-4 HTTP messages.

MESSAGE	EXPLANATION
GET	Request to read a web page
HEAD	Request to read the head section of a Firewall Forensics web page
PUT	Request to write a web page
POST	Request to append to a page
DELETE	Remove the web page
LINK	Connects two existing resources
UNLINK	Breaks an existing connection between two resources

TABLE 13-5 The HTTP response codes.

MESSAGE RANGE	MEANING
100–199	These are just informational. The server is telling your browser some information, most of which will never be displayed to the user. For example, when you switch from HTTP to HTTPS, a 101 message goes to the browser telling it that the protocol is changing.
200–299	These are basically "OK" messages, meaning that whatever the browser requested, the server successfully processed.
300–399	These are redirect messages telling the browser to go to another URL. For example, 301 means that the requested resource has permanently moved to a new URL, whereas message 307 indicates the move is temporary.
400–499	These are client errors, and the ones most often shown to the end user. You may be puzzled; how is "file not found" a client error? It is because the client requested a page that does not exist. The server processed the request without problem, but the request was invalid.
500–599	These are server-side errors. For example, 503 means the service requested is down, possibly overloaded. You will see this error frequently in DoS attacks.

Network Packet Analysis

It is important for any forensic analyst to be able to analyze network traffic. Many attacks are live attacks on a network, such as denial-of-service attacks. In this section you will learn more about network packets, network-based attacks, and tools for analyzing network traffic. Capturing packets is relatively easy and is accomplished by tools. However, once the network traffic has been captured, it is necessary to analyze the packets and determine what evidence they provide.

Network Packets

Data that is sent across the network is divided into chunks called **packets**. Those packets need to carry data, but they also need information to help devices move the packet to the appropriate destination. Therefor packets are divided into three sections. There are different types of packets, which all have the same general format of header, payload, and footer, though the specifics can vary. For example, **Asynchronous Transfer Mode (ATM)**, a high-speed connection technology, uses fixed-length, 53-byte packets called *calls*. But whether it is referred to as a frame, a packet, a cell, etc., a packet has to have the header, payload, and footer. The header may be the most interesting part in a forensic investigation. Understanding where the packet came from, and where it is addressed to, can be critical.

While the general structure is the same, there are some differences between packets, segments, frames, datagrams, etc. A more basic term is Protocol Data Unit (PDU). This refers to a unit of network transmission, regardless of the specifics. A PDU at the transport layer of the OSI model is a segment. At the network layer, a PDU is a packet. And at the data link layer, PDUs are referred to as frames.

Packet Headers

A unit of information being transferred can actually have several headers put on by different protocols at different layers of the OSI model. There is usually an Ethernet header from Layer 2, an IP header from Layer 3, a TCP header from Layer 4, and then appropriate higher-layer headers above that. Each contains different information. Combined, they have several pieces of information that will interest forensic investigators.

The Ethernet header has the source and destination MAC address. The IP header contains the source IP address, the destination IP address, and the protocol number of the protocol in the IP packet's payload. These are critical pieces of information. The TCP header contains the source port, destination port, a sequence number, and several other fields. The sequence number is very important to network traffic; knowing this packet is 4 of 10 is important. The TCP header also has synchronization bits that are used to establish and terminate communications between both communicating parties. It is also possible that certain types of traffic will have a User Datagram Protocol (UDP) header instead of a TCP header. A UDP header still has a source and destination port number but lacks a sequence number and synchronization bits. If encryption is used, such as with IPSec virtual private networks, or TLS, you will have an additional header.

TCP Header Synchronization Bits

The synchronization bits in the TCP header can also yield interesting forensic data. Here are the bits most often used and what they indicate:

URG (1 bit)—Traffic is marked as urgent, though this bit is rarely used. It is more common that the IP precedence bits are used for priority when there is a need.

ACK (1 bit)—Acknowledges the attempt to synchronize communications.

RST (1 bit)—Resets the connection.

SYN (1 bit)—Synchronize sequence numbers.

FIN (1 bit)—No more data from sender.

A normal network conversation starts with one side sending a packet with the SYN bit turned on. The target responds with both SYN and ACK bits turned on. Then the other end responds with just the ACK bit turned on. Then communication commences. When it is finished sending information, the connection is terminated by sending of a packet with the FIN bit turned on.

There are some attacks that depend on sending malformed packets. For example, some session hijacking attacks begin with sending an RST packet to attempt to reset the connection, so the attacker can take over. The SYN flood DoS attack is based on flooding the target with SYN packets but never responding to the SYN/ACK that is sent back.

Port Scanning

Also keep in mind that most skilled hackers start by performing reconnaissance on the target system. One of the first steps in that process is to do a port scan. Many port scanning tools are available on the web. The most primitive just send an ICMP packet to each port in order to see if it responds. But since this is rather obviously a port scan and some administrators block incoming ICMP packets, hackers have become more sophisticated. There are several more stealthy scans based on manipulating the aforementioned bit flags in packet headers. Seeing incoming packets destined for well-known ports, like the ones listed previously, with certain flags (bits) turned on, is a telltale sign of a port scan. Some of the more common scans are briefly described next so you will know what to look for.

FIN scan

A packet is sent with the FIN flag turned on. If the port is open, this will generate an error message. Remember that FIN indicates the communication is ended. Since there was no prior communication an error is generated, telling the hacker that this port is open and in use.

Xmas tree scan

The Xmas tree scan sends a TCP packet to the target with the URG, PUSH, and FIN flags set. This is called a Xmas tree scan because of the alternating bits turned on and off in the flags byte.

Null scan

The null scan turns off all flags, creating a lack of TCP flags in the packet. This would never happen with real communications. It, too, normally results in an error packet being sent.

This means when you are examining TCP/IP packet headers, you will need to look at the ports, IP address, and bit flags. You may also find useful information in the MAC address in the lower-layer part of the information transfer unit. This is in addition to searching the actual data in the packets.

Payload

The payload is the body or information content of a packet. This is the actual content that the packet is delivering to the destination. If a packet has a fixed length, then the payload may be padded with blank information or a specific pattern to make it the right size. If the traffic is encrypted, then you will not be able to decipher the payload. However, you can still gather information from the headers regarding the packet's protocol, source, and destination.

Trailer

The TCP (OSI Layer 4) and IP (OSI Layer 3) portions of a unit of information transfer only contain a header and payload. However, if the Layer 2 portion of a unit of information transfer is analyzed, then in addition to a header and payload, there is a part at the end called the trailer. The trailer may be part of the Ethernet or PPP frame or other Layer 2 protocol, often called a Data Link Layer protocol. An Ethernet frame, for instance, has 96 bits that tell the receiving device that it has reached the end of the transmission. A Layer 2 frame also has error checking.

Ethernet uses a 32-bit Cyclic Redundancy Check (CRC). The sender calculates the CRC using a very complex calculation based on the source address, destination address, length, payload, and pad, if any. The four-octet (32-bit) result is stored in the trailer by the sender and the frame is transmitted. The receiving device repeats the exact same calculation as the sender and compares the result to the value stored in the trailer. If the values match, the frame is good, and the frame is processed. But if the values do not match, the receiving device has a decision to make. The decision is made consistently based upon the protocol involved. In the case of Ethernet, the receiver discards the errored frame and sends no indication whatsoever that the frame has been discarded. The receiver usually does, however, update some internal counter, which can be queried to identify how may frames were discarded. There is also a counter that says how many frames arrived and passed the CRC check.

Ethernet relies on the fact that an upper-layer protocol may or may not request a retransmission of the errored frame and may or may not do something else, based on how the protocol works. In the case of Internet Protocol (IP), there is, likewise, no retransmission request for an errored or missing frame, nor is there a retransmission request in the UDP protocol. TCP, on the other hand, does request a retransmission. If a frame does not pass the CRC check of Ethernet, it is discarded. TCP knows that Ethernet discarded a frame because of the sequence number in the TCP header. If a lower-level frame is discarded, and therefore is missing from the sequence, then TCP will request a retransmission. It also will usually request a retransmission in the case of a sequence error.

Ports

A port is very much like a channel through which communication can occur. Just as your television may have one cable coming into it, but many channels you can view, your computer may have one cable coming into it, but many network ports you can communicate on. There are 65,635 possible ports, but some are used more often than others. There are certain ports a forensic analyst should know on sight. Knowing what port a packet was destined for (or coming from) will tell you what protocol it was using, which can be invaluable information. The following is a list of the ports you should memorize and the protocols that normally use those ports.

20 and 21—**FTP** (File Transfer Protocol): For transferring files between computers. Port 20 is for data; port 21 is for control.

22—**SSH** (Secure Shell): Used to remotely and securely log on to a system. You can then use a command prompt or shell to execute commands on that system. Popular with network administrators and more secure than Telnet.

23—**Telnet**: Used to remotely log on to a system. You can then use a command prompt or shell to execute commands on that system. Popular with network administrators but less common. SSH is preferred for its greater security.

25—**SMTP** (Simple Mail Transfer Protocol): Send email.

43—**WhoIS**: A command that queries a target IP address for information.

53—**DNS** (Domain Name Service): Translates URLs into web addresses and possibly retrieves other information about the system that matches the URL.

69—**TFTP** (Trivial File Transfer Protocol): A faster version of File Transfer Protocol (FTP).

80—**HTTP** (Hypertext Transfer Protocol): Displays web pages.

88—**Kerberos**: Authentication.

110—**POP3** (Post Office Protocol Version 3): Retrieve email.

137–138, 139—**NetBIOS.**

161 and 162—**SNMP** (Simple Network Management Protocol).

179—**BGP** (Border Gateway Protocol).

194—**IRC** (Internet Relay Chat): Chat rooms.

220—**IMAP** (Internet Mail Access Protocol): Email service.

389—**LDAP** (Lightweight Directory Access Protocol): User authentication.

443—**HTTPS** (Hypertext Transfer Protocol—Secure): Secure web page display.

445—**Active Directory / SMB** (Server Message Block protocol).

464—**Kerberos**: Change password.

465—**SMTP over SSL** (Simple Mail Transfer Protocol over Secure Sockets Layer): Secure email sending.

636—**LDAPS (SSL or TLS)**: (Lightweight Directory Access Protocol, Secure).

31337—**Back Orifice.**

54320/54321—**BO2K.**

6666—**Beast.**

23476/23477—**Donald Dick.**

43188—**Reachout.**

407—**Timbuktu.**

So what does it do for you to know these ports? Consider the information you gather from them. Assume you capture traffic going to and from a database server on port 21. This means someone is using FTP to upload or download files with that server. But you query the network administrator and find they don't use FTP on their database server. This is likely a sign of an intruder or, at the very least, of an insider who is not adhering to system policy. Or perhaps you see frequent attempts to connect to a web server on port 23 (Telnet). An old hacker trick is to attempt to Telnet into a web server and grab the server's banner or banners. This allows the hacker to determine the exact operating system and web server running unless the system administrator has modified the banner to avoid such a well-known hacker trick.

The last six items on the preceding list (starting with Back Orifice) may seem strange. The names are certainly a bit odd. These are all utilities that give an intruder complete access to the target system. Only one of them, Timbuktu, has any legitimate use. Timbuktu is an open-source alternative to pcAnywhere. It allows the program's user to log into a remote system and work just like they were sitting in front of the desktop. It is possible that technical support personnel are using Timbuktu to make support calls more efficient. But it is also possible that an intruder is logging in and taking over the system. The other five items are simply examples of back-door hacker software with no legitimate use. The list is not intended to be exhaustive—there are many more hacker programs and new ones are launched every day.

As you can see, just knowing ports, and seeing the ports in the TCP or UDP headers, can yield very valuable evidence. The next step is to start tracking down the source IP address. Assuming it is not a spoofed IP address, this may lead you directly to the culprit.

Network Attacks

There are certain computer attacks that actually strike at the network itself rather than a specific machine that is attached to the network. In some cases, these attacks are directed at a specific machine or machines but have an impact on the network itself.. A few of those attacks are discussed here.

> **NOTE**
>
> You might think that tracing back a source IP address is a waste of time. After all, it is not particularly difficult to spoof an IP address; you can even find instructions on how to do it on YouTube. So surely any cybercriminal would take the obvious step of hiding their real IP address. Well, consider more traditional crimes: Surely anyone committing a murder with a gun would immediately destroy the gun and dispose of the parts? However, law enforcement officers routinely find the gun used in a crime still in the suspect's possession. The same thing occurs with spoofing an IP. It is surprising how often criminals don't take this obvious step. And even if they do spoof their IP, they may not know to also spoof their MAC address. So absolutely take the time to trace back the origins of suspect packets using the information you find in the headers: A little effort could prove very fruitful.

13

Network Forensics

Denial of Service

This is the classic example of a network attack. A DoS attack can be targeted at a given server, but usually the increased traffic will affect the rest of the target network. In a DoS attack, the attacker uses one of three approaches. The attacker can damage the ability of the target machine(s) to operate, overflow the target machine with too many open connections at the same time, or use up the bandwidth to the target machine. In a DoS attack, the attacker usually floods the network with malicious packets, preventing legitimate network traffic from passing. The following sections discuss specific types of DoS attacks.

Ping of Death Attack

In a Ping of Death attack, an attacker sends an Internet Control Message Protocol (ICMP) echo packet of a larger size than the target machine can accept. At one time, this form of attack caused many operating systems to lock or crash, until vendors released patches to deal with Ping of Death attacks. Firewalls can be configured to block incoming ICMP packets completely or to block ICMP packets that are malformed or of an improper length, which is typically 84 bytes, including the IP header.

Ping Flood

Related to the Ping of Death is the ping flood. The ping flood simply sends a tremendous number of ICMP packets to the target, hoping to overwhelm it. This attack is ineffective against modern servers. It is just not possible to overwhelm a server, or even most workstations, with enough pings to render the target unresponsive. But, when executed by a large number of coordinated source computers against a single target computer, it can be very effective. This second variety of ping flood falls into the category called a distributed denial-of-service (DDoS) attack.

Teardrop Attack

In a teardrop attack, the attacker sends fragments of packets with bad values in them, which cause the target system to crash when it tries to reassemble the fragments. Like the Ping of Death attack, the teardrop attack has been around long enough for vendors to have released patches to avoid it.

SYN Flood Attacks

In a SYN flood attack, the attacker sends unlimited SYNchronize requests to the host system. The SYN requests, the first step in initiating communication, are supposed to be responded to by the attacker's system, but aren't. Essentially the attacker sends the target the starting SYN request. This causes the server to set up some resources to handle the connection, and respond to the client with both the SYN and ACK (ACKnowledgment) bits turned on, acknowledging the synchronization request. The attacker is supposed to respond with the ACK bit turned on. In this attack, the attacker just floods the target with SYN packets, never responding with ACK. This can overwhelm the target system with phantom connection requests and render it unable to respond to legitimate requests.

Most modern firewalls can block this attack. This is because most modern firewalls look at the entire "conversation" between client and server, not just each individual packet. So while a single packet with the SYN bit turned on from a specific client is totally normal traffic, 10,000 such packets in under 5 minutes is not, and will be blocked. The firewall won't let the server process them at all.

Land Attacks

In a land attack, the attacker sends a fake TCP SYN packet with the same source and destination IP addresses and ports as the target computer. Basically, the computer is tricked into thinking it is sending messages to itself because the packets coming in from the outside are using the computer's own IP address.

> **NOTE**
>
> The type of firewall technology that allows SYN flood attacks to be blocked is called Stateful Packet Inspection (SPI). While many operating system firewalls are just standard packet-filtering firewalls, most routers support SPI. Even inexpensive routers for home use will support SPI.

Smurf Attacks

A Smurf attack generates a large number of ICMP echo requests from a single request, acting like an amplifier. This causes a traffic jam in the target network. Worse still, if the routing device on the target network accepts the requests, hosts on that network will reply to each echo, increasing the traffic jam. A Fraggle attack is similar to a Smurf attack, except that it uses spoofed UDP packets instead of ICMP echo replies. Fraggle attacks can often bypass a firewall.

DHCP Starvation

If enough requests flood onto the network, the attacker can completely exhaust the address space allocated by the DHCP servers for an indefinite period of time. This is a DoS attack. There are tools such as Gobbler (*https://app.gobbler.com/security*) that will do this for you.

HTTP Post Attack

An HTTP post DoS attack sends a legitimate HTTP post message. Part of the post message is the `'content-length'`. This indicates the size of the message to follow. In this attack, the attacker then sends the actual message body at an extremely slow rate. The web server is then "hung" waiting for that message to complete. For more robust servers, the attacker will need to use multiple HTTP post attacks simultaneously.

PDoS

A permanent denial of service (PDoS) is an attack that damages the system so badly that the victim machine needs an operating system reinstall, or even new hardware. This is sometimes called *phlashing*. This will usually involve a DoS attack on the device's firmware.

Login DoS

The attacker could create a program that submits the registration forms repeatedly, adding a large number of spurious users to the application. The attacker may overload the login process by continually sending login requests that require the presentation tier to access the authentication mechanism, rendering it unavailable or unreasonably slow to respond. The attacker may enumerate usernames through another vulnerability in the application and then attempt to authenticate the site using valid usernames and incorrect passwords, which will lock out the accounts after a specified number of failed attempts. At this point, legitimate users will not be able to use the site.

Packet Mistreating Attacks

A packet mistreating attack occurs when a compromised router mishandles packets. This type of attack results in congestion in a part of the network.

Network Traffic Analysis Tools

A **sniffer** is computer software or hardware that can intercept and log traffic passing over a digital network. Sniffers are used to collect digital evidence. Commonly applied sniffers include Tcpdump (*http://www.tcpdump.org/tcpdump_man.html*) for various Unix platforms and WinDump (*http://www.winpcap.org/windump/*), which is a version of Tcpdump for Windows. These programs extract network packets and perform a statistical analysis on the dumped information.

Use them to measure response time, the percentage of packets lost, and TCP/UDP connection startup and end.

The following are some other popular tools for network analysis:

- NetIntercept (*http://www.sandstorm.net/products/netintercept/*)
- Wireshark (*http://www.wireshark.org*)
- CommView (*http://www.tamos.com/products/commview/*)
- Softperfect Network Protocol Analyzer (*http://www.softperfect.com*)
- HTTP Sniffer (*http://www.effetech.com/sniffer/*)
- ngrep (*http://sourceforge.net/projects/ngrep/*)
- OmniPeek (*http://www.wildpackets.com*)

Some software tools for investigating network traffic include:

- NetWitness (*http://www.netwitness.com*)
- NetResident (*http://www.tamos.com/products/netresident/*)
- InfiniStream (*http://www.netscout.com/products/infinistream.asp*)
- Snort (*http://www.snort.org*)
- Nmap (*https://nmap.org*)

When collecting evidence on a network, it is vital to document what you've collected. Specifically, note in detail who collected the evidence, when it was collected, where it was collected, and how it was collected. Then analyze the evidence to construct a clearer picture of all activities that have occurred. If possible, organize the evidence by time and function.

A few of these tools bear a closer look.

Wireshark

Wireshark (**FIGURE 13-1**) is a widely used packet sniffer, and my personal favorite. It is a free download (*http://www.wireshark.org*) available for several operating systems. Perhaps one of the things I like most about Wireshark is how easy it is to use. The user simply selects an interface (network card) and then starts the process.

From this screen, you can see the address the packets are either coming from or going to. You can also see what protocol they are using. At any time, you can stop the packet capture process and view individual packets. Then you click on any given packet and see the details of that packet. You can even expand the headers and see the details (**FIGURE 13-2**).

You can immediately see the source and destination MAC address, protocol, and much more. If you look at the bottom of that screen, you can actually see the data in the packet.

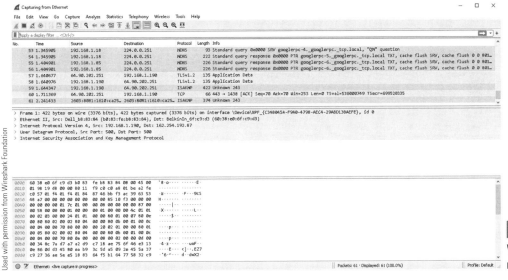

FIGURE 13-1

Wireshark main screen.

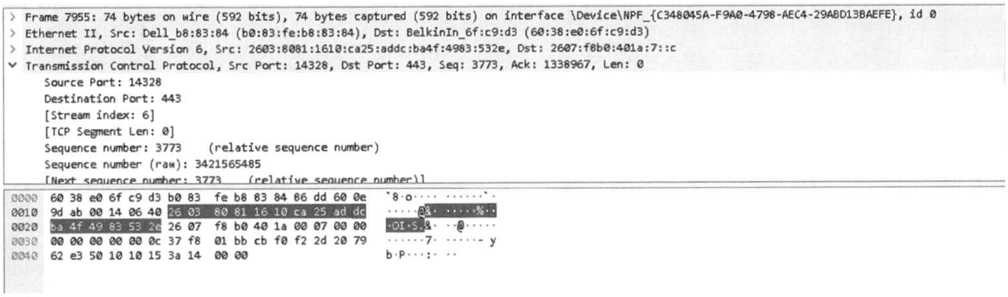

FIGURE 13-2

Wireshark packet details.

Now, the data won't always be readable. If the packet is an image file, you won't be able to read much of what is displayed.

You can also right-click on a packet, at which point you have a number of options. One is to follow the TCP stream. That will show you the entire conversation with that packet. The "follow TCP stream" option is shown in **FIGURE 13-3**. The items you send are shown in red (lighter gray in the figure), and the items received are shown in blue (darker gray in the figure).

From the menu at the top of Wireshark you have a number of options. There are statistics and analysis options that provide detailed information. For example, under statistics, you can choose to produce a graph of TCP packet sequences. This is shown in **FIGURE 13-4**.

13

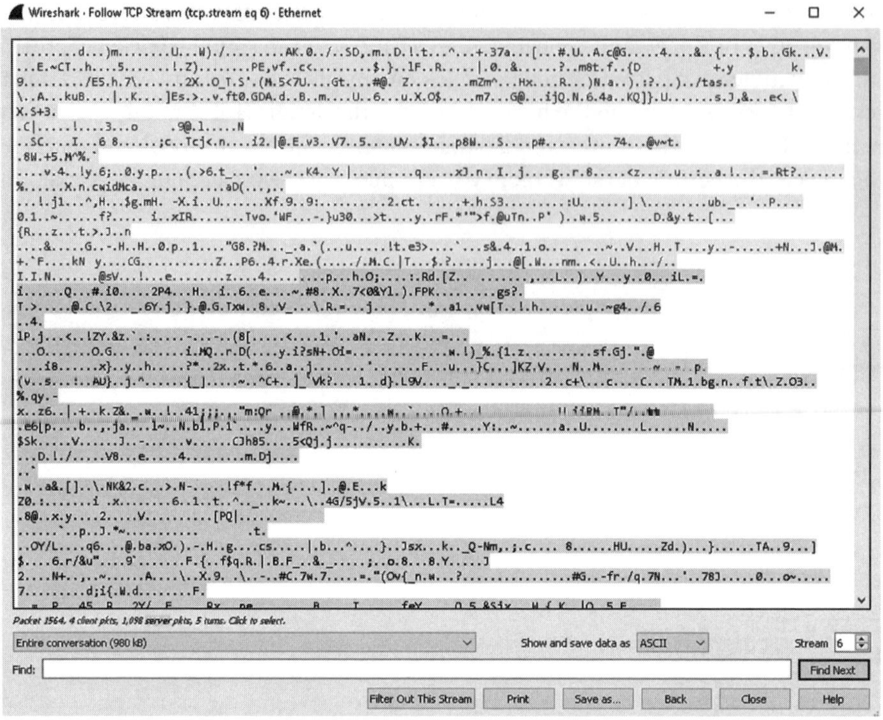

FIGURE 13-3

Wireshark follow TCP stream.

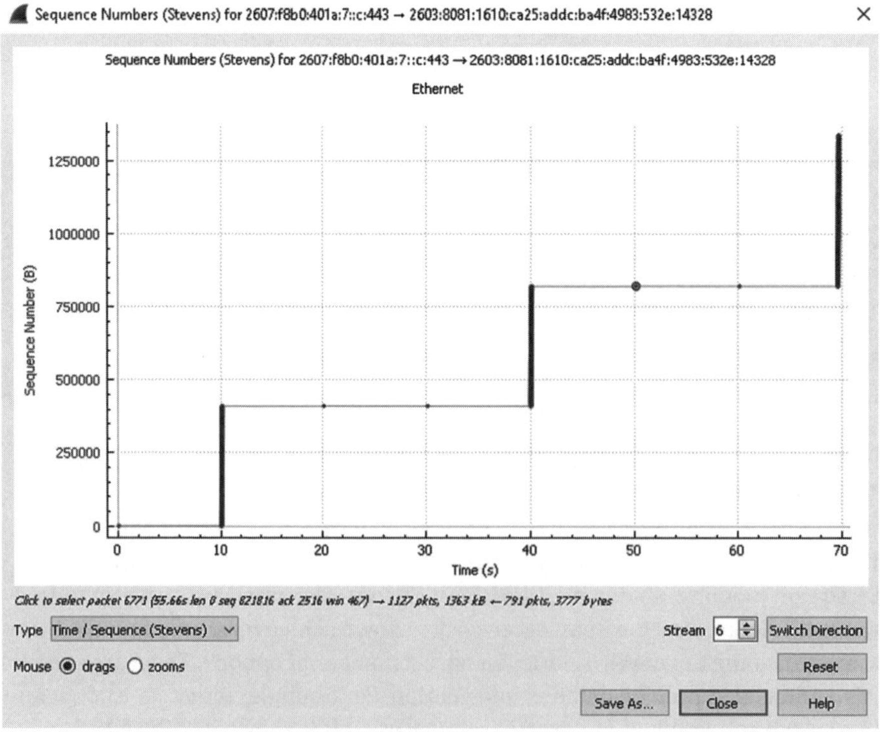

FIGURE 13-4

Wireshark TCP sequence statistics.

Nmap

Nmap is popular with both network security administrators and hackers. It allows the user to map out what ports are open on a target system and what services are running. Nmap is a command-line tool, but has a Windows interface that is available for free. It is shown in **FIGURE 13-5**.

This tool is popular with hackers because it can be configured to operate rather stealthily and determine all open ports on an individual machine, or for all machines in an entire range of IP addresses. It is popular with administrators because of its ability to discover open ports on the network. Such ports could indicate spyware, a backdoor, or many other attacks.

Tcpdump

One of the most common packet scanners for Linux is Tcpdump. It has also been ported to Windows. You will need to download it for Windows; you can get it from *http://www.tcpdump.org*. It works from the shell/command line, and it is relatively easy to use. To start it, you have to indicate which interface to capture packets on, such as:

```
tcpdump -i eth0
```

This command causes Tcpdump to capture the network traffic for the network card, eth0. You can also alter Tcpdump's behavior with a variety of command flags such as the following:

```
tcpdump -c 500 -i eth0
```

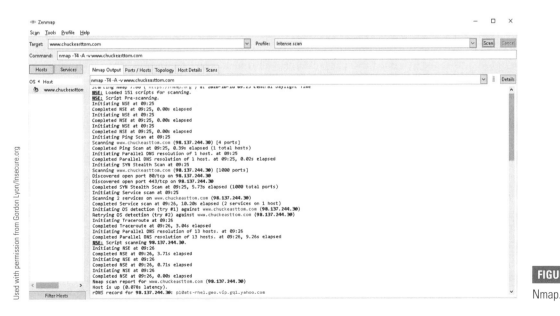

FIGURE 13-5

Nmap.

This tells Tcpdump to capture only the first 500 packets on interface eth0 and then stop.

```
tcpdump -D
```

There are several ways to use Tcpdump. Here are a few examples:

`tcpdump host 192.168.2.3` will only show you traffic going to or from 192.168.2.3.
`tcpdump -i` any gets traffic to and from any interface on your computer.
`tcpdump -i eth0` will only get traffic for the interface eth0.
`tcpdump port 3389` will only show traffic for port 3389.
`# tcpdump smtp` will only show traffic using the SMTP protocol.

Snort

Snort is primarily used as an open-source intrusion detection system. But it can also function as a robust packet sniffer with a lot of configuration options. For full installation instructions, visit *www.snort.org*. A free manual is available at *http://manual-snort-org .s3-website-us-east-1.amazonaws.com/*. For network analysis, you want to run Snort as a packet sniffer and configure it to log verbose data.

NetWitness

NetWitness is a product from RSA that has a freeware version (*http://www.emc.com/security /rsa-netwitness.htm#!freeware*). It is definitely worth taking a look, and the freeware version fits into any budget, even that of a college student! But this product is not nearly as easy to use as Wireshark is.

Network Traffic Analysis

Once you have access to the appropriate tools, you can examine either the live traffic or logs to determine if a crime has been (or is being) committed and to gather evidence about that crime.

Using Log Files as Evidence

An end-to-end investigation looks at an entire attack. It looks at how an attack starts, at the intermediate devices, and at the result of the attack. Evidence may reside on each device in the path from the attacking system to the victim. Routers, VPNs, and other devices produce logs. Network security devices, such as firewalls and intrusion detection systems (IDS), also generate logs. An IDS is software that automates the process of monitoring events occurring in a computer system or network, analyzing them for signs of possible incidents, and attempting to stop detected possible incidents.

A device's log files contain the primary records of a person's activities on a system or network. For example, authentication logs show accounts related to a particular event and the authenticated user's IP address. They contain date and time stamps as well as the username and IP address of the requestor. Application logs record the time, date, and application identifier. When someone uses an application, it produces a text file on the desktop system containing the application identifier, the date and time the user started the application, and how long that person used the application.

Operating systems log certain events, such as the use of devices, errors, and reboots. Operating system logs can be analyzed to identify patterns of activity and unusual events. Network device logs, such as firewall and router logs, provide information about the activities that take place on the network. You can also coordinate and synchronize them with logs provided by other systems to create a more complete picture of an attack. For example, a firewall log may show access attempts that the firewall blocked. These attempts may indicate an attack. Log files can show how an attacker entered a network. They can also help find the source of illicit activities. Log files from servers and Windows security event logs on domain controllers, for instance, can attribute activities to a specific user account. This may lead you to the person responsible.

Intrusion detection systems record events that match known attack signatures, such as buffer overflows or malicious code execution. Configure an IDS to capture all the network traffic associated with a specific event. In this way, you can discover what commands an attacker ran and what files he or she accessed. You can also determine what files the criminal downloaded, such as malicious code.

You may bump into a few problems when using log files, however. One is that logs change rapidly, and getting permission to collect evidence from some sources, such as ISPs, takes time. In addition, volatile evidence is easily lost. Another problem is that hackers can easily alter logs to include false information.

Wireless

Wireless networks are almost everywhere today—including homes, offices, hotels, airports, and coffee shops. Some cities even provide wireless network access to citizens in their areas. In fact, one can often access wireless networks while in flight! Wireless connections allow devices to connect to a network without having to physically connect to a cable. This makes it easy to connect computers and devices when running cables is either difficult or not practical.

Wireless, or Wi-Fi, is ubiquitous now. You probably have wireless internet in your home, and it is widely available at many public locations including fast-food restaurants, coffee shops, and retail stores. Therefore, you should be familiar with Wi-Fi technology. The standard for wireless networking is Institute of Electrical and Electronics Engineers (IEEE) standard 802.11. The various letter designations are used for denoting varying wireless speeds. The various wireless speeds, starting from the oldest to the current, are listed here:

IEEE 802.11a—This was the first widely used Wi-Fi; it operated at 5 GHz and was relatively slow.

IEEE 802.11b—This standard operated at 2.4 GHz and had an indoor range of 125 feet with a bandwidth of 11 megabits per second (mbps).

IEEE 802.11g—There are still many of these wireless networks in operation, but you can no longer purchase new Wi-Fi access points that use 802.11g. This standard includes backward compatibility with 802.11b. 802.11g has an indoor range of 125 feet and a bandwidth of 54 mbps.

IEEE 802.11n—This standard was a tremendous improvement over preceding wireless networks. It obtained a bandwidth of 100 to 140 mbps. It operates at frequencies of 2.4 or 5.0 GHz, and has an indoor range of up to 230 feet.

IEEE 802.11n-2009—This technology gets bandwidth of up to 600 mbps with the use of four spatial streams at a channel width of 40 MHz. It uses **multiple-input multiple-output (MIMO)**, which uses multiple antennas to coherently resolve more information than is possible using a single antenna.

IEEE 802.11ac—This standard was approved in January 2014. It has throughput of up to 1 gigabit per second (gbps) with at least 500 mbps. It uses up to 8 MIMO.

IEEE 802.11ad—Wireless Gigabyte Alliance. This supports data transmission rates up to 7 gbps—more than ten times faster than the highest 802.11n rate.

IEEE 802.11af—Also referred to as "White-Fi" and "Super Wi-Fi" and approved in February 2014. It allows WLAN operation in TV white-space spectrum in the VHF and UHF bands between 54 and 790 MHz.

IEEE 802.11aj—IEEE 802.11aj is a rebranding of 802.11ad for use in the 45-GHz unlicensed spectrum available in some regions of the world (specifically China).

Wi-Fi Security

Securing Wi-Fi has also evolved over the years. First there was WEP, then WPA, then WPA2, and more recently WPA3. You should be familiar with each of these technologies.

Wired Equivalent Privacy (WEP) uses the stream cipher RC4 to secure the data and a CRC-32 checksum for error checking. Standard WEP uses a 40-bit key (known as WEP-40) with a 24-bit initialization vector, to effectively form 64-bit encryption. In contrast, 128-bit WEP uses a 104-bit key with a 24-bit IV.

Because RC4 is a stream cipher, the same traffic key must never be used twice. The purpose of an IV, which is transmitted as plaintext, is to prevent any repetition, but a 24-bit IV is not long enough to ensure this on a busy network. The way the IV was used also opened WEP to a related key attack. For a 24-bit IV, there is a 50% probability the same IV will repeat after 5000 packets.

Wi-Fi Protected Access (WPA) uses Temporal Key Integrity Protocol (TKIP). TKIP is a 128-bit per-packet key, meaning that it dynamically generates a new key for each packet.

WPA2 is based on the IEEE 802.11i standard. It provides the following:

- The Advanced Encryption Standard (AES) using Counter Mode-Cipher Block Chaining
- (CBC)-Message Authentication Code (MAC) Protocol (CCMP), which provides data confidentiality, data origin authentication, and data integrity for wireless frames

WPA3 requires attackers to interact with your Wi-Fi for every password guess they make, making it much harder and time-consuming to crack. With WPA3's new "Wi-Fi Easy Connect," though, you'll be able to connect a device by merely scanning a QR code on your phone. One of the important new security features is that with WPA3, even open networks will encrypt your individual traffic

Other Wireless Protocols

While the 802.11 standard is most common, in recent years several other types of wireless protocols have become common. Some of these are used in Internet of Things (IoT) operations. Others are intended for specific applications.

There are several other wireless communication protocols. The most common are briefly described here:

* ANT+ is a wireless protocol often used with sensor data such as that obtained with bio-sensors or exercise applications.
* ZigBee is a standard developed by a consortium of electronic manufacturers for mainly residential applications of wireless devices as related to appliances and security and such. It is based on the 802.15.4 standard. What appears to be confusing is that the standard is represented by the name "ZigBee" rather than a number. The term ZigBee is used similarly to the way the term Wi-Fi is used.
* Z-Wave is a wireless communications protocol used primarily for home automation. It uses a low-energy radio for appliance-to-appliance communication using a mesh network.

Bluetooth is also a very common wireless protoco for short-distance radio using the 2.4 to 2.485 GHz frequency. The IEEE standardized Bluetooth as IEEE 802.15.1, but no longer maintains the standard. It enables devices to discover other Bluetooth devices within range. The name comes from king Harald Bluetooth, a 10th-century Danish king. He united the tribes of Denmark—thus the implication is that Bluetooth unites communication protocols. There have been different explanations for his name. One is that Harald had a bad tooth that was blue (i.e., rotted). Another explanation is that he was often clothed in blue. The Bluetooth speed and range depend on which version is used. The various versions are shown in **TABLE 13-6**.

Attackers may compromise a server to allow public access to stolen software, music, movies, or pornography. The following are the most important forensic concerns with wireless networks:

* Did a perpetrator use a wireless network entry point for a direct network attack or theft of data?

TABLE 13-6 Bluetooth.		
TABLE I	**TABLE II**	
3.0	25 mbps	10 meters (33 ft)
4.0	25 mbps	60 meters (200 ft)
5.0	50 mbps	240 meters (800 ft)
5.2	Released in December 2019, this revision adds new features. Low-energy options are the most obvious new feature.	

13
Network Forensics

- Did an attacker use a third-party wireless network, such as a hotel hotspot, to conceal his or her identity?

In addition to evidence that moves across wireless networking devices, you may find evidence in wireless storage devices. These devices include wireless digital and video cameras, wireless printers with storage capacity, wireless network-attached storage (NAS) devices, PDAs and smartphones, wireless digital video recorders (DVRs), and wireless game consoles.

There are several tools available just for discovering wireless networks. Some of the more popular tools include:

- NetStumbler (*www.NetStumbler.com*)
- MacStumbler (*www.MacStumbler.com*)
- iStumbler (*www.iStumbler.net*)

There are even apps available for both iPhone and Android that can scan for wireless networks. So Wi-Fi scanning can be accomplished with relative ease. If a hacker discovers a poorly secured wireless network, one thing they may try is to access the wireless access point's administrative screen. Unfortunately, too many people turn on these devices and don't think to change the default settings. There are websites that store default passwords that anyone can look up. One very popular website is *http://www.routerpasswords.com/*.

Router Forensics

Using network forensics you can determine the type of attack over a network. You can also in some cases trace the path back to the attacker. A router is a hardware or software device that forwards data packets across a network to a destination network. The destination network could be multiple networks away. A router may contain read-only memory with power-on self-test code, flash memory containing the router's operating system, nonvolatile random access memory (RAM) containing configuration information, or volatile RAM containing the routing tables and log information.

Router Basics

The basic networking hardware devices are:

- Network card
- Hub
- Switch
- Router

A network interface card (NIC) is an expansion board you insert into a computer or a motherboard-mounted bit of hardware that allows the computer to be connected to a network. A NIC handles many things:

- Signal encoding and decoding
- Data buffering and transmission
- Media access control
- Data encapsulation: building the frame around the data.

NICs are relatively simple devices and don't store information that you can examine for any appreciable period of time.

A hub is used to connect computers on an Ethernet LAN. Essentially a hub does not do anything to see that packets get to their proper destination. Instead, the hub will take any packet it receives and simply send a copy out every port it has, except the port on which the packet entered the hub. This is based on the theory that the packet is going somewhere, so send it out via all available avenues. This causes a lot of excess network traffic, which is why hubs are no longer used.

A switch prevents traffic jams by ensuring that data goes straight from its origin to its proper destination, with no wandering in between. Switches remember the address of every node on the network, and anticipate where data needs to go. A switch only operates with the computers on the same LAN. That is because a switch operates based on the MAC address in a packet, and that is not routable. It cannot send data out to the internet, or across a WAN. These functions require a router.

A router is similar to a switch, but it can also connect different logical networks or subnets and enable traffic that is destined for the networks on the other side of the router to pass through. Routers typically provide improved security functions over a switch. Routers utilize the IP address, which is routable, to determine the path of outgoing packets. Routers work at the network layer of the OSI model.

> **NOTE**
>
> In practice many of these definitions have become blurred. For example, if you go into your favorite electronics store and ask for a hub, they will probably hand you a switch, as these terms have become interchangeable. Also there are now specialized switches that use factors other than the MAC address to determine the path to send packets on. These devices have many names including upper-layer switches, application switches, etc.

The routers determine where to send information from one computer to another. Routers are specialized computers that send your messages and those of every other internet user speeding to their destinations along thousands of pathways. Routers maintain a **routing table** to keep track of routes: which connections are to be used for different networks. Some of these routes are programmed in manually, but many are "learned" automatically by the router. This is done by examining incoming packets and if one comes from an IP address the router has not seen before, adding that address to its routing table. Modern routers also inform each other about new routes and no longer working routes to make routing as efficient as possible.

Modern routers are complex devices. They handle packets, often have firewall and DHCP capabilities, are programmable, and maintain logs. The gold standard in routers is Cisco, and it is worthwhile to become familiar with at least the basics of working with a Cisco router.

For a good overview of Cisco routers, this document will be a great help: *http://www .ciscorebateprogram.com/en/US/docs/routers/access/800/850/software/configuration /guide/routconf.pdf*.

Types of Router Attacks

Routers can be vulnerable to several types of attacks, including router table poisoning. Router table poisoning is one of the most common and effective attacks. To carry out this type of attack, an attacker alters the routing data update packets that the routing protocols need. This results in incorrect entries in the routing table. This, in turn, can result in artificial congestion, overwhelm the router, or allow an attacker access to data in the compromised network by sending data to a different destination or over a different route than anticipated.

Getting Evidence from the Router

Even though a router is just a special-purpose computer running a routing program, getting evidence from a router is quite different that getting evidence from a PC, laptop, or server. The first major difference is that with a router, you do not shut down the device and image it. The reason is that once you shut it down, you will have potentially lost valuable evidence. For this reason, router forensics requires a great deal of care. You absolutely must make certain that you are careful not to alter anything, and you must be meticulous in documenting your process.

The first step is to connect with the router so you can run certain commands. Hyperterminal is a free tool that can be used to connect to and interact with your routers. Since the router is live, it is important to record everything you do. Fortunately, hyperterminal makes this easy.

There are several commands that are important to router forensics. The most important and commonly used commands from Cisco routers are described here. The commands for different brands of routers, or even different Cisco routers, may be different but there is an equivalent command

The `show version` command provides a significant amount of hardware and software information about the router. It will display the platform, operating system version, system image file, any interfaces, how much RAM the router has, and how many network and voice interfaces.

The `show running-config` command will get you the currently executing configuration.

The `show startup-config` command will get you the system's startup configurations. Differences between startup config and running config can be indicative of a hacker having altered the system.

The `show ip route` command will show the routing table. Manipulating that routing table is one primary way that hackers infiltrate routers.

These are a few commands you will probably find useful in your forensics examination. However, there are many others you may find useful, including:

```
show clock detail

show version

show running-config

show startup-config
```

```
show reload

show ip route

show ip arp

show users

show logging

show ip interface

show interfaces

show tcp brief all

show ip sockets

show ip nat translations verbose

show ip cache flow

show ip cef

show snmp user

show snmp group
```

The release of version 11.2 of Cisco IOS (operating system) introduced the new command `show tech-support`. This command has allowed for the collection of multiple sources of information concerning the router in a single command. This one command will output the same data as when running all of the following commands:

```
show version

show running-config

show stacks

show interface

show controller

show process cpu

show process memory

show buffers
```

For readers who are looking for more in-depth, highly technical router forensics information, the following papers might be interesting:

http://www.cs.uml.edu/~xinwenfu/paper/D-SPAN10_RouterForensics_Fu.pdf

http://www.recurity-labs.com/content/pub/RecurityLabs_Developments_in_IOS_Forensics_USA08.pdf

Firewall Forensics

Examining the firewall should be a fundamental part of any network forensic analysis. Since all external traffic must come through the firewall, it is imperative that the firewall's logs be examined carefully. They frequently contain valuable evidence.

Firewall Basics

Before you delve too deep into firewall forensics, you should ensure you have a basic, working understanding of firewalls. There are several ways to categorize firewalls, but there are two that are more basic than the rest.

Packet Filer

This is the most basic type of firewall. It simply filters incoming packets and either allows them entrance or denies them entrance based on a set of rules that were put into its configuration. A packet filer is also referred to as a screened firewall. It can filter packets based on packet size, protocol used, source IP address, etc. Many routers offer this type of firewall option in addition to their normal routing functions.

Stateful Packet Inspection

The Stateful Packet Inspection (SPI) firewall will examine each and every packet, denying or permitting them based on not only the current packet but also the previous packets in the conversation. This means that the firewall is aware of the context in which a specific packet was sent. This makes the firewall far less susceptible to ping floods, SYN floods, and spoofing.

Collecting Data

All the traffic going through a firewall is part of a connection. A connection consists of two IP addresses that are communicating with each other and two port numbers that identify the protocol or service. The concatenation of an IP address and a port number is called a socket and is unique while it is active. The three ranges for port numbers are:

- Well-known ports—The well-known ports are those from 0 through 1023.
- Registered ports—The registered ports are those from 1024 through 49151.
- Dynamic ports—The dynamic, or private, ports are those from 49152 through 65535.

Attempts on the same set of ports from many different internet sources are usually due to "decoy" scans. In a decoy scan strategy, an attacker spoofs scans that originate from a large number of decoy machines and adds his or her IP address somewhere in the mix.

Earlier in this chapter, you saw a list of common ports. You should carefully check the firewall logs for any sort of connections or attempted connections on those ports. You also learned about packet flags that might indicate a port scan. If your firewall logs such details, you will want to scan the log for any packets that might indicate a scan.

Using protocol analysis may help you determine who the attacker is. For example, you can ping each of the systems and match up the time to live (TTL) fields in those responses with the connection attempts. The TTL is not actually a time, per se, but rather the number of routers between a source and destination. The TTLs should match, plus or minus one or two, in case the route is slightly different. If the TTL of the captured traffic and the TTL of the test/trace traffic don't match, or aren't at least close, the addresses are being spoofed by an attacker. One drawback is that to know the actual number of hops, you must know the starting TTL that is being used. The idea of the TTL is that an IP packet is discarded when its TTL, decreased at each intermediate router, reaches zero before the packet gets to its destination.

Analyze the firewall logs in depth to look for decoy addresses originating from the same subnets. You will likely see that the attacker has connected recently, whereas the decoyed addresses have not.

13

Network
Forensics

CHAPTER SUMMARY

In this chapter, you learned about network packets, how to capture them, and how to analyze them. You were also introduced to the concepts of network analysis, including the use of popular network tools such as Wireshark. Then you learned about the basic functionality of routers, and how to perform basic router forensics. You also saw how firewalls work and how to perform a forensic analysis of the firewall logs.

KEY CONCEPTS AND TERMS

Asynchronous Transfer Mode (ATM)	multiple-input multiple-output (MIMO)	routing table sniffer

CHAPTER 13 ASSESSMENT

1. Which type of firewall is most likely to prevent SYN floods?

   A. Packet filtering
   B. Static
   C. Stateful Packet Inspection
   D. Dynamic

2. What does a 500 HTTP response indicate?

   A. Client error
   B. OK
   C. Redirect
   D. Server error

3. Why would you not turn off a router before examining it for evidence?

   A. You may destroy evidence.
   B. You would turn it off.
   C. It will lose its routing tables when powered off.
   D. It violates FBI forensic guidelines.

4. What does a router use to determine the path to send packets on?

   A. MAC address
   B. IP address
   C. Protocol used
   D. Next available port

5. Which header would have the senders MAC address?

   A. TCP
   B. IP
   C. Ethernet
   D. None

Memory Forensics

MEMORY FORENSICS IS NOT SOMETHING THAT NEEDS to be conducted with every investigation. In some cases, the evidence needed to fully understand the facts of the case can be determined without using memory forensics. However, some cases will require you to examine a computer's memory. This is particularly true when the case involves sophisticated malware. Often, it is only via memory analysis that a complete understanding of the malware is possible. Before we can delve into memory forensics, it is important to understand how memory functions. This will be covered in the next section.

When we speak about memory analysis, we are talking about volatile memory—that is, memory that can change. This is typically what one thinks about when one considers RAM (random access memory). Information in permanent storage is analyzed, typically, by imaging that drive and then examining the image. Information in volatile memory must first be "dumped" before that memory dump can be analyzed. This has been covered in detail in previous chapters.

Chapter 14 Topics

This chapter covers the following topics and concepts:

- Memory structure in modern computers
- Analyzing the evidence in memory

Chapter 14 Goals

When you complete this chapter, you will be able to:

- Capture memory using multiple tools
- Analyze memory using Volatility
- Evaluate memory using OSForensics
- Determine signs of malware in memory dumps
- Understand how malware functions

How Computer Memory Works

Volatile memories only hold their contents while power is applied to the memory device. This is one issue that makes such memory critical in forensics. Once the computer is shut down, that data in volatile memory is lost. Examples of volatile memories include static RAM (SRAM), synchronous static RAM (SSRAM), synchronous dynamic RAM (SDRAM), and Field Programmable Gate Array (FPGA) on-chip memory.

The most common type of memory today is **dynamic random access memory** or **DRAM**. SRAM is often used for CPU caches and registers, but those items are not part of our discussion of memory here. Whereas clusters and sectors are the fundamental building blocks of hard drives (traditional platter-based hard drives), RAM is different. In RAM, the memory cell is the fundamental building block. A **memory cell** is an electronic circuit that stores a bit of binary information. High voltage denotes a 1, whereas low voltage denotes a 0. There are a few different ways this can be done, such as a capacitor, field-effect transistor, and other options. But for our purposes, the specific circuitry is not relevant.

Memory within a RAM chip has specific addresses. A 4-bit RAM chip has four memory cells per address; an 8-bit RAM chip has 8 memory cells per address. You might think that with all modern computers being 64 bit, that the RAM is also 64 bit. That is not necessarily true.

Memory has various components, in addition to the aforementioned memory cells. There is the fetch/store controller that is used to either fetch data from memory addresses or store data in memory addresses. There is a **memory address register (MAR)** that holds the addresses in memory. The MAR is actually a CPU register, but it stores the memory addresses so data can be brought to the CPU or sent from the CPU to memory. There is also the **memory data register (MDR)**, which is also part of the CPU. The MDR stores data that is being transferred to and from memory. Consider for a moment how things work when you use a computer. If, for example, you open a document, that document is located on your hard drive or solid-state drive, then loaded into memory. This requires memory addresses to be located and the data that constitutes your document to be placed in those addresses. The address of the cell where the value should go is placed in the MAR, and then the new data is placed in the MDR. This is just a general overview of how memory and CPU work together.

Stack Versus Heap

Another issue to understand in memory is memory allocation. Those readers with a background in C or C++ programming are probably quite familiar with the heap and stack. For the rest of you, this section will provide an explanation.

The stack is computer memory that is automatically allocated and managed as needed for temporary variables within functions inside programs. The heap is not managed quite so tightly as the stack. The heap is memory that programs can allocate as needed. The heap is the source of what are commonly called "memory leaks." When a programmer writes code that allocates memory from the heap, but does not carefully deallocate that memory, then the program can begin consuming more and more memory until a system crash can occur. A great deal of malware is poorly written, and one can certainly encounter memory leaks in malware investigations.

Paging

A **page** table is a data structure. It maps virtual addresses to physical addresses. Processes use virtual addresses; hardware (more specifically RAM) uses the physical addresses. There is also auxiliary information about the page, such as a present bit, a dirty or modified bit, and address space or process ID information, among others. Basically, each process is using virtual pages to give the impression of working with contiguous sections of memory. However, the physical memory may or may not be contiguous.

The Memory Management Unit of the CPU stores recently used mappings. This is referred to as the **translation lookaside buffer (TLB)**. When a virtual address needs to be translated into a physical address, the first step is to search the TLB. Finding something in the TLB is called a *TLB hit*; if it is not found, it is a *TLB miss*. If there is a TLB miss, then the page table is searched (called a *page walk*).

Capturing Memory

The ability to capture the memory and then analyze it has important ramifications for forensic exams. Oftentimes, sophisticated malware is best detected by examining memory for specific traces of that malware. Fortunately, there are numerous options for capturing memory.

The first step is to capture the memory from a live machine. This can be done with several different tools, many of which are available for free.

One common tool that is free is the command-line tool DumpIt, shown in **FIGURE 14-1**. This tool will dump out the current memory in a file ending in the .raw extension. Note that this can take a few minutes. The DumpIt tool is popular, but can sometimes be hard to find on the internet. It is downloadable from *https://moonsols.com/resources.html*.

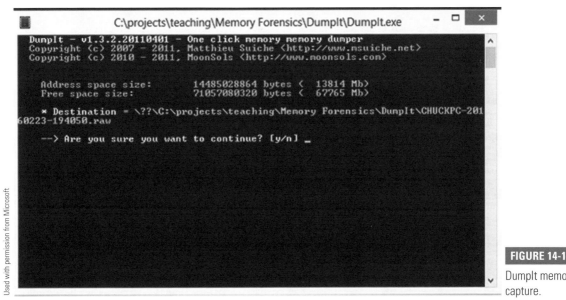

14

Memory Forensics

FIGURE 14-1

DumpIt memory capture.

Another popular memory capture utility is Ram Capturer from Belkasoft (*http://belkasoft.com/ram-capturer*). This tool as a graphical interface, rather than working from the command line. You can see this in **FIGURE 14-2**.

OSForensics also provides the option to capture live memory. That is shown in **FIGURE 14-3**.

There are other tools on the internet that can be used to capture memory, including the AccessData FTK imager you saw earlier in this book. FTK imager allows you to capture memory very easily. This is shown in **FIGURES 14-4** and **14-5**.

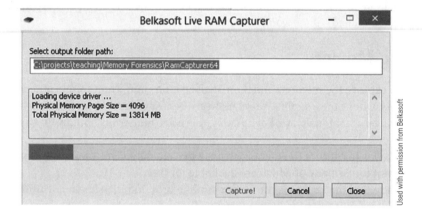

FIGURE 14-2

Belkasoft RAM Capturer.

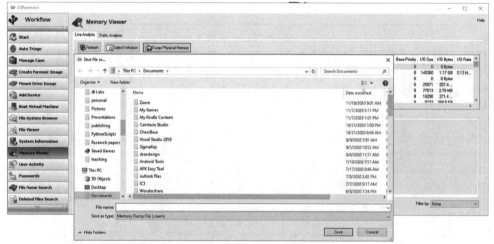

FIGURE 14-3

OSForensics memory capture.

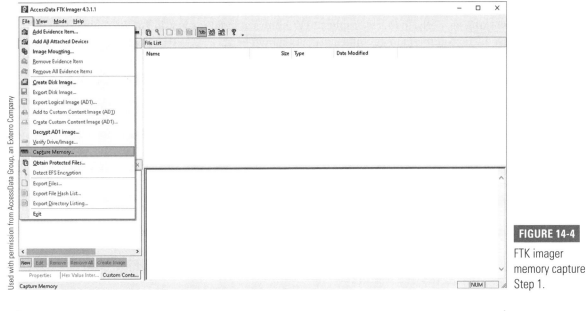

FIGURE 14-4

FTK imager memory capture Step 1.

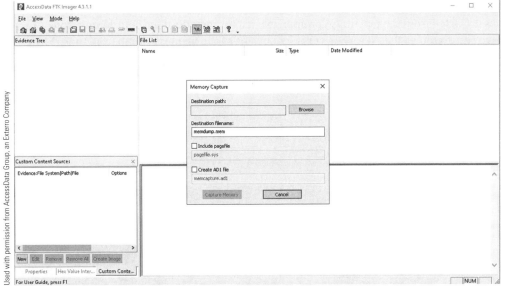

FIGURE 14-5

FTK imager memory capture Step 2.

14

Memory Forensics

Analyzing Memory with Volatility

Regardless of how you capture the memory, analyzing it is the important issue. Fortunately, the premier tool for memory analysis is also a free download. This tool is Volatility (*http://www.volatilityfoundation.org*). It is a command-line tool. Since 2016, up through early 2021, version 2.6 has been the current version of Volatility.

The first Volatility command is simply to get information about Volatility to ensure it is working properly. In this example, the Windows standalone version of Volatility is being used. The command to get information is shown here:

```
Volatility-2.6 standalone.exe --info
```

This command should fill the command window with a great deal of information. Among the information will be the profiles supported. The profile indicates the operating system of the machine the memory dump was taken from, not the machine you are running Volatility on. You can see the ``--info`` output, particularly the supported profiles, in **FIGURE 14-6**.

The basic format of commands is shown here:

```
volatility-version.exe commandname -f filepath –profile=profile
name
```

Here are examples:

```
volatility-2.6.standalone.exe pslist -f C:path\tovolatility\
dump.bin --profile=Win8SP0x64
volatility_2.6_win64_standalone.exe psscan -f dump.bin
--profile=Win8SP0x64
```

The commands, also called plug-ins, are modules used with Volatility to scan a memory dump for specific data. The memory dump file will have whatever name it was given when it was extracted from the machine. Common extensions include .mem, .bin, .dump, and .raw. The examples that follow use profiles specific to the memory dump used to perform the screen capture. You will need to use profiles that match your memory dumps. Don't be surprised when these commands take several minutes to provide results. The process is quite slow.

The ``plist`` Command

``plist`` is a basic command that lists the processes that were in the memory dump. For example:

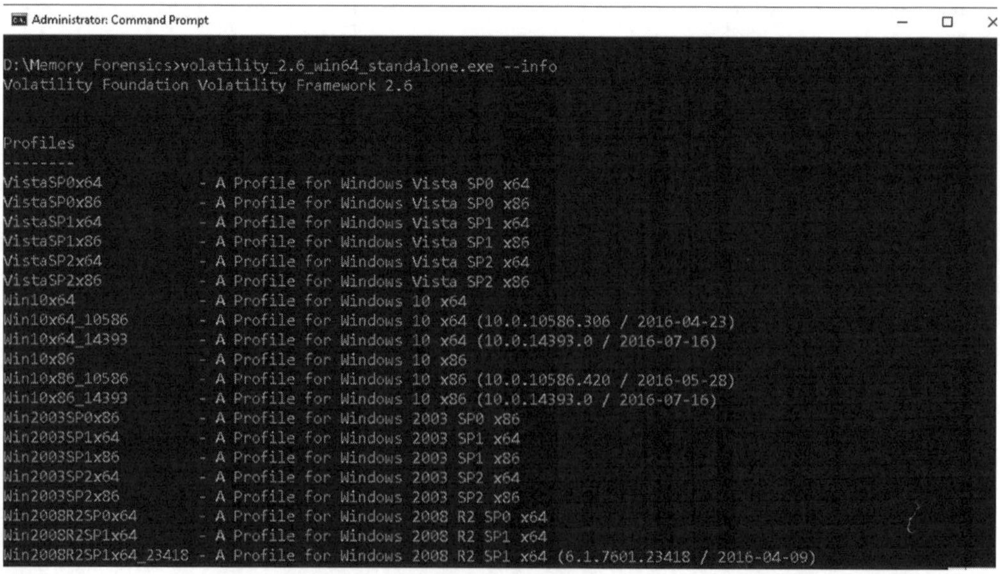

Used with permission from Volatility Foundation

FIGURE 14-6

Volatility ``--info``.

```
D:\Memory Forensics>volatility_2.6_win64_standalone.exe pslist -f memdump.mem --profile=Win8SP0x64
Volatility Foundation Volatility Framework 2.6
Offset(V)            Name            PID   PPID   Thds   Hnds   Sess  Wow64 Start
    Exit
-------------------- ----------- ------ ------ ------ ------ ------ ------ ------------------------------
--- ------------------------------
0xfffffa800c73a980 System              4      0    110      0 ------      0 2016-11-07 17:49:53 UTC+000
0
0xfffffa800cf90980 smss.exe          264      4      3      0 ------      0 2016-11-07 17:49:53 UTC+000
0
0xfffffa800d6ad080 smss.exe          392    264      0 --------      0      0 2016-11-07 17:50:05 UTC+000
0    2016-11-07 17:50:06 UTC+0000
0xfffffa800d183980 csrss.exe         408    392     10      0      0      0 2016-11-07 17:50:05 UTC+000
0
0xfffffa800c883980 smss.exe          468    264      0 --------      1      0 2016-11-07 17:50:06 UTC+000
0    2016-11-07 17:50:06 UTC+0000
0xfffffa800c881980 csrss.exe         476    468     13      0      1      0 2016-11-07 17:50:06 UTC+000
0
0xfffffa800c87f980 wininit.exe       484    392      2      0      0      0 2016-11-07 17:50:06 UTC+000
0
0xfffffa800d89e180 winlogon.exe      512    468      3      0      1      0 2016-11-07 17:50:06 UTC+000
0
0xfffffa800d0d2980 services.exe      572    484     13      0      0      0 2016-11-07 17:50:07 UTC+000
0
0xfffffa800d3f6980 lsass.exe         580    484      6      0      0      0 2016-11-07 17:50:07 UTC+000
0
0xfffffa800d3f0980 svchost.exe       688    572      7      0      0      0 2016-11-07 17:50:14 UTC+000
```

FIGURE 14-7

Volatility
pslist.

```
volatility_2.6_win64_standalone.exe pslist -f memdump.mem
--profile=Win8SP0x64
```

The output is shown in **FIGURE 14-7**.

The PID is the process ID for that specific process. The PPID is the parent process ID, the ID of the process that spawned this process. The value thds indicates how many threads that process has. Hnds is the number of handles; sess is the number of sessions. The start date/time is also shown.

The `pstree` Command

This is very much like `plist`, except it shows the processes in a hierarchical tree, making it very clear what process started a particular process. For example:

```
volatility_2.6_win64_standalone.exe pstree -f memdump.mem
--profile=Win8SP0x64
```

This is shown in **FIGURE 14-8**.

The `psscan` Command

This command is particularly interesting in malware investigations. `psscan` can find processes that previously terminated (inactive) and processes that have been hidden or unlinked by a rootkit. For example:

```
volatility_2.6_win64_standalone.exe psscan -f memdump.mem
--profile=Win8SP0x64
```

This is shown in **FIGURE 14-9**.

14

Memory
Forensics

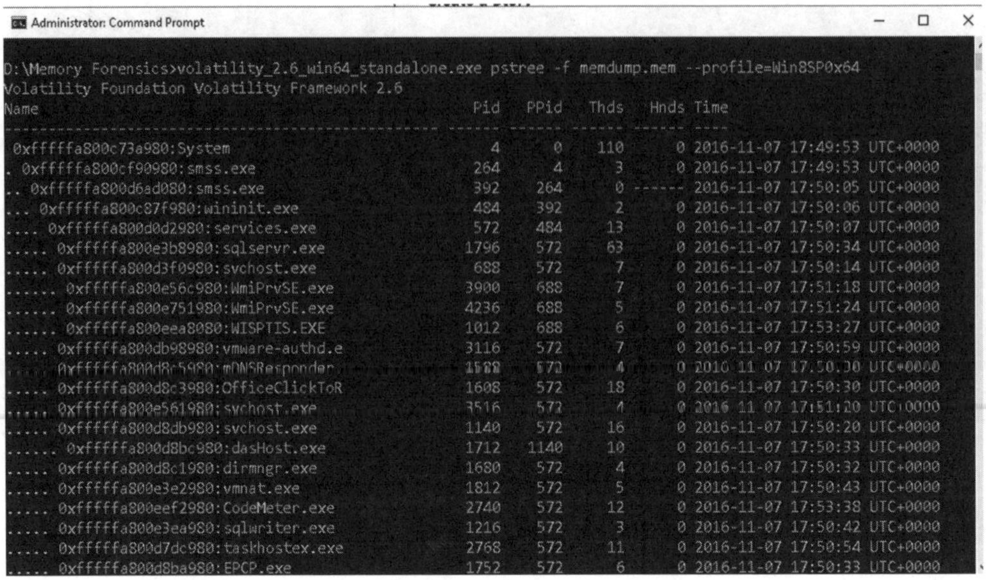

FIGURE 14-8

Volatility
`pstree`.

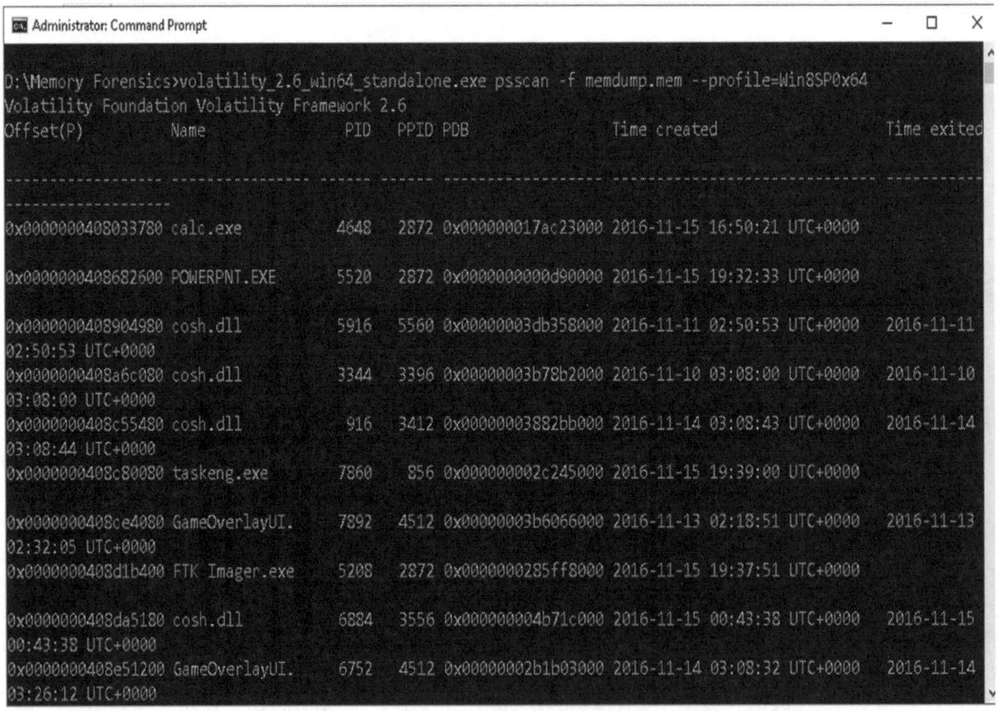

FIGURE 14-9

Volatility
`psscan`.

The `svcscan` Command

This command is very commonly used; it will list details of all services that were in memory when the memory dump was taken. For example:

```
volatility_2.6_win64_standalone.exe svcscan –f memdump.mem
--profile=Win8SP0x64
```

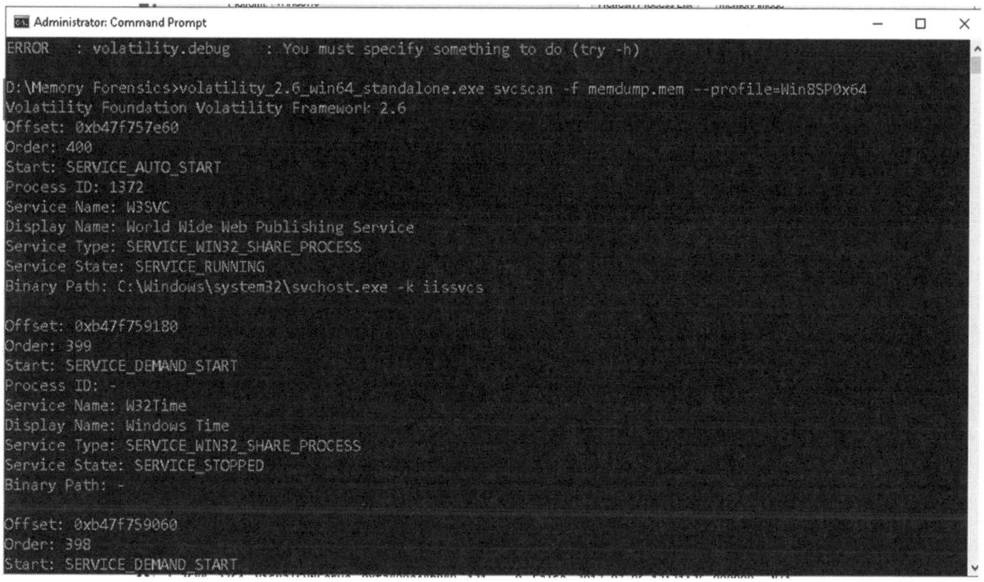

```
Administrator: Command Prompt                                    —  □  ×

ERROR   : volatility.debug    : You must specify something to do (try -h)

D:\Memory Forensics>volatility_2.6_win64_standalone.exe svcscan -f memdump.mem --profile=Win8SP0x64
Volatility Foundation Volatility Framework 2.6
Offset: 0xb47f757e60
Order: 400
Start: SERVICE_AUTO_START
Process ID: 1372
Service Name: W3SVC
Display Name: World Wide Web Publishing Service
Service Type: SERVICE_WIN32_SHARE_PROCESS
Service State: SERVICE_RUNNING
Binary Path: C:\Windows\system32\svchost.exe -k iissvcs

Offset: 0xb47f759180
Order: 399
Start: SERVICE_DEMAND_START
Process ID: -
Service Name: W32Time
Display Name: Windows Time
Service Type: SERVICE_WIN32_SHARE_PROCESS
Service State: SERVICE_STOPPED
Binary Path: -

Offset: 0xb47f759060
Order: 398
Start: SERVICE_DEMAND_START
```

FIGURE 14-10

Volatility svcscan.

This can be seen in **FIGURE 14-10**.

To understand svcscan, you need the following terms:

- Offset: Actual location in memory
- Order: The order in which the DLL was loaded into that process
- Start: How it starts
- Process ID: Standard PID
- Display Name and Service Name: Name of service
- Service Type: What specific type of service this is:
  - SERVICE_WIN32_SHARE_PROCESS: A service type flag that indicates a Win32 service that shares a process with other services
  - SERVICE_WIN32_OWN_PROCESS: A Win32 service that runs in its own process
  - SERVICE_KERNEL_DRIVER: A Windows NT device driver
  - SERVICE_FILE_SYSTEM_DRIVER: A Windows NT file system driver
  - SERVICE_ADAPTER: An interface for a Windows Service
  - SERVICE_INTERACTIVE_PROCESS: Service that can interact with the desktop
- Service State: Is it started, stopped?
- Binary Path: Path to executable

There are several other Volatility commands. This chapter has not provided an exhaustive coverage of all Volatility commands. A few others you may wish to try are:

Try to get LSASecrets L

```
volatility_2.6_win64_standalone.exe lsadump -f yourimage.dmp
-profile=Win8SP0x64
```

If truecrypt is present but the user is currently logged in, you may be able to get the keys:

```
volatility_2.6_win64_standalone.exe truecryptpassphrase
-f yourimage.dmp --profile=Win8SP0x64
```

14

Memory Forensics

```
volatility_2.6_win64_standalone.exe truecryptsummary -f
yourimage.dmp --profile=Win8SP0x64
```

The following command produces a color-coded graph of the memory processes. Just replace "PID" with an actual PID that you are interested in.

```
volatility_2.6_win64_standalone.exe vadtree -p PID --output=dot
--output-file=graph.dot -f yourimage.dmp --profile=Win8SP0x64
```

Another interesting command is hollowfind. This command is used to detect hollowing techniques. We will discuss these techniques later in this chapter. There are two flags you will want to use: -p to show information for a specific process ID, and -D to identify a directory to save the suspicious memory sections to.

```
volatility_2.6_win64_standalone.exe -f memdump.mem hollowfind -
p 10101
```

psxview searches for hidden processes:

```
volatility_2.6_win64_standalone.exe -f memdump.mem psxview
```

modscan searches for drives including unlinked drivers:

```
volatility_2.6_win64_standalone.exe -f memdump.mem modscan
```

moddump extracts kernel drivers:

```
volatility_2.6_win64_standalone.exe -f memdump.mem moddump
```

dlldump provides dynamic link libraries (DLLs) associated with specific processes. You can use -p to do this for just a single process:

```
volatility_2.6_win64_standalone.exe -f memdump.mem dlldump - p
10101
```

It is beyond the scope of this chapter to provide a complete coverage of all Volatility is capable of. However, the Volatility Foundation provides a cheat sheet: *http://downloads.volatilityfoundation.org/releases/2.4/CheatSheet_v2.4.pdf.*

Analyzing Memory with OSForensics

OSForensics includes a Volatility Workbench, and it can be downloaded as a separate, standalone program. This is essentially a graphical user interface for Volatility. It allows you to select the Volatility command you wish to execute, along with any flags needed. You can see the command list in **FIGURE 14-11**.

When you run specific scans, they work much the same way as the command-line Volatility. The only substantive difference is that the output is displayed within the Volatility Workbench interface. This is shown in **FIGURE 14-12**.

Understanding the Output

Now you have seen Volatility commands with both the command-line version of Volatility and the Volatility Workbench from OSForensics. It is important to fully understand what

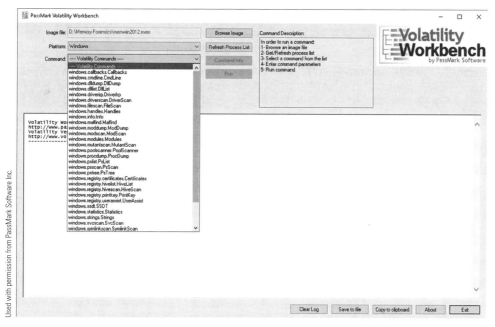

FIGURE 14-11

OSForensics
Volatility
Workbench.

FIGURE 14-12

OSForensics
Volatility
Workbench
output.

the different outputs mean. Some of the output parameters were discussed previously with respect to specific commands. Additional items you are likely to see in various Volatility outputs are given in **TABLE 14-1**.

Given that Windows is such a ubiquitous operating system, it is also important to understand the various Windows services and executables you are likely to see in many Volatility scans. The major Windows system services are listed and described here:

14

Memory
Forensics

TABLE 14-1 Volatility memory objects.

ITEM	DESCRIPTION
SERVICE_WIN32_SHARE_PROCESS	A service type flag that indicates a Win32 service that shares a process with other services
SERVICE_WIN32_OWN_PROCESS	A Win32 service that runs in its own process
SERVICE_KERNEL_DRIVER	A Windows NT device driver
SERVICE_ADAPTER	An interface for a Windows Service
SERVICE_INTERACTIVE_PROCESS	Service that can interact with the desktop
_FILE_OBJECT	Open file
_EPROCESS	A process
_ETHREAD	A thread within a process
_OBJECT_SYMBOLICLINK	Used with aliases
_TOKEN	Stores security context
_KMUTANT	Mutual exclusion for synching
gDesktop	The desktop
_DRIVER_OBJECT	A driver

Used with permission from Volatility Foundation

- Session Manager Subsystem (SMSS) first marks itself and its main thread as critical objects (note that you will see more than one SMSS).
- SMSS starts both Wininit and the CSRSS Client/Server Runtime Subsystem.
- Then Winnit starts services.exe.
- Services.exe starts all the other services. Expect to see many svchost.exe processes.
- Svchost.exe is a process on your computer that hosts, or contains, other individual services that Windows uses to perform various functions. For example, Windows Defender uses a service that is hosted by a svchost.exe process.

Putting It All Together

You have now learned about a wide range of Volatility commands, as well as various objects you are likely to see in the output. It is time to put all that knowledge together into a process you can follow in any investigation. It should be noted that as you gain more experience in memory forensics, you will develop your own process. However, this is a good starting point, particularly for those new to memory forensics.

1. `pslist` is a good place to start as your first Volatility command. Simply knowing what processes are listed in memory can be very beneficial.

2. Note any unexplained processes; processes with a parent process ID that is not listed; and processes that are spawning several processes that are not explained.

3. Then you can use `connections` (Volatility command) to see network connections and process IDs. Are any of the suspicious processes connecting?

4. Also check `sockets` to see if any suspicious process IDs have a socket connection.

5. Try the `malfind` plug-in. It at least attempts to identify malware.

6. Memory sections marked as `Page_Execute_ReadWrite`, which allows a piece of code to run and write itself, can be a sign of code injection.

7. The `handles` plug-in identifies handles.

8. The `-t Mutant` option will show only mutants (or mutexes); these are used to control access to shared resources and could indicate malware. Many malware memory artifacts have been documented.

This should give you a starting point to begin analyzing memory dumps with Volatility or with Volatility Workbench. You can use this process to begin to explore the data found in memory dumps and to understand that information.

Malware Techniques

Generally, memory forensics is most often used in malware investigations. Therefore, it is advantageous to have an understanding of malware and malware techniques. In Chapter 2 we briefly introduced malware, but in this section, we will explore the topic in more depth. Malware can be divided into several categories. It should be noted that these categories are not strict. Many instances of malware fit into multiple, overlapping categories. However, these categories can be helpful for analysis.

Viruses

Viruses are any software that self-replicates. Some sources state that a virus attaches to a legitimate file, but that is not the definition we will use. There are many types of viruses. For example, macro viruses are viruses that are created via macros in documents. Polymorphic viruses are viruses that alter some of their characteristics periodically, thus making them more likely to avoid antivirus tools.

To better understand viruses, let's examine a few rather famous viruses from recent years. In March 2017, Wannacry hit the world in a storm of activity. However, this virus will be studied for many years to come. There are several reasons for this. The first reason this virus is noteworthy is that there was a patch for the vulnerability it exploited, and that patch had been available for weeks. This illustrates why patch management is such an important part of cybersecurity.

Any modern conversation about viruses must include a discussion of ransomware. One of the most widely known examples of ransomware is the infamous Crypto Locker, first discovered in 2013. Crypto Locker utilized asymmetric encryption to lock the user's files. Several varieties of Crypto Locker have been detected. Crypto Wall is a variant of Crypto Locker first found in August 2014. It looked and behaved much like Crypto Locker.

In addition to encrypting sensitive files, it would communicate with a command-and-control server and even take a screenshot of the infected machine. By March 2015 a variation of Crypto Wall had been discovered that is bundled with the spyware TSPY_FAREIT.YOI. It actually steals credentials from the infected system, in addition to holding files for ransom.

Worms

A worm is essentially a computer virus that self-propagates. Put another way, the worm is a more virulent virus. This is an excellent example of how categories overlap. Many instances of malware that are referred to as viruses are actually worms.

Spyware

Spyware is software that monitors the computer's activities in some fashion. Keyloggers are one example. Keyloggers simply record the keystrokes. Screen capture software periodically takes a screenshot. For any spyware, one issue is data exfiltration. The data must be sent to some outside party. This is one place where memory forensics can be very helpful. Searching for processes that are creating sockets to outside IP addresses can reveal spyware that is exfiltrating data. Spyware can be legitimate. For example, software for monitoring minor children's online activities is quite popular with parents. And some employers use certain kinds of spyware to monitor how their employees use company-owned machines while working remotely. However, placing such monitoring software on a machine you don't own without the owner's consent is a criminal act.

There have been some famous instances of spyware. FinFisher was software made for the use of law enforcement, by the company Lench IT Solutions. However, it was leaked to the general public and widely used.

Zwangi was another famous spyware. This malware would take two actions. The first was to redirect URLs that are typed into the address bar of the browser and take the user to www.zwangi.com. However, the second activity was to take periodic screenshots of the computer.

Logic Bomb

Logic bombs execute their malicious activity when some logical condition is met. This is often a time, but it can be any factor at all. For example, there have been multiple cases of programmers putting a logic bomb into a company's computer that would delete important files, should that programmer's employment be terminated. One famous case was that of David Tinley. In 2019, Tenley pleaded guilty to programming and deploying logic bombs within software he had created for the Siemens Corporation. The goal of the logic bomb was to cause the software to fail after a period of time, thus causing Siemens to have to hire him again to fix the problem.

Trojan Horse

A Trojan horse is more of a delivery mechanism than a separate category of malware. One can use a Trojan horse to deliver a virus, spyware, logic bomb, etc. Essentially, a Trojan horse is software that appears to have some legitimate purpose. But when one executes the software, a second payload, the malware, is delivered. Due to the legitimate activity of the Trojan horse, it is much easier to entice users to download the malware.

One of the most famous Trojan horses is a bit dated. The infamous Gh0st RAT that emerged in 2008 was a Trojan horse that provided remote access to the infected machine. The acronym RAT refers to Remote Access Trojan.

Malware Hiding Techniques

Malware uses various techniques to covertly execute code on systems. One such technique is DLL injection. DLL injection involves causing code to execute within the address space of some other process. This is accomplished by forcing the targeted program to load a DLL. Multiple techniques can be used to accomplish this kind of attack. Specific registry keys can be useful. As one example, every DLL that is listed in the registry entry HKEY_LOCAL_MA-CHINE\SOFTWARE\Microsoft\Windows NT\CurrentVersion\Windows\AppInit_DLLs is loaded into every process that loads User32.dll. User32.dll is commonly used by many programs. Therefore, if the attacker can get their DLL listed in that registry entry, it will be loaded along with a great many programs.

Another registry key that can be used for DLL injection is HKEY_LOCAL_MACHINE\SYSTEM\CurrentControlSet\Control\Session Manager\AppCertDLLs. Any DLL listed in this registry entry will be loaded into every process that calls the Win32 API functions CreateProcess, CreateProcessAsUser, CreateProcessWithLogonW, CreateProcessWith-TokenW, and WinExec. This also encompasses a large number of programs.

Volatility has commands for examining the registry, including:

* `hivescan`
* `hivelist`
* `printkey`

The last one, `printkey`, is probably the one most useful in examining DLL injection. This Volatility command allows the user to view any particular registry key. That would include the two registry entries previously discussed in this section.

Another technique is process hollowing, which is also known as process replacement. This is a technique wherein the malware is disguised as a legitimate system process, without the risk of crashing the process. The key to process hollowing is creating a process in a suspended state. This is accomplished by loading the process into memory by suspending its main thread. The program will remain inert until an external program resumes the primary thread, causing the program to start running.

Signs of process hollowing or process injection can be found in memory dumps. Look for calls such as `–VirtualAllocEx( )` and `CreateRemoteThread( )` `–SetWindowsHookEx()`. These can be part of normal software, but they also could indicate DLL injection. Review memory sections marked as `Page _ Execute _ ReadWrite` and having no memory-mapped file present. This can also be a sign of hollowing or injection.

Density Scout

There is yet another tool that can be used to find malware. This is not actually memory forensics, but it can often be used in conjunction with memory forensics. The application Density Scout has options shown here:

`-a`	Show errors and empties, too
`-d`	Just output data (Format: density|path)
`-l density`	Just files with density lower than the given value
`-g density`	Just files with density greater than the given value
`-n number`	Maximum number of lines to print
`-m mode`	Mode ABS (default) or CHI (for file size > 100 Kb)
`-o file`	File to write output to
`-p density`	Immediately print if lower than the given density
`-P density`	Immediately print if greater than the given density
`-r`	Walk recursively
`-s suffix(es)`	File type(s) (e.g., dll or dll,exe,...)
`-S suffix(es)`	File type(s) to ignore (e.g., dll or dll,exe)
`-pe`	Include all portable executables by magic number
`-PE`	Ignore all portable executables by magic number

Here is an example command to explore files in Windows\System32:

```
densityscout -d -o results.txt c:\Windows\System32
```

You can see this command in **FIGURE 14-13**.

Nothing is printed to the screen; rather, the output is in results.txt, which is also shown in Figure 14-13. A partial listing of what is in the results.txt is shown here:

0.02548|c:\Windows\System32\mcupdate_GenuineIntel.dll

0.05214|c:\Windows\System32\WdfCoInstaller01009.dll

0.05728|c:\Windows\System32\WdfCoInstaller01011.dll

0.06189|c:\Windows\System32\WdfCoInstaller01007.dll

0.07584|c:\Windows\System32\DisplayAudiox64.cab

0.08219|c:\Windows\System32\cp_resources.bin

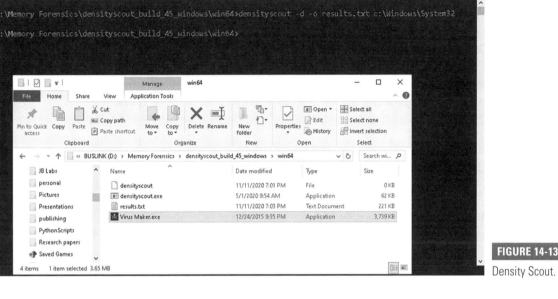

FIGURE 14-13

Density Scout.

0.08965|c:\Windows\System32\Windows.UI.PicturePassword.dll

0.09582|c:\Windows\System32\appverif.chm

0.09873|c:\Windows\System32\FilmModeDetection.wmv

0.12906|c:\Windows\System32\WinUSBCoInstaller2.dll

0.13074|c:\Windows\System32\ImageStabilization.wmv

0.14987|c:\Windows\System32\WinUSBCoInstaller.dll

0.16818|c:\Windows\System32\wpcatltoast.png

0.17130|c:\Windows\System32\DesktopKeepOnToastImg.gif

0.17688|c:\Windows\System32\IMAX Hubble.scr

0.17799|c:\Windows\System32\MaxxAudioVnA64.dll

As you can see, this is a density rating for various files found in Windows\System32. What you are looking for are files that have an odd density. That would mean density that is substantially different than known good files of the same type. If you look at the preceding list, there are eight DLLs with density values from 0.02548 to 0.17799. This is a rather large range. Note that these are not, for the most part, Windows System DLLs.

CHAPTER SUMMARY

This chapter introduced you to the fundamentals of memory forensics. You learned essential facts about memory structure and function, as well as the use of Volatility. We also explored the nature of malware and the techniques that can be used to hide malware. Malware forensics is often memory forensics. Memory forensics is a common aspect of digital forensics. This is an essential skill for any forensic examiner.

KEY CONCEPTS AND TERMS

DLL	MAR	Memory cell
DRAM	MDR	Page

CHAPTER 14 ASSESSMENT

1. What best describes DLL injection?

A. Forcing a program to load a particular DLL

B. Injecting malware into a DLL

C. Injecting a malicious DLL into the Windows\System32 directory

D. Injecting a malicious DLL into the boot sequence

2. The _____ is memory that programs can allocate as needed.

A. stack

B. MDR

C. MAR

D. Heap

3. What maps virtual addresses to physical addresses?

A. MDR

B. Page

C. MAR

D. Heap

4. What is a Volatility profile for?

A. The memory profile of the computer you are doing the examination with

B. The memory profile of the memory image

C. The profile of the parameters of your memory scan

D. A script for automating Volatility

5. The following image was most likely generated from what Volatility plug-in?

Used with permission from Volatility Foundation

A. pstree

B. pslist

C. psscan

D. psxview

Trends and Future Directions

A S WITH ANY TOPIC RELATED to science and technology, the field of digital forensics is changing rapidly. A substantial part of this change is due to the fact that the underlying technology changes rapidly. There are widely used technologies today that did not even exist a few years ago. However, changing technology is not the only issue facing digital forensics examiners. The legal environment is changing as well. New laws can change how an analyst approaches investigation. Techniques also evolve over time. In this chapter, we will explore the latest trends and what they might mean for the near future of computer forensics.

Chapter 15 Topics

This chapter covers the following topics and concepts:

- Technology trends and their impacts on forensics
- Legal and procedural changes in forensics

Chapter 15 Goals

When you complete this chapter, you will be able to:

- Understand how increasing computing power affects forensics
- Understand the impact of new technology on forensics
- Investigate methods for extracting evidence from new technology
- Understand how new laws affect evidence collection

Technical Trends

Digital forensics is a relatively new field in comparison to other forensic disciplines such as DNA forensics, fingerprint forensics, etc. The field of digital forensics as a scientific discipline is still growing. Standards are still evolving. This fact, coupled with the changing technology, makes for a very dynamic environment. That is why it is important for the forensic examiner to keep up with changing trends.

One of the earliest uses of digital systems was to compute payroll. One of the earliest digital crimes was taking the "round-off"—the half-cent variance resulting from calculating an individual's pay. A criminal would move that round-off to his or her own account. In this type of fraud, a perpetrator stole very small amounts each time. However, the number of paychecks calculated made the total theft quite large. This showed that digital crime is relatively easy to commit and difficult to detect. To make the situation worse, the courts frequently sentenced perpetrators to probation instead of prison, so digital criminals faced relatively minor consequences if they did get caught.

Digital technology provides many benefits and reduces costs in a number of ways. Therefore, the use of digital technology to support business processes and nearly every other facet of modern life has increased. In parallel, criminals have made increasingly innovative use of digital techniques in their activities. The methods of protecting digital systems and associated assets have also grown. However, they haven't grown fast enough to keep pace with the growing number and complexity of attacks. Attackers now realize that there are many ways to illegally obtain benefits from digital systems. They can steal money and identities, and they can even commit blackmail. For example, perpetrators have stolen customer data and held it for ransom.

In a 1965 paper, Gordon E. Moore, co-founder of Intel, noted that the number of components in integrated circuits had doubled every 18 to 24 months from the invention of the integrated circuit in 1958 until 1965. He predicted that this trend would continue for at least 10 more years. In other words, he predicted the number of transistors on an integrated circuit would double every two years for the next 10 years. This statement regarding the progression of integrated circuit capacity and capability became widely known as **Moore's law** or **Moore's observation**. More importantly, though, each doubling of capacity was done at half the cost. This means that a component that cost $100 would have twice the capability but cost only $50 within 18 to 24 months. This can be seen in hundreds of modern digital devices from DVD players and cell phones to computers and medical equipment.

Moore's law achieved its name and notoriety because it proved to be an accurate representation of a trend that continues today. Specifically, the capacity and capability of integrated circuits has doubled, and cost has been halved, every 18 to 24 months since Moore noted the trend. Further, Moore's law applies to more than just integrated circuits. It also applies to some of the other primary drivers of computing capability: storage capacity; processor speed, capacity, and cost; fiber-optic communications; and more.

Only human ingenuity limits new uses for technological solutions. In the 1950s, the UNIVAC I, the first commercial digital computer, was touted as having the capability to meet an organization's total computing requirements. Today, a typical low-end mobile phone has more capability and capacity than the UNIVAC I.

Moore's law also applies to digital forensics. You can expect to conduct investigations requiring analysis of an increasing volume of data from an increasing number of digital devices. Unfortunately, in the forensics world, Moore's law operates as if it's on steroids.

For example, digital storage capacity for a particular device might double in a year. The data that you might need to analyze could easily experience twice that growth level. For example, a standard point-and-shoot digital camera now takes five-megapixel photos. High-end cameras take 16-megapixel—or larger—photos. A typical Windows XP build consumes roughly 4 gigabytes (GB) of disk space. A typical Windows 8 build consumes 8 GB to 10 GB. Although a single copy of a file or data record might be maintained for active use, you must often locate and examine all prior copies of that file.

Because of Moore's law, forensic specialists must develop new techniques, new software, and new hardware to perform forensic assessments. New techniques should simplify documentation of the chain of custody. You will have to determine what techniques have the greatest potential for obtaining needed information. In most investigations, analyzing all available data would be so costly as to be infeasible. Therefore, selectively evaluate data. Such selectivity is not unique to the digital world. It is the same concept that investigators have used for years to follow leads. For example, they often start by interviewing the most likely suspects and follow where the data leads to reach a conclusion. However, the U.S. legal system, helped by advertising and popular television, expects digital forensics to be unconstrained by such mundane factors as time, money, and available technology.

Today the situation is even more difficult to predict. There are countless new devices, including Internet of Things (IoT), smart TVs, cloud storage, and even quantum computing looming on the horizon. All of these new technologies will present challenges for digital forensics.

What Impact Does This Have on Forensics?

How does increasing computing power impact forensic investigations? The most obvious impact is the need for more storage on forensics servers. Most forensics labs use servers to store forensic images of suspect machines. If even the most low-end laptop has 500 GB to 1 terabyte (TB) in hard drive storage, the forensic server must be able to accommodate many TBs of data.

The process of imaging a disk will also be slower due to the increased size. For example, utilizing the forensics DD utility with the `netcat` utility to image a suspect machine requires transmitting the image over a network. Clearly, the larger the drive being imaged, the more bandwidth will be required. It is recommended that forensics labs use the highest-capacity cabling available for the forensics lab, even possibly optical cable. To do otherwise will impact the efficiency of future forensics investigations.

Software as a Service

It is also the case that not all forensic evidence will be on a single device or drive. When computing first entered the marketplace, computer manufacturers typically provided software as part of a bundled product. A bundled product includes hardware, software, maintenance, and support sold together for a single price. It wasn't long before the industry recognized that it could sell software products individually. This resulted in the rise of companies such as Microsoft.

Another approach to selling software arose. This approach involves selling access to needed software on a time-sharing basis. The price of the software was essentially embedded in a mathematical algorithm, and a user paid for software based on his or her usage profile. This pricing model continued into personal computer and server technology.

Then the pricing algorithm was changed to address a number of concurrent users, a number of instances, or some other model. In addition, the idea of buying use of a software product morphed into the concept of software as a service (SaaS)—that is, software that a provider licenses to customers as a service on demand, through a subscription model.

The model under which an organization obtains software is important to forensic analysis because it affects four areas of an investigation:

- Who owns the software? Know whom to talk with to obtain information regarding the functionality and patch levels of software.
- How can you get access to the program code? When software is obtained as a shared service, access is usually not possible. In such cases, use alternative techniques.
- What assurance do you have of the safety of a software product? You need to know that a particular software product doesn't contain malware that could alter the investigation.
- How can you keep the status of shared software static until the forensic investigation is complete?

SaaS has expanded substantially. There are now many variations, including infrastructure as a service (IaaS). With IaaS, the entire network infrastructure is virtualized. That includes the routers, switches, and servers. Platform as a service (PaaS) provides individual operating systems as a service. If a programmer normally uses a Macintosh computer, but needs a Windows machine for a specific project, they need not set up a Windows computer; instead, they can simply have a PaaS provide a Windows environment to work on. In addition to these services, it is quite common now to have virtual systems on a desktop. We will discuss such virtual systems in a subsequent section.

The Cloud

It seems in any conversation about computer networks today, one will hear mention of "the cloud." What exactly is it and how does it affect forensics? These are important questions now and will become more so in the next few years.

What is the cloud? In short, it is network redundancy taken to new level. In order to address disaster recovery, it is imperative for a robust network to have multiple redundant servers. In this way, if one fails, the organization simply uses the other server. In the simplest configuration, there are two servers that are connected. They are complete mirror of each other. Should one server fail for any reason, then all traffic is diverted to the other server.

This situation works great in environments where there are only a few servers, and the primary concern is hardware failure. But what if you have much larger needs—for example, the need to store far more data than any server can? Well, that led to the next step in the evolution of network redundancy, the storage area network (SAN). In a SAN, there are multiple servers and storage devices all connected in a high-speed small network. This network is separate from the main network used by the organization. When a user on the main network wishes to access data from the SAN, it appears to the user as a single storage device. The user need not even be aware a SAN exists; from their perspective, it is just a server. This not only provides increased storage capacity, but also provides redundancy. The SAN has multiple servers, and should one of them fail, the others will continue operating— and the end user will not even realize a failure occurred.

There are two problems with the solutions mentioned so far. The first is capacity. Even a SAN has a finite (though quite large!) capacity. The second is the nature of the disaster they can withstand. A hard drive failure, accidental data deletion, or similar small-scale incident will not prevent a redundant network server or SAN from continuing to provide data and services to end users. But what about an earthquake, flood, or fire that destroys the entire building, including the SAN? For quite some time, the only answer to that was an off-site backup network. If your primary network was destroyed, you moved operations to a backup network, with only minimal down time.

Eventually, the idea was formed to take the idea of a SAN and the idea of off-site backup networks and combine them. Thus, **cloud computing** was born. When a company hosts a cloud, it establishes multiple servers in diverse geographic areas, with data being re-dundantly stored in several servers. There may be a server in New York, another in San Francisco, and another in London. The end user simply accesses "the cloud" without even knowing where the data actually is. It is hard to imagine a scenario wherein the entire cloud would be destroyed. The basic architecture of a cloud is shown in **FIGURE 15-1**.

From the standpoint of a forensic examiner, though, the cloud is being used increasingly to create a physical distance between important elements. As an example, storage as a service (STaaS) allows a computer in one place to connect to actual storage embedded in the

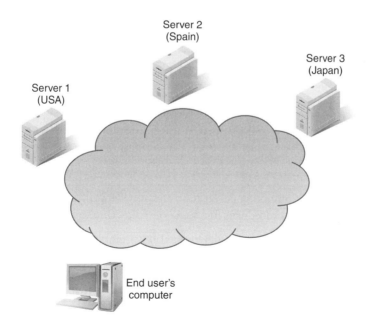

FIGURE 15-1

The cloud.

■ NOTE

It may be urban legend but the origin of "the cloud" is often traced to an IBM sales representative, his customer, and a chalkboard in late 1973 or early 1974. Upon return from an internal training class on the then-new IBM Systems Network Architecture (SNA), the technically astute sales rep attempted to explain mainframes, 3270 terminals, front-end processors, and a myriad of SNA logical unit and physical unit designations and definitions and drew this new IBM world on a chalkboard as he spoke. As the sales rep talked, the customer became wearier, and his eyes glazed over at all of the new jargon and complexity. The customer finally asked if it was necessary to understand all of the complexity before placing an order. Of course not, explained the IBM sales rep. He quickly erased what was on the chalkboard between the mainframe computer and the end-user terminal—and what was left looked like a cloud connecting the two. From that time forward, the complexity of the network and all of its connections has been known as "the cloud," which is a simplified way of envisioning the connectivity. The cloud has existed for a long time, but the big deal is that the cloud is being used for more than basic connectivity, which is to say networking; the cloud now houses valuable services.

cloud. Not only is it usually less expensive, but there are a number of pluses such that the information is automatically backed up and is available from many locations and even from different computers, potentially to other users. It is clear that the additional ease of access from additional locations and potentially additional people changes the forensics outlook on computer storage and potentially adds a number of additional considerations, such as tampering, chain of custody, and even evidentiary value of the information.

Cloud providers are everywhere. Microsoft is increasingly emphasizing its Azure cloud service. In fact, as of 2020, most Microsoft certifications are Azure-focused. Amazon cloud services are also widely used in business. Many individuals store data in Google Drive, Microsoft One Drive, or Dropbox—all cloud providers.

What Impact Does Cloud Computing Have on Forensics?

Cloud computing impacts digital forensics in several ways. First and foremost, it makes data acquisition a little more complicated. If a website is the target of a crime, and the server must be forensically examined for evidence, how does one collect evidence from the cloud? Fortunately, each individual hosted server is usually in a separate virtual machine. The process, then, is to image that virtual machine, just as you would image any other hard drive. It does not matter if the virtual machine is duplicated or distributed across a cloud. However, a virtual machine is hosted on a host server. That means that in addition to the virtual machine's logs, you will need to retrieve the logs for the host server or servers.

Another issue in cloud forensics involves the legal process. Since a cloud could potentially be transnational, the investigator must be aware of the rules of seizure, privacy, etc. in each country that hosts data that will be retrieved. With the growing popularity of cloud computing, these issues are likely to become more common in the coming years. This is why it is important for a forensic investigator to have at least some familiarity with laws related to computer forensics, even in other countries.

The U.S. National Institute of Standards and Technology (NIST) published document NISTIR 8006, "NIST Cloud Computing Forensic Science Challenges," in August 2020. It outlines forensic challenges and procedures for cloud forensics. Quoting from that document:

> NIST defines cloud computing as a model for enabling ubiquitous, convenient, on-demand network access to a shared pool of configurable computing resources (e.g., networks, servers, storage, applications, and services) that can be rapidly provisioned and released with minimal management effort or service provider interaction. This

cloud model is composed of five essential characteristics, three service models, and four deployment models. Cloud forensics is a process applied to an implementation of this cloud model.[1]

NIST reemphasizes that the eight general principles of forensics are still applicable to cloud forensics. Those eight principles are:

1. **Search authority**. Legal authority is required to conduct a search and/or seizure of data.
2. **Chain of custody**. In legal contexts, chronological documentation of access and handling of evidentiary items is required to avoid allegations of evidence tampering or misconduct.
3. **Imaging/hashing function**. When items containing potential digital evidence are found, each should be carefully duplicated and then hashed to validate the integrity of the copy.
4. **Validated tools**. When possible, tools used for forensics should be validated to ensure reliability and correctness.
5. **Analysis**. Forensic analysis is the execution of investigative and analytical techniques to examine, analyze, and interpret the evidentiary artifacts retrieved.
6. **Repeatability and reproducibility (quality assurance)**. The procedures and conclusions of forensic analysis should be repeatable and reproducible by the same or other forensic analysts.
7. **Reporting**. The forensic analyst must document his or her analytical procedure and conclusions for use by others.
8. **Presentation**. In most cases, the forensic analyst will present his or her findings and conclusions to a court or other audience.[1]

The NIST document mainly focuses on documenting the challenges of cloud forensics. It does not provide specific solutions, but instead gives general recommendations. Among other issues, it is usually not possible to "image" a cloud. You will most often either conduct live forensics or need to make a logical copy of the data. This is a departure from how forensics is often done with computers, laptops, and similar devices.

New Devices

While it is true that computers are becoming more powerful every year, that is not the only challenge facing forensics. Another important issue is the emergence of new devices. Consider smartphones and tablets: These are both relatively new devices. With any new computing device, it is safe to assume that it will eventually become the target of a forensic investigation.

Cars

For several years cars have become increasingly sophisticated. GPS devices within cars are now commonplace. Many vehicles have hard drives for storing music to be played. These technological advances can also be repositories for forensic evidence. For example, GPS data might establish that a suspect's car was at the scene of a crime when the crime took place. That alone would not lead to a conviction, but it does help to build a case.

Vehicles now often have infotainment systems that have complete computers with operating systems. One example is Android Automotive OS, an Android-based infotainment system that is built into vehicles. The car's system is a standalone Android device that is optimized for vehicles. The operating system was first announced by Google in March 2017 (*https://source.android.com/devices/automotive*). This system is found on a wide range of car models. The general architecture is shown in **FIGURE 15-2**.

Medical Devices

An increasing number of medical devices are built to communicate. For example, there are insulin pumps that send data regarding insulin usage to a computer via a wireless connection. There are pacemakers that operate similarly. This leads to the question as to whether medical wireless communication can be compromised. The unfortunate fact is that it can be. Multiple news sources have carried the story of a pair of researchers who discovered they could hack into pacemakers to shock the wearer[2]; they also found they could hack wireless insulin pumps and alter the wearer's insulin dosage, even to fatal levels.[3] The pumps were later recalled by the manufacturer.[4]

Many medical devices incorporate wireless communication in order to facilitate remote monitoring. This includes implantable cardiac devices. In 2017, the U.S. Food and Drug Administration

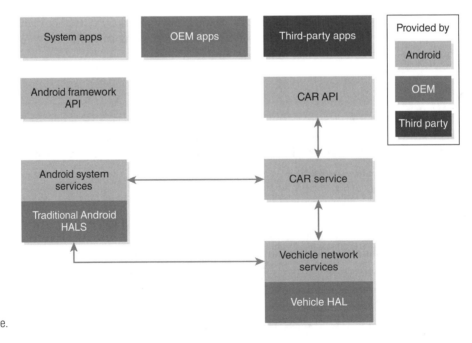

Android Automotive.

(FDA) issued a warning related to the essential programming functions of pacemakers. These issues included the potential for unauthorized access and modification. While cardiac devices were the focus of this particular FDA alert, the danger is not limited to such devices, but rather impacts a wide range of implantable medical devices.

Threats to insulin pumps had been documented even earlier. In 2013, the hacker Barnaby Jack revealed a technique that would allow an attacker to take control of an insulin pump remotely.[5] In that attack scenario, the attacker was able to cause the insulin pump to completely dispense its contents in a single dose. If this were done on a live human subject, the result would most likely be death. Whether it is an insulin device or a cardiac device, the cybersecurity issues are considerable. Unfortunately, while the literature has significant coverage of the vulnerabilities, there is far less discussion of broad-based solutions.

With the increasing complexity of medical devices, it could eventually become commonplace to forensically examine them in cases where foul play is suspected—just as it is now commonplace to forensically examine any phone seized in relation to a crime.

GPS Forensics

During any forensic examination involving cell phones, it is a common practice to extract data from cell phone usage records. This is a common practice in criminal investigations as well as some civil investigations. Cell phone records acquired from cell phone carriers will indicate the particular tower that an individual cell phone is connected to at a specific time. This is often referred to as cell site analysis. These records have been used to attempt to locate individuals in both criminal and civil investigations. This approach to using historical cell phone records is flawed for multiple reasons. The primary reason this approach is scientifically invalid is that the latitude and longitude records from the cell phone tower logs are for the cell, not for the individual phone.

In general, a location defined by latitude and longitude, found in historical cell phone records, can only identify that the cell phone was within range of a specific cell phone tower. Cell towers have a rough general range of 5 to 10 kilometers but can extend for tens of kilometers. However, this range can be reduced by factors in the terrain, including extensive mountains, particularly those with metal ores, and large urban constructions. It is also true that when there is a high density of cell phone towers in a given geographic region, a cell phone will be handed off to another tower when in range of that second tower. Thus, cell tower density can reduce the range that a given cell tower covers.

Given that a cell tower can have a range between 5 to 10 kilometers, and occasionally beyond that, the cell's GPS location provides a large area in which the device could be. NIST states, in its 2014 *Guidelines on Mobile Device Forensics*, that cell phone towers can be servicing phones as far away as 35 kilometers (21.74 miles). This presents a very large range that a cell phone could potentially be in and be connected to that tower. NIST is very clear in what cell phone usage records can and cannot demonstrate:

> While plotting call record locations and information onto a map can sometimes be useful, it does not necessarily provide a complete and accurate picture. Cell towers can service phones at distances of up to 35 kilometers (approximately 21 miles) and may service several distinct sectors.[6]

The NIST standards document goes on to state that these records can only give you a general area a phone was in, and a general direction of motion. The preceding quote should clarify the problematic nature of attempting to geolocate a particular phone based solely on historical cell phone records.

Smart Televisions

Smart televisions have become ubiquitous. It is important to bear in mind that these devices are not merely televisions, but rather fully functioning computers with internet connectivity, applications, and internal storage. As such, these devices can be a subject of digital forensics investigations. It is certainly possible to find forensically relevant data on a smart television. It is also the case that ignoring the examination of smart televisions can lead a forensic analyst to miss valuable evidence. As early as 2013, there were discussions about forensically analyzing smart televisions. Related to the topic of smart television forensics, there has been growing interest in Internet of Things (IoT) and smart home forensics. Only limited work has been done specifically on smart television forensics. However, there have been some studies regarding extracting data from related devices such as Amazon Fire Stick.

As of 2020, the majority of smart televisions utilized the Android operating system, or some variation thereof. Android TV is used by Toshiba, Asus, LG, Sony, Sharp, and many other vendors. Google TV was previously utilized by several vendors, including LG and Sony, but was supplanted by Android TV. Roku TV uses a custom Linux distribution named Roku OS. Given that Android is based on Linux, many techniques used for Android TV will also work on Roku televisions. Some LG televisions utilize webOS, but it is also a Linux-based operating system. Samsung has utilized Tizen and Oray as operating systems. However, both of those are Linux-based systems.

The data regarding widely used smart television operating systems strongly suggests that focusing on Android and variations will provide a broad-based methodology that can be utilized with a wide array of televisions. The bulk of that methodology will also be applicable to other Linux-based television operating systems. Utilizing an Android-based approach will provide a methodology that is applicable to the largest number of different brands of smart TVs.

There are two approaches that meet the requirements of being forensically sound and readily usable by a broad range of forensic examiners. The first is using Android Debugging Bridge (ADB). ADB is already widely accepted for forensics. You saw this in the chapter on cell phone forensics. Therefore, utilizing ADB for forensic analysis is scientifically sound. Any Android TV can be accessed using ADB. Given that not all smart TVs allow a USB connection, the best way is to use ADB via a network. Android Debugging Bridge (adb) is a versatile command-line tool that lets you communicate with a device. The adb command facilitates a variety of device actions, such as installing and debugging apps, and it provides access to a Unix shell that you can use to run a variety of commands on a device.

Connecting is a straightforward process. From the command line, use the following command (replacing the IP address with the IP address of the smart TV in question):

```
adb connect 192.168.1.85:5555
```

This is shown in **FIGURE 15-3**.

By typing adb devices, one can verify there is a connection. Then, executing adb shell provides a shell on the target device and the ability to execute a range of Linux

```
D:\platform-tools>adb connect 192.168.1.85:5555
already connected to 192.168.1.85:5555

D:\platform-tools>adb devices
List of devices attached
192.168.1.85:5555       device

D:\platform-tools>adb shell
kanda:/ $ ls
acct        charger default.prop init             init.usb.configfs.rc mnt  product sys
bin         config  dev         init.environ.rc   init.usb.rc          odm  sbin    system
bugreports  d       etc         init.rc           init.zygote32.rc     oem  sdcard  ueventd.rc
cache       data    factory     init.recovery.m5621.rc lost+found      proc storage vendor
kanda:/ $
```

FIGURE 15-3

ADB connect.

commands. The shell can be exited at any time by typing `exit`. A first step, done from without the shell, is to back up the device:

```
adb backup -apk -shared -all -f C: \backup.ab
```

After backing up the target device, it is necessary to document details about the device. The `adb shell getprop` command can be useful for this purpose.

This general overview of how to use ADB to obtain forensically relevant information from a smart TV leads naturally to a need for a step-by-step process. This is a process that can be generally applied to any Android TV. The steps are as follows:

Step 1: Turn on USB debugging on the target device.

Step 2: Connect to the smart TV from a forensic workstation using `adb connect 192.168.1.85:5555`.

Step 3: Back up the device using `adb backup -apk -shared -all -f C: \ backup.ab`.

Step 4: Utilize `adb shell getprop` to gather details about the smart TV. These details are necessary for thoroughly documenting the forensic investigation. It may be useful to get all properties via `adb shell getprop > properties.txt`.

Step 5: Now utilize `adb` commands as needed to locate relevant data, and copy that data back to the forensic workstation using `adb pull`. The specific commands used will depend on the nature of the incident being investigated as well as the evidence found.

Legal and Procedural Trends

The legal environment in which forensics is conducted changes slowly, but it does change. Normally, the enactment of new laws has very little effect on how evidence is examined; rather, it affects how it is seized. For example, the U.S. Supreme Court ruled in June 2013 that law enforcement officers could collect DNA evidence from suspects without their consent in certain cases. This significantly changes the collection of evidence, but not the analysis of it.

15

Trends and Future Directions

Changes in the Law

Some laws do make changes to the process of seizing evidence. Laws can alter the requirements for a warrant, exceptions to warrant requirements, and issues of consent to search.

The USA PATRIOT Act

The most obvious change to U.S. law in reference to forensics in recent years has been the USA PATRIOT Act of 2001, most often just called "the Patriot Act." The Patriot Act was designed to combat terrorism. It was not created with computer crime as its focus. However, it has impacted computer crime. For example, prior to the Patriot Act, internet service providers (ISPs) were very limited in what they could share with law enforcement without warrants or subpoenas. Now they can choose to notify law enforcement if they reasonably believe that they have found evidence of an imminent crime that would endanger lives.

Section 816 of the Patriot Act—titled the "Development and Support of Cybersecurity Forensic Capabilities"—calls for the U.S. Attorney General to establish regional computer forensic laboratories. This led to the creation of the Electronic Crimes Task Force, which operates computer forensics labs in many major cities. This task force also includes members of local law enforcement.

Private Labs

Private forensics labs are becoming more common. These laboratories handle forensic examinations for private companies, attorneys, and sometimes law enforcement agencies. More and more forensic investigations are being done in private labs. This has become routine in other areas of forensics, such as DNA testing.

In the case of civil litigation, it is usually necessary to hire private forensics labs to process evidence. Private labs can gather evidence, analyze it, and produce reports regarding their findings. This data might be used in civil litigation or simply to ascertain the cause of an incident.

Defense attorneys will often want their own lab to examine evidence, in order to challenge the findings of the state's lab. The goal may be to confirm or deny what the prosecution has presented or to find some flaw in the methodology utilized by the prosecution. In some cases, the defense is simply seeking grounds for a reasonable doubt that their client committed the crime. For example, if the defendant is accused of sending a virus to a victim, and that virus along with virus creation utilities are found on their computer, it may seem a hopeless case. However, if the defense can show that other people had access to the computer, or even that other users logged on around the time the virus was sent, this provides reasonable doubt.

It is becoming increasingly common for smaller police departments to outsource their computer forensics to private labs. It is often far more cost-effective. In smaller towns and cities, the cost of equipping the police department with a full computer forensics lab and adequately trained staff may simply be beyond their budget. In those cases, it is more cost-effective to outsource computer forensics examinations.

It should be noted that many states require a private citizen to hold a valid private investigator's license in order to practice digital forensics. You should check with the law in your state. In those states that do require a private investigator's license, it is actually a misdemeanor to perform a digital forensics exam without a license.

International Issues

Clearly, the cloud presents international legal issues for forensics examiners, but there are other issues as well. What happens when a case is transnational in nature? Cases of bank fraud, identity theft, and money laundering frequently cross national boundaries. Consider an identity theft scheme where a server in Malaysia is used to steal identities, and then the perpetrator uses their laptop while in Spain to take money from a victim's accounts. If the victim lives in yet a third country, such as the United States, this crime now involves three different international jurisdictions.

You might think that in such cases the only answer is to be aware of the laws in each country and ensure they are all obeyed. However, that is rarely necessary. Usually taking the national laws that are most restrictive to your investigation and following those will satisfy the legal requirements of the less restrictive jurisdictions.

Techniques

Techniques are always evolving. Due to the Daubert Standard, which requires that the scientific evidence presented in court be generally accepted in the relevant scientific field, new techniques need to be verified before being used in court. This means it is unlikely that a new tool will be released and immediately utilized in court. However, as time passes and the new tool is tested, often in academic settings, it gains wide acceptance in the field and finds its way into court.

For this reason, it is important that a forensic investigator be aware of changes in technology and have at least a basic familiarity with emerging technologies and techniques. Even if they are not yet being used in court, they could be soon.

CHAPTER SUMMARY

This chapter gave an overview of how technology is changing and how that affects forensics. Even technology that has been in place for many years, such as the personal computer, is changing as increased storage, speed, and performance are developed. New technologies, such as smart TVs, smart automobiles, etc., are emerging and will require forensic analysis.

There are also new laws and new techniques being developed. These impact how evidence is both collected and processed. It is imperative for a forensic investigator to be familiar with them.

KEY CONCEPTS AND TERMS

Cloud computing   Moore's law

CHAPTER 15 ASSESSMENT

1. Which of the following is the main advantage of cloud computing?

A. Speed of accessing data
B. Fault tolerance
C. Both A and B
D. Ease of use

2. Moore's law concerns which of the following?

A. How to seize evidence
B. Who can seize evidence
C. How fast computing power improves
D. How long it takes new devices to be adopted

3. When performing forensic analysis on devices from diverse jurisdictions, the proper approach is to:

A. adhere to the jurisdiction with the least restrictive requirements.

B. adhere to the jurisdiction with the most restrictive requirements.
C. adhere to international requirements.
D. use your own best judgment.

4. How would you connect to a smart TV with ADB?

A. Connect a USB device and use `adb`
B. Use `adb connect ipaddress`
C. Connect from the TV to the computer
D. Use the same approach as when connecting to a smartphone

References

1. Herman, M., Iorga, M., Salim, A.M., Jackson, R., Hurst, M., Leo, R., et al. (2020). *NIST Cloud Computing Forensic Science Challenges*. Gaithersburg, MD: National Institute of Standards and Technology. Retrieved from https://csrc.nist.gov/publications/detail/nistir/8006/final on February 23, 2021.

2. Newman, L. H. (2018, August 9). A new pacemaker hack puts malware directly on the device. *Wired*. Retrieved from https://www.wired.com/story/pacemaker-hack-malware-black-hat/ on February 23, 2021.

3. Newman, L. H. (2019, July 16). These hackers made an app that kills to prove a point. *Wired*. Retrieved from https://www.wired.com/story/medtronic-insulin-pump-hack-app/ on February 23, 2021.

4. Krakow, M. (2019, June 28). Insulin pumps are vulnerable to hacking, FDA warns amid recall. *The Washington Post*. Retrieved from https://www.washingtonpost.com/health/2019/06/28/insulin-pumps-are-vulnerable-hacking-fda-warns-amid-recall/ on February 23, 2021.

5. Infosecurity Group. (2011, October 25). Barnaby Jack hacks diabetes insulin pump live at Hacker Halted. Retrieved from https://www.infosecurity-magazine.com/news/barnaby-jack-hacks-diabetes-insulin-pump-live-at/ on February 23, 2021.

6. Ayers, R., Brothers, S., & Jansen, W. (2014). *Guidelines on Mobile Device Forensics*. NIST Special Publication 800-001, Revision 1. Retrieved from https://csrc.nist.gov/publications/detail/sp/800-101/rev-1/final on February 23, 2021.

Answer Key

Chapter 1	Introduction to Forensics
	1. C 2. B 3. B 4. C 5. B 6. D 7. B 8. B
Chapter 2	Overview of Computer Crime
	1. C 2. A 3. A 4. B 5. A 6. A 7. C 8. D
Chapter 3	Forensics Methods and Labs
	1. C 2. C 3. C 4. D 5. A 6. C 7. A
Chapter 4	Collecting, Seizing, and Protecting Evidence
	1. C 2. C 3. D 4. B 5. B 6. B 7. A
Chapter 5	Understanding Techniques for Hiding and Scrambling Information
	1. A 2. B 3. B 4. D 5. C 6. A 7. B 8. C 9. D 10. A 11. B 12. D
Chapter 6	Recovering Data
	1. B 2. C 3. B 4. A
Chapter 7	Incident Response
	1. B 2. C 3. B 4. C
Chapter 8	Windows Forensics
	1. C 2. C 3. B 4. A
Chapter 9	Linux Forensics
	1. A 2. B 3. A 4. C 5. C 6. `pstree` 7. A 8. C
Chapter 10	Mac OS Forensics
	1. A 2. C 3. A 4. A 5. A
Chapter 11	Email Forensics
	1. B 2. A 3. C 4. B 5. D
Chapter 12	Mobile Forensics
	1. A 2. C 3. A 4. B 5. C
Chapter 13	Network Forensics
	1. C 2. D 3. A 4. B 5. C
Chapter 14	Memory Forensics
	1. A 2. D 3. B 4. B 5. C
Chapter 15	Trends and Future Directions
	1. C 2. C 3. B 4. B

Standard Acronyms

3DES	Triple Data Encryption Standard
ACE	AccessData Certified Examiner
ACK	acknowledgment
ADB	Android Debugging Bridge
ADRAM	asynchronous dynamic random access memory
AES	Advanced Encryption Standard
AFF	advanced forensic file format
AFS	Apple File System
ALE	annualized loss expectancy
ANSI	American National Standards Institute
AP	access point
APFS	Apple file system
API	application programming interface
APIPA	Automatic Private IP Addresses
ARO	annual rate of occurrence
ASCLD	American Society of Crime Laboratory Directors
ATM	asynchronous transfer mode
BAM	background activity monitor
BCP	business continuity planning
BIOS	basic input/output system
CALEA	Communication Assistance to Law Enforcement Act
CAP	Certification and Accreditation Professional
CAUCE	Coalition Against Unsolicited Commercial Email
CCNA	Cisco Certified Network Associate
CERT	Computer Emergency Response Team
CFE	Certified Fraud Examiner
CHFI	Certified Hacking Forensic Investigator
CISA	Certified Information Systems Auditor
CISM	Certified Information Security Manager
CISSP	Certified Information System Security Professional
COOP	continuity of operations plan
DAM	desktop activity monitor
DBMS	database management system
DC3	U.S. Department of Defense Cyber Crime Center
DDoS	distributed denial of service

DDR	double data rate
DES	Data Encryption Standard
DFRWS	Digital Forensic Research Workshop
DHCP	Dynamic Host Configuration Protocol
DLL	dynamic link library
DNS	domain name service
DoD	U.S. Department of Defense
DoS	denial of service
DOS	Disk Operating System
DPI	deep packet inspection
DRAM	dynamic random access memory
DREAD	Damage Potential, Reproducibility, Exploitability, Affected Users, and Discoverability
DRP	disaster recovery plan
DSS	Digital Signature Standard
EDO RAM	extended data out dynamic random access memory
EIDE	Enhanced IDE
ELF	Executable and Linkable Format
EMR	electromagnetic radiation
EnCE	EnCase Certified Examiner
EPROM	erasable programmable read-only memory
ESN	electronic serial numbers
EXT	extended file system
FAT	file allocation table
FBI	Federal Bureau of Investigation
FDA	U.S. Food and Drug Administration
FISA	Foreign Intelligence Surveillance Act
FRE	Federal Rules of Evidence
FTC	Federal Trade Commission
FTP	File Transfer Protocol
GIAC	Global Information Assurance Certification
GIMP	GNU image manipulation program
GPEN	GIAC Penetration Tester
GPS	global positioning system
GUI	graphical user interface
GUID	globally unique identifier
HSM	hierarchical storage management
HTTP	Hypertext Transfer Protocol
HTTPS	HTTP over Secure Socket Layer
ICCID	integrated circuit card identifier
ICMP	Internet Control Message Protocol
IDS	intrusion detection system
IEEE	Institute of Electrical and Electronics Engineers
IETF	Internet Engineering Task Force
IMAP	Internet Message Access Protocol

IMEI	International Mobile Equipment Identity
InfoSec	information security
IoT	Internet of Things
IP	Internet Protocol
IRC	internet relay chat
IRS	Internal Revenue Service
(ISC)²	International Information System Security Certification Consortium
ISCP	information system contingency plan
ISO	International Organization for Standardization
ISP	internet service provider
LAN	local area network
LDAP	Lightweight Directory Access Protocol
LTE	Long-Term Evolution
MAC	media access control
MAR	memory address register
MBR	master boot record
MDR	memory data register
MIME	Multipurpose Internet Mail Extensions
MPE	mean percentage error
MSD	mean squared deviation
MTD	maximum tolerable downtime
MTTF	mean time to failure
MTTR	mean time to repair
NAND	Negated AND
NIC	network interface card
NIST	National Institute of Standards and Technology
NTFS	new technology file system
OS	operating system
OSI	Open System Interconnection
PATA	parallel advanced technology attachment
PCI	Payment Card Industry
PDF	Portable Document Format
PDoS	permanent denial of service
POP	Post Office Protocol
PROM	programmable read-only memory
PUK	personal unlocking code
RAID	redundant array of independent disks
RAM	random access memory
RCFL	Regional Computer Forensics Laboratory
ReFS	resilient file system
RMON	Remote Network MONitoring
ROM	read-only memory
RPO	recovery point objective
RSA	Rivest, Shamir, and Adleman (algorithm)
RTO	recovery time objective

SaaS	software as a service
SAM	security accounts manager
SAN	storage area network
SATA	Serial Advanced Technology Attachment
SCSI	Small Computer System Interface
SDRAM	synchronous dynamic random access memory
SHA	Secure Hash Algorithm
SLE	single loss expectancy
SMSS	Session Manager Subsystem
SMTP	Simple Mail Transfer Protocol
SNMP	Simple Network Management Protocol
SQL	Structured Query Language
SRUM	system resource usage monitor
SSCP	Systems Security Certified Practitioner
SSD	solid-state drive
SSL	Secure Sockets Layer
SWGDE	Scientific Working Group on Digital Evidence
SYN	synchronize
TCP	Transmission Control Protocol
TLB	translation lookaside buffer
UEFI	Unified Extensivle Firmware Interface
URL	universal resource locator
USB	universal serial bus
US-CERT	U.S. Computer Emergency Readiness Team
VLSM	Variable Length Subnet Mask
VoIP	Voice over Internet Protocol
VPN	virtual private network
WAN	wide area network
WLAN	wireless local area network

Glossary of Key Terms

A

American Standard Code for Information Interchange (ASCII) | A set of codes defining all the various keystrokes you could make, including letters, numbers, characters, and even the spacebar and return keys.

Anonymous remailing | The process of sending an email message to an anonymizer. The anonymizer strips identifying information from an email message before forwarding it with the anonymous mailing computer's IP address.

Anti-forensics | The actions that perpetrators take to conceal their locations, activities, or identities.

Asymmetric cryptography | Cryptography wherein two keys are used: one to encrypt the message and another to decrypt it.

Asynchronous transfer mode (ATM) | A high-speed connection technology that uses fixed-length, 53-byte packets called calls.

Authenticate | To verify the identity of a person, or to verify evidence.

B

Base transceiver station (BTS) | The part of the cell network responsible for communications between the mobile phone and the network switching system.

Basic input/output system (BIOS) | The basic instructions stored on a chip for booting up the computer.

Bit-level information | Information at the level of actual 1s and 0s stored in memory or on the storage device.

Block cipher | A form of cryptography that encrypts data in blocks; 64-bit blocks are quite common, although some algorithms (like AES) use larger blocks.

Bootstrap environment | A special program, such as U-Boot or RedBoot, that is stored in a special section of the flash memory.

Brute-force attack | An attack in which the attacker tries to decrypt a message by simply applying every possible key in the keyspace.

Business continuity plan (BCP) | A plan for maintaining minimal operations until the business can return to full normal operations.

Business impact analysis (BIA) | An analysis of how specific incidents might impact the business operations.

C

Caesar cipher | The method of cryptography in which someone chooses a number by which to shift each letter of a text in the alphabet and substitute the new letter for the letter being encrypted. For example, if your text is "A CAT," and you choose to shift by two letters, your encrypted text is "C ECV." This is also known as a monoalphabet, single-alphabet, or substitution cipher.

Carrier | The signal, stream, or data file in which the payload is hidden.

Cell-phone forensics | The process of searching the contents of cell phones.

Chain of custody | The continuity of control of evidence that makes it possible to account for all that has happened to evidence between its original collection and its appearance in court, preferably unaltered.

Channel | The type of medium used to hide data in steganography. This may be photos, video, sound files, or Voice over IP.

Clean room | An environment that has a controlled level of contamination, such as from dust, microbes, and other particles.

Cloud computing | The practice of delivering hosted services over the internet. This can be software as a service, platform as a service, or infrastructure as a service.

Computer forensics | The use of analytical and investigative techniques to identify, collect, examine, and preserve computer-based material for presentation as evidence in a court of law.

Consistency checking | A technique for file system repair that involves scanning a disk's logical structure and ensuring that it is consistent with its specification.

Cryptanalysis | A method of using techniques other than brute force to derive a cryptographic key.

Curriculum vitae (CV) | An extensive document expounding one's experience and qualifications for a position, similar to a résumé but with more detail. In academia and expert work, a CV is usually used rather than a résumé.

Cyberstalking | The use of electronic communications to harass or threaten another person.

D

Data consistency | The act of ensuring the data that is extracted is consistent.

Daubert standard | The standard holding that only methods and tools widely accepted in the scientific community can be used in court.

Demonstrative evidence | Information that helps explain other evidence. An example is a chart that explains a technical concept to the judge and jury.

Denial-of-service (DoS) attack | An attack designed to overwhelm the target system so it can no longer reply to legitimate requests for connection.

Digital evidence | Information that has been processed and assembled so that it is relevant to an investigation and supports a specific finding or determination.

Digital forensics | Computer forensics expanded to include smartphones, smart watches, and other current and forthcoming digital media and devices.

Disaster recovery plan (DRP) | A plan for returning the business to full normal operations.

Disk forensics | The process of acquiring and analyzing information stored on physical storage media, such as computer hard drives or smartphones.

Disk Operating System (DOS) | A command-line operating system.

Disk striping | Distribution of data across multiple disk sectors to improve speed (also called RAID 0).

Distributed denial-of-service (DDoS) attack | An attack in which the attacker seeks to infect several machines, and use those machines to overwhelm the target system to achieve a denial of service.

Documentary evidence | Data stored in written form, on paper or in electronic files, such as email messages and telephone call-detail records. Investigators must authenticate documentary evidence.

Drive geometry | The functional dimensions of a drive in terms of the number of heads, cylinders, and sectors per track.

Dump | A complete copy of every bit of memory or cache recorded in permanent storage or printed on paper.

E

Electronic serial number (ESN) | A unique identification number developed by the U.S. Federal Communications Commission (FCC) to identify cell phones.

Email forensics | The study of the source and content of email as evidence, including the identification of the sender, recipient, date, time, and origination location of an email message.

Enhanced data rates for GSM evolution (EDGE) | A technology that does not fit neatly into the 2G/3G/4G spectrum. It is technically considered pre-3G but was an improvement on GSM (2G).

Euler's Totient | The total number of coprime numbers. Two numbers are considered coprime if they have no common factors.

Expert report | A formal document prepared by a forensics specialist to document an investigation, including a list of all tests conducted as well as the specialist's own curriculum vitae (CV). Anything the specialist plans to testify about at a trial must be included in the expert report.

Expert testimony | The testimony of an expert witness, one who testifies on the basis of scientific or technical knowledge relevant to a case, rather than personal experience.

Feistel function | A cryptographic function that splits blocks of data into two parts. It is one of the most influential developments in symmetric block ciphers.

File allocation table (FAT) | The table used to store cluster/file information.

File slack | The unused space between the logical end of file and the physical end of file. It is also called *slack space*.

Foreign Intelligence Surveillance Act of 1978 (FISA) | A U.S. law that prescribes procedures for the physical and electronic surveillance and collection of "foreign intelligence information" between foreign powers and agents of foreign powers, which may include U.S. citizens and permanent residents suspected of espionage or terrorism.

Fraud | A broad category of crime that can encompass many different activities, but essentially any attempt to gain financial reward through deception.

Global System for Mobile (GSM) communications | A standard developed by the European Telecommunications Standards Institute (ETSI). Basically, GSM is the 2G network.

Grand Unified Bootloader (GRUB) | A newer Linux boot loader.

Graphical user interface (GUI) | A point-and-click user interface.

grep | A popular Linux/UNIX search tool.

Hash | A function that is nonreversible, takes variable-length input, produces fixed-length output, and has few or no collisions.

Heap (*H*) | Dynamic memory for a program comes from the heap segment. A process may use a memory allocator such as malloc to request dynamic memory.

Hierarchical storage management (HSM) | Continuous online backup storage.

High-level format | Setting up an empty file system and installing a boot sector in a drive. Also called a *quick format*.

Hive | One of the five sections of the Windows Registry.

Home location register (HLR) | The database used by the MSC for subscriber data and service information.

Identity theft | Any use of another person's identity.

Inode | A data structure in the file system that stores all the information about a file except its name and its actual data.

Integrated circuit card identifier (ICCID) | A unique serial number that identifies each SIM. These numbers are engraved on the SIM during manufacturing.

International Mobile Equipment Identity (IMEI) number | A unique number identifying GSM, LTE, and other types of phones. The first 8 bits of the ESN identify the manufacturer, and the subsequent 24 bits uniquely identify the phone.

Internet forensics | The process of piecing together where and when a user has been on the internet.

Internet Message Access Protocol (IMAP) | A protocol used to receive email that works on port 143.

Intrusion detection system | A system that monitors network traffic looking for suspicious activity.

ISO9660 | A file system used with CDs.

Kasiski examination | A method of attacking polyalphabetic substitution ciphers by deducing the length of the keyword. This is sometimes also called Kasiski's test or Kasiski's method.

Kerckhoffs' principle | The principle that the security of a cryptographic algorithm depends only on the secrecy of the key, not the algorithm itself.

Key space | The total number of keys.

L

Least significant bit (LSB) | The last bit or least significant bit is used to store data.

Life span | A term that refers to how long data will last. The term is related to volatility. More volatile data tends to have a shorter life span.

LILO (Linux Loader) | One of the Linux boot loaders.

Live system forensics | The process of searching memory in real time, typically for working with compromised hosts or to identify system abuse.

Locard's principle of transference | The forensics principle that states you cannot interact with an environment without leaving some trace.

Logic bomb | Malware that executes its damage when a specific condition is met.

Logical analysis | Analysis involving using the native operating system, on the evidence disk or a forensic duplicate, to peruse the data.

Logical damage | Damage to how the data is stored—for example, file system corruption.

Logical imaging | Use of the target system's file system to copy data to an image for analysis.

Long Term Evolution (LTE) | A standard for wireless communication of high-speed data for mobile devices. This is what is commonly called 4G.

Low-level format | Creation of the structure of sectors, tracks, and clusters in a drive.

Master boot record (MBR) | The record on the hard drive partition used to initiate booting that partition.

Maximum tolerable downtime (MTD) | The length of time a system can be down before the business cannot recover.

Mean time before failure (MTBF) | The average length of time before a given piece of equipment will fail through normal use.

Mean time to failure (MTTF) | How long, on average, before a given piece of equipment will fail through normal use.

Mean time to repair (MTTFR) | The average time needed to repair a given piece of equipment.

Memory cell | The fundamental building block of memory.

Metadata | Data about the data, including information about when a file or directory was created, when it was last modified, and so forth.

Mobile switching center (MSC) | A switching system for a cellular network.

Moore's law | The observation by Gordon Moore of Intel Corporation that capacity would double and price would be cut in half roughly every 18 to 24 months for products based on computer chips and related technology.

Multiple-input multiple-output (MIMO) | The wireless technology that uses multiple antennas to coherently resolve more information than is possible using a single antenna.

Network forensics | The process of examining network traffic, including transaction logs and real-time monitoring.

Packets | Chunks of data sent across a network.

Page | A data structure that maps virtual addresses to physical addresses.

Payload | The data to be covertly communicated. In other words, it is the message you want to hide.

Permanent denial of service (PDoS) | an attack that damages the system so badly the machine needs a full reinstall of its OS and potentially even new hardware.

Personal identification number (PIN) | An ID number for a cell phone user.

Personal unlocking code (PUK) | A number for unlocking a cell phone.

Physical analysis | Offline analysis conducted on an evidence disk or forensic duplicate after booting from a CD or another system.

Physical damage | Damage to actual hard drive parts; for example, a damaged platter or spindle.

Physical imaging | Making a physical copy of a disk.

Post Office Protocol version 3 (POP3) | A protocol used to receive email that works on port 110.

Power-on self-test (POST) | A brief hardware test the BIOS performs upon boot-up.

Probative value | The value of evidence in helping determine the facts in a case.

Protected computer | Any computer at a financial institution of any kind or a government agency.

R

Rainbow table | Type of password crackers that work with precalculated hashes of all passwords available within a certain character space.

Real evidence | Physical objects that can be touched, held, or directly observed, such as a laptop with a suspect's fingerprints on it or a handwritten note.

Recover time objective (RTO) | The time that the system is expected to be back up. This must be less than MTD.

Recovery point objective (RPO) | The amount of work that might need to be redone, or data lost.

Routing table | A table used with routers to track what IP addresses are connected to ports on the router.

Rules of evidence | Rules that govern whether, when, how, and why proof of a legal case can be placed before a judge or jury.

Scrubber | Software that cleans unallocated space. Also called a *sweeper*.

Simple Mail Transfer Protocol (SMTP) | A protocol used to send email that works on port 25.

Slack space | The unused space between the logical end of file and the physical end of file. It is also called *file slack*.

Slurred image | The result of acquiring a file as it is being updated.

Sniffer | Computer software or hardware that can intercept and log traffic passing over a digital network.

Social engineering | Nontechnical means of obtaining information you would not normally have access to.

Software forensics | The process of examining malicious computer code.

Spoofing | The act of making an email message appear to come from someone or someplace other than the real sender or location.

Stack (*S*) | Memory is allocated based on the last-in, first-out (LIFO) principle.

Steganalysis | The determination of whether a file or communication hides other information.

Steganography | The art and science of writing hidden messages.

Steganophony | The use of steganography with sound files.

Stream cipher | A form of cryptography that encrypts the data as a stream, one bit at a time.

Subnetting | Dividing a network into smaller portions.

Subscriber Identity Module (SIM) | A card that identifies a phone with a user and a number.

Substitution | In cryptography, the method of changing some part of the plaintext for some matching part of ciphertext.

Swap file | A virtual memory extension of RAM that can be temporary or permanent.

Sweeper | A kind of software that cleans unallocated space. Also called a *scrubber*.

Symmetric cryptography | Those methods where the same key is used to encrypt and decrypt the plaintext.

Temporary data | Data that an operating system creates and overwrites without the computer user taking a direct action to save this data.

Test system | A functional system compatible with the hard drive from which someone is trying to recover data.

Testimonial evidence | Information that forensic specialists use to support or interpret real or documentary evidence; for example, to demonstrate that the fingerprints found on a keyboard are those of a specific individual.

Three-way handshake | The process of connecting to a server that involves three packets being exchanged.

Transposition | In terms of cryptography, the swapping of blocks of ciphertext.

U

Unallocated space | Free space, or the area of a hard drive that has never been allocated for file storage.

Unicode | The international standard for information encoding.

Universal Disk Format (UDF) | A file system used with DVDs.

Universal Mobile Telecommunications System (UMTS) | A 3G standard based on GSM.

USA PATRIOT Act of 2001 | An act passed into law as a response to the terrorist attacks of September 11, 2001, that significantly reduced restrictions on law enforcement agencies' gathering of intelligence within the United States; expanded the Secretary of the Treasury's authority to regulate financial transactions, particularly those involving foreign individuals and entities; and broadened the discretion of law enforcement and immigration authorities in detaining and/or deporting immigrants suspected of terrorism and related acts.

Vigenère cipher | A method of encrypting alphabetic text by using a series of different monoalphabetic ciphers selected based on the letters of a keyword. A polyalphabetic cipher.

Virus | Any software that self-replicates.

Visitor location register (VLR) | A database used by the MSC for roaming phones.

Volatile data | Data that changes rapidly and may be lost when the machine that holds it is powered down.

Volatile memory | Computer memory that requires power to maintain the data it holds, and can be changed. RAM is highly volatile; EEPROM is very nonvolatile.

Volatile memory analysis | A live system forensic technique in which you collect a memory dump and perform analysis in an isolated environment.

Zero-knowledge analysis | A technique for file system repair that involves recovering data from a damaged partition with limited knowledge of the file system.

Index

Note: Page numbers followed by *f* and *t* indicate figures and tables, respectively.

Index